GCE **AS Level** **Double Award**

AS Level for AQA

Travel & Tourism

Peter Hayward • Alan Marvell • Hayley Reynolds • Sue Stewart

www.heinemann.co.uk
✓ Free online support
✓ Useful weblinks
✓ 24 hour online ordering

01865 888058

Heinemann

Inspiring generations

Heinemann Educational Publishers
Halley Court, Jordan Hill, Oxford OX2 8EJ
Part of Harcourt Education

Heinemann is a registered trademark of
Harcourt Education Limited

Text © Alan Marvell, Peter Hayward, Hayley Reynolds, Sue Stewart 2005

First published 2005

09 08 07 06 05
10 9 8 7 6 5 4 3 2 1

British Library Cataloguing in Publication Data is available
from the British Library on request.

10-digit ISBN 0 435 44658 4
13-digit ISBN 978 0 435 44658 1

Designed by Lorraine Inglis
Typeset and illustrated by 🖋 Tek-Art, Croydon, Surrey

Original illustrations © Harcourt Education Limited, 2005
Cover design by Wooden Ark Studios
Printed by Bath Colourbooks Ltd
Cover photo: © Robert Harding

Contents

Acknowledgements

The publishers wish to thank the following for their kind permission to reproduce the photos in this book.

Alamy 95, 101, 128, 130, 130, 136 (bottom), 159, 160, 197, 199, 231, 236, 247; Alamy/Travel Ink 97 (bottom left); Alamy/Travel Shots 14; BAE Systems 112; Britainonview 154, 210; Britainonview/Ingrid Rasmussen 36; Butlins 21; Centre Parcs 158; Corbis 2 (bottom right), 16, 20, 44, 59, 99, 102, 119, 134, 135; easyJet 31; Getty 186 (top); Getty AFP 264; Getty Images/Photodisc 94 (bottom left and right), 96, 97 (bottom right), 136 (top); Getty News & Sport 201; Harcourt Education Ltd/Debbie Rowe 11; Harcourt Index, 153, 234, 255, 284 (top), 285 (top and bottom); Jane Hance 58; www.johnaparicio.com/Thomas Cook 186; Lonely Planet Images 2 (bottom left), 19, 129, 191, 194, 211, 216, 272, 273, 275, 284 (bottom); Rex Features 35; Scottish Viewpoint 206; Superstock (bottom) 273

Every effort has been made to contact copyright holders of material reproduced in this book. Any omissions will be rectified in subsequent printings if notice is given to the publishers.

Introduction

Travel and tourism is one of the world's fastest growing industries with over two million people employed in tourism-related industries in the UK. The AS GCE Travel and Tourism (Double Award) has been designed as a qualification that provides knowledge and understanding of this dynamic industry. The qualification will enable you to progress to the GCE A2 Advanced Level Travel and Tourism qualification and other qualifications in further and higher education, training or employment.

This book has been produced to meet the requirements of the AQA AS GCE Travel and Tourism (Double Award) qualification. It has been specifically written by a team of experienced authors to enable you to get the most from your course.

The book is set out in the order of the units that you will be studying:

* Unit 1 Inside Travel and Tourism
* Unit 2 Travel and Tourism – A People Industry
* Unit 3 Travel Destinations
* Unit 4 Working in Travel and Tourism
* Unit 5 Marketing in Travel and Tourism
* Unit 6 Tourism in the UK
* Unit 7 Overseas Destinations Study.

During the course you will study six units. You will either study Unit 6 Tourism in the UK or Unit 7 Overseas Destinations Study, but not both. Your tutor will give you further details as to which unit you will study.

Each unit in this book has been written with essential information that you need to know along with a range of examples, case studies, activities and practice questions:

* **Key terms** – These provide you with concise definitions of important words and phrases
* **Case study** – These provide you with detailed examples to show you how key ideas relate to the travel and tourism industry

* **Think about it** – These provide you with an opportunity to think, discuss and reflect on important questions affecting the industry
* **Skills practice** – These allow you to research and investigate ideas related to the information that has been discussed and to begin working towards your portfolio
* **Knowledge check** – These allow you to check your understanding of what you have learnt before you start work on your portfolio
* **Portfolio practice** – These provide you with activities and examples of the type of work that you will be expected to produce as part of this course and helps you to build your own assessment portfolio.

How will I study?

You will be researching and investigating a wide range of issues relating to travel and tourism. These will be based around a series of assignments that are agreed with your tutor. You will be expected to use a variety of different sources, some of which can include:

* Libraries and information centres
* Internet searches
* Travel brochures and guidebooks
* News reports and advertisements from a variety of different media
* Visiting and talking to people in the travel and tourism industry
* Using industry reports and trade journals
* Learning from guest speakers
* If it is possible, work experience with a travel and tourism company.

How will I be assessed?

Two-thirds of the qualification is assessed by a portfolio of activities that are set out in the AQA specification. Your tutor will give you a copy. The portfolio is based on coursework and other activities as specified by your tutor. You must make sure that you follow the instructions carefully and that the portfolio is all your own work. This book provides you with examples and suggestions on where to find information.

The other third of the qualification is a test that contains short-answer and extended-answer questions. This book prepares you for the test with hints, suggestions and practice questions.

We hope you enjoy using this book and good luck with your course.

UNIT 1

Inside travel and tourism

Introduction

This unit introduces you to travel and tourism. You will learn that the travel and tourism industry is complex and diverse and is made up of a large number of different organisations. You will also discover that organisations in the industry are interrelated and interdependent. You will investigate the development and growth of travel and tourism and the roles of the different sectors of the travel and tourism industry.

This unit provides the foundation for supporting the more detailed study of the travel and tourism industry in other GCE units, as well as an overview of the nature and growth of the UK travel and tourism industry.

How you will be assessed

Assessment for this unit is through an externally assessed written paper. The paper will be two hours long and will comprise short and extended answer questions.

To help you prepare for the written paper you will need to study at least two destinations in the UK and overseas.

Throughout the unit, activities and tasks will help you to learn and remember information in preparation for your external assessment.

After studying this unit you need to have learned:

* To define travel and tourism and know the main types of tourism
* To understand the nature of the travel and tourism industry
* To be able to describe the main historical developments and factors that have led to the growth of the industry into its current characteristics
* To be able to identify the roles of the different sectors of the travel and tourism industry
* To understand the areas of overlap and the nature of the relationships between sectors within the travel and tourism industry.

Defining travel and tourism

Two weeks in the sun; a business trip to see customers; visiting relatives in Australia. All of these are examples of travel and tourism activities and there are a variety of organisations involved in supplying travel and tourism products and services to customers.

This section aims to examine what is meant by travel and tourism, the different parts of the industry and the range of tourism destinations travellers visit.

In the section you will learn:

✷ The main types of tourism

✷ The main reasons people travel

✷ Different types of travel and tourism products and services

✷ The size of and role of organisations in the industry

✷ The industry is dominated by commercial organisations

✷ The support and influence of public and voluntary organisations within the industry

✷ Internal and external pressures on the industry

✷ The impact of travel and tourism activities on destinations and host communities.

What are travel and tourism?

Travel and *tourism* is concerned with people travelling away from home on a temporary basis – i.e. they intend to return home at a given point in time. The reasons people choose to travel are varied and these shall be examined later in this section. The destinations people travel to are also varied and range from UK seaside resorts to exotic, little-visited faraway places.

A traditional UK seaside resort and an exotic overseas beach location

The demand for travel and tourism products and services has created a large and dynamic industry that continues to grow. Covering a number of activities and organisations, travel is seen as the key component in the industry as it concerns how people actually get to their chosen destination and how they travel around the area they are visiting. Without travel there would be no tourism and without tourism there would be little demand for travel services.

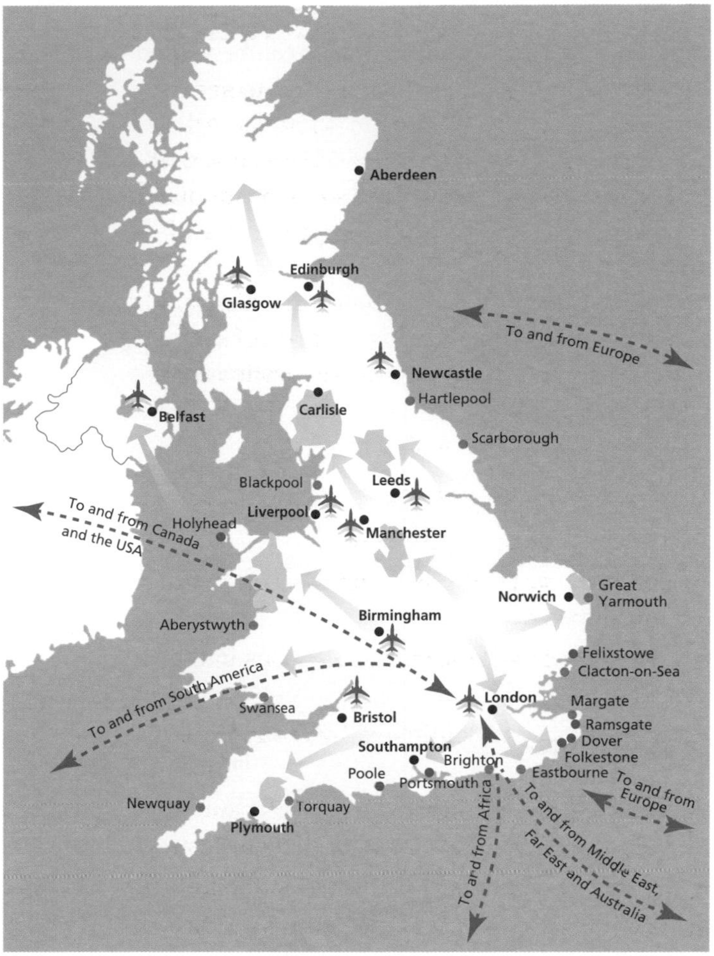

Figure 1.1 The UK's main flows of tourism

Key terms

Travel Travel is concerned with how people get to their chosen destination and how they travel around the area they are visiting.

Tourism Tourism is 'the temporary, short-term movement of people to destinations outside the places where they normally live and work and the activities they take part in during their stay at those destinations.' (*Tourism Society*, 1976)

Think about it

In groups of three or four, list as many methods of transport as you can think of. Then consider the advantages and disadvantages of each method.

Skills practice

1 Visit your local tourist information office to collect information about five different local tourist attractions.

2 Imagine you are working at promoting your local area. Prepare a PowerPoint presentation selling the local attractions you have collected information on to attract visitors to the area.

Are we coming or going?

Tourism can be classified into three main types:

* Domestic
* Inbound
* Outbound.

Domestic tourism involves UK residents visiting locations within the UK either for a day trip, visiting friends or relatives, or for a holiday. The UK has a wealth of many towns and cities that attract tourists every year.

Skills practice

1 Write a list of as many places as you can think of in the UK which attract tourists to visit them.

2 Compare this list with a colleague who has also completed Task 1.

3 Draw a large outline (possibly big enough for a wall display) of a map of the UK. On to this map, mark all the UK tourist spots you identified in Tasks 1 and 2.

The UK, even though only a small country, has different types of destinations that can be visited by tourists.

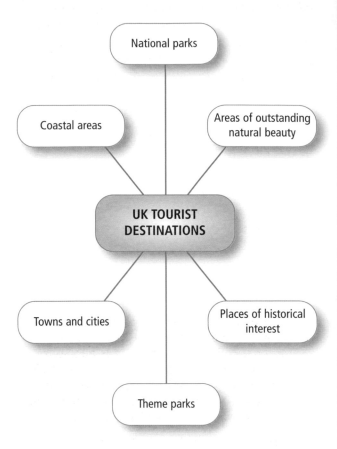

Figure 1.2 The range of UK tourist destinations

For each of the above types of UK tourist destination, you need to be able to name different destinations for each type. Using your own knowledge and a map of the UK to help you, create a list of five destinations for each category.

ICT can be used to help you with this task, either for research purposes or presenting your findings.

As part of your external examination, you need to be able to interpret and analyse data collected on the travel and tourism industry. The next activity contains data about the most visited places in the UK. This is a great opportunity to practise your skills of interpretation and analysis for your examination.

National Tourist Board regions	Number of trips made by UK residents (millions) in 1996	Number of trips made by UK residents (millions) in 2002
United Kingdom	154.2	167.3
Northumbria	3.7	4.8
Cumbria	3.7	4.3
North West	11.9	14.5
Yorkshire	11.9	12.2
East of England	15.8	14.5
Heart of England	18.9	24.6
London	12.9	16.1
Southern	11.5	14.6
South East England	11.9	10.9
South West	17.5	21.0
England	117.3	134.9
Wales	13.6	11.9
Scotland	19.6	18.5
Northern Ireland	3.8	2.8

Source: United Kingdom Tourism Survey, sponsored by the National Tourist Boards; International Passenger Survey, Office for National Statistics

1 What is the above data showing? (2 marks)

2 From 1996 to 2002, some areas of the UK have experienced an increase in the number of visitors to their area. Identify two of these areas. (2 marks)

3 The East of England is an area of the UK that has seen a decrease in the number of visitors between 1996 and 2002. As a hotel owner in Norwich (which is in the East of England), these figures have concerned you. What could you do as the hotel owner to try and attract tourists, and their money, to the area? (6 marks)

4 What factors do you think have contributed to the general increase in the number of visits made from 1996 to 2002? (6 marks)

5 Calculate the percentage change in number of visitors from 1996 to 2002 for London and Wales. (4 marks)

6 These figures show that overall there has been an increase in domestic tourism between 1996 and 2002. Despite the increase, what do you think are the challenges facing organisations involved in the domestic travel and tourism industry? (8 marks)

CASE STUDY

Mary, Ray and their friends

Mary and Ray are both in their seventies and have been retired for a number of years. They enjoy visiting Spain and the Canary Islands in the cold winter months for the sunshine and warmth. However, through the rest of the year Mary, Ray and several of their friends take pleasure in going on several trips to various UK destinations. Their trips take them all over the UK and last for five days, usually starting on a Monday and finishing on a Friday. They travel on organised coach tours. Recent places they have visited include Blackpool, Edinburgh, Truro and Eastbourne.

1 **Mary, Ray and their friends are part of an increasing group of senior citizens who have money to spend on travel and tourism. What do you think are the requirements of such travellers?**

2 **Most of Mary and Ray's holidays are organised group trips. Why do you think they prefer this to travelling alone?**

3 **Imagine you are working for 'Speedies', an organisation which specialises in coach trips for the over 65s. Choose a UK destination and conduct some research to plan a five-day holiday itinerary for Mary, Ray and their friends. You need to find a hotel with bed, breakfast and evening meal options, plan three-day trips and nightly evening entertainment.**

Inbound tourism

When you visit another country you are an *inbound tourist* to whichever country you are visiting. Therefore, visitors from other countries to the UK are inbound tourists. The UK is popular with inbound tourists and particularly with visitors from the USA due to the history and culture of this country. The idea of visiting royal palaces and castles and the birthplaces of famous writers such as Shakespeare, is a magnet to many inbound tourists.

Think about it

What makes the UK attractive to overseas visitors?

Skills practice

1 Prepare a questionnaire which includes questions about where travellers to a particular area have originated from. Include questions that will help you to discover where the traveller started their journey, how they travelled, why they are visiting a particular area and how long they are planning to spend in that area.

2 Visit an airport, railway station or bus station close to where you live to survey people who have just arrived at that destination to find out where they have come from. Use the questionnaire you prepared in Task 1 and remember to ask the permission of both individuals and the authorities of where you plan to survey travellers.

3 Analyse your results to draw conclusions about the origins of travellers. Use ICT to help present your findings in a professional manner. Analysis must also be numerical as well as written so use bar charts and pie charts etc. to illustrate your findings.

CASE STUDY

The Braithwaites

John and Colleen Braithwaite live in a suburb about twenty miles southeast of Sydney in New South Wales, Australia. John and Colleen have taken early retirement after selling their hardware business, which they ran for many years. After having spent several months travelling around Australia, they now want to visit the UK and Europe. John and Colleen have visited Europe before but only for a short period of time. They now wish to spend three months visiting the UK and continental Europe.

1   **John and Colleen are inbound tourists. In your own words what does this mean?**

2   **Suggest two ways John and Colleen could book their tour to the UK and Europe. For the two suggestions you make, consider the advantages and disadvantages of using those methods.**

3   **As inbound tourists John and Colleen contribute to the UK economy in many ways. How do you think they will contribute to the UK economy?**

4   **John and Colleen want to visit London as part of their trip. They have three days in the capital and want to visit at least five cultural tourist attractions. Use the Internet to plan an itinerary for John and Colleen based on their requirements.**

Skills practice

The UK is often very expensive for inbound tourists to visit. This is due in part to the high cost of living in the UK but is also due to the value of the pound and exchange rates. Carry out some research to answer the following questions, remembering that textbooks are also a great way to find out information, as is the Internet:

1   What are exchange rates?

2   If the value of the pound is high, what impact will this have on the number of tourists visiting the UK from overseas?

3   How can UK destinations and tourism agencies attract overseas visitors and overcome the problem of the UK being perceived as an expensive place to holiday in?

Outbound tourism

Leaving the UK in search of warmer weather and sunnier climes makes people outbound tourists. *Outbound tourism* involves UK residents leaving the UK and spending their holidays (and their money) in another country. Money spent by outbound tourists benefits the economies of the countries they visit and provides jobs and wages for local people.

In recent years, UK tourists have become much more adventurous in their choices of overseas destinations. In the 1950s and 1960s, the majority of outbound tourists from the UK would visit the Mediterranean resorts in Spain, such as Benidorm, Torremolinos and Lloret de Mar. During the 1980s, America and in particular the 'Sunshine State' of Florida became popular with UK tourists. The 1990s saw a growth in short-stay visits to cities and resorts in the Caribbean and the Far East, and South America also became popular.

The majority of destinations visited by tourists from the UK are accessed by air travel. Holidays involve either *short-haul* flights or *long-haul* flights. The distinction between the two is the length of flight needed to reach a particular destination. Short-haul flights usually take less than five hours and include destinations such as Greece, Spain, Portugal and other parts of Europe. Traditionally, short-haul destinations have been the major market for UK tourists visiting overseas, however the long-haul destinations have stolen some market share in recent years, as discussed earlier. Long-haul destinations take more than five hours to reach by air and this is the fastest growing segment of the holiday market.

Skills practice

You are a writer for a local newspaper and have been asked to contribute to the next edition's travel section. You have to write about the attractions of one long-haul destination from a choice of the Dominican Republic, Goa or Hong Kong. You need to include the following details:

• Where in the world the destination is

• How long it takes to reach the destination

• Attractions of that destination.

Domestic tourism UK residents visiting UK destinations for holidays and day-trips.

Inbound tourism Tourists from other countries visiting the UK for their holidays.

Outbound tourism UK residents visiting other countries for travel and tourism purposes.

Short-haul flights These flights are less than five hours long and mainly to European destinations.

Long-haul flights Flights to destinations, such as the USA, Caribbean and Africa, that take more than five hours.

Just like domestic tourists, outbound tourists are looking for a holiday to suit their own individual requirements and this has been a contributing factor in the variety and number of resorts visited by UK outbound tourists.

Skills practice

You are to imagine that you are working in a local travel agency and a variety of different customers have been to see you about finding a resort that would be suitable for their particular needs. Read the following descriptions and suggest resorts for these groups of people, stating why the resorts would be suitable.

1 Anne is a nineteen-year-old university student who wishes to go on holiday in the summer with five other friends who are the same age. The girls have a limited budget of £400 each and want to go away for one week only. The girls also want lazy days sunbathing and a resort with good nightlife.

2 James is an old romantic and wants to take his wife away for a surprise anniversary trip. Ideally, James would like to visit a city in Europe which is rich in culture, has good restaurants and breathtaking sights.

3 Steve and Vicky are intrepid travellers and each year try to visit a country they have never visited before. This year the couple have saved hard and have three weeks off work. They also like to take part in new and extreme sports. Over the last five years they have travelled to America, Italy, China, Mexico and France.

Skills practice

For your external examination you need to be able to interpret statistical information on types of tourism. Using your research skills, visit the website of the Office of National Statistics to find data on the most popular overseas destinations visited by UK tourists. Once you have collected this data, you can write a report showing your findings, using these guidelines:

- Which countries do UK tourists like to visit?
- Why do you think these resorts are popular?
- Do you think these destinations will still be as popular in ten years' time?

Why do people travel?

People travel for leisure, for business or to visit friends or relatives. These are the three main reasons people choose to travel. For each of these reasons, tourism can be domestic, inbound or outbound. For example, a group of friends visiting the Lake District for a weekend of walking would be classed as domestic tourists and the reason behind their trip would be leisure. Directors from a Japanese company who have opened a factory in the UK would be inbound tourists visiting the UK on business purposes. A brother and his wife visiting a relative who lives in New Zealand would be outbound tourists and the purpose of their visit is visiting friends and family.

Different reasons for travel mean that tourists have different needs and requirements based upon the purpose of their travel. A businessman when visiting London on a business trip may wish to stay in a hotel with conference facilities and which is close to an airport to receive international guests. However, the same businessman will have very different requirements when he visits London for the weekend with his family. He may want to stay in a hotel that is in the centre of London, close to all the main attractions, and which offers family rooms and children's meals. Therefore, the same tourist has very different requirements depending on the reason or purpose of his travel.

Leisure tourism

For many people, travelling away from home for a temporary period is for *leisure* purposes. Summer holidays, day trips to the seaside, shopping expeditions, all have leisure as the underlying reason. Holidays for leisure purposes can be classified into several categories.

Figure 1.3 Categories of leisure holidays

Skills practice

For each of the types of holiday for leisure purposes, write a definition. Once you have written a definition, use holiday brochures to find an example of each type of holiday.

Sightseeing and visiting attractions, whilst not strictly holidays, are still tourism activities with leisure at their core.

Skills practice

Conduct some research to find out about the visitor attractions in your local area.

Visiting friends or relatives

People today are more mobile than they have ever been. We move around the country and the world for work and therefore have *friends and relatives* living in different geographical areas. In 2001, this type of tourism accounted for 25 per cent of all holidays taken by UK tourists.

A beach holiday at home or abroad is one of the most popular leisure activities among UK tourists

Visiting loved ones and those close to you usually has one major advantage – free accommodation. Because of this tourists visiting friends and family tend to spend money saved on eating out, visiting leisure facilities and travelling around the area.

CASE STUDY

Travelling around the UK

Giovanni and Helen have lived in Leeds for the last three years. The couple met at university and after having lived in London for several years, and working hard and playing even harder, decided to move to be close to family.

Helen is from the Leeds area originally but Giovanni is from Brighton. The couple, wanting to settle down and start a family, felt that they wanted to be near to one set of family to help and support them. House prices were cheaper in the north and this swayed their decision to move to Leeds.

Most weekends, Helen and Giovanni either travel to stay with family or friends or have guests at their home. Their university friends live in different parts of the country especially between Nottingham and Bristol.

1   Why do Helen and Giovanni travel to certain parts of the country at weekends?
2   If friends and family visit Helen and Giovanni in Leeds, they do not have to pay for accommodation. How do these visitors contribute to the local economy of Leeds if they are not paying to stay in hotels?
3   Leeds is a very popular city and attracts many visitors because of its shopping attractions. It also has many cultural attractions such as the Royal Armouries. Conduct some research to find out about this attraction and suggest to Helen and Giovanni whether or not it is worth visiting.

Business tourism

Travel and tourism is not just for leisure and pleasure purposes. Many people have to travel as part of their jobs and this travel can be international as well as national. With a global economy, many companies operate in more than one country and employees may be required to visit other parts of the business in different countries.

Business travel is often quite luxurious, with first-class travel and accommodation in the best hotels. It may also often be viewed as a perk of a job and a real bonus.

Business people need to travel for several reasons. These may include:

* business meetings
* exhibitions and trade fairs
* conferences and conventions.

You work for a travel agent that specialises in making travel arrangements for local business people. An architect has approached you to organise a business trip for herself and three other colleagues to the Ideal Home Exhibition at the NEC in Birmingham. You need to:

* make travel arrangements by rail from your local railway station
* book tickets for the exhibition
* find overnight accommodation in Birmingham
* book a table for an evening meal at a top Birmingham restaurant
* fully cost the whole trip for the four architects.

CASE STUDY

Business travel

Phil Reynolds works as a Store Planner for Marks & Spencer Plc. Phil's job role is varied and his work takes him all over the UK and the Republic of Ireland (Eire). As a result, Phil travels a lot.

Phil's job role is primarily to design the interior and layout of Marks & Spencer stores. This ranges from refitting and refurbishing older stores to designing the layout and look of brand new stores for the company. Phil works as a member of a small team who between them look after all of the company's 360 stores.

Marks & Spencer Plc has had stores in Eire since the late 1970s. Due to the recent relaxation of planning laws in Eire, Marks & Spencer has followed an ambitious programme of opening new stores. As a Store Planner, Phil has done work in Eire on these new stores. He lives in North Nottinghamshire and regularly has to fly to Eire for work.

1   Why do you think Marks & Spencer pays for Phil to travel to Eire rather than employ a Store Planner in that country?
2   Phil lives in a small village in North Nottinghamshire, which is twenty miles from Nottingham city centre and twenty miles from the centre of Doncaster in South Yorkshire. Conduct some research into which airport would be best for Phil to travel from – Nottingham East Midlands or Leeds/Bradford? Consider the cost of flights, flight times, distance from home and frequency of flights to Eire. Use this information to fully justify your answer.
3   The arrival of low-cost airlines has made Phil's return journeys to Eire much cheaper. Why do you think airlines such as British Midland have made many of their flights much cheaper and marketed them under the banner of bmibaby, their low-cost carrier?
4   Phil takes responsibility for booking the majority of his own flights. The Internet is an invaluable tool for him as he books all his flights online. Why do you think Marks & Spencer prefer him to do this rather than use their agent American Express to book tickets?
5   Business travellers often have very specific requirements that they wish to be met. Make a list of these requirements and suggest how airports and airlines can meet these needs.

The nature of travel and tourism

The travel and tourism industry is continually developing to meet changing consumer needs, tastes and fashions. The characteristics of today's industry reflect its dynamic nature and the uniqueness of the products and services available.

Nature of products and services

Travel and tourism products and services are intangible, perishable and non-standardised

Travel and tourism products and services take on many different forms, such as holidays, excursions and holiday insurance. All of these products have one thing in common – they are *intangible*. Imagine you are going for a haircut. Your hair is cut to the required style and length and you pay for the service. You walk out of the hairdresser's and even though you have spent money you do not actually leave the shop with anything physical in your hand. You have though enjoyed a service that has been performed for you. Holidays and other travel and tourism products and services are like this. You pay to travel on an aeroplane to a chosen destination but you do not pay to own and take away part of the aircraft. Staying in a hotel, you sleep in a bed for a night but at the end of your stay you do not take the bed away with you.

As well as being difficult to handle physically, travel and tourism products have a limited life – i.e. they are perishable. Compare a holiday to food in your fridge at home. The food in the fridge has an expiry date on it and will be no good to eat after that date. With holidays, you only stay at your destination for a given period of time and at the end of your two-week stay in Spain, for example, the holiday also expires and you have to return home.

Travel and tourism products and services are also *non-standardised*. This means that they are all different. Consider two different families. Both the Smith family and the Jones family stay in the same hotel, in the same resort on the island of Gran Canaria for the same week in July. However, the two families have two completely different holiday experiences. The Smith family are happy to lie by the pool all week soaking up the sun. The Jones family on the other hand are much happier going on excursions to see other parts of the island, para sailing and scuba diving. The same holiday booked does not mean that the whole experience will be the same for all involved and therefore standardised.

Unlike buying a car, holidays and travel and tourism products and services cannot be test driven or sampled by a customer before they decide to purchase. This is why travel and tourism products and services are presented in a glossy, colourful, highly appealing way in travel brochures, as this is often what customers are going to base their purchasing decisions on. Many holidaymakers, however, do choose to visit resorts and destinations recommended by family and friends who have already experienced the holiday and can advise from first-hand knowledge. Some

tour operators send travel agents on trips to resorts they wish to promote in order to acquire first-hand knowledge that they can use when selling tour operators' products and services. Some tour operators are finding new ways to market and promote their products and services. For example, the promotion of Disneyland Paris and Disney World in Florida can be experienced in the comfort of your own home through videos produced by the Disney corporation to encourage people to purchase holidays to its resorts.

Key terms

Intangible products These are services that have been performed for you.

Perishable products These have a limited life span.

Non-standardised products The experiences of the products vary from person to person.

There is a vast range of travel and tourism products and services to choose from, as you can see from the brochures displayed at this travel agency

For each of the travel and tourism products and services listed below, write about how they are intangible, perishable and non-standardised.

- Cruise holiday
- A city-break holiday to Prague
- Holiday insurance for a skiing trip to France
- Services supplied by a resort representative
- Car hire
- A day excursion to a traditional market in Spain, as part of a two-week holiday.

Range of products and services

The travel and tourism industry is composed of a large number of small to medium-sized enterprises whose roles are interrelated

The number of providers of travel and tourism products and services is vast. Look in your local business directory and you will see there are many organisations that can sell you a holiday, provide transportation or accommodation. Some of these organisations are part of larger regional, national or international chains, however the majority are small to medium in size and their roles are interrelated. This means that they either offer similar products and services or provide products and services that need another organisation to provide other products and services to make a customer's travel and tourism experience complete. For example, a bed and breakfast accommodation provider located near to Sherwood Forest relies on the local council properly maintaining the Sherwood Forest Country Park and the Major Oak. If these are not well looked after, then visitors will not want to come to the area and the bed and breakfast provider will experience a downturn in guest numbers.

This task involves researching the provision of travel and tourism products in your local area.

You need to research all the enterprises, individuals and organisations that provide tourist products and services and describe how their roles are interrelated.

Commercial organisations

The travel and tourism industry is dominated by commercial organisations

Travel and tourism organisations have many different aims and objectives. Generally they want to provide the general public with a quality service and value for money. However, the main motivation behind doing this is to make a profit. Many millions of pounds are spent each year on travel and tourism by consumers and each organisation providing the products and services wants a share of the money spent.

Commercial organisations are those that operate to make a profit and are therefore in the private sector of the economy. The private sector of the economy is made up of organisations that are started by entrepreneurs, individuals or groups. The government provides no resources to this sector of the economy.

The main purpose of commercial organisations is to make a profit

Many of the largest companies in the UK are involved in travel and tourism. Examples include British Airways, Forte (hotels) and the Tussaud's Group that owns attractions including Madame Tussaud's and Alton Towers.

Public and voluntary organisations

The travel and tourism industry is supported and influenced by public and voluntary organisations

Commercial organisations may dominate the travel and tourism industry, however both the public and voluntary sectors of the economy play a role in supporting and influencing the industry.

Public sector facilities are funded and controlled by the government. This could be national government or local government, such as local councils. The government has become involved in tourism because of the positive effects of tourism and the income and jobs that are created by the industry.

Voluntary sector organisations are funded and run by volunteer organisations. Most of their income comes from membership fees, gifts, legacies, selling merchandise and public appeals. Organisations in the public or voluntary sectors do not aim to make a profit; they merely provide services and support the industry. So, how do these two sectors support and influence the travel and tourism industry?

Public sector organisations involved in travel in tourism include the British Tourist Authority (BTA), the English Tourism Council (ETC), the Wales Tourist Board (WTB) and the Scottish Tourist Board (STB). These organisations are funded by central government (national

government) and in 1999–2000 the Department for Culture, Media and Sport gave just under £50 million to the BTA and ETC. The STB and WTB both received over £15 million each from their own executives. Services provided by these tourism authorities include providing tourist information offices, funding marketing campaigns and funding new tourism facilities. They also play an advisory role in helping principals in the private sector to make decisions and respond to current trends and fashions by providing information on visitor numbers, for example.

One way in which the public sector has worked to support tourism is by scrapping admission fees to many of London's top museums and attractions. In the year 2003–2004, visitor numbers to these attractions were thought to have increased by around 50 per cent.

Voluntary organisations in the travel and tourism industry are generally formed to

✳ meet a particular interest or need in the community, for example a sport

✳ raise interest in a particular problem, such as a conservation issue

✳ encourage constructive use of leisure time, for example Scouts and Guides.

The National Trust is probably the most important voluntary sector organisation involved in tourism. Its work ranges from protecting historic buildings, gardens and coastlines, which attract millions of visitors a year. In recent years, the organisation has also run conservation holidays for volunteers who want to do something useful with their leisure time. Activities for volunteers can range from conducting wildlife surveys to laying new hedgerows. The National Trust runs working holidays called Acorn Projects and Oak Camps. The Royal Society for the Protection of Birds (RSPB) also offers holidays in its reserves for volunteers who want to do conservation work.

The National Trust offers holiday facilities such as accommodation and attractions such as historic buildings

Skills practice

Visit a local National Trust attraction. Take a tour of the attraction to get a sense of the work undertaken by the organisation. Try to find out information on visitor numbers.

Think about it

What contribution do you think voluntary sector organisations make to the tourism industry?

Very often organisations in the private, public and voluntary sectors work together, for example on conserving and maintaining tourist attractions.

Key terms

Private sector This comprises those organisations that operate to make a profit.
Public sector This comprises those organisations that are funded and controlled by government.
Voluntary sector This comprises those organisations that are funded and run by volunteer agencies.

Think about it

How do you think organisations in the private, public and voluntary sectors can work together?

Internal and external pressures

The travel and tourism industry is vulnerable to internal and external pressures

What stops you doing what you want to do? Is it that you don't have enough money to go on a dream holiday or do your parents insist that you are back home by a certain time in the evenings? Or was the concert you had booked tickets for months in advance cancelled because the lead singer of the band was ill? Some of these effects on your life are *internal* and can be controlled to a certain degree by yourself. Other effects are *external* and you have no control over these. The travel and tourism industry is no different as it is also vulnerable to internal and external pressures.

Examples of the internal pressures on the travel and tourism industry are health and safety issues and the need to rationalise costs.

Think about it

What other internal pressures do you think organisations in the travel and tourism industry are under?

External pressures are more difficult to control. Even though organisations can plan to deal with

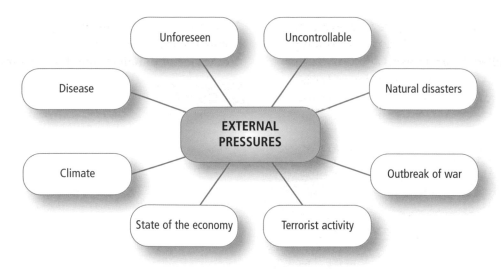

Figure 1.4 External pressures are more difficult to control than internal pressures

these pressures, the responses to them are primarily reactionary in nature.

The principals of the travel and tourism industry (the different organisations who offer different products and services) must find ways to deal with both internal and external pressures to minimise their impact on operations and revenues/profits.

Recent pressures on the travel and tourism industry have mainly been external in their nature. Examples that have had a huge impact on the travel and tourism industry include the 9/11 attacks on New York, the SARS virus, the Iraq conflict and the South East Asian tsunami.

Skills practice

In 2001, an outbreak of Foot and Mouth disease swept across the UK. Carry out research to answer the following questions.

1 What is Foot and Mouth disease and whom does it affect?

2 Which areas of the UK were most affected by the outbreak of the disease?

3 What measures were put in place to reduce the spread of the disease?

4 How do you think the outbreak of the disease affected the UK tourism industry? Consider the impact on both domestic and inbound tourism.

CASE STUDY

9/11

A day that shook the world – September 11th 2002. This was the day terrorists hijacked passenger aircraft and flew them into the Twin Towers buildings of the World Trade Organisation in New York. These huge, impressive buildings crumbled to the ground and thousands of people lost their lives.

1 **What impact do you think this tragic event had on travel and tourism?**

2 **Why do you think the numbers of people travelling globally, not just in America, declined after this event?**

3 **As a result of 9/11, security in airports the world over has been stepped up to try and prevent another tragedy such as this. What do you think have been the consequences of improved and heightened security measures for ordinary travellers?**

4 **What do you think are the challenges facing tourism officials in America in the aftermath of this event?**

Tsunami sweeps South East Asia

Boxing Day 2004, thousands of tourists were waking to another day in paradise. The beaches of South East Asia were beginning to fill with holidaymakers ready to soak up the sunshine of a glorious day. Resorts in Thailand, Indonesia, India and Sri Lanka were busy and full of European tourists escaping the traditional cold weather of the festive period in Europe.

At around 9.30 in the morning local time, the unthinkable happened. An underwater earthquake measuring approximately 9 on the Richter scale, the world's fourth worst earthquake since records began, shook the area without warning and created gigantic tidal waves which pounded coastal areas in the region. Whole towns and resorts were destroyed, hundreds of thousands lost their lives, disease became a real threat and supplies of fresh water and food ran out.

The rest of the world launched massive relief projects to help the people and local economies of those areas affected. Tourists who were left with little more than the clothes they had on were flown home, whilst others continued their holidays.

1 Tourism has played a major part in supporting the economies of less economically developed countries in South East Asia. What impact do you think the tsunami will have had on tourism in the area?

2 As a tourism official in one of the affected countries, how would you try to attract visitors back to the area?

3 Those tourists who survived unscathed from the tsunami and continued with their holidays were criticised in the media for enjoying themselves sunbathing and drinking in the midst of such tragedy. Do you think the tourism authorities in affected countries would have been pleased that tourists behaved in this way? Explain your answer.

4 Natural disasters happen all over the world. Can you think of any other tourist destinations that have been hit by a natural disaster in recent years?

An example of the devastation caused by the tsunami that struck coastal resort areas of South East Asia on Boxing Day 2004

The economic climate in a country also has an impact on tourism. Economies behave in a cyclical fashion. At times economies and countries are prosperous, with the majority of people in work earning money and spending that money. The opposite of this boom situation is a recession. If a country's economy is in recession, then unemployment is high and people have less money to spend on luxuries and non-necessities such as travel and tourism.

Impact of travel and tourism

Travel and tourism activities impact on destinations and host communities

Governments across the world are keen to promote and support tourism, as the industry is a major provider of foreign investment and jobs. However, not all the impacts of tourism on host destinations and communities are seen as positive. Both the positive and negative impacts of tourism is examined below in terms of their effects on the economy, culture and environment of host communities. *Host communities* are the people who live in the areas that tourists visit.

Positive economic impacts of tourism

✳ Job creation – employees are needed to work in hotels, restaurants and other facilities aimed at attracting tourists.

✳ Wealth creation – local people employed in the travel and tourism industry earn money and in turn demand and consume more products and services. This has an impact on jobs in other industries.

✳ Other parts of the world become aware of the host destination and community, and so trade other than tourism may result from this.

✳ The infrastructure of an area is improved. Roads and airports are built to deal with the increased number of visitors, again increasing job and earning opportunities.

✳ Tourists spend money on food and drink, accommodation and entertainment. This money is spent at local businesses and some of this is then invested in providing new facilities that locals as well as tourists can use and enjoy.

Negative economic impacts of tourism

✳ Prices of goods, services and houses tend to rise in tourist areas. These prices often rise too high for the people of the host communities to afford.

✳ Seasonal work. Many jobs that are created by the tourism industry are only temporary, so local workers may have reduced incomes during the 'off-season', when no or fewer tourists visit.

✳ Tourism depends on other economies flourishing. For example, if lots of German tourists visit a particular resort each year, and then the German economy goes into recession with increases in taxation, interest rates and unemployment, this may mean that many Germans can no longer afford to holiday at the resort.

✳ Loss of local services. Shops may become more geared towards serving tourists than locals, with, for example, the sale of souvenirs taking over from the sale of groceries.

✳ Jobs in tourism are notoriously low paid.

✳ Many hotels are owned by companies based in other countries. The profits from these hotels therefore do not stay in the host community but flow out to another country. This has an impact on future development of the area.

Positive cultural impacts of tourism

✳ Host communities have contact with the outside world and the people become more educated, for example learning other languages to be able to communicate with tourists.

✳ As facilities increase, the social life of the population increases.

✳ Rather than dying out with older generations, cultures and traditions can be preserved and remembered because tourists find them interesting.

Negative cultural impacts of tourists

✳ Loss of identity. Host communities can feel like strangers as the tourists take over.

✳ Bad habits and practices can be spread, for example tourists introduce smoking, drinking and recreational drug-taking that host communities may not have been exposed to before.

✳ Traditions and religions can become ignored because tourists have no knowledge of them.

✳ Host communities can be exploited by tourists.

Positive environmental impacts of tourism

✳ Derelict and run-down areas are cleaned up and regenerated.

✳ Old buildings are converted into tourist accommodation.

✳ Areas are pedestrianised and signposting is improved.

Negative environmental impacts of tourism

✳ Physical erosion of landscapes and coastlines.

✳ Litter.

✳ Increased pollution – air, sea and noise pollution.

✳ Increased traffic congestion.

✳ Disturbance of wildlife.

✳ Reduction of natural habitats.

✳ Alteration of landscapes.

✳ Encouragment of inappropriate development.

Skills practice

Tourism is a developing industry in many countries, particularly as travellers want to visit more exotic locations. You are to write a project on the impact of tourism on either The Gambia or Phuket in Thailand. Your project should have the following structure:

• Where the destination is located and what facilities it has

• Economic impacts on host communities of tourism (positive and negative)

• Cultural impacts on host communities of tourism (positive and negative)

• Environmental impacts on host communities of tourism (positive and negative)

• Evaluation – overall do you think tourism has benefited or hindered the destination you have investigated?

Think about it

How can tourist destinations work to reduce the negative impacts of tourism?

Moves have been made in recent years to take a more responsible attitude towards tourism, especially where it is a growing industry in the less economically developed countries. The aim has been to protect host communities from being exploited and to reduce the impact of pollution on natural environments.

Key terms associated with this movement are *responsible tourism*, *sustainable tourism* and *eco-tourism*. *Responsible tourism* refers not only to developers taking a sensible approach towards the development of tourist resorts but also to the way in which tourists behave and the activities they take part in whilst in a resort. For example, responsible tourism can include the choice of souvenirs that tourists choose to purchase. An example of this is tourists to Africa not buying souvenirs made from ivory and therefore not supporting the illegal trade of elephant hunting and ivory poaching.

Sustainable tourism seeks to tackle the long-term environmental and social issues surrounding uncontrolled tourism development. Much development in tourist destinations has taken place on an ad hoc basis and has become disjointed because there has been little formal planning and control. Sustainable tourism aims to strike a healthy balance between conserving areas of natural beauty, meeting the needs of local people and the desire to attract tourists and meet their demands.

The natural beauty of New Zealand is one of the great attractions for tourists

Green issues and the environment have become important issues in the travel and tourism industry. Global warming and climate change have been at the centre of many concerns and *eco-tourism* is an ethos that promotes environmentally friendly tourism. This involves resorts and accommodation being built out of locally sourced materials that are also replenishable. Some resorts in Indonesia have been built using such materials and are also powered by solar power.

The development of the travel and tourism industry

To help you understand the nature of today's travel and tourism industry, it is important that you realise how the industry has developed over a long period of time. This section will examine the historical developments and factors that have contributed to creating the dynamic, ever-changing and still-developing travel and tourism industry of today.

In this section you will learn:

✱ The factors contributing to the emergence of mass tourism, rather than tourism for the wealthy elite

✱ The technological developments relating to infrastructure, transport and information systems and their impact on tourism destinations

✱ The product development, innovation and the major developments which have shaped the industry

✱ The needs of consumers, their expectations and fashions change, and organisations in the travel and tourism industry must respond to these changes.

Tourism for all?

One hundred and fifty years ago holidays were a luxury only the wealthy could afford to enjoy. The UK seaside resorts, for example, were once the

In Victorian times only those who were rich enough could afford to take holidays

preserve of rich Victorians who took the sea air as part of their health regimes. So how has the travel and tourism industry developed so that the majority of people now participate in travel and tourism activities in some way?

There are various factors that explain the emergence of the mass tourism. These include:

* Socio-economic influences
* Technological developments
* Product development and innovation
* Changing consumer needs, expectations and fashions.

The development of the travel and tourism industry has taken place over many years and the growth of leisure travel has its origins in the nineteenth century.

Travel and tourism in the nineteenth century

Finding a cure for medical ailments led to the introduction of holiday centres in the eighteenth century. For the wealthy who could afford to travel and who also had time for cures to take effect, the spa towns of Bath, Scarborough and Cheltenham, and coastal towns such as Brighton and Bognor Regis, became popular. The wealthy who visited these resorts believed that taking to the waters would cure a range of illnesses and conditions, from rheumatism to gout. As the number of visitors to these resorts increased, the demand for entertainment and accommodation grew. At this time overseas travel was the

preserve of the aristocracy and those who were extremely well-connected and wealthy. Young aristocrats were often sent on a 'Grand Tour' of European cities as this was believed to be a valuable part of their education.

It was not until the emergence of the railways in the nineteenth century that the less wealthy began to enjoy visiting seaside resorts. Resorts such as Margate, Blackpool and Southport grew as a result of direct transport links with major cities. People also travelled to the resorts by road, often by stagecoach, but this was slower than travelling by rail and was more expensive. Hotels were built close to many of the new railway stations to service the growing demand for travel and accommodation.

As well as developments in transportation, the nineteenth century saw a shift in the geographical distribution of people from rural locations to new urban areas. As workers moved from the countryside as a result of the Industrial Revolution to take jobs in the new mills and factories, the earning potential of this group increased. This in turn meant that more people had disposable income to spend on leisure pursuits, transport and travel. However, only a minority of people could afford to access travel and transportation; the majority of the population were still excluded by the cost.

Overseas travel also became increasingly popular during the latter half of the nineteenth century. The Great Exhibition at Crystal Palace in 1851, for example, attracted visitors from all parts of the British Empire.

Carry out research using your library to help you answer the following questions.

1 What was the Great Exhibition of 1851?

2 Who organised the Great Exhibition?

3 What effect do you think the Great Exhibition had on tourism in the UK?

Travel and tourism in the twentieth century

During the twentieth century, the travel and tourism industry grew rapidly into the industry it is today. For socio-economic and technological reasons, many more people were able to participate in travel and tourism activities and this developed into mass tourism.

Pollution, congestion, and parking difficulties are common problems we face with modern motoring and the use of cars. However, this has not always been the case. At the beginning of the twentieth century, car ownership was restricted to the wealthy few and cars were not viewed as the reliable mode of transport they are today. During the inter-war years (1919–1938), car ownership grew as cars were manufactured more cheaply and prices fell. New tourist areas were opened up, particularly those that had previously been inaccessible by ferry or train. With improved road networks, more restaurants, hotels and caravan sites emerged as travellers could go further than ever before. Bus and coach companies also flourished as travellers became more adventurous and paid holidays gave the working classes the opportunity to take time off work and afford to spend a holiday away from home, even if only for a week.

Before travel to overseas destinations became popular with UK tourists from the 1950s onwards, most people would holiday in the UK, particularly in holiday resorts such as Butlins and Pontin's, which became popular for family holidays. The resorts (which were called 'camps' at the time) provided all the necessary facilities on site and they could be accessed from any part of the country by way of the extensive network of dual carriageways and major roads that had been built.

The development of the travel and tourism industry is a key component of Unit 1 for the Applied GCE in Travel and Tourism. The external examination requires you to be able to write confidently about some of the major developments in the industry, such as the creation of holiday resorts in the UK, which was a major turning point in the working classes accessing holidays and becoming tourists. The following activity will not only help to improve your research skills but will help in building your knowledge for your examination.

Conduct as much research as you can on Billy Butlin, the man who founded Butlins' holiday resorts, and create a report using the following as headings to guide your research. Your report should be in a formal business style.

1 How it all began – the first holiday resort, Skegness 1937

2 The growth of the holiday resorts

3 Competitors to Butlins

4 The 1970s and 1980s – why did visitor numbers to holiday centres fall?

5 The 1990s – making holiday resorts attractive again

6 Now and the future – what is on offer at the holiday resorts today and what does the future hold?

A modern Butlins holiday resort

Holiday resorts such as Butlins and Pontin's enjoyed great popularity; some employers even developed resorts just for their own staff to visit and use. The civil service was one example, where the idea was to provide employees with subsidised holidays to keep them motivated, as it was believed that staff who played together would also work much better together!

As travel by road became increasingly popular, fewer people were travelling by sea and rail than in the nineteenth century. Car ownership and the technological innovations in the air travel industry meant that travel by road and air became the preferred methods of transport by most travellers by the end of the twentieth century.

The development of fighting airforces in the First and Second World Wars paved the way for much of the development in the air travel industry. The advances made in knowledge and technology was transferred to commercial airlines, so that by 1952 travellers were being transported from the UK to the other side of the world using new turbojet technology. Air travel was twice as fast at the end of the Second World War as it had been at the beginning. The need for trained pilots during the war meant that after the end of hostilities, many men were qualified to fly and were employed by the new and emerging commercial passenger airlines.

CASE STUDY

Growing up on a holiday camp

Paul is now in his fifties, but recounts growing up on a holiday camp run by the civil service for their staff. His parents worked in the holiday camp.

'We lived in a cottage tied to the holiday camp. It was quite primitive really – no mains electricity, no running water and no indoor loo. It was really bleak and a far cry from the holiday camp where civil service staff would come in the summer for their one or two week holiday.

'The holiday camp was just outside Scarborough in Yorkshire and my parents had moved from London to Scarborough to find work there. Dad worked as a chef and Mum as a cleaner. I'm not sure how good a chef Dad was, but he got the job as he'd been in the army catering corps during the war. Mum cleaned out the chalets, which were like rows of Nissan huts and I suppose they were quite simple inside. I have photographs of my parents with the rest of the camp's staff from each year they worked there. Dad looked all smart in his chef's whites, Mum had a tunic-type uniform and the staff who ran all the sporting activities for guests wore crisp white uniforms and looked quite fearsome!

'As a child I was allowed free roam of the holiday camp during the school summer holidays. I would help out and watch all the different activities. The holidays were really hectic, with guests running from one activity or contest to the next. It didn't seem very relaxing to me! Meal times were always fascinating to watch. Guests queued up to take their seats in the large restaurant and would be called up table by table to help themselves from the buffet. It was more like a work's canteen actually, but the food always smelt good and there never seemed to be any left. Perhaps Dad was an okay cook after all!

'We left the holiday camp when Dad went to work for the local water board. I still remember it well though'

1 Do you think that today's tourists would enjoy staying at a holiday camp like the one described in the case study? Explain your answer.
2 Why do you think employers who ran such holiday camps closed them down in the 1960s and 1970s?

The UK holiday resorts were able to provide all the entertainment, food and other facilities for a family holiday, however there was one thing they couldn't guarantee – good summer holiday weather. So the idea of taking holidays overseas where the weather was guaranteed to be dry, hot and sunny had considerable appeal to the British holidaymaker; and the package holiday was born.

The British were soon flocking to the Spanish Mediterranean resorts of Benidorm, Lloret de Mar and Torremolinos on package holidays. Spain offered great weather, another culture and cheap food and wine. Costa Brava, Costa Dorada, Costa del Sol and Costa Blanca also became popular with UK tourists, and early holidaymakers to these resorts paid as little as £50 for their holiday in paradise. As package holidaymakers became more adventurous, they began travelling to Portugal, Greece and Turkey, for example.

CASE STUDY

Marjorie and George

Marjorie and George live in Derby and go on holiday at least three times a year to an overseas destination. Their favourite destinations include Benidorm in Spain, Santa Ponsa on the Spanish island of Majorca and Playa de las Americas on the island of Tenerife. They first started visiting Mediterranean resorts in the early 1960s and discuss some of their experiences here.

Marjorie: Before we started going to Spain, we would visit UK seaside resorts such as Skegness, Bridlington and Blackpool. I really liked those places, they were good fun.

George: If what you describe as running from one bus shelter to the next and from café to café to avoid the rain as fun, then I suppose it was. I remember going to Skegness one year and it rained so much that the caravan we were staying in sank in the field. We left the caravan only a handful of times during the week we were there.

Marjorie: That's why we first started going abroad. One of George's friends from work had been to Spain the same week we spent in the caravan at Skegness. They came back all nice and brown and we came back soggy! I said to George that I'd love to feel the sunshine on my face and Spain seemed so exotic.

George: I agreed to go and we've never looked back since. We went to Benidorm the first time and stayed in a lovely, brand-new hotel. It was all shiny marble and white and clean and absolutely nothing like our old caravan. I was sold. No more summers in the rain in caravans or guesthouses where you have to be out all-day and back in at 11 at night.

Marjorie: The freedom was great. The weather was great. And most of all the wine was great. It was all so different from going on holiday at home. We saw flamenco dancers at night, sat on the beach during the day and ate in the hotel three times a day. Our neighbours were so jealous when we returned and everyone wanted to see our photos.

George: And we got to fly, so no driving for me. Even now, it's Spain every time for us when we go on holiday.

1 Why do you think Mediterranean resorts became centres for mass tourism?
2 When Mediterranean resorts first became popular what do you think was the impact on British resorts?
3 Not everybody likes to go overseas for his or her holidays. Why do you think some tourists prefer to holiday at home?
4 Many resorts in the UK have to compete with overseas resorts for holidaymakers. Imagine you work for a local tourist board and want to attract tourists to your area. How could you do this?

Travel to overseas destinations meant that UK residents were spending their money abroad and not in this country. This, coupled with a decline in visitor numbers to UK destinations, led to the Development of Tourism Act of 1969. Tourism potentially earned the country a great deal of money and provided many jobs. Around the world economies were growing and booming as most of the world recovered from the struggle of the post-war years. People were more inquisitive and wanted to travel and explore, so the 1969 Act aimed to coordinate marketing activities of promoting the UK as a holiday destination to foreigners and to improve facilities that would attract tourists. Regional tourist boards were also established to help promote tourism in particular areas of the UK.

Skills practice

Contact your local tourist board to find out about the range of activities they are involved in to promote your area as a tourist attraction.

Throughout the twentieth century, travel and tourism continued to evolve and to provide a host of products and services tourists could choose from. From the introduction of holiday camps to the emergence of the package holiday to overseas destinations, tourism was certainly very different at the end of the century than at the beginning. Consumer needs have changed dramatically and the choice of holidays is wide-ranging, including beach holidays, long-haul destinations, activity holidays, short breaks, self-drives and fly-drives.

Travel and tourism in the twenty-first century

Technology and the sophistication of modern tourists have ensured that already in this century the travel and tourism industry has seen many changes.

The growth in the use of personal computers has had a huge impact on the travel and tourism industry and poses a threat to many of the traditional principals involved in servicing customers. Product development and innovation has played a large role in the changing face of the industry. Internet travel companies such as lastminute.com and ebookers enable tourists to become more independent and avoid the services of a travel agent. Package holidays are still popular but there has been considerable growth in the cruise sector. This sector was previously seen as catering for the older generation but now taking a cruise is seen as being in a 'floating hotel', with all amenities under one roof and providing the opportunity to visit different destinations.

Developments in travel and tourism

The brief history of the development of the travel and tourism industry has given an insight into how the industry has reached its current position. Tourism and travel provide in the region of two million jobs in the UK and more than 25 million overseas visitors are attracted to the UK each year. The industry is of utmost importance to the UK economy. Some of the main historical developments and factors that have led to the growth of the industry and its current characteristics will now be examined in more detail.

Changes in socio-economic circumstances

We have already seen that over the last two centuries travel and tourism has become more accessible to the working classes. Traditionally, only the wealthy could afford to travel, so how have the working classes been able to increasingly participate in travel and tourism?

Better pay and conditions for workers is the key to why more people could afford to travel and spend a holiday away from home. Legislation compelled employers to treat their workers better and in 1938 the government passed the Holidays with Pay Act. This increased the potential for holidaymaking among workers. Previously holidays were unpaid or unauthorised, which meant that workers would either lose money or their jobs. However, the 1938 Act was not strictly observed until a decade after it was introduced, and it was then that people's travel behaviour really began to change.

Paid holidays, as well as reduced working hours, gave workers more leisure time and more disposable income. Disposable income is what you have left to spend after all of your bills and overheads have been paid. Having more money enabled the working classes to take daytrips, buy cars and go on holidays. So, the changes in their socio-economic circumstances enabled the working classes to take part in tourist activities.

Technological developments

Technology has played a major role in the growth of the travel and tourism industry. In particular, the development of transport systems and infrastructure has allowed visitors to access previously inaccessible destinations. The introduction of the railways, passenger ferries, cars and aeroplanes has enabled people to travel, and without them travel tourism would not exist.

As well as the building of railway tracks and stations, motorways and airports, the development of new materials offering greater flexibility, durability and strength has affected the design of aeroplanes, cars and communication systems, making them cheaper and longer lasting. These costs are then in turn passed on to customers.

The use of computers has revolutionised many aspects of the travel and tourism industry. Notable examples include air traffic control, automated aircraft flying and landing procedures, computerised navigation, automated baggage handling, hotel management and security systems and payment systems.

Booking holidays has become easier due to advances in technology. Travel arrangements can now be made much more quickly and easily through central reservation systems which travel agents can access. These central reservation systems allow the travel agent to book, confirm and issue tickets instantly and whilst the customer is in the shop. Walk into almost any travel agent and each sales consultant will be equipped with a personal computer on their desk that allows them to access information from a range of tour operators. The central reservation systems hold banks of information about available holidays, scheduled airline bookings, car rental, hotel accommodation and the booking of excursions, activities and other entertainments. A queuing system is used to manage incoming messages and requests for travel arrangements and a customer's details can be saved and held ready for when they wish to make a reservation. Tour operators are also able to respond quickly to unsold holidays by offering special deals and promotions to travel agents, and ultimately to customers.

Computers have revolutionised the travel and tourism industry, particularly in air traffic control

Product development, innovation and changing consumer needs

The range of products and services offered to customers has become increasingly sophisticated, a long way from the early days of excursions offered by Thomas Cook. Through any travel agent you can book a holiday and you can purchase insurance, organise car rental and book airport car parking.

Tourists have also become more sophisticated and knowledgeable, and therefore more demanding in what they want. They look for new places to visit and better offers from travel and tourism organisations. Those organisations which fail to meet these sorts of demands risk going out of business. The following are examples of product development and innovation over time:

∗ Thomas Cook's first overseas tour to the USA in 1855

∗ Billy Butlin opens his first holiday resort in 1937

∗ Package holidays introduced to the Mediterranean in the 1950s and 1960s

∗ Growth of budget airlines offering customers cheap flights to a range of destinations in the 1990s

∗ Growth of the cruising sector and the cruise ship as 'floating hotel' in the early 2000s.

Not only have the products changed dramatically over the years, so have the ways you can buy these products. Thomas Cook pioneered the idea of travel agents operating from an office through which customers can make their travel arrangements. Some tour operators then decided to cut out the 'middle man' and sell their holidays direct to the general public. People could then book holidays by filling out and sending off an order form or by using the telephone to contact the tour operator. Other tour operators use new technologies to promote and sell holidays, for example on television information systems such as Teletext and through advertising on commercial television channels. Viewers can browse through hundreds of offers and then telephone tour operators to take advantage of the offers. In recent years the growth of satellite and cable television channels has stimulated the setting up of channels dedicated to informing viewers about particular holiday destinations and selling a variety of holidays to them.

Television is a powerful medium for advertising and selling holidays. However, the Internet has made the greatest impact on the travel and tourism industry in recent times. There are many websites selling holidays to travellers who are increasingly confident about making their own travel arrangements. Lastminute.com and ebookers are well-established websites that bring together different elements of the travel and tourism industry and often have special offers saving tourists lots of money.

ICT has played a major role in changing the travel and tourism industry. Another major influence has been the changing requirements of customers. Tourists have become more sophisticated and demanding in their needs, with the result that destinations and resorts fall in and out of fashion as tourists satisfy those needs. Early travel companies offered customers only a narrow range of holidays, so in that sense they dictated what kind of holidays people had. However, tourists are now much more sophisticated and through what they demand from a holiday they dictate what the travel companies must be prepared to offer. Travel companies must now follow fashions and the requirements of customers if they are to stay trading.

The Mediterranean resorts became so popular in the 1960s because of the way they were marketed to people, the majority of whom had never been overseas before. At the time these resorts were perceived as exotic, however as tourists became more knowledgeable about the destinations and confident about travelling to holiday at these, they began demanding different holiday destinations, so that in the 1980s and 1990s holiday fashions moved from the Mediterranean to Greece, America, the Caribbean and the Far East.

The needs of consumers have changed and they now expect so much more from their travels. They now demand many different types of holidays. Examples include:

* Short-breaks to city destinations
* Long-haul holidays to exotic destinations
* Activity holidays – skiing, cycling, painting
* Self-drive
* Fly-drive
* Self-packaging (independently booking and organising holidays without the help of travel agents).

Skills practice

For your external examination, you need to study at least two destinations in the UK and overseas. In preparation for the examination, the next activity will provide you with case studies that you can then use in your examination answers.

CASE STUDY

Benidorm

Changing consumer needs, expectations and fashions have had a significant influence on the travel and tourism industry. Benidorm in Spain has long been a favourite of British holidaymakers and it is your task to conduct research on this Mediterranean resort. Once you have collected research to answer the questions below, you will be able to make judgements about the success of the resort using your skills of analysis and evaluation.

1   **Whereabouts in Spain is Benidorm located? Which airport serves the resort? How far away are any of Spain's large cities?**

2   **How did Benidorm grow into the resort it is today? (This needs to include information about the historical development of the resort.)**

3   **When and why did Benidorm become so popular with British tourists?**

4   **What attractions and facilities does Benidorm have today to attract tourists?**

5   **How many British tourists visit Benidorm each year?**

6   **Is Benidorm as popular today as it once was? Why?**

7   **What threats are there to Benidorm continuing as a holiday hotspot?**

8   **How can the resort respond to any threats and changes in consumer demands?**

As another case study of an overseas resort, this task can be repeated for Florida or for the resort of Kardamena on the Greek island of Kos.

Paris

Sacré-Coeur, the Champs Elysées, the Eiffel Tower and the fine restaurants, just a few of the attractions and delights of Paris, the French capital. All of this and only an hour's flight from some UK airports. Always popular with UK tourists, Paris has seen an increase in the number of UK visitors within the last few years.

1 **What reasons can you think of have contributed to the growth in the number of UK visitors to Paris?**
2 **Paris is a popular short-break destination. Can you name five other short-break destinations?**
3 **Choose a large city that is located near to where you live. What attractions does this city have that could attract short-break holidaymakers?**

The following are the milestones in the development of travel and tourism.

1700s	Paid employment and regulated working hours
1750s	Beginning of the Industrial Revolution
1815	First steam-driven sea voyage (Glasgow to Dublin)
1830	First passenger train service (Manchester to Liverpool)
1840s	Cunard began a regular shipping service to America. P & O sailed regularly to India and the Far East
1841	Thomas Cook's first 'day' excursion from Leicester to Loughborough via rail
1851	The Great Exhibition at Crystal Palace attracts visitors from far and wide
1855	Thomas Cook organises his first overseas tour to the Paris Exhibition of 1855
1860	Invention of bicycle – independent travel for the masses
1860s	Regular ferry services to Ireland and across the Channel were in operation
1865	Thomas Cook opens an office in London
1866	Thomas Cook organises first tour to America
1869	The opening of the Suez Canal makes India and the Far East easier to travel to
1869	The USA could be completely crossed by rail as a link between the Union Pacific and Central Pacific railways is opened
1870	60-hour working week became the standard. Half-day holiday introduced on Saturday afternoon, later known as the weekend
1871	Bank Holiday Act establishes four public Bank Holidays
1880s	The first skiing holidaymakers travelled from the UK to Switzerland
1885	Invention of the motorcar
1900s	Vast improvement in road, rail, sea and air transport
1918	After the First World War, bus and coach services began to appear

1920s	Air services develop mainly to transport mail to the British colonies and to carry military personnel. Air travel is still expensive and unreliable at this time	**1970**	First Boeing 747 carries 352 on a transatlantic flight
1935	Approximately 500,000 visitors crowded into Brighton on August Bank Holiday. The majority arrived by rail or specially organised coach services	**1971**	BOAC and BEA merge and are administered by the British Airways Board

1920s   Air services develop mainly to transport mail to the British colonies and to carry military personnel. Air travel is still expensive and unreliable at this time

1935   Approximately 500,000 visitors crowded into Brighton on August Bank Holiday. The majority arrived by rail or specially organised coach services

1935   Gatwick aerodrome opened to relieve congestion at Croydon. At this time Gatwick could handle six aircraft at a time

1936   First train ferry service between Dover and Dunkirk. Passengers would leave London Victoria station at 10 pm and arrive in France at 8.55 am, the next day

1937   The first Butlins holiday resort is opened in Skegness

1938   Holidays with Pay Act

1939   First transatlantic passenger flight

1940s   London's main air terminal transferred from Croydon to Heathrow. British airlines include British Overseas Airways Corporation (BOAC) and British European Airways (BEA)

1945   After the Second World War, there was a dramatic increase in air travel due to the number of trained pilots available

1950s   Construction and opening of the motorway network is under way

1950   First package holiday organised by Horizon to Corsica. Other tour operators quickly organised packages to other Mediterranean resorts

1952   First jet airline passenger service from London to Johannesburg

1960s   Introduction of 37-hour working week

1968   First cross-Channel hovercraft service

1969   The Development of Tourism Act sees the establishment of tourist boards, showing the government's recognition of tourism as an income generator and as an employer

1970   Travel allowance charged by the government for people wishing to travel overseas is abolished

1970   First Boeing 747 carries 352 on a transatlantic flight

1971   BOAC and BEA merge and are administered by the British Airways Board

1974   Clarksons, a major holiday company, goes out of business, stranding 50,000 tourists abroad. Issues highlighted include the structure of pricing for holidays and consumer protection

1976   Concorde goes into service

1977   Laker Airways is established to challenge major national airlines with cheaper transatlantic air tickets

1978   Spending by British holidaymakers overseas exceeds their spending on domestic tourism for the first time

1980   The International Leisure Group starts to offer cheap package holidays to Florida

1982   Laker Airways goes out of business

1990s   Eurotunnel carries first passengers

1991   The International Leisure Group, which had organised cheap package holidays to Florida, go out of business due to the Gulf War and recession in the UK

1991   A national marketing campaign, 'Discover the English Seaside', was launched in an attempt to arrest the decline of traditional UK seaside resorts

1992   The number of foreign visitors to the UK grows to 18.5 million

1992   Euro-Disney (later known as Disneyland Paris) is opened

1995   More people are finding out about the Internet and more people start to travel independently, organising travel and accommodation online

2000s   Low-cost airlines offering reduced price tickets to a number of European destinations are established and become very popular with a new breed of independent travellers. Examples include easyJet, Ryanair, Go and bmibaby

2003   Concorde decommissioned from service

A television producer has approached you about a new television series for the Applied GCE in Travel and Tourism. The aim of the television series is to cover the main units of the qualification and each thirty-minute programme is to feature a different unit. For Unit 1, Inside Travel and Tourism, you have been asked to write a script for the development of the tourism section of the first programme. Use the following brief to help write your script:

• Your script should be in the form of a documentary – therefore it should be informative and authoritative.

• You have a five-minute slot in the programme.

• You need to include information on travel and tourism in the nineteenth century, travel and tourism in the twentieth century, reasons for developments in the industry and the future of the industry.

Different sectors of the travel and tourism industry

As we have already examined in earlier sections the travel and tourism industry is large, forever changing and consists of many organisations. These organisations range in size from individual to multinational companies. Most of them are commercial and therefore in the private sector. Some, such as tourist information offices, may be funded by local and/or national government and are in the public sector. A small number are run by charities. These organisations are usually interested in sustainable tourism and help to protect host destinations from exploitation and pollution.

Organisations in the travel and tourism industry can be grouped into different sectors depending on the types of products and services they offer.

In this section you will learn about:

✱ The different sectors of the industry

✱ The types of organisation within each sector of the industry

✱ The role of organisations within each sector.

Each sector of the travel and tourism industry will be investigated in turn.

Figure 1.5 Sectors of the travel and tourism industry

Transport providers

This is concerned with the range of travel options available to independent tourists, package holidaymakers and business travellers. Transport is needed within the traveller's own country of residence and/or in an overseas destination. Many travellers also need to travel to a terminus such as an airport, railway station or ferry port before they embark on the main part of their journey.

Think back to your last holiday or day trip. How did you travel to your destination? Did you use more than one method of transport? If so, why?

Travellers require transport systems to be quick and efficient, whether they involve travel by road, rail, air or sea. Travellers today expect to be able to travel far and wide and their choice of transport depends on several factors. These include:

Price Today, with the introduction of low-cost air carriers such as easyJet, Ryanair and bmibaby, people can now reach European destinations that

Budget airlines have made air travel much more affordable

previously were too expensive to reach. For example, a return flight to Dublin from a UK airport in the early part of this century could cost anything between £200 and £300. Now the budget airlines can do the same journey for as little as £29 return.

Those travelling for leisure purposes rather than for business may choose not to travel during peak times in order to take advantage of cheaper fares offered by train companies, for example.

Think about it

On the same scheduled flight to exactly the same destination, passengers will have paid different amounts of money for their ticket depending on which class they travel in. Why do you think some passengers are willing to pay more to travel in business or first class rather than in economy class?

Destination Not all destinations are serviced by a range of transport providers and a traveller's choice may be limited by this. An example of this is tourists visiting some of the smaller Greek islands. They may fly into Athens airport but then have to transfer to a ferry to reach their holiday destination. This is because the island that is their final destination has no airport.

Time How much time a traveller has available to them can dictate their choice of transportation. A week's leisurely holiday along the canals of East Anglia may be a holiday idyll for some travellers. The chance to meander along waterways in a barge only covering thirty miles in a week is ideal for the relaxed holidaymaker, but for a business

person travelling the length and breadth of the UK, speed is of the essence. Speed in this case would, ultimately, be the key to choosing a travel and transport provider.

Reason Visiting friends or relatives, business or leisure.

The need for speed, the time available to travel and the reason to travel, all combine to influence a traveller's choice of travel and transport provider. As for price, business travellers may be prepared to pay more for their travel, if it is necessary for getting their work done efficiently and because they may not be personally responsible for the costs, as their companies will be paying. To reduce costs and to benefit from bulk-buying discounts, companies often have special arrangements with certain transport providers to provide services at specially negotiated prices.

Departure points How easy is it to get to a departure point? For example, if a small town had a bus/coach station but not a railway station, then travellers in that area may not see travelling by train as a viable option.

Skills practice

Draw an outline of a map of the UK. Mark on your map the main air and ferry ports.

Skills practice

A new airport was opened in South Yorkshire in March 2005. Formerly RAF Finningley, the new airport is named the Robin Hood Doncaster/Sheffield airport.

Try to find out about the new airport and why it was opened? Answer the following questions:

1 How can this new airport be accessed? Consider both road and rail links.

2 Why do you think a new airport was opened in this area?

3 Demand for air travel has grown in recent years. Why do you think this is?

4 Many existing airports want to extend and build additional runways. Local residents are opposed to these plans. What arguments would you use to justify extending our airports?

A traveller's choice of transport provider is influenced by a number of factors. These include:

- Price of travel
- Destination being travelled to
- Time available to travel
- Reason for travel
- Accessibility of departure points.

The development of transport systems

The development of transport systems can be attributed to technological advances. During the reign of Queen Victoria in the 1800s, travelling by steam train was seen as a major technological breakthrough in travel, however many people were nervous of a machine that could travel at speeds of up to thirty miles per hour. It wasn't until the Queen travelled by train herself that many people's fears were allayed about the dangers of such speeds!

The introduction of the steam train, the motorcar and the jet engine have all contributed to the growth of travel systems and the organisations that provide transportation for travellers.

The role of transport providers is integral to the whole tourism industry in physically moving tourists and travellers to and around their destinations.

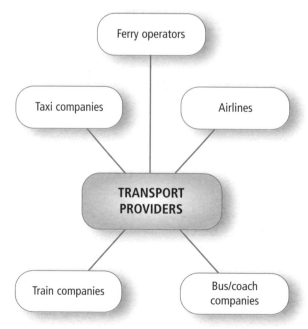

Figure 1.6 Transport providers of the travel and tourism industry

CASE STUDY

M25 – Motorway or car park?

The London Orbital, or the M25 as it is known to most of us, was opened in the early 1980s to ease the problem of congestion in the nation's capital city. Intended to send travellers around London and not through the city, the motorway is often referred to as the M25 car park because of the number of traffic jams endured by those who use the road.

Sections of the motorway can only be accessed by motorists who pay a toll, to travel through the Dartford Tunnel or across the Queen Elizabeth II Bridge.

1 **On a map of the UK mark the major cities and major motorways.**
2 **Tolls are used on UK motorways to try and restrict the number of people travelling on them. Why in the case of the M25 do you think that the toll charges do not stop as many people using the road?**
3 **We constantly hear about our congested roads through the media. Why do you think people are reluctant to give up travelling by car and using our busy motorways?**
4 **London has recently seen the introduction of congestion charges for motorists wishing to travel in the centre of the city. What impact do you think this has had on tourist attractions in the city? Fully explain your answers.**

1 Look through your local telephone or business directory to find transport providers in your area.
2 Create a table recording the number of providers of different modes of transport.
3 Select one of the organisations you have identified that provides transport for travellers and research this organisation further. Find out:
   - How long the business has been established
   - The services offered by the organisation
   - The cost of services
   - The availability of services.

Research could be conducted by visiting an organisation's website, writing to them or interviewing an employee of the business.

CASE STUDY
The Bal family

Raj, Rapinder and their two children, Kuldeep and Gurjit, are eagerly awaiting their forthcoming trip to Florida to visit some of the world's most famous theme parks.

Naturally the children are excited about the trip, but Rapinder is worrying about the amount of travel involved. The family will fly out of Manchester Airport and when they arrive in the USA, their hotel is approximately a seventy-five-minute drive from the airport. The family have a fly/drive package organised by their local travel agent in Wakefield.

1 **List all the methods of transport you think the family will need to use for this trip. Consider every part of their journey.**

2 **For each of the methods of transport you have listed in Task 1, write about why you consider that method the most appropriate.**

3 **For families travelling with young children, what type of services would you expect transport providers to offer?**

4 **Price may not be the most influential factor taken into account by young families when deciding on transport to a particular destination. Discuss the extent to which you agree with this statement. Explain your answer fully.**

Skills practice

National Express are a coach company which runs services all over the UK. Visit the organisation's website to research the destinations and departure points serviced by the company.

Once you have a 'feel' for the organisation, answer the following questions:

1 Who are National Express' customers?

2 Who do you consider to be National Express' main competitors?

3 With increasing congestion on our roads and more stringent environmental laws being made, how do you think National Express can move forward into the future?

CASE STUDY
'Le Chunnel'

The Channel Tunnel was opened in the early 1990s, finally linking mainland UK to continental Europe. With a terminus in Ashford, Kent, at the end of the M20 motorway and one at Waterloo railway station in London, travellers can travel directly to European cities in the comfort of their own cars or a high-speed train (Eurostar).

The concept of a tunnel under the English Channel had been dreamt of for many years. Attempts to link England and France had been made since Napoleonic times. Resistance to the tunnel being built came from local residents in Kent and ferry operators feared they would lose customers and, ultimately, profit.

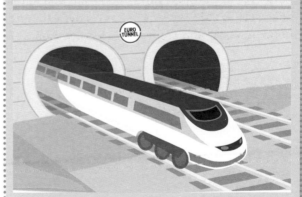

Though it is a major feat of modern engineering, the Channel Tunnel has been controversial and rarely out of the media spotlight. It is used by the white van brigade as the main route for transporting into this country the cheaper alcohol and cigarettes they buy in France. Industrial action and fires have disrupted services to passengers and the tunnel has become a favourite route of illegal immigrants into the UK.

1 Why do you think the Channel Tunnel is a popular route with many travellers?

2 As a cross-channel ferry operator, how would you tackle competition from the Channel Tunnel?

3 Safety has obviously been an issue in the Channel Tunnel, given that vehicles have caught fire whilst in the tunnel. On the list of travellers' requirements, safety is paramount. Imagine you are working as a marketing manager for the Channel Tunnel, devise a marketing campaign designed to promote the tunnel as a safe means of transport.

4 Eurostar is the name of the high-speed train which takes travellers from London to continental Europe. Use your research skills to find out where in Europe the Eurostar travels to.

5 The Channel Tunnel employs approximately 5000 people. What type of job opportunities do you think are offered by the Channel Tunnel?

Accommodation providers

Where to stay and how much to pay for accommodation are factors in choosing where to holiday and visit for many tourists. After

transportation, this is possibly the second-most crucial part of the industry and many people are employed in a variety of different job roles. From top quality hotels offering every luxury imaginable to a youth hostel offering a bed in a shared dormitory, the traveller has many options of where to stay.

Below is a diagram showing examples of different types of accommodation. This is not meant to be exhaustive.

Think about it

For each of the types of accommodation listed, try and write a definition.

Location is usually important to travellers when choosing accommodation. Finding accommodation in exactly the right place can be tricky and often very pricey. Certain types of accommodation are only available in certain locations. For example, gîtes are only found in rural areas of France. Location also affects the type of accommodation on offer. For example, in a city location there is likely to be a wide range of hotels, from five-star luxury to small

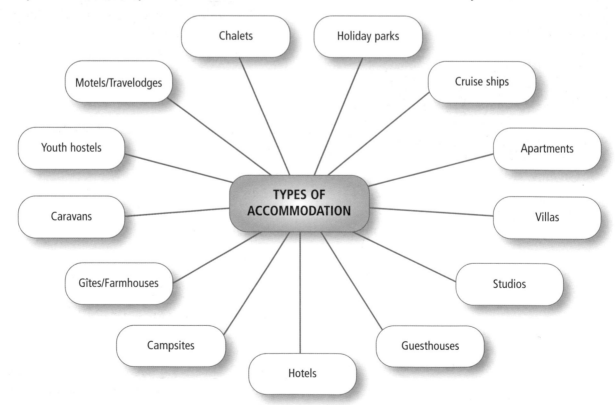

Figure 1.7 Types of accommodation in the travel and tourism industry

independently owned hotels. In cities you are also more likely to find hotels that belong to a chain. Lots of hotel chains today are not only national but also international and can be found in a number of destinations in a number of countries. Examples of these include Holiday Inn, Ibis, Marriott, Sheraton and Hilton.

Smaller towns and rural areas are more likely to offer guesthouses and bed and breakfast accommodation facilities. Some rural areas offer country house hotel accommodation, combining the luxury of top city hotels with the genteel rural life and settings. Seaside resorts offer a mixture of accommodation: hotels, guesthouses, flats and caravan sites. Hotels can be categorised according to their location:

* City centre hotels
* Beach hotels
* Resort hotels
* Country house hotels.

A country house hotel combines luxury with a rural setting

Skills practice

Tourists have different needs and different budgets. For each of the types of hotel write a profile in terms of age, socio-economic grouping, activities, likes and dislikes.

CASE STUDY

The Crouches – taking a baby on a holiday

Jonathan and Donna have recently had their first baby, Rowan. To take full advantage of Donna's maternity leave, the family are planning to go on a relaxing holiday for a week in the Spanish holiday resort of Fuengirola. Jonathan wants to stay in a hotel so that neither he nor Donna have to cook. When the family travel, Rowan will be six months old.

1   As a family with a young child, the Crouches will have many specific requirements. Create a list of as many requirements you can think of that will meet the needs of the Crouch family.
2   The Crouches want to stay in a hotel. What type of facilities do you think the hotel will need to have to meet the requirements of the family?
3   Log on to the website of one of the major travel agents and find a hotel that is suitable for the family to stay in. Remember their requirements and fully price the cost of the holiday.

Accommodation can be divided into two categories:

* *Serviced accommodation* – where meals are provided, for example hotels and guesthouses
* *Self-catering accommodation* – such as farmhouses, chalets and some hotels.

In serviced accommodation, tourists may have a choice of eating arrangements to choose from. The options available include:

* Full board – also known as the 'American Plan', three meals a day are provided for tourists
* All-inclusive – the cost of food and snacks and a selection of drinks is included in the price of the holiday

* Half-board – known as the 'modified American plan', breakfast and one other meal is offered to guests

* Bed and breakfast – known as the 'Continental plan', tourists pay for their room and their breakfast. The cost of other meals is extra.

Price can also be a contributing factor in a traveller's choice of accommodation. The price of accommodation is determined by the facilities on offer. The more and better the facilities are, the more it costs to stay. Accommodation is usually graded to help tourists in making their decision. There are a number of organisations that accredit hotels, for example the RAC and the AA both classify a large number of hotels, bed and breakfasts and guesthouses, and travellers use these as a guide to the quality and facilities on offer. The English Tourism Council also visits a wide range of tourist accommodation and annually assesses accommodation, so tourists can be confident that where they are staying has been thoroughly checked out. All the assessing bodies use these general guidelines when grading accommodation in terms of quality:

* A star rating of between one and five stars is awarded to hotels and self-catering accommodation. Stars are awarded for quality in terms of décor and furnishings and for facilities such as lifts, swimming pools, and entertainment systems in bedrooms. The greater number of stars awarded, the better the facilities and services offered.

* Holiday, touring and camping parks inspected by the English Tourism Council are also given ratings of between one and five stars. The AA, however, awards pennants (flags) for the same types of accommodation. With both schemes, the number awarded is based on the quality of service, cleanliness, environment and facilities provided.

* Other accommodation, such as guesthouses, bed and breakfasts, inns and farmhouses, are awarded between one and five diamonds. Again, the more diamonds that are awarded, the better quality of the services and facilities provided.

The use of stars is one way tourist accommodation is graded

Skills practice

You work for the RAC as a hotel inspector. You travel the length and breadth of the country, visiting hotels and awarding them with stars. The better the accommodation, the more stars awarded.

You are looking to be promoted and have been asked to rewrite the evaluation form used by inspectors when assessing hotels. This you feel is your opportunity to really impress your bosses.

It is your task therefore to write a new evaluation form considering all the different aspects you may be looking for when awarding ratings.

Skills practice

Following on from your task to write a new evaluation form for hotel inspectors, visit a local hotel and use your form to assess the facilities on offer.

Remember to ask permission from the manager.

Skills practice

City Hotels, an international chain of hotels, has asked you, a renowned hotel designer, to decide on the facilities to be installed in its newest hotel development. The new hotel will be located in Liverpool and is aimed at business people during the week and families at the weekend.

Tour operators

Every year when it comes to deciding where to go on holiday, we find ourselves flicking through a number of brochures, looking for the perfect holiday destination.

Weighing up the relative merits and demerits of each resort and type of accommodation, where we can fly from and at what time of day the flights are, we give little thought as to how the whole package is organised. Tour operators are responsible for combining the key elements of a holiday, namely transport and accommodation, into the package holiday, which we spend so much time choosing.

There are two main types of tour operators:

* *Wholesale operators* – these put together and organise package holidays that are then only sold through retail travel agents.

* *Direct sell operators* – these do not use travel agents as facilitators in selling their packages, but sell their package holidays direct to the general public.

Tour operators generally specialise in domestic, outbound or inbound travel. Domestic tour operators arrange packages to destinations within the UK; outbound tour operators arrange packages to overseas destinations; and inbound tour operators arrange packages for overseas visitors visiting the UK. Some tour operators provide both domestic and outbound package holidays, for example Wallace Arnold.

The role of tour operators is to act as the intermediaries or 'wholesalers' in the retail distribution chain. They provide, for example, the link between the hotels, airlines and the travel agents on the high street, where we book our holidays.

Tour operators have traditionally had considerable control over the types of destinations visited by travellers as they are responsible for planning and marketing holidays to selected destinations. The role of tour operators is varied and complex and comprises the following activities:

* Organising travel and accommodation

* Setting prices for holidays based on budgeted costs of a package

* Producing marketing materials, especially brochures advertising the holidays arranged

* Distributing brochures to travel agents.

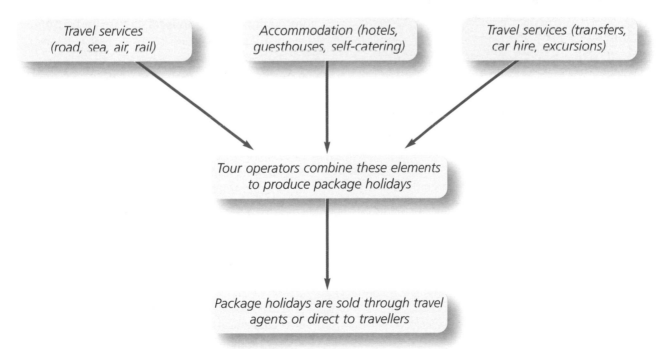

Figure 1.8 The holiday retail distribution chain

The process of organising a package holiday has to be done well in advance of any customer's commitment to purchase. Customers expect all the planning and organisation to have been done so that they are buying a package that is complete and ready to be used and enjoyed. Working in conjunction with travel agents, tour operators aim to provide 'hassle-free' holidaying for the traveller. Brochures promoting the holidays are printed anything from six months to a year in advance of when holidays will actually be taken, which also meets the needs of customers who like to book their preferred choice well in advance.

The first step in putting together a package holiday is the selection of resorts and destinations by tour operators. Larger tour operators have marketing departments which research current market trends to find out what customers want, how much they are willing to spend, how far they are willing to travel and how many want to visit new destinations. In recent years tour operators have extended their offerings beyond the much-loved Spanish resorts and islands, to destinations such as the Greek islands, Florida and Mexico.

Think about it

Why do you think resorts such as Florida and Cancun in Mexico have become more popular with tourists from the UK?

Tour operators generally select organisations on the basis of five essential criteria:

1 Accessibility
2 Attractions
3 Quality of local facilities and services
4 Availability of excursions
5 Political stability of the area.

Skills practice

Select one of the following destinations: Cancun in Mexico, Skanes in Tunisia or Eilat in Egypt. For the resort you have chosen, use the five essential criteria used by tour operators to make a judgement on how suitable these resorts are to be offered to customers.

Accommodation selected by tour operators has to be checked well in advance for its suitability for the tour operators' customers. Tour operators generally guarantee hotel owners that they will take a number of rooms in advance. These rooms in selected accommodation are then featured in brochures.

Skills practice

Imagine you work for one of the major tour operators selecting hotels and self-catering accommodation in a number of popular tourist destinations. You have been asked to create a new checklist to be used in assessing the suitability of accommodation. It is your task to create this checklist, taking into consideration factors such as facilities, star rating, location and proximity to beaches.

Brochures are not only marketing materials that aim to persuade travellers to choose the package holidays of one particular tour operator, they also need to be informative. Travellers rely on tour operators to provide them with all the information they need to know about a particular destination. This can range from entry requirements (e.g. visas), health regulations (vaccinations needed), time zones, currency used, language spoken, local festivals and bank holidays, and any other information relating to local culture and customs.

Skills practice

Mauritius is an island in the Indian Ocean. You work for a major tour operator who is extending the number of destinations they offer and Mauritius is to be included as one of the new destinations for next year. Your task is to research the island and create the text to be included in the brochure to inform travellers about the destination. You need to research:

• Entry requirements
• Health regulations
• Time zones
• Currency used
• Language spoken
• Local festivals
• Local culture and customs.

Costing package holidays can be very difficult for tour operators. The most difficult to cost is air travel. Tour operators charter flights up to eighteen months in advance and these need to be 80 per cent occupied if the tour operator is to cover the costs. Flight costs are especially hard to calculate as the cost of aviation fuel can vary enormously depending on external factors which tour operators have no control over, such as the supply of aviation fuel, political situations, taxation and the general state of the economy.

Value for money and quality are features which most customers are looking for when choosing holidays. Tour operators must convince customers that their products and services are value for money. When tour operators calculate the cost of holidays, they consider the following.

✱ The type of accommodation – is it serviced or self-catering?

✱ The number in the party – different rates are charged for children and discounts can be given for larger groups.

✱ The type of transport used – to get to some destinations and resorts, a variety of modes of transport may be needed.

✱ The point of departure – where the traveller leaves from at the start of their journey.

✱ The time of year – during the summer when the weather is usually better in most resorts and during peak times such as school holidays, tour operators charge more as there is greater demand for their products and services.

Once tour operators have completed the organisation and planning of package holidays they have to sell them to travel agents who will in turn sell them to the general public. Tour operators visit travel agents to update them on the range of holidays offered. Travel agents will then sell the tour operators' holidays and receive a commission, usually a percentage of sales, in return. Occasionally, larger operators will send travel agent staff to particular resorts to promote holidays offered by that tour operator.

Apart from the services offered to travellers before they depart for their holiday destination, many tour operators offer services when they arrive. The most common service is that of resort representatives. Their role is to welcome guests, organise excursions and deal with any emergencies guests may have. Representatives

CASE STUDY

July and August – the most expensive months of the year

'Have you seen the difference in prices?'

Andy was not impressed that the same holiday he had selected from the new brochure of 'Go Far' was £450 more expensive in July than in May. Granted that July is always warmer than May, but why the difference in price for one week in the same three-star hotel in Torremolinos, Spain?

Andy and Jill and their three children were planning their annual holiday, but were utterly dismayed by the cost in the school summer holidays. The cost of the holiday in July was too high for the family's limited budget and Andy made the following decision.

'We're going in May. The greedy tour operators are not ripping me off. The kids can miss a week of school!'

1 Why do you think tour operators charge more for holidays during school holidays?

2 Do you think it is ethical for tour operators to charge more for holidays when they know demand will be greater for their products and services?

3 Many families feel they have no alternative but to take children out of school during term time. Other people believe that this is wrong. How could overseas travel contribute to a child's education?

also monitor the quality of the tour operator's services and customers' opinions whilst on holiday.

Large tour operators tend to organise package holidays to the most popular resorts, whilst smaller tour operators tend to specialise in offering packages that fill a niche in the market that meet specific needs. For example, there are tour operators who specialise in packages for travellers who want to participate in a range of extreme sports. There are also operators specialising in packages to specific destinations such as Australia and New Zealand.

Skills practice

You can use a spreadsheet package for this activity to practise your ICT skills.

1 Create a list of twenty tour operators.

2 For each of the tour operators, state whether they offer domestic, outbound or inbound package holidays. Remember some may offer a combination of more than one type of package holiday.

3 Add to your list whether the tour operator is a wholesale tour operator or a direct seller.

Despite the availability of tour operators, there are travellers who prefer to arrange their own holidays. This is getting easier as people become more confident about travelling and as they get accustomed to booking holidays through the Internet.

Think about it

What do you think are the advantages of travelling independently?

Travel agents

The travel agent's role is that of 'retailer'. Travel agents sell holidays on behalf of tour operators as well as selling other products and services supplied by principals, such as airline tickets and hotel bookings. They also sell and provide other products and services, including travel insurance, currency exchange, traveller's cheques, guided tours and tickets for entertainments. As travel agents are selling holidays to the general public they tend to be located in areas where there is high customer traffic, such as high streets and major centres in towns and cities.

Skills practice

Visit your local high street or shopping centre to conduct a survey about the number of travel agents located there and the products and services they offer.

The main aims of travel agents are:

* to sell holidays and associated products such as insurance, car hire and currency exchange

* to advise clients

* to provide information.

Travel agents sell their products and services in much the same way as most other retailers on the high street. However, as they are selling the products of other companies (such as airlines, hotels, rail companies, tour operators) they are only paid a commission by those companies on the money they receive from the customers.

Travel agents either specialise in a particular market or sell a wide range of products and services to a wide range of people. The travel agents who specialise in selling holidays to Australia, for example, are usually independents, not part of a national chain. Even a travel agent

A travel agent sells holidays and associated products, advises clients and provides information

who has up to six shops/offices can be classed as independent. Independents are generally located in smaller premises in suburban or village locations and often in less prominent positions, such as above another retail outlet.

Travel agents that are part of a larger nationwide chain are known as multiples. Examples include Thomas Cook and Lunn Poly. These offer a wide range of products and services to a wide range of destinations and resorts. They are also retail travel agents, not just business travel agents who arrange business trips. Business travel agents operate in much the same way as retail travel agents, in booking flights and accommodation for their clients. Large organisations such as Boots Plc and Marks & Spencer have their own business travel agents to arrange travel and accommodation for their staff. Profits are often higher for business travel agents but many trips are arranged at short notice.

Think about it

What are the key differences between independent and multiple travel agents?

Skills practice

Write definitions for the following:
- Retail travel agent
- Business travel agent
- Independent travel agent
- Multiple travel agent.

Skills practice

Refer back to the second section of this unit, 'The development of travel and tourism'. Technological advances, such as central reservation systems, have impacted on the work of travel agents. How do you think these systems have helped travel agents and what are the advantages and disadvantages of using the systems?

To protect tourists from the unscrupulous, all travel agents are required to hold a licence from the International Air Transport Association (IATA) to sell airline tickets. Travel agents may also register with the Association of British Travel Agents (ABTA) to improve their reputation and to provide customers with a guarantee that they will not lose money if the travel agency goes out of business.

Skills practice

ABTA is an association to help protect travellers from losing money if a travel agency stops trading or from being stranded overseas if one of the travel principals goes out of business.

Research the role ABTA plays in the travel and tourism industry by finding out in detail what the association stands for and how it operates.

Travel agents – the future

For many years, travel agents were where most travellers went to book a holiday. The boom years for travel agents were the 1960s–1980s when all sorts of people started to travel overseas on package tours to popular destinations such as Spain, Balearic Islands and the Canary Islands. The travel agent was seen as a 'one-stop shop', where the traveller could book their holiday, buy insurance, change their currency and book a car parking space at the airport. The last twenty years has seen more people booking their holidays and arranging their own travel arrangements independently. One of the major reasons for travellers becoming more independent in planning their travel, itineraries and accommodation, is undoubtedly the growth of the Internet and personal computer ownership.

Threats to traditional travel agents

The travel agency sector of the travel and tourism industry is highly competitive. However, the major threat to travel agents today is technology, as it enables travellers to become more independent and dispense with the services of the travel agent.

Think about it

Technology is a threat to travel agents. What other threats do you think travel agents face today?

Imagine you are the managing director of a small chain of four travel agents in your local area. You need to put together a one-page summary of how you are going to react to threats facing travel agents. Your summary needs to include:

- A list of what you consider to be threats to your business

- What products and services you will offer to make you stand out from the competition

- How you will price the products and services you sell

- How you will promote your business to ensure customers will keep using your services.

CASE STUDY

Anne – 13 years in the business

Anne has worked in the travel agency business for more than thirteen years. She has always worked for the larger nationwide chains of travel agents and has recently been interviewed to give a real insight into the life of a travel agent, the changes that have impacted on the industry and what the future holds for traditional high street travel agents.

Hayley: Anne, you've worked in a travel agency for a long time now, what do you think have been the major changes since you started work in the industry?

Anne: It's now thirteen years I've been working as a travel agent. I started work for Lunn Poly as soon as I left school at sixteen. Things are so different now to when I first started working. The main difference is the customers. People are so demanding these days and customers know what they are talking about. People have travelled more and are more experienced. They know what type of holiday they want and how much everything costs. Of course, customer knowledge is no bad thing, but people are always quoting prices from other travel agents, and especially from the Internet travel companies.

Hayley: So the Internet has had a real impact on your business then?

Anne: The Internet has had a massive impact on the amount of business we do. It's made a really big difference. Price is the main way that the Internet travel companies have affected our business. They can offer holidays cheaper than we can as they don't have the same costs and overheads to cover. We have to pay for staff, shop rental, electricity, etc.

Hayley: If travel agents can't compete on price, how can they compete with such fierce rivals?

Anne: We can compete on price to a certain extent. Where I work now, we have a price watch promise and we can match quotes of other high street travel agents. As for the Internet travel companies, we can offer the face-to-face contact that they can't. There's also still a whole generation, particularly older people, who don't know how to use computers or don't have one at home, and it's these people who still use our services. It'll probably be different though in the next ten to twenty years as technology will become even cheaper and everybody will have access to the Internet.

Hayley: The future for high street travel agents is okay then?

Anne: I wouldn't go that far! In the future, we'll see less and less of what we see now on the high street. I think most travel agents will either become huge holiday supermarkets or telephone call centres with no shops. Competition is fierce now and I think it'll get worse as customers become more sophisticated and price sensitive.

Hayley: Do people demand different products and services today than they did thirteen years ago?

Anne: Yeah, people are much more adventurous today. They want to go further afield and the Caribbean has become really popular. People also like to go to places like that to get married. They are guaranteed good weather and don't have to invite members of the family they never see to the wedding!

Hayley: Apart from the increase in long-haul destinations, what other changes have you noticed?

Anne: A real noticeable change has been the increase in cruising. When I first started work, cruises were for the over-sixties but now they are aimed at the family market. People like the idea of everything being under one roof and visiting different places in one holiday. Modern ships are huge and the entertainment is non-stop. It's a bit like an upmarket floating Butlins holiday resort with sports and activities organised by a team of staff.

Hayley: Has the technology used in shops changed much?

Anne: No, not really. We've had new computers and I suppose communication lines don't go down and fail as much as they used to, but the reservation systems we use are more or less the same as they were when I started working. Travel agents invested loads of money years ago into reservation systems and the like, but little has been spent in recent times. Costs are always being cut and I don't think updating systems is a priority at the moment. It's a real pain when systems do fail though. It's really embarrassing when you have a client with you and you have to try and get through on the telephone. It also takes ages as if a system crashes, it usually crashes nationally and every travel agent is trying to book holidays over the telephone. Sometimes you can even lose customers as they are annoyed that the system has crashed. Our shop doesn't even have its own email link. It's a real pain.

Hayley: What events outside of your control have had an impact on business?

Anne: Without a doubt the latest conflict in Iraq and the Gulf has had a real impact on business. Coupled with 9/11, these two events have made people more apprehensive to travel. Also people don't want to travel to destinations in the Middle East, such as Dubai, as they are scared of terrorist attacks. People's attitudes have changed. They now think much more about the political situation of the destinations they are travelling to, which I suppose is sensible. People generally think much more about their own personal safety and that of their family.

Hayley: Do you still enjoy working as a travel agent?

Anne: On the whole I love the job. As I said earlier, customers are so demanding but I'm sure anybody who works with the general public feels that way. Some months we are set really hard sales targets to achieve and that can really put the pressure on. The money could be better, the hours could be shorter but I'm sure that's the same with every job!

1   **What does Anne identify as major changes in the travel and tourism industry?**

2   **According to Anne, what has been the impact of Internet travel companies on traditional high street travel agents?**

3   **What does Anne believe the future will hold for travel agents?**

4   **What other external influences or events, apart from the conflict in Iraq and 9/11, do you think have had an impact on the travel and tourism industry?**

5   **Anne has worked in a travel agency for thirteen years. What skills and qualities do you think Anne needs to be able to do her job well?**

Think about it

Currency exchange has always been a service offered by travel agents to their customers. With the introduction of the Euro as the currency of many continental European countries, there has been less demand for many different types of currency. Travel agents have always charged commission to change currency. With the introduction of the Euro, do you think travel agents have had less call for their currency exchange services?

Visitor attractions

Visitor attractions provide recreation, leisure and entertainment facilities for visitors to particular destinations. The attractions vary in nature and may be provided and managed by public, private or voluntary organisations. They can be categorised into natural attractions such as country parks, purpose-built attractions such as theme parks, historic and cultural attractions such as Stonehenge, and events such as major sporting competitions like the football World Cup.

Think about it

For each of the categories of visitor attraction, list five different places to visit in the UK.

- Natural attractions
- Purpose-built attractions
- Historic and cultural attractions
- Events.

Visitor attractions can be a real 'pull' to a certain area, with visitors making special trips to the area to see a particular attraction. For example, many people visit Wiltshire to see Stonehenge, the ancient stone circles.

Stonehenge is a major historic attraction for tourists

CASE STUDY
London and the Olympic Games

London, along with other major cities in the world, is competing to hold the 2012 summer Olympic Games. Plans have been submitted to the International Olympic Committee as to how London will be redeveloped to cater for all the sporting events in the Games and how the city will cope with the number of visitors that will be drawn by the Games. Not only would new stadia have to be built but also London's transport system would need to be overhauled to be able to swiftly transport visitors around the capital.

1 What would be the economic costs of London holding the 2012 Olympic Games?
2 What would be the economic benefits of London holding the 2012 Olympic Games?
3 How would London holding the 2012 Olympic Games be of benefit to the travel and tourism industry of the whole of the UK?

CASE STUDY
Alton Towers

Alton Towers is the country's premier theme park, situated in Staffordshire. Originally the site of a stately home and extensive gardens, the theme park has been developed to attract thousands of visitors a year. A hotel has been built to provide accommodation and evening shows and concerts are held in the grounds of the park. Each year a new ride or attraction is added to the theme park.

1 Why do you think the Tussauds Group, which owns Alton Towers, added a hotel to the facilities of the theme park?
2 Evening concerts and shows are being put on at Alton Towers. Why do you think this is so?
3 Alton Towers is well promoted through a series of TV advertisements. What is the purpose of spending money on such expensive campaigns?

Support services

The role of support services depends upon the nature of the service. Support services could, for instance, include ancillary services offered as optional extras to package holidays, for example excursions and day trips. These enhance the holiday experience for the holidaymaker while offering alternative sources of income for the organisation. Representatives who work for tour operators in destination resorts offer many of these support services, and, as well as providing information and guidance to tourists in the resort, they sell excursions. Many of the representatives earn commission for the number of excursions they sell. This commission acts as an incentive for the representatives to boost their usual wage, as well as boosting revenues for tour operators.

Support services are not only provided by commercial organisations, they are also provided by public sector organisations. Tourism is seen as big business and it supports many jobs in the UK. The government has a vested interest in supporting tourism and provides support through a number of publicly funded organisations.

Think about it

What type of information do you think the English Tourism Council could provide to organisations in the travel and tourism industry to help them plan for the future?

National and regional tourist boards and information centres are funded by national and local government. These support services to the travel and tourism industry market and monitor the quality and development of the particular tourism area they serve.

Support services can be both revenue spinners and information providers for commercial

A welcome meeting for holidaymakers

organisations. Another support service is that of guiding services. The aim of guiding services is to make any guided tour as interesting and informative as possible. Guided city tours, such as open-top bus tours of London, are known throughout the world and are an attraction to tourists, enhancing their experience of a city. Many guided tours provided in stately homes and places of historic interest are led by volunteers who have a wealth of knowledge and a passion for these attractions.

Think about it

Can you think of any other support services in the travel and tourism industry?

The relationships between sectors and their interdependency

Being interdependent means relying on others. We all rely on others for help and support in our lives and at work; it is almost impossible to do a job without somebody else having already done another task. This idea of relying on others filters through to the travel and tourism industry, and the different sectors of the industry, described in the third section, also rely upon each other for customers and work. There are many areas of overlap in the industry and many organisations depend directly upon the activities and success of others.

The success of tour operators and the number of holidays they sell depends very much on how well travel agents are promoting the products and services of the tour operator and how successful they are at persuading customers to purchase particular holidays. If the travel agent is not selling holidays, then neither is the tour operator, thus illustrating the interdependency of these two sectors. Another example is visitor attractions experiencing a downturn in the number of visitors due to problems with transport systems and accessibility.

Think about it

Can you think of any other examples of how sectors in the travel and tourism industry are interdependent of each other?

As a tour operator you may be concerned about the way in which travel agents sell your products and services, especially if a travel agent is also selling the products and services of other tour operators. The travel agent may in turn be concerned about the quality of service offered by an airline that it sells tickets for. If the quality of service from the airline is poor, then the reputation of the travel agent could be damaged as it is seen as recommending inferior services to its customers. Travel agents may also be put in a compromising position if they send customers to a hotel that is not of a very high standard.

Think about it

How can tour operators and accommodation providers work together to promote and encourage business? What benefits would this have?

Customers trust the different sectors of the travel and tourism industry to provide them with value-for-money products and services. However, because the different principals involved in providing a holiday – tour operator, travel agent, hotelier – can be individual, unrelated companies, each of the organisations involved could have conflicting aims and objectives for what they want to achieve. To gain more control over the whole chain of the holiday experience, several organisations have become vertically integrated.

Vertical integration occurs when a single company extends its activities into another stage of the distribution process. A company may wish to gain a controlling interest in a tour operation, a travel agency and an airline. This enables the company to sell its own products without paying commission and gives it priority in purchasing airline seats. It also allows significant economies of scale, lowering costs because of the increased purchasing power of a larger organisation. Examples of vertical integration include

Thomas Cook, the travel agent owning the Iberostar hotel chain with hotels in the 'summer sun' resorts and the Thomas Cook airline, and the Thomson tour operator owning Britannia airlines.

Think about it

Think about it

What do you foresee as some of the problems of vertical integration?

Skills practice

As a director of a tour operator, you are concerned about the future of your organisation and see vertical integration as a way of gaining control over the sale of your holidays in uncertain times for the travel and tourism industry. Your task is to prepare a presentation to persuade the other directors that vertical integration is the best option to take the business forward.

In your presentation you need to include the following:

- An explanation of what vertical integration is
- Examples of how your tour operator could vertically integrate with other sectors
- The advantages of vertical integration
- The disadvantages of vertical integration (to show that you appreciate the limitations of vertical integration as well as the benefits)
- Your plans – how you aim to vertically integrate.

Skills practice

There have been concerns that vertical integration of organisations in different sectors of the travel and tourism industry leaves the customer with less choice. Some cases of organisations integrating have been taken to the Competition Commission.

1 What is the role of the Competition Commission?

2 Why do you think there is a need for such a body as the Competition Commission?

3 Can you think of an example of integration in the travel and tourism industry that may be stopped from going ahead in the interests of maintaining competitiveness in the market?

Many organisations have sought vertical integration, giving them greater control of all aspects of their business. One of the major reasons behind seeking vertical integration is to provide a wider range of products and services and to offer a more extensive portfolio of products. Careful planning and marketing of all products and services is needed to ensure that all processes in the distribution channel are well managed and that quality, value for money and service is maintained.

Think about it

As well as vertical integration, organisations in the travel and tourism industry can integrate horizontally. What do you think this means?

UNIT ASSESSMENT

The aim of this section is to help prepare you for your external examination by having you answer a variety of questions on the material covered for this unit. You will be required to demonstrate your knowledge, apply this knowledge to vocational contexts, analyse information and perform evaluations based on these skills.

Defining travel and tourism

1 Name the three main types of tourism. (3 marks)

2 What is the difference between the three main types of tourism? (6 marks)

3 What are the three main reasons why people travel? (3 marks)

4 The following table includes data collected about overseas visitors to the UK and the purpose of their visit.

COUNTRY	LEISURE VISITS (000s)	BUSINESS VISITS (000s)	VISITING FRIENDS AND RELATIVES (000s)
Australia	355	75	240
Canada	246	83	266
France	1085	1112	695
Germany	1130	853	552
India	75	51	38
Italy	396	331	171
Japan	292	111	32
Spain	249	263	201
USA	1876	851	803

Adapted from *Number of visits, nights and spending by overseas visitors to the UK 1999*, Office for National Statistics

a   What does the above data set show? (1 mark)

b   This data set contains data collected on the three main purposes of travel. List two other reasons why people may travel. (2 marks)

c   From the data provided, which is the main reason for why people travel to the UK? (1 mark)

d   In what units have the number of visits to the UK been measured? (2 marks)

e   What factors do you think have an impact on the number of travellers from other countries to the UK? (6 marks)

f   The UK is thought by people in many countries to be a very expensive country to visit. If the pound is strong against other currencies, what will be the likely effect on the number of tourists visiting the UK? Explain your answer fully. (8 marks)

g Working for the British Tourism Authority, you are devising a new marketing campaign to attract overseas visitors to the UK. Why do you think public money is invested in promoting the UK as a tourist destination? (6 marks)

5 Many tourists from the UK choose to holiday overseas. The data below shows the countries visited by UK tourists in 1999.

COUNTRY	PERCENTAGE
Spain	27
France	20
USA	7
Greece	6
Eire	6
Italy	4
Portugal	4
Cyprus	2
Netherlands	2
Turkey	2
Belgium	2
Caribbean	2
Germany	2
North Africa	1
Other countries	1

Adapted from *International Passenger Survey*,
Office for National Statistics 1999

a Which country was most visited by UK tourists in 1999? (1 mark)

b In the category of other countries, give two examples of destinations that this may include. (2 marks)

c European destinations appear to be very popular with UK tourists. What factors do you think contribute to this popularity? (6 marks)

d Using an example of a resort you have studied, describe the attractions in that resort that may attract tourists from the UK. (8 marks)

e Domestic tourism has become more popular in the early twenty-first century, with more people choosing to holiday at home. What events do you think have led to this recent trend? (8 marks)

6 What is the difference between organisations in the private, public and voluntary sectors of the travel and tourism industry? (4 marks)

7 Using an example of an external pressure on the travel and tourism industry, evaluate the impact that pressure has had on tourism. (8 marks)

8 Host communities both gain and lose from the development of tourism in their areas. To what extent do you agree with this statement? (12 marks)

The development of the travel and tourism industry

1 What influence do you think Thomas Cook had on the travel and tourism industry in the UK? (8 marks)

2 There is no longer a need for traditional high street travel agents due to the emergence of online travel companies. Evaluate the extent to which you believe this statement to be correct. (12 marks)

3 Tourism is an activity which the majority of the population can today access. What historical developments have led to tourism for the masses rather than just for the wealthy elite? (8 marks)

4 Travellers today are becoming much more sophisticated, confident and independent. How do you think travellers have reached this point? (8 marks)

5 The travel and tourism industry is dynamic and forever evolving. What do you think will be future developments in the industry? Fully explain your answer. (8 marks)

Different sectors of the travel and tourism industry

1 Name the six different sectors of the travel and tourism industry. (6 marks)

2 What factors are taken into consideration by a tourist when choosing transportation? (4 marks)

3 What is the purpose of grading schemes for accommodation in the travel and tourism industry? (4 marks)

4 With the increase of online travel companies, there will be an increase in the number of direct sell tour operators. To what extent do you believe this statement to be true? (12 marks)

Relationships between sectors and their interdependency

1 Sectors in the travel and tourism industry are said to be interdependent. What does this mean? (4 marks)

2 Explain how organisations in the travel and tourism industry depend directly upon the activities and success of others. (6 marks)

3 What is vertical integration? (3 marks)

4 Using an example of a company you have studied, describe the benefits and drawbacks of vertically integrated companies in the travel and tourism industry. (12 marks)

Total marks: 180

UNIT 2

Travel and tourism – a people industry

Introduction

This unit introduces you to customer service as provided by travel and tourism organisations. It shows you why it is important for these organisations to provide excellent customer service in an industry where organisations offer similar products and services to each other. It is usually the quality of customer service that is the deciding factor as to which organisation customers use. Owners and managers therefore need to view customer service as necessary to the survival, development and success of the organisation.

The unit helps you understand how important training and induction are in preparing staff to provide customer service. You also learn how important a good level of product knowledge is in providing high levels of customer service. Finally, you will learn that customers have different needs and that the customer service skills you develop can be applied to a variety of situations in which customers' needs have to be met.

How you will be assessed

The unit is assessed by portfolio evidence based on an investigation into aspects of customer service in a chosen travel and tourism organisation.

Your portfolio should include:

✱ A review of induction procedures and training provided by your chosen organisation

✱ A record of customer service role plays, demonstrating how you would meet the needs of different types of customer of your chosen travel and tourism organisation

✱ An investigation into the product knowledge required by employees of the organisation

✱ An evaluation of the range of skills required to deliver customer service.

After studying this unit you need to have learned:

* The principles of customer service
* The needs of internal and external customers
* The significance of induction and training
* The significance of product knowledge
* The importance of customer service skills
* Dealing with different types of customer
* The technical skills that contribute to operating effectively in travel and tourism organisations.

Through studying this unit you will acquire valuable skills and understanding which you can use in studying other units in the AS Double Award: Unit 4 Working in Travel and Tourism and Unit 5 Travel and Tourism. For the A2 qualification understanding and the practice of customer service skills will be necessary for Unit 8 Marketing in Travel and Tourism and Unit 9 Travel and Tourism – People and Quality, which are both compulsory units. This unit therefore provides essential skills and understanding to achieve success in the AS and A2 qualifications.

What is customer service?

A *customer* is an individual with specific needs when buying products and services and expects a very high level of service in meeting those needs. *Customer service* involves providing products and services that meet the needs of the customer and satisfy their demands. This particularly applies to travel and tourism – a people industry – where the success of any business depends on providing customers with a high level of customer service.

Customer service is crucial to the success of a travel and trourism business

CASE STUDY

Customer service at the travel agents

There are three travel agents in town and Sophie and Rick decide to visit all three to find the best deal for a two-week holiday in Bulgaria.

The first travel agent had a dazzling window display showing all the late deals and special offers. It looked very inviting. Everyone else must have thought the same as there must have been ten other people waiting to see the one travel consultant on duty.

Sophie and Rick were greeted with 'Take a seat. Both my colleagues are at lunch but they will be back in forty-five minutes. Feel free to look at the brochures.'

Rick and Sophie moved on to the next travel agent.

This one was just off the high street. It too had an enticing window display showing promises of free insurance and commission-free currency exchange. There was only one member of staff on duty and she was working on a computer. Sophie and Rick sat down and waited for the travel consultant to finish her work on the computer. This lasted five minutes and they still hadn't been greeted with an 'Hello' or 'Be with you in one minute.'

The consultant was about to turn her attention to them when the phone rang. Again no apology to her two clients. A five-minute conversation with head office followed.

Finally, after putting some more chewing gum in her mouth, she was ready to focus on Sophie and Rick, who were already on their way out.

Third time lucky was what Sophie and Rick thought. The third travel agency was again busy but at least there were three consultants dealing with their clients. One of them greeted Sophie and Rick with a smile and asked them to take a seat, saying they would be attended to as soon as possible.

Rick helped himself to a free cup of coffee and they both watched a promotional video about the products and services the travel agency offered.

After about three minutes a very welcoming travel consultant apologised for the wait and invited them to her desk. She asked what type of holiday Sophie and Rick were looking for, the price range they were aiming at, the type of accommodation they preferred and the airport they wanted to fly from. Throughout the conversation the travel consultant was making eye contact, listening closely and thinking about what would match Sophie and Rick's needs. And all this time, she never once looked at her computer!

1 **How could the customer service be improved in the first two travel agents?**
2 **Why is it important to treat customers appropriately?**

Skills practice

When customers visit a travel and tourism organisation for the first time they tend to react to two things: the staff and the physical surroundings. The first reaction is to the tangible, i.e. what they perceive through their senses; the second is to the non-tangible, i.e. the emotional effect. Examples of the tangible are staff uniforms and the directional signs; examples of the non-tangible are the friendliness of staff and the atmosphere.

On your own, list some of the features that might create a pleasant visit for
- a family group visiting a theme park
- a guest in a hotel
- a passenger on an aeroplane.

Think about it

One way of knowing if customers are satisfied with the service they received in a restaurant is the amount of tips in the 'tips' jar. An empty jar is not encouraging!

Think about other ways which show that customers have been happy with the service they received.

In recent times the UK economy has increasingly moved away from the primary and secondary sectors towards the service sector. Travel and tourism plays a major part in the service sector in that it employs thousands of people and is totally geared towards providing the services that its customers need and want.

Figure 2.1 This is what customer service is all about

The diagram shows **CUSTOMER SERVICE IS ALL ABOUT:** with the following connected points:

- Putting the customer first and at the centre of everything
- Exceeding customer expectations
- Finding out what the customer wants and making sure it is delivered
- Getting the details right, every time
- Making sure there is every chance the customer will recommend the organisation

Organisations that fail to appreciate that customers must come first, will find themselves inundated with complaints, poor staff morale and a bad reputation. Those which train their staff thoroughly in all aspects of customer service, will be successful through increased sales, an enhanced reputation and a satisfied and confident workforce.

The principles of customer service

Why customer service is so important

In recent years customers have come to expect more from the products and services they are buying. What once may have been an added extra is now often a necessity. This is especially so in the travel and tourism industry. For example, en suite facilities in hotel bedrooms, new rides at theme parks, a drinks service on long coach journeys are now expected services and not extras.

Customer service also involves the way staff treat customers. Never ignore a customer or belittle them. How would you feel if you were treated in this way? Remember, the way you treat customers will have a major effect on how the customer views the organisation. Travel and tourism depends on customers, not the other way round.

It is important that a flexible customer service policy is developed by an organisation. In the past, customers had to take or leave the level of service offered. This is no longer the case. Travel and tourism is now far more diverse and there is intense competition between organisations for a limited number of customers. This means that staff and organisations have to be far more flexible. The aim is to have satisfied customers who will return with repeat business, so retaining the customer base. Potentially, satisfied customers also give an organisation a competitive advantage through personally recommending the organisation, as well as enhancing its image.

CASE STUDY

The Portland Hotel

Here are some of the customer service features that the Portland Hotel provides for its business guests.

- Guests who book on a regular basis are allocated their own car-parking space during their stay. This saves time and the pressure of driving round looking for somewhere to park.

- A monthly newsletter is sent out to regular guests giving details of new restaurants and what's on at the local theatre. This means that businesspeople can plan their time to relax after a hard day on the road.

- The hotel's administrative staff are available to deal with any business-related tasks the businessperson has to complete, for example sending faxes, emailing important information, word processing documents. This service is free of charge. Once again this saves time and eases pressure.

1 What do you think the Portland Hotel is trying to achieve by offering these extra services?

2 Do you think the benefits would justify the costs?

Making your business succeed

Travel and tourism organisations must recognise that their survival and continued success will depend on the way their customers are treated.

Customer service means putting customers first. Successful organisations make a point of putting their customers' needs at the heart of their policies and procedures.

Giving excellent customer service plays an important part in helping travel and tourism organisations keep their existing customers and attract new ones. This is brought about by people recommending to friends and relatives the organisation's products and services, and, just as important, the way they are treated.

Success comes in the form of increased sales, fewer complaints, satisfied customers and an enhanced reputation. The ultimate test of excellent customer service is the amount of repeat business an organisation generates, that is loyal customers returning on a regular basis.

Poor service is bad news! If you have ever received poor service in a restaurant, shop or hotel then the chances are you will not go back. You are more likely to go to their nearest competitor.

Poor service makes customers unhappy and creates a poor image of the company

Business surveys indicate that organisations lose customers for the following reasons:

* 1% die
* 3% move away
* 4% float from one organisation to another
* 7% change organisations on the recommendation of friends
* 9% change because they can buy more cheaply elsewhere
* 76% stop dealing with organisations because sales staff and others giving service are indifferent and show little interest in them or their needs.

Selling products and services

Income is generated by the sale of products and services. This means costs are covered and profits can be made.

The majority of selling in travel and tourism is made through face-to-face communication with the customer. The travel agent (the seller) tries to persuade the potential client (the customer) to buy a holiday, therefore knowledge of selling and sales techniques is essential in these situations. Sales techniques are discussed in more detail on page 80.

Effective selling skills contribute to customer satisfaction as customers can be provided with the products that suit their needs. This can lead to future business (repeat business) and can guarantee long-term success for the organisation due to this established business.

You may know people who have used the same travel agent for years. This doesn't happen by chance. Many travel and tourism organisations try to build up an almost family-type of atmosphere when developing relationships with customers.

Increased sales and profitability

All travel and tourism organisations have to make profits, otherwise they would go out of business. The first contact a customer has with an organisation can be the deciding factor as to whether that customer buys the product or service on offer.

An organisation with an excellent reputation for looking after its customers and providing what they want, is usually able to increase its customer base through recommendation from its satisfied customers. This leads to increased sales and more profit that can be used to expand the organisation and thus offer more choice to customers.

Though the private and public sectors are different in that private industry aims to make a profit from its activities, the public sector organisations, like museums and tourist information centres, nevertheless adopt the same standard of customer service as those in the private sector. After all, they also want to increase usage.

The English Tourism Council has the following customer service policy aimed at providing customer satisfaction:

* Exceeding customers' expectations

* Making sure that every customer recommends us

* Putting the customer first and at the centre of everything.

These aims would help all organisations meet sales and profit targets.

Increased reputation

All travel and tourism organisations like to promote the fact that they have a good reputation and a good public image. This is a way of showing customers that the products on offer are good value for money and that the service they receive is second to none.

If an organisation has a positive image then customers will have more confidence in it. So if the organisation can improve and develop its reputation then it should be able to increase its sales and attract customers as more people become aware of what the organisation offers to those customers. Competition between travel and tourism organisations is fierce and if one organisation is able to offer better quality of service than a competitor it stands to get more business.

A good public image can be created by using endorsements from satisfied customers. This strengthens the image of the organisation by showing that the customers who use that organisation are happy with the service they have received and the products they have bought. Travel and tourism organisations also use photographs showing people enjoying themselves because they are using the organisation's products and services. The aim of this is to project a good image, encourage new custom and build up loyalty.

CASE STUDY

Increasing sales

Travel and tourism organisations have to make a profit in order to stay in business. Increased sales can lead to profits. However, survival is not the only aim, an organisation has to develop and expand so that new products and services can attract existing and potential customers.

A theme park, for example, aims to provide customers with fun, thrills, excitement and value for money. Customers either pay an entrance fee allowing them to go on any ride or buy tickets for individual rides.

1   How can the theme park encourage customers to return year after year?

2   What products and services can it offer so that ancillary or secondary sales, that is those that are additional to the main product, will increase?

Building a good reputation

Newark Tourist Information Centre provides a variety of services. Information about places to visit within the town is available to local people and overseas visitors.

The information it gives includes accommodation availability, restaurant prices, entertainment venues, antique fairs and tourist attractions. It also gives a five-day weather forecast.

The products it sells includes maps, souvenirs such as key rings, pens and posters.

Twice a year an undercover inspector posing as a customer assesses the quality of service given by the staff, who are judged on their performance in answering the phone, the response time to requests for information and general efficiency.

Last year the centre was voted the best in the region for customer service.

1 **How has the Tourist Information Centre built up a first-class reputation?**
2 **What do we mean by the expression 'Reputations take a long time to build but can be lost overnight'?**
3 **How could the staff at Newark Tourist Information Centre be classed as salespeople?**

A competitive edge

Organisations which care about their customers will try to provide high-quality service which gives them an edge over the competition. This can be achieved by providing a wider range of products, effective promotion and, most of all, higher standards of customer service. For example, this could be by anticipating customers' needs and offering extra services, such as a hotel which offers guests a choice of newspapers or an airport which offers a free bus service from the car park to the terminal buildings.

Many travel and tourism organisations offer similar products, for example all travel agents sell holidays and insurance, all hotels offer rooms, all airlines sell seats. In some cases, customers prefer to stay with the same travel and tourism organisation even though its products and services aren't as wide-ranging as others; it's the standard of customer service that attracts them!

A competitive edge

Two coach operators in the Midlands specialise in day trips for senior citizens. Staff in both organisations are friendly and well trained and drivers are encouraged to build up a rapport with their passengers.

One of the coach operators picks up and drops off its passengers at their doorsteps. It also provides bingo, raffles and quizzes to help make the journeys more interesting and fun. It also gives each passenger a small gift on the return leg of the trip.

These three small extras give this coach operator the edge over its competitor.

How could the other coach operator improve its customer service to compete on the same level?

Customer satisfaction and repeat business

Nowadays customers expect more than just the basic product and will only use an organisation again if they feel confident in the type of service they have received. This in turn will lead to repeat business, increasing sales even further.

Satisfied customers are those who are satisfied with the products and services they have paid for and the way they have been treated. They are also satisfied because they have

* received value for money
* been treated with respect
* had their needs fulfilled.

For example, a family group may have paid £5000 for a holiday in Florida. At the airport they were met by the organisation's representative and were transferred to their resort in an air-conditioned coach. The hotel was clean and near to all the attractions, including the beach.

A babysitting service was provided for the children and a free taxi was provided for mum and dad so that they could have a few drinks in the nearby restaurant, knowing they didn't have to drive back.

Going-away gifts were presented to the children on the last day and the holiday rep stayed at the airport with them to ensure they boarded their plane on time.

Travel and tourism organisations must meet customers' needs and expectations. To achieve this they must be committed to providing the highest standards of customer service and therefore must

* develop the right mix of products and services
* ensure high-quality delivery

Travel and tourism organisations must provide the right mix of products and services for customers

* measure customer satisfaction
* train staff in customer service.

Never underestimate the importance of providing customer satisfaction and always recognise the danger of leaving customers dissatisfied!

Key terms

Competitive edge This is when organisations strive to achieve an advantage over the competition, in being better than they are at providing products and services. This could be achieved by better customer service, providing a wider range of products or giving better value for money.

Repeat business Customers who are happy with the service and the products they have received from an organisation usually return for more of the same because they are satisfied with the way they have been treated.

Value for money This is when customers feel satisfied with the products they have bought and believe their money has been well spent.

Skills practice

People tend to be creatures of habit. Once they find something they enjoy they will tend to stay with it. Eighty per cent of business in the travel and tourism industry comes from regular customers, so it makes good business sense to ensure that their visit or experience is as good as, if not better than, the last one. Likewise, unhappy customers will tell between ten and fifteen people about their experience.

Answer the following questions on the value of customer satisfaction and repeat business:

1 What are the benefits of having a loyal customer base?

2 How does this reduce advertising costs?

3 What effect does repeat business have on staff?

First impressions are lasting impressions

Providing a warm welcome for customers means going beyond basic manners and politeness. It is being willing to go 'the extra mile'. This is what

The first impression you make on a customer is crucial to being successful

makes a true, professional customer service employee stand out.

Customers notice almost immediately how clean and tidy any facility is kept, whether it is a hotel reception or even the inside of a plane. Who would want to spend ten hours on a flight with litter on the floor and the remnants of someone's meal on their seat? What state would the toilets be in on such a flight?

Customers also notice whether the person dealing with them is neat, clean and well groomed, and whether that person is working in an efficient and orderly manner. For example, is the travel consultant wearing a smart uniform? Do they answer the phone in the correct way? Do they make eye contact with the person they are dealing with?

Customers will not only make a judgement about the person attending them and about how well they are meeting their needs, they will also make a judgement about the organisation that person is representing.

Research has shown that first impressions are formed within seven seconds and embedded within thirty seconds, and it is almost impossible to change a customer's opinion if the initial contact has not been positive. In short, first impressions are lasting impressions. The implications of this are that customers will not buy products and services from an organisation which does not immediately impress them either because of their staff or the environment.

> ### Key term
>
> **First impressions** This is the image presented by staff of the facility itself that immediately decides whether or not a customer likes what he or she sees, which is why it is vital to make an excellent first impresison.

Uniforms and dress code

Many travel and tourism organisations provide staff with uniforms. You have only to look at travel agency staff or air cabin crew to see how smart they look. Among the advantages of providing staff with uniforms are that they

* are functional

* present a professional image

* make it easy to recognise staff as being part of the organisation

* give staff a sense of belonging to a team and so loyalty is also promoted.

There are usually certain codes that organisations insist on. For example, men are not allowed to wear earrings, their hair must be tidy and smart, beards and moustaches are not allowed, and tattoos must not be visible. In the case of women, make-up should be conventional and not excessive.

CASE STUDY

First impressions

The Regional Manager of a well-known travel agency states 'We encourage our staff to create a really positive impression. Their uniforms are extremely smart and everyone wears a polished name badge . . . along with a big smile.'

He goes on to say that staff are able to put customers at ease and are able to listen to and understand the needs of their customers.

1 **What rules regarding dress code would you put in place for your staff?**
2 **How would you know if your staff were creating a favourable impression?**

A dress code creates a professional image

Clothes not only say a lot about you personally, they also say something about the organisation. Basic rules should apply to appearance, for example clothes should be clean and ironed and appropriate to the role. For example, 'T' shirts are not acceptable in business situations, even if they are the latest designer fashion costing over £60!

Skills practice

Customers judge staff and therefore the organisation for which they work by the way they look and act, that is their appearance and attitude.

As the manager of a travel agency you have noticed recently that one of your travel consultants has started to come in looking a little unkempt and haggard.

1 How would you handle this situation?

2 Why would you have to deal with it as a priority?

You could act this out with a colleague.

Attitude and behaviour

The expression 'Your attitude is showing' means that you can't hide how you are feeling. That is why it is always wise to adopt a positive approach to work.

Your behaviour will have a profound effect on customers. No one can actually see your thoughts and feelings, they can only see how you behave and what you say, and this is what customers base their impressions of you, and your organisation, on.

In travel and tourism staff are providing services to other people, so the attitude adopted by them towards customers could make the difference between people returning to buy the product or not. Having a positive attitude is made up of believing in yourself, taking pride and belief in your organisation and having respect for the customer. Someone who believes in the values and aims of their organisation will be enthusiastic towards customers, whereas someone who is critical of their organisation can have a damaging effect.

Respect for the customer has to be genuine – you can't fake sincerity! Training can help instil this respect, however staff must have a natural, genuine interest in people if they are to offer the right level of customer service. Take, for example, a receptionist who has dealt with hundreds of customers at a theme park in the first hour of opening. An enthusiastic receptionist may feel tired but doesn't show it. She has told herself to treat every customer as if they were the first. This is thinking positive.

Take the trouble to project a belief in yourself and adopt a positive attitude. This can make you feel good about yourself and others. This approach willl certainly be appreciated by customers.

Your behaviour is like a beacon, sending out signals to all the people with whom you have dealings. The signals you send out are vital because they are a major influence on the reactions of the customer. They can either help or hinder any transaction you make with them. Remember, enthusiasm and a positive attitude enable you to build up relationships with customers quite quickly. On the other hand, misery spreads!

Having a positive mental attitude enables you to tackle problems or situations you wouldn't have thought possible. By adopting a positive mental attitude, how would you handle the following situations:

1 You have to tell a group of passengers their flight has been delayed for twelve hours.

2 A family of four has to move hotel due to a double booking.

3 There are rumours of redundancies being made at your organisation.

Discuss with another student or as a class.

Think positive!
Act positive!
Be positive!

Travel Assistant

Even the most professional employee can sometimes feel less than enthusiastic towards customers. This could be the result of lack of sleep or even a hangover. The latter could be reflected in the smell of alcohol on your breath or the smell of stale cigarettes on your clothes. It is one thing to try and disguise the way you feel; it is a bigger challenge to disguise the way you look.

How do you think customers would react to the above situation?

Recognising customer needs

The needs of customers are an important consideration for all travel and tourism organisations because they have a direct bearing on the demand for products and services. According to Maslow (1943), people's needs must be satisfied in some hierarchical order, starting first with physical needs then followed by social and psychological needs.

Maslow believed that the order of the levels of need were important. As needs at level 1 are satisfied, so those on the next level become more dominant, and so on.

Figure 2.2 Maslow's pyramid of needs

These needs can be related to a travel and tourism product such as a holiday:

* Physiological needs — warmth, food, drink, sleep
* Safety needs — secure environment, safe destination
* Social needs — belonging, socialising, making new friends
* Esteem — status, travelling first class
* Self-fulfilment — learning a new skill, for example paragliding, surfing

After the physiological needs have been met, the second need of customers is safety. Customers will want to make sure that equipment checks have been carried out when they take part in high-risk activities on holiday, such as paragliding, water-skiing or bungee jumping. They also want to know if staff are trained and qualified when they take part in sports like sub-aqua diving.

Imagine you are on holiday in Spain and have the opportunity to take part in relatively high-risk sports activities. In terms of safety, what would be the order of priority of your needs?

Most people have wants but they cannot afford to satisfy them. However, when you have the money to back up your desires, wants become demands which, in the travel and tourism industry, can be expressed in many ways, such as the number of overseas holidays taken or the amount spent on tourist attractions in a year.

A person's needs will vary with age and family circumstances and will affect demand for travel and tourism products and services. It is therefore vital that customer needs are recognised and met accordingly.

The specific needs of travel and tourism customers cover many areas including the following.

Products

Market research is conducted to find out what customers are looking for. If you don't give people what they want you are not providing good customer service and they will go elsewhere. For example, a couple on honeymoon may want secluded beaches on a paradise island, whereas a family group may want a self-catering holiday in Crete. Providing the right product to the right people is fundamentally important in customer service.

CASE STUDY

Identifying underlying needs

A young man walks into a restaurant to book a table for two. What he actually wants to do is to propose to his girlfriend in a romantic setting.

1 **As the restaurant manager how could you find out exactly what your customer's needs are?**

2 **How could you fulfil them?**

Help

Customers usually look to travel and tourism staff for practical help, such as the directions to the nearest restaurant or carrying a guest's luggage from the taxi to the hotel.

Advice

Customers ask for advice because they want to be sure that the activities they want to take part in are suitable and safe, for example asking if a particular theme park ride is suitable for children or asking a travel consultant about the different types of insurance.

Think about it

An American backpacker walks into a tourist information centre wanting to know about cheap, local accommodation near to the railway station so that he can catch the early morning train to London.

It would be irresponsible of the receptionist to say something like, 'If you look in Yellow Pages you might find what you are looking for.'

The correct procedure would be for the receptionist to phone a bed and breakfast nearest to the station and book it for him.

What other information could the receptionist give to the American visitor?

Information

Customers may need information because they are unfamiliar with a place. Travel and tourism staff need to know how to give this information, either by face-to-face communication or in the form of brochures and leaflets. The information customers may require could range from 'What type of visa will I need for visiting South Africa?' to 'What time does the park close?'.

Safety and security

Ensuring customer safety and security is a vitally important part of customer service. Customers need to know that they and others with them will be safe. This is why airports check luggage, why safety deposit boxes for passports and valuables are available at hotels, why fire exits are kept clear, why theme park rides are checked regularly. All these procedures are carried out to give customers peace of mind.

To be understood

This need can be fulfilled by staff who listen carefully to what customers need and can empathise with their situation. For example, holidaymakers looking for peace and quiet don't want nightclub music blasting out until all hours of the morning. They didn't pay £3000 for that. In this case a transfer to another, more peaceful hotel would seem appropriate.

Made to feel welcome

When people arrive at a new place for the first time they are often anxious about fitting in and meeting other people. Travel and tourism staff should be aware of this and act as good hosts. A friendly greeting and a warm smile makes customers feel welcome. This in turn makes them more relaxed and gives them confidence in the staff charged with looking after them.

Feeling important

One way of making people feel important is to call them by their name. 'Good morning Miss Beadle, how are you today?' sounds a lot better than a plain 'Good morning' or even 'Good morning madam'. People like to be recognised and called by their name; it makes them feel important and wanted. Customers have every right to feel important, especially if they have spent a lot of money on the organisation's products and services.

Think about it

If someone calls you by your name it makes you feel important and you appreciate that they have taken the trouble to find it out.

How could you find out a customer's name in advance so that when you greeted them you could use their name?

Feeling comfortable

A warm, friendly environment puts people at their ease and gives them a sense of comfort and security. This may be fulfilled when all other needs have been taken care of.

The aim of meeting customers' needs is to provide customer satisfaction. It is therefore imperative to recognise and fulfil these needs, given that the success of the business will be affected by the recommendations of satisfied customers.

People working in travel and tourism have to be thoroughly trained to recognise and satisfy customers' needs. The organisations themselves need to invest heavily in customer service training so that the employees know how to treat and look after customers properly. Making such an investment should pay off in terms of increased sales and satisfied customers.

CASE STUDY

Meeting needs is no accident

Ricky Aston was, at twenty-seven, one of the youngest hotel managers in London. The guests of his hotel included foreign politicians, pop stars, celebrities and even royalty.

Naturally these sorts of guests have particular needs. Ricky found it very exciting but at times quite daunting dealing with some of the guests. There were things that had to be handled with extreme sensitivity, like security or television interviews and press conferences. Ricky seemed to be able to take these in his stride.

He started his career in a small Brighton hotel and studied part-time for a Diploma in Management. After two years he was promoted to assistant manager in charge of twenty staff.

Further part-time study in Hospitality Management followed. This was extremely challenging as he had to attend college three hours every Monday evening, complete ten

hours coursework each week and hold down a full-time job which included shift work. He fulfilled one of his ambitions at the age of twenty-three when he became deputy manager of a top London hotel. Four years later he was promoted to his present position.

A combination of study, training and experience had enabled Ricky to manage staff effectively and recognise and satisfy customers' needs as a top priority.

1 What skills and qualities do you think you need to reach the top of your chosen profession?
2 What sort of on-the-job training would Ricky have received?
3 What topics would have been included in Ricky's studies?

The needs of external customers

External customers are those outside the organisations of the travel and tourism industry who are purchasing the products and services of those organisations: visitors, clients, guests, the public. All of them have needs which they satisfy by purchasing products and services from organisations, and they must be given the best customer service possible as they expect value for money and will recommend any organisation that provides it, which will contribute to the success of the business.

Satisfying customer needs is vital to the success of an organisation, as are the following points employees are trained to bear in mind when dealing with customers, namely that customers

* are always right
* pay our wages
* are the main purpose of our job
* are not to be argued with
* are people with feelings and needs, not statistics
* trust our expertise to give them what they want.

The following is used by many travel and tourism organisations as a reminder of the importance of customers.

Rule 1 The customer is always right
Rule 2 If the customer is ever wrong, re-read rule 1!!!

Key terms

Customer charter A document produced by an organisation that sets out the minumum levels of service and standards that customers should receive when they use the organisation.

External customers People from outside the organisation who pay for the organisation's products and services.

Skills practice

The two rules above were written by an American entrepreneur. Other expressions include 'The customer is King' and 'No customers, no business'.

Working alone or with another student, devise three expressions which show the importance of customers and how they are looked after.

THE CUSTOMER IS KING!

NO CUSTOMERS
NO BUSINESS!

THE CUSTOMER IS
ALWAYS RIGHT!

Customers are treated as individuals, however they can also be identified and treated as groups of individuals sharing certain characteristics. This applies to any organisation in the service sector. To identify the special needs of groups of people enables an organisation to make sure it provides the products and services that meet the needs of the individuals in those groups.

The following are the sorts of groups of customers the travel and tourism industry has to provide products and services for:

* Other organisations in the travel and tourism industry, e.g. coach operators who would be seen as customers of a theme park

* People of different ages

* People from different cultural backgrounds

* People with specific needs.

It isn't easy to provide high customer service to a wide range of customers with different needs. To succeed staff need to be appropriately trained to do the job, enthusiastic, committed and hard working.

Obviously there are times when the customer is not always right. They may have misinterpreted information or possibly have been told by friends that they were entitled to certain discounts when in fact they didn't fall into that particular category. These situations have to be dealt with sensitively and with tact. This is dealt with in more detail on page 83.

Individuals

An organisation may only have to satisfy the needs of one person who wishes to buy the products and services of that organisation. Having to satisfy only one person's needs can simplify the task. However some individuals can be a problem, making awkward requests or being demanding just for the sake of it. If you are faced with such a customer and feel isolated or exposed, always seek support from your manager. Remember, asking for support is a strength, not a weakness.

In dealing with individual customers try to find out their name and use it. This is one way you can make the customer feel important and at ease, and make it easier for you to deal with them. 'Good morning Mr White, good to see you again'

is one way of making a customer feel good and putting them at ease.

Individual customers may feel awkward when visiting a travel agent, for example, so the staff should make a special effort to make the customer feel relaxed and at ease. A warm welcome from a well-presented, friendly member of staff goes a long way to putting someone at ease.

CASE STUDY
Putting people at ease

Some people are excellent at making customers feel welcome and relaxed. It seems to come naturally to them. They tend to be staff who are genuinely interested in customers and can build up a rapport in minutes.

Some young people may feel shy when talking to older people. Perhaps they feel older people may be intimidated by young people.

You will probably find that gradual exposure to customer service will build up your own confidence as you develop your customer service skills.

Many people believe you have to be an extrovert to work in the travel and tourism industry and be blessed with a sparkling personality. This is not so. Anyone with a pleasant personality who is capable of listening can succeed.

1 How would you rate yourself as someone who could provide excellent customer service?
2 How would you deal with a customer who came into your travel agency looking extremely unsure of himself, ready to bolt to the nearest exit?

Customers have basic needs: to be understood, to feel comfortable, to feel welcome, to feel important. So how do you find out an individual's needs? It is quite easy, really. Use an open question like 'How may I help you?' Asking questions increases the possibility of the customer doing the talking.

The following are examples of the needs of an individual that need to be satisfied by a travel and tourism organisation:

* A businessperson staying at a hotel wants the *Daily Telegraph* left outside their bedroom door each morning. This is because he may have a breakfast meeting or an early morning business meeting and needs to gather the latest financial news.

* A customer in a travel agency may want an adventure holiday. This is because they have been on holiday to the usual places but now want to go trekking in the Himalayas to fulfil their spirit of adventure.

Whatever the circumstances, it is vital that travel and tourism organisations recognise the needs of customers and provide for their needs.

Groups

A group is a number of people who want to take part in the same activity. For example, holidaymakers gathered together to listen to the travel representative's talk would be classed as a group. The advantage of dealing with groups of customers is that it can save time, as it is possible to deal with several customers at once. This means that groups are good for business. Every group booking involves less sales time and reduced staff time. One advantage for the customer is that group bookings often attract discounts.

However, travel and tourism staff must realise that although groups might be made up of families, young couples, senior citizens and people holidaying alone, each group member has to be treated as an individual.

It requires special skills to take into account the needs of individual customers while dealing with the group as a whole. Groups can be disruptive or threatening to individual customers, if only through the sheer numbers in the group, for example a coach load of football fans spilling into a pub.

Group members can also become angry and frustrated if their visit is not managed well, as in the case of having to queue up for thirty minutes to collect tickets you paid for the previous day.

There are several ways of managing groups which may help avoid irritation. These include:

* A separate entrance for groups to allow speedy access
* Advance booking – reduces bottlenecks at entry
* Identifiable guide to sort out the problem
* Re-emphasising group benefits – discounts on admission, priority bookings for the future.

Information for the group is usually communicated by the leader, for example a holiday representative or tour guide. It can be quite daunting for most people to stand up and speak to twenty or more people. However, these reps are fully trained and exude a confidence that wins over most groups. The situation needs someone who can raise their voice, make the information sound interesting and keep the group within earshot and eye contact. You also need to catch and keep people's attention.

Managing groups can be made easier if

* their needs are met fully
* group members are recognised as individuals and not numbers
* they have a leader in whom they have confidence.

People of different ages

Staff who work in the travel and tourism industry have to communicate with people of widely differing ages. Age affects people's behaviour and needs. Customer age groups can be classified as children – from babies to teenagers – and adults – from young adults to senior citizens.

A group of customers may consist of adults with young children or parents with grandchildren, a combination of ages. This means that travel and tourism staff will need to identify and satisfy the specific needs of each age group. For example, a family group on holiday may look like this: gran and granddad want to relax by the pool; mum and dad want to go to the beach; the children want to join in the organised games.

> ## CASE STUDY
> **Holiday differences**
>
> Holidays are supposed to be occasions when you can relax and do whatever you like. The pressures of work have been forgotten and it is now time to busily employ yourself in rest and relaxation.
>
> Sometimes there are obstacles preventing this taking place, especially when the occasion involves a family group consisting of people of different ages who have different needs.
>
> **Identify the needs of the different people in this family group and come up with ideas to meet their needs: grandma and granddad; mum and dad; Sue aged 17; Josh aged 13; twins Sarah and Jack aged four.**

Let's look at the different age categories in more detail and identify their needs.

Under-fives

Many travel and tourism organisations promote specific services and facilities for babies and toddlers. This is a way of encouraging parents to visit a destination because they know the needs of their youngsters will be met.

The under-five age group's needs can be met by providing child-friendly facilities such as baby changing rooms, special family areas in restaurants, play areas and a crèche. Airlines may provide a 'sky cot' and jars of food for babies.

Good customer service provides alternative options for children while adults follow their own pursuits. For older children and teenagers a variety of exciting, safe activities can be provided by travel and tourism organisations, especially during family holidays. These include ten-pin bowling, paintballing, laserquest, go-karting, karaoke competitions and of course having fast-food meals.

Young adults

This age group also has its particular set of needs. Tour operators organise holidays specifically for 18–30-year-olds consisting of activities like beach parties and barbecues, themed evenings and fancy dress parties. The main aim is to provide fun, excitement, opportunities for socialising and romance so that everyone can concentrate on having a good time.

Older people

Travel and tourism organisations now recognise that people over sixty years of age have spending power, and tour operators such as Saga target this particular age group, in fact they target the fifty-plus market.

Demographic factors concerning the age structure of the population influence the travel and tourism industry. For example, there is an increasing number of older people in the UK, due to the increase in life expectancy because of improved levels of healthcare and advances in medicine, which is pushing back the definition of the 'elderly'. As a result there is a new market for products and services in travel and tourism for the older customer as their disposable income increases along with better pension schemes.

The number of over sixty-five-year-olds is forecast to grow. This should be looked on as a positive trend for the travel and tourism industry because many potential customers in this age group have paid off their mortgages and no longer have children to support. This 'grey' market has time and money to spend on leisure pursuits like holidays. In Australia this age group is known as 'Grey Nomads', such is their love of travel.

Traditional stereotypes do not apply any more when it comes to older people. It is not unheard of for people of sixty years plus to go trekking in the Himalayas. Obviously some older customers do have requirements traditionally associated with their age, like mobility, hard of hearing or poor sight problems.

As in the case of all customers, a level of respect and patience is required when dealing with older people, although travel and tourism employees should not make assumptions about someone's needs based solely on their age. They should judge each customer's case individually.

Skills practice

It is tempting and convenient to stereotype older people as being inactive and dependent on others. This is an untrue generalisation.

Answer the following questions, conducting research wherever necessary:

1 What sort of things do older people look for in a holiday?

2 In what ways do you think your age group is stereotyped?

3 How do you think older people are stereotyped?

4 Think about the older people you know. What do they like to do in their leisure time?

Customers from different cultural backgrounds

Culture is associated with people's tastes, traditions and way of life. It is important to understand someone's cultural background so that they can be provided with the most effective type of customer service. Customers from different cultures may still speak English but have different ways of doing things. You may have experienced different cultures when you have been abroad on holiday and you may experience cultural differences in your own country which include diet, language and dress.

Cultural differences can include handshakes and body language. For example, making a circle with the forefinger and thumb in the UK means everything is OK. However in Brazil it is classed as a very rude gesture.

HSBC bank promotes itself as 'The world's local' bank. Its advertisements show people in different countries adopting different habits to us. For example, showing the soles of your feet in Thailand is extremely rude or eating all your food in Japan is a sign that you are not fully satisfied with the food provided. HSBC's message is quite simple: people in different countries have different ways of doing things and HSBC recognises these needs through the way they treat their customers.

Skills practice

Many people in the UK expect everyone to speak English when they go abroad. In the same way, many of us expect overseas visitors to speak fluent English when they come to the UK. Obviously this is not always the case.

Answer the following questions:

1 How would you prepare yourself for receiving customers who do not speak English?

2 How would you prepare your workplace, for example a hotel, for non-English speaking guests?

A question asked is 'How can travel and tourism employees recognise cultural differences?' Air cabin crew and holiday representatives are encouraged to do this through reading, talking to friends and colleagues from other cultures or experiencing the culture themselves by spending time in that country.

As with other aspects of customer service, dealing with customers from different cultures is not simply a case of being nice. It takes training and practice. This can help reduce any misunderstandings and should ensure that customers from different cultures are treated properly and that all their needs are met.

Cultural differences

Cultural differences are apparent in diet, language and dress.

In Spain, shops usually close at lunchtime because of the heat so a siesta is taken in the afternoon. The nightlife starts at 11 pm and goes on until 6 am.

In France, breakfast may consist of coffee and croissants.

In Australia, Christmas dinner may be a barbecue on the beach.

In the UK the local pub is still a focal point for many people.

Using your experience from holidays abroad, reading or talking to friends, try and identify specific examples of culture that relate to different countries.

Customers with specific needs

All customers have their own special needs and wants. Some customers have more specific needs and require extra understanding and sensitive treatment. These include people needing wheelchair access, those with sensory disabilities and people with young children.

When they recognise that customers have specific needs, travel and tourism staff should choose an appropriate means of communication, either spoken or written, or think about any special information the customers need, such as disabled facilities.

Skills practice

The Disability Discrimination Act 1995 covers customer service for people with disabilities or specific needs. Facilities now have to ensure that people with disabilities are able to access and have the opportunity to take part in activities like anyone else. For example, theme parks will need to provide adapted seats on rides for people with disabilities.

Carry out research into the Act in order to answer the following question.

What provisions for specific needs do you think other travel and tourism organisations will have to make in order to comply with this legislation?

Of course we should see customers as people with particular needs, not as difficult people. People with specific needs want the same level of service that every customer receives, with possibly a little more understanding. Visitors with restricted mobility include those in wheelchairs to those who have stiff joints. It also includes people who are temporarily disabled through, for example, breaking a leg.

Not all travel and tourism facilities are ideally constructed or equipped to deal with this type of disability. The situation can be helped by considering the following points:

* Is there enough space for them to sit/stand/move/manoeuvre?

* Is there a shorter route they can take with fewer obstacles/changes of level?

* Can they reach handles, controls, shelves, and telephones or will they need help?

* Will they need help to carry things, or open doors if they are on crutches, for example?

* Do you need to slow down if you are guiding them somewhere?

Visually-impaired visitors

Many people have some form of visual impairment, but only a small proportion are totally blind and some only experience lack of colour definition. Information in large print format or printed text in Braille can be useful. The following points could be considered.

* When guiding a blind person, ask how they would like you to guide them. Most prefer you to walk slightly ahead while they take your arm.

* Explain exactly what obstacles are ahead, for example a set of stairs going up.

* Avoid intrusive background noise, such as loud piped music – blind people rely more on hearing their way than sighted people.

* When introducing yourself to a blind person who does not recognise your voice, tell them who you are, and address them by their name if you know it.

Hearing-impaired visitors

Again the nature of disability varies from person to person. The following points may aid communication.

* Face the person on the same level, with your face to the light and not in front of a bright window.

* Keep your hands or pen away from your face and do not eat whilst speaking.

* Check that background noise is kept to a minimum.

* Make sure the hearing impaired person is looking at you – attract their attention if necessary.

* If the topic of conversation is changed, make sure the hearing-impaired person knows.

* Speak the words clearly, maintaining a normal rhythm of speech.

* Do not shout as it distorts the visual effect of words.

* Use visual material and gestures where it helps understanding, but avoid exaggerated or inappropriate facial expressions.

* Remember that phrases and sentences are easier to understand than isolated words.

* If a word/phrase is not understood, use different words with the same meaning rephrased.

* Allow more time for the person to absorb what you are saying.

* Remember that lip reading can be very tiring.

It is important to remember that a person is not disabled by their impairment but by the environment and attitudes of the people they encounter.

People with young children

People with specific needs also include customers with young children who may be restricted by the needs of the children.

In the example of a theme park, these needs can be met by providing breastfeeding and crèche facilities, baby-changing rooms, special family areas in the catering areas and use of free pushchairs.

All customers have needs and expectations, some more than others. Travel and tourism staff have to recognise this needs something which can only usually be achieved by thorough training and experience. It is not easy to satisfy all customer needs but practice and experience will help you deal effectively with all customer service requirements. In time, your confidence and experience will grow.

The needs of internal customers

Internal customers are employees who work in different sections or departments of an organisation. Everyone in a travel and tourism organisation must work well together so that the organisation can give excellent customer service.

Internal customers may also include other organisations such as catering franchises operating in a theme park. At the same time, organisations must treat the internal customers to the same degree as their external customers in order to get the best out of them and establish good working relations between colleagues, managers and staff teams.

It might at first seem strange to think of your colleagues as customers, but you have the same responsibility to each other as you have to external customers.

Good levels of communication between different departments are required to ensure that travel and tourism organisations operate smoothly to meet the needs of external customers. For example, imagine you work in a travel agency. We know that your external customers are the people who want to book a holiday or arrange travel insurance. To reach that stage in the transaction, head office would have provided you with the posters to advertise the holidays, the computer systems to enable you to make a reservation and the skills you need to operate the computers.

In this case, you are the internal customer because you need the product. Your requests have been communicated to the departments and they have responded positively so that the external customers' needs are fulfilled. If organisations

Employees of a company are internal customers

treat staff well it eventually reflects on the level of service that is delivered to customers. A happy and efficient workforce who provide good service to each other is more likely to provide good customer service to external customers.

It can take a while to get used to the idea of regarding your colleagues at work as customers. However, it must be emphasised that staff who come into direct contact with customers cannot provide them with excellent customer service unless they receive the same type of service and support from colleagues.

In many travel and tourism organisations, employees work in teams and members of these teams work together to deliver high-quality customer service.

People who work well together usually enjoy their work more. A happy workforce leads to good teamwork and greater efficiency. Job satisfaction leads to greater motivation and leads to a sense of pride in the organisation, an increase in self-confidence and the motivation to continue to do well.

People who can work well with others tend to be able to motivate them. This is especially useful in supervisory and management positions. Providing excellent internal customer service will not only improve external customer service but can result in co-operation from colleagues, recognition from management and improved chances of promotion.

CASE STUDY

Internal customers working together

People who work well together usually enjoy their jobs more. This can lead to effective teamwork and greater efficiency, and as a result the external customer will receive excellent customer service.

Unfortunately this doesn't always happen. For example, a travel agent may sell a holiday to a regular customer with whom they have built up a friendly relationship over the years. This relationship could be spoiled somewhat when the customer receives a very formal letter from head office two days' later saying that payment is due within the next five days and the booking cannot be confirmed until this payment is received.

1   How could this situation be corrected?
2   How would you encourage teamwork in your organisation?
3   How do travel and tourism organisations motivate their employees to work more effectively?

Key terms

Internal customers These are the people who work within the same organisation as colleagues, who should support each other and co-operate with each other in order for the organisation to be a success. An internal customer should be given the same respect as an external customer.

Job satisfaction This is the degree to which employees enjoy their work and feel motivated to do it well.

The significance of induction and training

Induction is concerned with providing a new member of staff of an organisation with a structured introduction to the organisation and its employees.

An induction programme will help them become familiar with their duties and responsibilities. This will help them deliver effective customer service. The programme should be designed to help new members of staff familiarise themselves with their new work environment, settle into their new jobs and establish good working relations with other members of staff.

Starting a new job can be quite a daunting experience. In fact it can be very stressful and nerve-racking. A good induction programme should aim to make the new employee feel relaxed yet motivated about his/her new workplace.

Some organisations appoint an existing member of staff to assist the new employee to settle into their new surroundings. This is called mentoring. The mentor plays an important role in the induction process in that he/she can motivate and enthuse the new employee into working for an organisation that looks after its employees both during their induction and throughout their career.

Skills practice

Studying for qualifications and training to learn new skills will play a major part in your career progression. Your studies could include working towards certificates, diplomas or degrees. Your training could include using information technology, marketing and management.

You will need to do research to carry out the following:

1 Make a list of the courses which would be applicable to you if you were to continue your studies in travel and tourism.

2 What skills and qualifications would you need to become: a cabin crew manager; a travel consultant; a regional manager for holiday resort reps?

Recruiting a new employee is a big investment. A structured and well thought out induction programme will help ensure this investment pays dividends.

Many travel and tourism organisations provide their employees with some form of manual or booklet outlining the structure of their new organisation and including a number of important points of information, including health and safety, first aid, disciplinary procedures, as well as details about social clubs, pension arrangements and trade union membership.

The following example of an induction checklist shows what the new employee can expect during the first month in their new job.

Sherwood Health Club

Induction for Leisure Assistants

Name _____

Date _____

First day activities:
- Tour of club
- Introduction to staff
- Evacuation procedures
- Staff room and locker key issue
- Issue of staff uniform and name badge
- Staff handbook and club procedures booklet issued

First week activities:
- Shift rotas
- Pension schemes
- Annual leave
- Sickness procedures
- 'Shadowing' supervisor

Additional aspects to be covered:
- Organisational structure
- Career prospects
- Training programmes
- Community links
- Competition

Signed..................................... Manager

Signed..................................... Leisure Assistant

Date..

A good induction programme will ensure that new employees feel they have a valued part to play in their new organisation and should motivate them to want to do the very best for their new employer.

Imagine you work in the Human Resource department of Thomas Cook and are responsible for the induction programmes for all new trainee travel consultants. Work out an induction programme for them which would include their first day at work until they have finished their one year probationary period.

Many travel and tourism organisations, such as theme parks and tourist attractions like Blackpool Pleasure Beach, employ seasonal and part-time staff. It is just as important to provide a full induction programme to these staff as it is to full-time staff because they still have to look after customers, carry out any emergency procedures and know the layout of the organisation. Imagine on your first day at Alton Towers being told to operate 'Oblivion'! You may be inclined to ask, 'How'? 'Where is it'?' What happens if it breaks down'? 'Who will be my supervisor'?

This situation would never happen at Alton Towers, which is well known for giving excellent staff induction programmes followed up by additional training.

It is important to make sure all new staff are aware of their responsibilities towards customers. This is especially so when a large number of staff are starting their employment at the same time. In such cases travel and tourism organisations organise group induction sessions. This saves time and money and helps build teamwork right from the start as newcomers can get to know each other before they start their jobs.

CASE STUDY

A question of communication

Rio Fourget was staying with a friend in London for six months. He applied for a job in a restaurant by letter saying that he had worked as a kitchen hand and then as a waiter in a busy restaurant overseas.

To his surprise he received a letter back within three days asking him to come to the restaurant and be ready to start that day as the restaurant was very short of staff.

Rio turned up on time, looked extremely smart and was asked to start work in the café bar. Everything looked perfect. The manager came down to observe this very smart, friendly looking new member of staff. He was about to congratulate his assistant manager on this latest appointment when they discovered all was not well. They watched together as Rio took his first order. The customer seemed to be talking for quite a while, repeating his order. Was Rio hard of hearing? Was the customer a foreign visitor with limited English? The answer to both of these was a definite No! It was Rio who couldn't speak a word of English!

It is highly unlikely that a situation like this would ever occur. However it highlights the importance of ensuring the right procedures are followed to employ the right staff.

1 What process should be followed when recruiting and selecting staff to work in travel and tourism?
2 What questions would you ask at an interview of someone wanting to be an air cabin crew member?
3 It is often said that interviewing is a skill. Why is that?

Inductions should be made as interesting and motivating as possible. This helps create a positive first impression of the organisation for new staff as well as giving the impression of efficiency and careful planning.

Effective induction programmes should include guided tours, videos showing details of the organisation, team-building exercises and activities to 'break the ice' between new and existing employees. This helps get people talking and getting to know exactly what is involved in the job they have just taken on.

> **Key term**
>
> **Induction training** The training that new employees receive at the start of their employment to introduce them to the organisation's policies and procedures. The training can last for up to a year.

On-going training

Training should start on day one. A well-trained workforce will be productive because training will improve their knowledge of the job. They will also be more motivated, as people enjoy what they are doing if they know they are good at it.

Many travel and tourism organisations provide staff with on-going customer service training.

Customer service includes all contact with the customer whether it is face-to-face or dealing with letters of complaint. Travel and tourism organisations should provide quality training before allowing staff to deal with the public. It should be emphasised to staff during training that good customer service is one of the main aims of the organisation. Role-play situations are introduced so that new staff either play the part of a customer or play the part of sales staff. This gives them a good idea of what it is like in real life to be a customer on the receiving end of both good and bad service.

Types of training

After staff have gone through induction training there are ways they can improve their skills by taking additional training.

The first type of training is *on-the-job training*, which is basically learning by doing. This is the most common type of training and involves the employee learning how to do the job better by being shown how to do it, and then practising. It is also known as internal training.

The advantage of this type of training is that it is cost-effective for the employer in that the employee continues to work while learning. There is, however, one disadvantage. An experienced work colleague often carries out the internal training, so bad practices can be passed on to the new member of staff.

Another type of training is called *off-the-job training*, through which an employee learns away from their workplace, although on some occasions the training is still carried out internally if the organisation has a separate training division.

Off-the-job or external training often takes place at college. It can be more expensive than on-the-job training but it is often of a higher quality because better-qualified people teach it. This type of training is best used when introducing new skills or training people for promotion. Training will help with employees' personal development and enable them to take additional responsibilities.

> **Skills practice**
>
> On-going training for new employees, especially those straight from school or college, could include both off-the-job and on-the-job training.
>
> What would you include in both types of training for an eighteen-year-old travel consultant?

The travel and tourism industry is highly competitive and every organisation must constantly be looking to improve and update to remain competitive. All organisations should aim to maximise the potential of each employee. This development benefits the person and the organisation.

The result of a planned professional development programme is that the employee is able to complete their job as effectively as possible.

The significance of product knowledge

Customers are likely to ask a range of questions relating to the products and services provided by an organisation. In order to sell its products, staff need to have a wide knowledge of the products and services offered by the organisation. This means that staff can answer specific questions or queries that may arise and can quickly and efficiently deal with problems.

Product knowledge is an essential requirement of a successful sales process. Staff working in travel and tourism must have regular training to help them learn about the features and benefits of the products they are selling. Good product knowledge creates the impression of a professional organisation as staff can suggest alternatives if a customer's first choice of product is not available, or provide in-depth information on the range of products available.

In the travel and tourism industry product knowledge is sometimes gained by staff experiencing the products first hand, for example familiarisation trips for travel consultants. Sometimes it is not always easy to obtain a working level of product knowledge, particularly when you first start a new job, but it is important that you take every opportunity to gain as much information as possible. In many cases, work colleagues are usually helpful in providing the relevant information.

So that travel and tourism staff can give information and advice about products, they need to know about

* the range of products available, for example holidays, rooms available, flight times

* who the products are suitable for, for example holidays for 18–30-year-olds, meals for vegetarians.

Armed with this type of information, staff can advise customers what to buy or use based on what's available and the customer's needs. Customers also require information about the prices of products, opening times and the location of different facilities.

The more you know about the organisation you work for, the area in which you work and the travel and tourism industry in general, the more you will be able to help your customers. Imagine someone has spent fifteen hundred pounds on a holiday. He or she would expect to be given detailed information about the resort, the accommodation and the transfers.

Experience is something you can't replace and coupled with study and a thirst for more knowledge, staff can become experts in their particular field and so provide customers with all the information they need.

Think about it

Product knowledge is an essential part of the salesperson's armoury. If he/she doesn't know enough about the product or the benefits it offers it is highly unlikely that he/she will make the sale.

What do you think you would need to know if a potential visitor rang up and asked you if it was worth visiting the theme park where you work?

The importance of customer service skills

Travel and tourism organisations rely on customers for their revenue, and travel and tourism staff rely on them for their jobs. That's why providing the right type of customer service is so important. That's why people working in travel and tourism should possess the necessary personal skills so that customers will buy their products, hopefully on a continuous basis.

Communicating with customers is a skill every employee working with customers should be taught. Possibly the most important aspect is understanding. Staff can talk to or write to customers as much as they like but if customers don't understand what is being stated there would be little point.

Using appropriate language

The way in which we say things is just as important as what we say. Travel and tourism employees who use language well will communicate clearly with their customers. Verbal communication, either face to face or on the phone, will have an effect on what customers think of staff and the organisation.

In customer service situations the language used should be simple and easy to understand. This is because communication is not just about sending a message; it is about receiving and understanding it.

There are some simple tips to remember when communicating with customers. First of all, any communication should not be complicated by using difficult language. Speaking clearly and concentrating on what is being said helps get the message across. This is especially true in using the phone when your voice should be made to sound interesting by altering its pitch and tone. This prevents the person at the other end losing interest. Listen to a travel consultant in action on the phone to see how it is done properly. Their enthusiasm is almost but not quite overwhelming.

Think about it

Research shows that words play a small part in communication. It is in fact tone, speed, rhythm and emphasis of the voice that are largely influential. Think about this when you next talk to your friends, relatives or employer. Try and work out if it makes any difference to the reaction you get.

How do you think a receptionist who has to repeat the same information over and over again about prices and opening times can maintain an interest in what she says and so keep her voice interesting?

Positive body language

Not all communication involves using words. Feelings, thoughts and attitudes can be conveyed without speaking by using gestures or facial expressions. This is known as non-verbal communication or body language.

Because sight is a more developed sense than hearing, body language is a very powerful form of face-to-face communication. In fact, 80 per cent of all communication is non-verbal. The ability to read someone's body language, especially when dealing with customers, allows travel and tourism staff to work out how their customers are feeling. This is a very powerful tool to possess. It becomes

even more powerful when you are able to be aware of the messages your own body language is sending.

Positive body language includes making eye contact to show that you are listening to and are interested in the person who is talking to you. Open body language using welcoming gestures and smiles says to the customer you are not aggressive or hostile. Perhaps the most powerful and positive type of body language is a smile. This says two things: you like the customer and want to help them; you like your job and take pride in what you do.

Key term

Body language This refers to non-verbal communication where our feelings and emotions are transmitted even though we may not be aware of it. Knowing how to read someone's body language is a very useful skill in the travel and tourism industry as it can help you judge the way a customer may be feeling.

CASE STUDY
Body language at its best

A couple walk into a restaurant and are met by a friendly, smiling restaurant manager who uses a good, firm handshake to welcome them.

He shows them to their table and makes sure they are sitting comfortably by adjusting their chairs.

A click of the fingers and a slight wave brings over the drinks waiter who duly obliges by showing the customers the wine list.

The positive welcoming body language of the restaurant staff has reinforced the spoken word.

One of the best ways of seeing your own body language is to see yourself on video. It is hard to tell how you appear to other people, so being able to see yourself is a great help.

Think of a customer service situation you can role play with a colleague and identify the effectiveness of your body language. Assess each other's performance. Also look at your effectiveness at giving information (speaking) and receiving information (listening). Suggest ways they could be improved.

Listening to customers

Travel and tourism employees have to listen carefully to customers at all times and ensure they understand what a customer is asking for.

Listening is the receiving role in spoken communication and is just as important as sending information accurately. Some reminders to ensure good listening skills include:

* Listen with an open mind; everyone's range of interests has its limits. We have a tendency to ignore ideas that are of no personal interest to us. This is a natural human trait.

* Be aware of your own prejudices; try to listen from a neutral position rather than let your own views colour your judgement. Guard against the tendency to resist or dismiss ideas if they do not coincide with your own views.

* Listen all the way through. Do not jump to conclusions. Remember the ratio of listening to talking should be 80:20.

* Learn to use thinking time wisely; try to identify the theme of the other person's message and check your understanding of facts by asking questions.

* Practise active listening skills; in some situations, particularly when there has already been a misunderstanding, it is important that the other person is reassured that you have fully understood their point of view.

Active listening is made up of

* mirroring . . . reflecting back the feelings
* paraphrasing . . . reflecting back the facts
* summarising . . . reflecting back the facts and feelings.

Listening can be hard work and requires concentration. However it is a skill that can be developed and it will help you gain valuable customer feedback, which can be used to improve the service even more.

Skills practice

This activity will test your listening skills. Working in pairs, one of you has to play the part of a customer, the other a travel consultant.

* The customer has to prepare a script lasting about two minutes describing the fantastic time he has just spent on holiday. It would actually bore most people to death but as a travel consultant you have to look interested. When the customer has finished you have to prove you have been paying attention by repeating the main details about the holiday.

* Reverse the roles but use a different situation, for example a day out at a theme park.

Dealing with customers over the phone

Customers use the phone when they want to communicate or find out information quickly. Many travel and tourism organisations, such as reservations centres, use the telephone as the main method of communication when dealing with customer enquiries.

Good telephone skills enable the standard of service customers expect to be met or even exceeded as good telephone techniques can create an excellent impression of the organisation.

A good telephone manner is an important communication skill for all travel and tourism employees who have to make or receive calls as part of their job.

Research by BT shows that on the telephone 14 per cent of our total communication is transmitted by the actual words used and 86 per cent by the way they are vocalised – i.e. how they sound.

The following techniques give an idea of how telephone communication should be carried out.

Taking a phone call

* Answer the call within three rings.

* Greet the caller with 'Good Morning' or 'Good Afternoon' and give the name of the organisation.

* Ask, 'How may I help you?'

* Sound bright and friendly by smiling – it makes a big difference to the sound of your voice.

* Keep paper and pencils next to the phone and make clear notes. To assure the caller that all details have been recorded accurately, read them back.

* Don't keep the caller holding on for a long time while you look for information or for the person they want to speak to.

* When transferring a call, give the caller any important information (such as the name of the person to whom you are transferring).

* Give your colleague important information (such as who it is on the line and what they need) before putting the call through.

* At the end of the call, check that the caller is satisfied with what you have said and done and are going to do.

* Use the caller's name when saying goodbye. Thank them for calling and let them put down the receiver first. This is not only polite, but also gives them a final chance to ask any more questions.

Making a phone call

The same techniques apply when making an outgoing call. Be clear about what you want to say and make notes of the key points you want to cover and have to hand any additional information such as the customer file or correspondence. This will also help if you need to leave a message on the answer phone.

Taking phone messages

If a message for a colleague or customer is not taken and delivered accurately, the impression of the organisation is likely to be poor. Try to follow a set procedure when taking messages and include:

* The name, title and telephone number of the caller

* The date and time of the call

* A clear and concise message

* The name of the person taking the message.

Make sure that everybody knows the system for messages reaching their destinations – are they delivered, do people have to collect them?

Dealing with answer phone messages

When a customer gets through to an answer phone or voicemail that too is creating an impression. The pre-recorded message should be clear and the instructions should be easy to follow. Also be sure to check all messages left on the answer phone as soon as possible, so that callers get a timely response. This applies equally to e-mail messages.

Think about it

What do you think the following expressions mean in relation to using the phone:
* 'Smile as you dial and dial a smile'
* 'Don't phone a groan'
Why should you sound enthusiastic on the phone? How can you sound enthusiastic on the phone?

Written communication

The way communication is presented in writing can affect customers' overall impression of the organisation. In other words, poor grammar, spelling mistakes and a format which is set out incorrectly, create a bad impression.

The importance of the written word is that is should mean exactly what it says. This refers again to all types of written communication including e-mails, letters, memos, faxes and notes.

CASE STUDY

Getting it 'write'

The following letter was sent out by a coach operator to a customer confirming a booking for a weekend trip to the Lake District. Identify the deliberate mistakes.

> 16 St Mary's Court
> New Street
> Oldham
>
> Hayward's Coaches
> High Street
> Blackburn
>
> 30/09/05
>
> Dear Sir,
>
> Thank you for your booking of last week for a 3 day trip to the lake district. The total cost is £250 and I look forward to recieving your payment in a weeks' time.
>
> The accommodation will be in a 4 star hotel and will cosist or breakfast and evening meal.
>
> Here's hoping you enjoy yourselves.
>
> Yours sincerely
>
> Peter Hayward
>
> Mannager
> Hayward's coaches.

In travel and tourism, written communication includes brochures, tickets, timetables, advertisements and information guides. In all these examples, written communication should be easy to understand and properly set out.

Written requests from customers not only need to be answered clearly but also speedily. This shows they are not being ignored, so an acknowledgement and response in writing, say within three days, will show the customer their request is being dealt with speedily. It also shows the organisation values the customer's correspondence.

Successful selling techniques

There have probably been more books written on 'How to Sell . . .' than any other subject, probably because without successful sales businesses will not survive, hence the demand for such books.

Selling is a technique. There is no such thing as a 'born salesman' (salesperson). Products can look attractive and be affordable but they won't sell themselves, they need someone to say why customers really need them.

In order to attract and keep customers, travel and tourism organisations need to sell their products and services. Everyone who works in the industry, not just the sales department, has a part to play in selling the product to the customer. That's why it's important that travel and tourism organisations train their staff not only in selling specific products like holidays but also in selling the organisation as a whole by being able to provide product information, maintain good relations, handle complaints and generally give quality customer service.

More specifically, every travel and tourism organisation has to be profitable and the sale of products keep organisations in business as income is generated, costs are covered and profits are made. There's an expression which goes, 'Selling ain't telling, it's asking'. Basically this means that you first have to find out what customers really want from a product, then, and only then, can you sell the benefits of the product.

Let us look at a sales situation step by step.

Step 1 Creating a good first impression In general people will only buy a product if they can like and trust the person who is doing the selling. If customers are suspicious that they are being 'sold to', dislike the salesperson or feel tense in any way, they become sales resistant. It is therefore essential that the first impression customers receive is one of warmth, trust and friendliness. This puts the customers at ease and helps the salesperson establish a rapport with them.

Step 2 Find out what the customer wants This can only happen by listening to them and asking questions. For example, a customer in a travel agency might want a holiday in Spain. In order to establish exactly what they want the travel consultant can ask:

* When would you like to go?

* What type of area do you want to visit?

* What price range are you looking at?

* How long do you want to go for?

* How many people will be going?

* What sort of hotel would you like to stay in?

* What do you want out of your holiday?

Do not think you are being nosy by asking all these questions. The customer will realise that you are taking a great interest in them and will be only too happy to answer your questions.

Step 3 Sampling the products Once you have established what the customer wants, you can then give them a sample of products they may be interested in. Again, listen to what they say, look at their body language and answer any questions they may have.

Now is a good time to sell the benefits of the products, in other words what advantages there will be to the customer if they buy your products. For example,

'You can fly from Nottingham East Midlands Airport, which means you only have half an hour drive from home.'

or

'The hotel is less than half a mile from the beach so you will only have a five-minute walk before you get down to some serious sunbathing.'

or

'If you travel just before the high season you will save up to £200 per person.'

These are all attractive benefits which any customer will have difficulty resisting.

Step 4 Closing the sale This is a part of the sale that many people shy away from. It is easy to lose everything at this stage. No sale is made until it is closed, and that is when the customer decides to buy. The open questions you have asked previously can now be changed to closed questions that require a 'yes' or 'no' answer.

This is also a time for reiterating the information the customer has given, allowing him or her to add extra information if you have missed anything, and then justify your choice of product by relating it back to the needs the customer has mentioned and confirmed to you.

If people were unwilling to enter into a financial exchange for the product you are offering, they would have stopped the conversation before this stage.

Skills practice

Working in pairs take it in turns to act as a salesperson and customer. Choose two products connected with the travel and tourism industry and sell them to your colleague using the sales techniques already outlined.

Selling and self-confidence

Selling doesn't come easy. Employees need to be trained in the art of selling. This can include role-play situations and watching salespeople in action. Practising sales skills helps build subject knowledge and leads to an increase in self-confidence.

Making that first sale is almost like an obstacle to overcome, and the feeling an employee gains from making a sale gives them satisfaction and motivation to sell even more. Motivation is even more apparent if sales are linked to commission, that is the more you sell, the more you earn.

Salespeople are made not born. Thorough training along with personality, a positive attitude and good subject knowledge will give the salesperson every chance of making the sale. They will need to have the confidence to show the customer the benefits of buying the product and the value it will have for them.

Telesales

Many sales are made other than through face-to-face meetings. Telephone selling has grown hugely in recent years and demands special techniques of selling.

It may begin with a potential customer phoning a travel agent to ask about holidays. Obviously the customer wants to go on holiday and there are clear 'buying signals' if they start asking about prices, dates and accommodation. Faced with such situations the travel agent needs to have the required product knowledge to answer the customer's questions confidently, quickly and satisfactorily.

Telephone selling of products and services is also initiated by companies. They will phone an existing customer or a potential new customer with details and special offers on products or services without knowing whether the person they are calling is interested in buying these. This is called 'cold selling'. It is a practice used to sell various kinds of products and services, for example double glazing, motor insurance and financial products. Many travel and tourism products are also sold in this way, using a database of information about consumers to target prospective customers.

Though many people are offended by this selling techique and refuse to purchase in this way, there are many who find it convenient and are willing to purchase, for example, last-minute low-price holiday deals over the phone.

The Internet

The Internet has had a huge impact on the purchasing behaviour of consumers in recent times. New companies have been formed and existing ones have developed their marketing to take advantage of the potential of the Internet for selling products and services to consumers.

The travel and tourism industry has recognised the trend towards buying holidays or making travel arrangements through the Internet. The products of the industry are now extensively advertised through company websites, giving consumers easy access to information and choosing the arrangements that suit them: flights, accommodation, insurance and car hire can all be organised in this way.

Even travel agents, who experienced a downturn in business because of the effect of the Internet, have set up their own websites to compete with those organisations that sell their products solely through the Internet. However, the Internet still exerts considerable pressure on the business of travel agents.

Think about it

There will be times when a customer decides not to buy. You have to try and accept this with good grace. There's nothing wrong by saying to the customer, 'If you have a change of mind you know where to contact us.'

Many salespeople hate it when a customer says 'I will think about it'. Why is this?

Tact and diplomacy

There are occasions when a customer thinks he or she is right when in fact they are not. Take for example a customer who returns from holiday and complains to the travel agent that the location of the hotel, the entertainment offered and the types of excursions they could go on were not as described in the brochure. It turns out that the hotel they had looked at was not their hotel but one in a nearby resort! How do you handle that? The following action could be taken:

* Most importantly, listen to all the facts and do not interrupt – this gives you time to come up with a suitable response

* Remain calm and don't argue

* Check the brochure details and point out that the description applied to another hotel but you can see why they thought it was applicable to their hotel because it was on the same page

* Empathise with the customer and say that you understand how the misunderstanding arose

* Say you will communicate how the misunderstanding occurred to the marketing department in charge of the brochure production

* Once again, apologise that they were disappointed with their holiday.

Sometimes in situations like this customers will see the funny side of the misunderstanding or happily accept your explanation of how it came about. That will at least overcome any resentment. However they may be reluctant to book another holiday with you out of embarrassment or they may well return saying 'Remember us?'

Remaining calm

No matter how good your service, you will never please everybody all the time. However, you will be more prepared to deal with any situation that arises if you are confident of your customer service skills, aware of the sort of things likely to cause problems and know the correct procedure to use in difficult situations.

The use of active listening techniques without arguing with a customer who is complaining will help the situation, especially if you can reassure the customer you have understood.

Try to remain calm and in control. If one person is calm and the other angry and out of control, onlookers are likely to think that the calm person is right, even if this is not the case.

If you don't have the authority or knowledge to deal effectively with a situation, refer it on to someone who does. Always make sure the customer knows what is going on and that colleagues are aware that dealing with this customer could be sensitive.

In some travel and tourism organisations, the responsibility for solving problems rests with managers and supervisors. However, it is useful to remember that 'a customer with a problem is everybody's problem'.

Dealing with different types of customers

Awkward customers

Some people are naturally awkward. There is no particular reason for being so, it's just part of their character. However awkward they are, they still have to be treated properly and if it means remaining even cooler and calmer than normal, so be it.

Such people tend to complain more readily than other customers and know their rights. They are also aware that many organisations will offer some type of compensation if a customer complains.

Some of them will visit different places such as supermarkets, electrical goods stores, restaurants, pubs and travel agents, usually in search of compensation or to avoid paying the full price of a product by making a complaint about it. Eventually they become well known to these organisations who will tend to refuse them future service.

Travel and tourism organisations usually have procedures for dealing with customers who are unreasonable and abusive. Fortunately this type of customer is in the minority.

The procedures include staying calm and controlled and calling for support from a senior member of staff, if required. Some customers become angry, not necesarily because they are displeased with the product or even with the way they have been treated, but because of some problem in their personal life. So, you must listen and observe very closely to what they are saying and doing and act accordingly. However, never accept verbal abuse! If this occurs, call for support from your colleagues, or if it is serious enough, call the police.

Employees in the travel and tourism industry are trained to handle difficult situations. This is done through lectures on the issues and in role-play activities. The training has to be as realistic as possible in order for the employees to acquire the knowledge and confidence required for actually dealing with awkward customers.

People with special needs and disabilities

Anyone who works in customer service needs to understand the needs of customers with disabilities – whether mobility, sensory or learning impairment. It is particularly important to know about the specialist equipment and facilities available to customers. Many organisations, such as high street shops and hotels, deal with people with disabilities by providing lifts, ramps and wider car spaces near entrances to buildings.

Technical skills in travel and tourism

The travel and tourism industry has moved with the times when it comes to handling new technology. Employees are trained to operate Viewdata and reservations systems as well as process payments and exchange currency. These skills are learned through both internal and external training. This results in professional employees who are competent at using a wide range of skills necessary for working in the travel and tourism industry in the twenty-first century.

Knowledge check

1 What do we mean when we say organisations try to go the 'extra mile' to achieve customer satisfaction?

2 What do you think the term 'you only get one chance to make a good first impression' means?

3 What are the two most likely outcomes for a travel agent if clients leave feeling they have received 'value for money'?

4 How do you think customers feel about travel and tourism organisations that deal with complaints in a positive way?

5 Why is it important to make the induction process as interesting and motivating as possible for a new employee?

6 Why is training and development important to both the organisation and to the employee?

7 What does the following expression mean, 'Selling ain't telling, it's asking'?

8 How can travel and tourism organisations create a good public image?

9 What promotes good teamwork amongst staff?

10 How could you motivate employees who are not satisfied with their jobs?

11 Why is it important for employees in the travel and tourism industry to have in-depth product knowledge?

12 Why is it important nowadays to have the appropriate technical skills to work in the travel and tourism industry?

13 All customers have different needs. How different are the needs of the following people: individuals, groups, people with disabilities, senior citizens?

14 What is the best way of dealing with a very angry customer?

15 All customers think they are right, even when they are not! How would you deal with this type of customer?

UNIT ASSESSMENT

For this unit you have to produce a portfolio based on an investigation into aspects of customer service in a chosen travel and tourism organisation. You need to be aware of the importance of choosing an appropriate organisation to work with because input from the organisation and the collection of appropriate literature and resources is essential. So it may be an idea to choose an organisation with which you are familiar.

This unit makes up one-third of the total AS marks Single Award. It is assessed by your centre and moderated externally.

Your portfolio should include a review of induction procedures and training by your chosen organisation; a record of customer service role plays, demonstrating how you would meet the needs of different types of customer in your chosen organisation; an investigation into the product knowledge required by the organisation's employees; an evaluation of the range of skills required to deliver customer service.

You will be required to demonstrate your knowledge, understanding and skills of customer service and be able to apply such skills. You will have to use appropriate research techniques to obtain and analyse information, and finally you will have to evaluate that information in order to make judgements, draw conclusions and make recommendations.

Scenario

You are a management consultant who advises travel and tourism organisations on customer service. Your chosen organisation has invited you to advise them on how to improve their customer service as their sales have slumped recently and they have put this down to the level of service their clients have been receiving. Your job is to reverse this trend by reviewing the organisation's induction procedures, show staff how to meet the needs of different customers, investigate the amount of product knowledge the staff possess and the skills required in dealing with customers.

Task 1

Produce a thorough and detailed review of the appropriateness of the organisation's induction and training procedures, indicating how they benefit customers and the organisation. (up to 15 marks)

Task 2

Demonstrate in role-play situations a wide range of skills relating to the needs of different customer groups, showing sound product knowledge. You must try and respond in a positive way, successfully meeting the needs of different customer types. (up to 18 marks)

Task 3

Use your research skills independently to analyse how induction and training procedures provide employees with the product knowledge to enable them to provide first-class customer service. (up to 18 marks)

Task 4

Evaluate the full range of skills required to deliver customer service within the organisation and make sure all evidence is evaluated for appropriateness. You have to ensure your evaluation is well-structured and provides a full and detailed conclusion. (up to 9 marks)

Travel destinations

Introduction

This unit is about the main travel destinations in Europe and North America visited by UK tourists and why people visit them. By the end of the unit you will be able to locate where the popular destinations are and identify the main transport routes and travel times to these places.

Different destinations appeal to different types of tourists. You will be able to consider the advantages and disadvantages of a variety of travel options for different types of tourists.

How you will be assessed

You will be assessed on your research skills by producing a portfolio of travel information for different types of customers travelling from the UK to two contrasting destinations, one in Europe and one in North America. Your portfolio will contain information on where these destinations are located and a description of their key geographical characteristics and main attractions.

You will be asked to produce a script for a welcome meeting at each destination linking suitable tourist facilities to different customers. You will need to advise on the best method of travel to each destination and produce maps to inform your clients.

To complete the assessment you will need to provide research evidence to evaluate the appeal of each destination to different groups of tourists and evaluate their future popularity as a travel destination.

After studying this unit you should have learned about:

* The range of tourist destinations
* Research skills
* Tourist generating and receiving areas
* Tourist appeal
* Different types of transport.

The range of tourist destinations

A *travel destination* is the end point of a journey. People travel to a destination for a variety of different reasons, including holiday, business or visiting friends and relatives. A *tourist destination* combines travel with facilities and attractions that appeal to tourists. People working in the travel and tourism industry need to know where the major tourist destinations are and be able to describe the main features of these destinations.

People working in the travel and tourism industry need to be able to identify:

* The location of continents and oceans
* The location of major tourist destinations
* The location of major cities
* The climate of major destinations
* The natural and built attractions of major destinations
* The tourist facilities at the destinations
* Travel times to different destinations
* The main travel routes and gateways to major destinations.

This knowledge is important when advising clients about their travel plans, for example when working in a travel agency. You may be required to develop new tourism products seeking out potential tourist destinations for a tour operator. You may also be working with other travel and tourism organisations in different places around the world so a familiarity with tourism geography will help you gain an understanding of different places.

Key terms

Travel destination The end point of a journey.
Tourist destination A place with facilities and attractions that attract tourists.

The location of continents and oceans

A *continent* is a large continuous area of land on the surface of the Earth. There are seven continents:

* Africa
* Asia
* Australia
* North America
* South America
* Europe
* Antarctica.

An *ocean* is a large area of salt water on the surface of the Earth. Oceans cover 71 per cent of the Earth's surface. The five major oceans are:

* Antarctic (or Southern)
* Arctic
* Atlantic
* Indian
* Pacific.

Skills practice

Using an atlas identify each of the continents and the oceans.

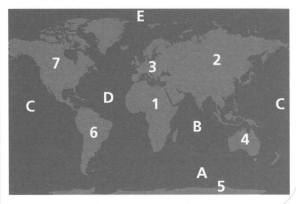

The location of major tourist destinations

Major tourist destinations have developed because they have good transport networks and are able to cater for the needs of large numbers of tourists. A destination that is a relatively short flight of less than five hours from the UK is known as a *short-haul* destination. The major short-haul tourist destinations are found within Europe, the most popular being Spain and France. *Long haul* describes flights of more than five hours, which tend to be beyond Europe, the most popular destinations being the USA and Canada.

Europe is defined by the countries in geographical Europe, within which some countries have joined the European Union.

Key terms

Short-haul destinations These are places to which it takes less than 5 hours to fly to.
Long-haul destinations These are places to which it takes more than 5 hours to fly to.

Skills practice

1 Using an atlas and a blank map of Europe (on page 142) identify each of the countries represented by geographical Europe.

2 Using the information in Table 3.1, add the information to your map of Europe. You may wish to use a colour code key.

3 Suggest reasons why Spain and France are popular travel destinations with tourists from the UK.

Table 3.1 The top 10 short-haul destinations from the UK in 2004

Rank order	Country	Number of visits abroad by UK residents (000s)
1	Spain	13,807
2	France	11,602
3	Irish Republic	4112
4	Italy	2968
5	Greece	2701
6	Germany	2332
7	Netherlands	2161
8	Belgium	1799
9	Portugal	1797
10	Cyprus	1280

In comparison the USA receives 4,173,000 visits and Canada receives 615,000 visits as long-haul destinations from the UK.

Source: Office for National Statistics (2005)

Within the countries in Table 3.1 certain destinations become popular with tourists and develop attractions and facilities that makes them into major tourist resorts. These places continue to attract large numbers of UK tourists.

The choice of destination can depend on the season. Both summer sun and winter sun holiday brochures suggest an escape to warmer climates, however some destinations are more popular at different times of the year. The most popular travel destinations for UK tourists buying package holidays with TUI are:

Summer	Winter
1 Majorca	1 Tenerife
2 Ibiza	2 Costa Blanca
3 Costa Blanca	3 Gran Canaria
4 Costa del Sol	4 Lanzarote
5 Tenerife	5 Costa del Sol
6 Minorca	6 Majorca
7 Corfu	7 Paphos, Cyprus
8 Paphos, Cyprus	8 Fuerteventura
9 Gran Canaria	9 Tunisia
10 Lanzarote	10 Sharm El Sheikh

Source: TUI (2004)

Skills practice

1 Label the top 10 summer and winter travel destinations on the blank map of Europe (on page 142), using a suitable key.

2 Identify which destinations are long haul and which are short haul.

3 Which destinations appear as both summer and winter resorts? Suggest why they are popular all year round.

4 Would the list of popular travel destinations be different for another tour operator? Give reasons for your answer.

Major travel destinations that are popular with UK tourists include:

The Algarve, Portugal
The Algarve is located on the southern coast of Portugal and is surrounded on both sides by the

Figure 3.1 The Algarve

Atlantic Ocean. It has an attractive coastline with nearly one hundred sandy beaches. The resorts are relatively low key (few night clubs but many quiet local bars and restaurants) and the area has many world-class golf courses. The long summers are hot and dry. The region receives the most international visitors to Portugal and the majority are from the UK.

The Spanish Costas, Spain

Figure 3.2 The Spanish Costas

The Spanish Costas are found along the southern coastline, on the shore of the Mediterranean Sea.

These areas are some of the most popular tourist destinations in Europe and are known for their sandy beaches and their high-rise hotels. By moving along the coastline away from the Costas quieter beaches can be found along with more historical and cultural attractions.

Costa del Sol stretches from Almeria to Tarifa. The main resort of Torremolinos has a reputation for being overcrowded due to its rapid development and its popularity with tourists.

Costa Brava lies northeast of Barcelona. Some of the resorts, such as Tossa de Mar, remain largely undeveloped, despite attracting large numbers of visitors, compared to resorts such as Loret de Mar.

Costa Blanca has also seen much recent development with the towns of Benidorm and Alicante becoming major tourist resorts. Temperatures are warmer than on the Costa Brava and the beaches are wider. The Terra Mitica Theme Park, Benidorm, offers an alternative to those who wish to venture away from the beaches.

Florida, USA

Figure 3.3 Florida

Florida is famous for its built attractions of Disney World, Universal Studios, Sea World and Busch Gardens in Orlando. To the south, Florida Keys offers many beaches and clear blue waters that are popular with divers. The city of Miami offers the chance for a city break and a visit to Miami Beach that is often frequented by celebrities.

The Grand Canyon, USA

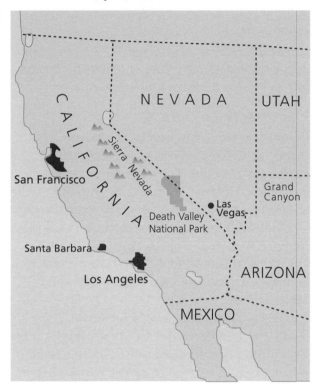

Figure 3.4 The Grand Canyon

The Grand Canyon is found in the Grand Canyon National Park in the state of Arizona and has been described as one of the 'must see' natural attractions in the world. The valley is visited by 5 million people each year and is over 1.61 kilometres (1 mile deep) and between 6.44 to 18.96 kilometres across (4 to 18 miles).

Think about it

In groups consider why these holiday destinations are popular with UK tourists.

Skills practice

1 Using a range of travel brochures identify five travel destinations in Europe and five travel destinations in the USA and Canada that are popular with UK tourists. Locate each destination on a map.

2 Identify the main attractions of each travel destination and suggest the types of tourist who would be interested in visiting them.

The location of major cities

Major cities provide a destination for city breaks, which is the fastest growing sector of international travel. It is not just the capital cities that benefit, other large cities offer services for conference visitors. Most people who go on city breaks tend to be from the middle- to high-income groups and therefore city breaks are less affected by economic decline. Europeans tend to take two or more city breaks a year in addition to their main annual holiday. Low-cost airlines have expanded the choice of destinations even further.

The most popular cities visited by UK tourists are:

1 Paris   6 Brussels
2 Amsterdam   7 Bruges
3 Dublin   8 Barcelona
4 Rome   9 Venice
5 Prague   10 Vienna.

Source: ABTA (2004)

Skills practice

1 Locate each of the ten most popular cities in Europe visited by UK tourists on the blank map of Europe (see page 142).

2 For each of the most popular cities visited by UK tourists, identify one major visitor attraction in each city.

3 Using a range of travel brochures identify ten cities in the USA and Canada that are visited by UK tourists. Plot these on the blank outline map (see page 143).

The climate of major destinations and why this affects their appeal

Think about it

Why is climate important in attracting visitors from the UK?

Climate affects the appeal of destinations. It is the second most important reason for choosing a holiday destination, after the price of the holiday. Climate is important because warmer climates are more often attractive to tourists from the UK.

Climate is a measure of atmospheric conditions such as temperature, sunshine and rainfall that are based on yearly or monthly averages over a period of not less than thirty years. These figures are usually displayed in holiday brochures, holiday guides and atlases.

Weather conditions are events that occur daily and form part of the climate for the destination. People prefer warm, bright sunny conditions rather than cold, damp and overcast ones. Comfort is very important; whether a person is sunbathing or skiing, they must feel comfortable otherwise they will not enjoy their holiday.

Major destinations tend to be in warmer climates. Colder climates also have an appeal but receive smaller numbers of visitors. One exception to this rule is the popular ski resorts that rely on an abundance of snow.

Precipitation

Precipitation is the measure of rainfall, snow or hail. Climate data can show the average amount of precipitation per month and is usually displayed in millimetres (mm). This gives the visitor an idea whether they are visiting during a wet or dry season.

Temperature

Temperature can be measured in degrees Centigrade (°C) or degrees Fahrenheit (°F). In Europe most of the travel brochures display temperatures in Centigrade, in America most of the travel brochures display temperatures in Fahrenheit. Although 75°F sounds a lot more than 24°C, in fact they are the same temperature. Travel brochures often display average monthly temperatures or average minimum and maximum monthly temperatures.

Humidity

Humidity describes the amount of water vapour that is present in the atmosphere and is measured as a percentage. The warmer the atmosphere is, potentially the more water the atmosphere can hold. High humidity over 70 per cent can make visitors feel sticky and uncomfortable. Where areas of high humidity and high temperatures exist, these are potentially unsuitable for tourist development.

Hours of sunshine

Hours of sunshine depends on the amount of cloud. The more cloud there is the less sunshine there is.

The UK receives on average 53 days of sunshine each year; this is one reason why so many Britons travel overseas to search for more sun.

The effects on climate

Destinations that have a similar climate can experience differences in sunshine, temperature, rainfall and humidity. These differences are due to geographical features, including the proximity of the sea, being inland, height of land and wind direction.

Destinations that are close to the sea tend to be cooler in the summer and warmer in the winter, whereas destinations in the middle of continents or inland, tend to have warmer summers and colder winters.

The height of the land affects climate. The higher the land the colder it is. For example, in the Alps the temperature drops by 0.75°C for every 100 metres ascent on north-facing slopes. Higher altitudes also mean more precipitation. This is particularly important in alpine regions where winter sports destinations rely on a generous amount of snow. In Southern Europe mountain regions have allowed the development of some winter sports, including the Sierra Nevada in Spain. Winter sports are also popular in the USA; Aspen, Colorado, in particular is famous for its skiing.

Adventure holidays and package tours have extended the choice of locations into the fringes of hot desert areas and cold regions. These give tourists a different experience and are usually made available during the most favourable times of the year due to the extreme climatic conditions.

Air pollution can also affect the amount of sunshine. In Los Angeles the amount of smog caused by air pollution reduces the amount of sunlight.

Key terms

Climate The average temperature, sunshine and rainfall of an area or place over a period of time.
Weather The climatic events on a particular day at a particular area or place.

CASE STUDY

Hurricanes in Florida

An important affect on the appeal of major destinations is the threat of hazardous climatic conditions. The Caribbean Islands and the state of Florida, USA, both suffer from hurricanes and tropical storms. The official hurricane season lasts from 1 June to 30 November with early to mid-September receiving most of the storms. Hurricanes tend not to affect the tourism industry but in September 2004 four hurricanes hit the American state of Florida, the first time that this has happened since records began in 1851. Wind speeds were recorded between 75 and 140 mph. Over 2.5 million residents were evacuated.

Tourism is Florida's largest industry and is worth $50 billion a year. It is America's second-most popular holiday destination after California. The hurricanes caused the major tourist attractions including Sea World, Universal Studios and Disney World to temporarily close. Hotel bookings began to decline as hotels in Miami and Tampa received 22 per cent fewer bookings than the same time the previous year.

During the hurricanes most UK tour operators allowed visitors booked to travel to Florida to make changes to their travel plans free of charge, as many had decided to change their choice of destination.

CASE STUDY

Tourism threatened by climate change

Heat waves, droughts, rising seas, flash floods, forest fires and diseases could turn profitable tourist destinations into holiday horror stories according to new research published by the World Wildlife Fund. Tour operators and countries relying on tourism will need to take into account the potential impacts of climate change when planning new resorts or upgrading their facilities.

Dr David Viner, Senior Research Scientist at the University of East Anglia, who compiled the study, warned: 'Areas such as the Mediterranean, a popular destination for British tourists, could become unbearable during the traditional summer holiday season. As temperatures begin to soar, many tourists will stay away.'

Source: World Wildlife Fund UK (1999)

Skills practice

1 Using the above two case studies explain how climate has an important impact on the appeal of travel destinations.

2 What are the problems associated with extreme weather and climate in tourist areas?

3 What can be done to help reduce the effect of extreme changes in climate? Explain how your recommendations will have an impact on the tourism industry.

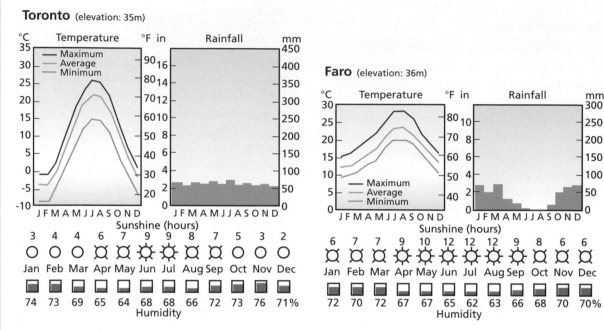

Figure 3.5 Climate graphs for Toronto and Faro

1 Using an atlas locate the two destinations above on a map.

2 For each destination identify the hottest month and the coldest month of the year in °C.

3 For each destination compare the annual temperature range (hottest to coldest monthly average) in °C.

4 For each destination what is the annual average temperature?

5 For each destination identify the wettest and the driest months.

6 For each destination identify the month that receives the most sunshine.

7 Which is the most popular holiday destination? Give reasons for your answer.

The natural and built attractions of major destinations

Major destinations can either provide natural or built attractions or both.

Natural attractions

Natural attractions are based on the *topography* or shape of the land. Each destination has its own unique topography, which can be attractive to tourists.

Natural attractions can include:

* Lakes
* Rivers
* Caves
* Volcanoes
* Forests
* Mountains
* Coastlines
* Waterfalls.

Think about it

Discuss a natural attraction that you have visited and give reasons as to why you found it interesting.

Lakes

Lakes are large inland areas of water. They provide an attraction to tourists, including those seeking scenic beauty and water sports.

CASE STUDY

The Italian Lakes

The Italian Lakes is a popular destination for UK tourists. Based in the region of Trentino in the north of Italy, the lakes are surrounded by the Dolomite Mountain range to the north. The lakes are deep and have steep sides producing a dramatic landscape.

There are four main lakes:

- Lake Como
- Lake Garda
- Lake Lugano
- Lake Maggiore.

Lake Garda is the largest lake in Italy and is the most developed in terms of tourism with many small towns and camping sites situated along the shore. A mild climate and rich fertile soils have encouraged olives, lemon trees and grape vines to flourish. The steep sides of Lake Garda can reach up to 1750 metres (5775 feet) at Monte Baldo. Views across the Lake are possible from a panoramic rotating cable car.

The Trentino Tourist Board has encouraged the growth of tourism based on natural attractions. These include:

- Wine tourism
- Dairy and local food tourism
- Mountain bike holidays
- Horse riding holidays through the mountains
- Windsurfing holidays.

Skills practice

Complete the following table for one lakeland region in Europe and one in North America:

	One lakeland region in Europe	One lakeland region in North America
Location		
Appeal of the main attractions		
Description of climate		

Rivers

Lakes and oceans are fed by a series of *rivers*. Rivers can be a popular destination for their scenic beauty, wildlife and fishing. Over sixty per cent of UK river cruise passengers travel to European destinations. The large European rivers of the Rhine and the Danube are linked by the Main River and a series of canals. This allows cruises to take place from the North Sea to the Black Sea along 3500 kilometres (2200 miles) of waterway. Popular cruises include trips from Frankfurt to Munich and from Amsterdam to Vienna and Budapest.

Cruises on the River Rhine allow passengers to explore towns and cities and the many castles that can be seen from the river.

The top five European destinations for UK river cruise passengers in 2002 were:

1   River Rhine and Moselle
2   River Danube
3   River Rhone and Seine
4   The Russian waterways
5   River Po.

Source: Mintel (2004)

Forests

Forests provide unique habitats for wildlife and are popular destinations for walking and activity holidays. The Black Forest in southern Germany is famous for its highland scenery, cuckoo clocks, fairy-tale castles and the cherry schnapps that is used to make the famous Black Forest Gateau. The forest is over 200 kilometres (125 miles) long and 60 kilometres (37 miles) wide, with mountain peaks of up to 1500 metres (5000 feet). The Black Forest runs along a stretch of the River Rhine and also borders other tourist regions that are famous for their natural attractions; these include Lake Constance in Switzerland and the Alsace region of France.

Mountains

Mountains form dramatic landscapes that often have snow on the highest peaks. This is in contrast to the deep valleys that often contain lakes and rivers. The Rocky Mountains extend from Alaska, through Canada and the USA, to Mexico. The valley beneath the Canadian Rockies contains Highway 93, which allows visitors to explore the National Parks of Banff and Jasper. These tourist destinations have been popular for over one hundred years and combine summer hiking with winter skiing.

Skills practice

Using the blank outline maps of Europe and North America (pages 142 and 144) and an atlas, identify the mountainous areas and using a key mark on your map ten popular mountainous tourist destinations, five in Europe and five in North America.

Mountains provide dramatic landscapes for tourists to explore

Forests provide opportunities for activity holidays

Caves

A *cave* is a natural hole in a rock, occurring most commonly in areas of limestone, although caves can occur in any type of rock. Caves can be spectacular and have columns of stalagmites that rise from the floor and stalactites that hang from the ceiling.

CASE STUDY

Show caves at Nerja, Spain

The show caves at Nerja, on the Costa del Sol in Spain, are situated 3 kilometres (1.9 miles) from the coast on the slopes of the Sierra Almijara mountains. The caves are 4823 metres (15,916 feet) long and over five million years old, and have been carved out by the gradual erosion of water. They have the widest column of rock in the world, the grand centre column found in the *Sala del Cataclismo* (Cataclysm Hall), which is 32 metres (105 feet) high, and 13 × 7 metres (43 × 23 feet) wide. Ancient wall paintings can also be seen in the caves as they were inhabited from 25,000 BC until the Bronze Age. The centre of the caves has been transformed into a performance area where music concerts and ballets are accompanied by a light show that illuminates the large columns of rock.

Show caves at Nerja

Skills practice

Describe another cave that attracts tourists from the UK, in either Europe or North America. Suggest why people visit this natural attraction.

Volcanoes

A *volcano* is an opening of the Earth's surface where magma, molten rock or ash erupts, often violently. Most volcanoes tend to be conical in shape and are found where there is a weakness in the Earth's crust. Volcanoes are popular with tourists who enjoy watching the spectacle from a safe distance, but when volcanoes are active they are dangerous.

Mount St Helens in Washington USA, stands at 2549 metres high (8411 feet) and erupted on 18 May 1980 with devastating effect. Over 400 metres of the volcano was blown away and the eruption cloud stood at 19 kilometres (12 miles) high. During the eruption 57 people lost their lives and the damage caused by the volcano cost over $1 billion. Further eruptions were recorded in 2004 with accompanying earthquakes. Mount St Helens is becoming more active and potentially could erupt again at any time in the near future.

Think about it

Discuss the impact that Mount St Helens has on tourism to the local area.

Skills practice

Complete the details for Mount Etna and Mount Vesuvius in following table:

	Mount Etna, Italy	Mount Vesuvius, Italy
Location		
Date of last eruption		
Description of the eruption		
Why tourists visit the volcano		

Coastlines

Coastlines are the most popular natural attractions. They can be dramatic with steep cliffs and crashing waves. These areas are exposed to powerful waves that erode the coastline. Other parts can be relaxing with sandy or pebble beaches. The coastline can offer many leisure opportunities, from sitting in the sun to taking part in water sports, beach sports or children's entertainment.

The coastlines in Europe are awarded a Blue Flag when the beach and water quality meets the standard of the European Union Bathing Water Directive. The eco-label is administered by the Foundation for Environmental Education in Europe (FEEE) and beaches are assessed on an annual basis. If a beach does not match the required standards the award can be taken away. The award has been given to nearly 3000 beaches and marinas in 24 countries across Europe and has been extended to South Africa.

The top ten countries in Europe with the largest areas of coastline are:

1	Norway	6	Turkey
2	Greece	7	Croatia
3	UK	8	Iceland
4	Italy	9	Spain
5	Denmark	10	Estonia.

Canada has the largest coastal area in the world with 202,080 kilometres (125,492 miles) and the United States has 19,924 kilometres (12,373 miles) of coastline.

Think about it

Discuss the reasons why some areas of coastline are developed for tourism whilst others are left in a relatively natural state.

Skills practice

1 For each of the top ten countries in Europe with the largest areas of coastline identify one major coastal resort and list the main attractions that exist.

2 Using a range of travel brochures identify five popular coastal resorts in Canada and five in the United States. List their main attractions and identify the type of visitor they would appeal to.

Skills practice

1 Is it important that a beach resort receives a Blue Flag? Give reasons for your answer.

2 Does a similar beach eco-label scheme exist in North America? Give examples of areas of coastline that are considered to be of high environmental quality.

Waterfalls

Waterfalls can be an impressive sight and are popular with visitors. Niagara Falls is the second largest waterfall in the world after Victoria Falls in southern Africa. Niagara Falls is located between Lake Erie and Lake Ontario on the border between Canada and the United States and is comprised of three waterfalls: the American Falls, the Bridal Veil Falls and the Canadian/Horseshoe Falls. The height of the waterfalls stands at approximately 52 metres (170 feet) with the water flowing at speeds between 150,000 and 600,000 US gallons per second. At the bottom of the Niagara Falls the water travels for 9.3 kilometres (15 miles) along deep and narrow valleys, known as gorges, until entering Lake Ontario. Niagara Falls attracts over 12 million tourists each year. At night the waterfalls are illuminated by powerful coloured spotlights, providing a colourful spectacle.

Think about it

Why do you think people find waterfalls so appealing?

Niagara Falls

Built attractions

Built attractions include a wide variety of purpose-built venues. Some have been adapted to meet the needs of tourists.

Built attractions include:

* Theme parks

* Indoor arenas

* Historic buildings

* Ancient monuments

* Museums and art galleries.

Theme parks

Theme parks are purpose-built visitor attractions offering a wide range of facilities including shopping, restaurants and gardens. The parks are themed around historic events, fantasy, childhood or a futuristic world. Many contain 'white knuckle rides' but increasingly they have become more sophisticated in terms of their use of fantasy and illusion.

Theme parks offer value for money in that they provide a full day's entertainment at a fixed price. Pricing structures often allow discounts for groups and for families. Details of special offers are usually displayed on a theme park's website. Even when the weather conditions are poor many theme parks contain attractions which people can enjoy in the wet as well as having a range of indoor attractions and facilities. Some theme parks are specifically targeted at families and younger children, whereas others have more exhilarating rides attracting teenagers and young adults. Although most visitors to theme parks are day visitors, many theme parks are encouraging visitors to stay overnight in purpose-built themed accommodation.

Skills practice

Complete the following table with the details and main features of popular theme parks in Europe:

THEME PARK	LOCATION	MAIN FEATURES
Disneyland	Paris	
Efteling		
Europa Park		
Futuroscope		
Gardaland		
Legoland		
Parc Asterix		
Phantasialand		
Port Aventura		
Tivoli Gardens		

Purpose-built attractions such as theme parks provide a wide range of facilities for visitors

Popular theme parks

The Magic Kingdom at Florida's Disney World is the number-one most visited theme park in the world, with 14 million visitors per year. It is not just a theme park but a purpose-built resort in its own right, including hotels, shops, entertainment, live music venues, a sports complex and six golf courses. The emphasis is on family fun and the attractions have been designed with this in mind. For younger visitors It's a Small World and The Magic Adventures of Winnie the Pooh contrast with Splash Mountain and Space Mountain for the older and more adventurous visitors. The Magic Kingdom covers 122 square kilometres (47 square miles), however not all the land has been developed as 25 per cent of the resort has been designated as a wilderness preserve. The Magic Kingdom is the largest employer in Florida, employing 50,000 people. More than 46 million colas are consumed each year at Disney World Resort along with 7 million hamburgers and 5 million hot dogs.

The top ten most visited theme parks in North America (2003) are:

1 The Magic Kingdom at Disney World, Lake Buena Vista, Florida (14 million visitors)

2 Disneyland, Anaheim, California (12.7 million visitors)

3 Epcot at Disney World, Lake Buena Vista, Florida (8.6 million)

4 Disney-MGM Studios at Disney World, Lake Buena Vista, Florida (7.8 million visitors)

5 Disney's Animal Kingdom at Disney World, Lake Buena Vista, Florida (7.3 million visitors)

6 Universal Studios at Universal Orlando (6.8 million visitors)

7 Islands of Adventure at Universal Orlando (6 million visitors)

8 Disney's California Adventures, Anaheim, California (5.3 million visitors)

9 SeaWorld Florida, Orlando, Florida (5.2 million visitors)

10 Universal Studios Hollywood, Universal City, California (4.5 million visitors).

Source: Amusement Business (2004)

Think about it

Why do the top ten theme parks in the United States attract so many visitors?

Indoor arenas

Indoor arenas provide a variety of public exhibitions, entertainment, music events and sporting facilities, as well as business exhibitions (trade shows) and conventions. They are large enough to support exhibitions and events on a grand scale and usually include:

* Conference rooms and meeting rooms

* Registration and welcome areas

* Box office services for public events

* Good transport access – road, rail and air

* Car parking facilities

* Support services for exhibitors and event organisers

* Food and catering facilities

* Adequate toilet facilities

* Easy access for visitors with special needs

* Nearby hotel accommodation.

Madison Square Garden in New York describes itself as the world's most famous arena. It first opened in May 1879 but has been rebuilt four times. It combines 76,178 square metres (820,000 square feet) of indoor space which includes a 20,000 seat arena, a 5600 seat theatre and a 3344 square metres (36,000 square feet) exposition rotunda. It is home to the New York Knicks basketball team and the New York Rangers ice hockey team. Seating arrangements vary between events. Such events include concerts, basketball, ice hockey, wrestling, boxing, tennis, the Ringling Brothers Circus, horse shows, ice shows, track and field events. For further information visit http://www.thegarden.com

Historic buildings

Historic buildings include stately homes, castles, royal palaces, birthplaces and houses of famous people. They have been adapted to allow tourists to visit, have improved health and safety features and incorporated additional tourist facilities such as guides, toilets and souvenir shops. Historic buildings help visitors understand the history and culture of the country they are visiting.

CASE STUDY

Versailles, France

The Palace of Versailles is one of the most famous historic buildings in Europe, with three chateaux and extensive gardens. It was originally built as a hunting lodge in 1624 and became the royal palace of King Louis XIV. Until 1789 it remained the seat of the monarchy in France and its design reflects its power and wealth. The buildings contain 700 rooms and 67 staircases, highly decorated and beautifully preserved. The most popular attraction is the Hall of Mirrors, a magnificent room that was the focus of grand celebrations and royal marriages. The parkland covers some 800 hectares and includes over 200,000 trees.

The royal palace is also historically significant as the place where Germany signed the Treaty of Versailles in 1919 to signify the end of the First World War and claim responsibility for the lives lost.

The Royal Palace of Versailles in France

Complete the following table with details of one historic building in Europe and one in North America:

	HISTORIC BUILDING IN EUROPE	HISTORIC BUILDING IN NORTH AMERICA
Name		
Location		
Main attractions		
Important events that took place		

Ancient monuments and historic monuments

An *ancient monument* or *historic monument* is a site that was built before the end of the Western Roman Empire, 476 AD, and represents a good example of the past.

Monuments can include:

* Buildings
* Forts
* Burial grounds
* Henges
* Stone circles
* Field systems
* Mines
* Hilltop enclosures
* Villas
* Roads.

One of the most visited ancient or historic monuments in Europe is the Roman town of Pompeii in southern Italy. In AD 79 Mount Vesuvius erupted burying the town of Pompeii. The remains were discovered in 1750, including

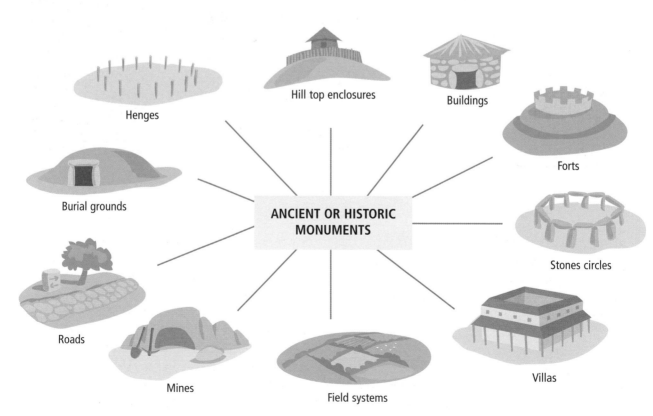

Figure 3.6 Ancient or historic monuments are among the most popular tourist attractions

buildings, temples and the remains of people who lived there. Excavations are on display in the National Archaeological Museum in Naples, including colourful paintings and mosaics. The buildings in Pompeii are very well preserved, including the Forum, the centre of civic and religious functions, the gladiators' barracks, theatres and many fine houses.

Skills practice

1 Locate and describe an ancient monument in Europe. Why is it popular with visitors?

2 Locate and describe an ancient monument in North America. Why is it popular with visitors?

3 Suggest why it is more difficult to locate an ancient monument in America than in Europe.

Think about it

Over 2.5 million people visit Pompeii each year. Why do you think this is such an interesting place to visit?

The Forum at Pompeii, Italy

Museums and art galleries

Millions of people visit *museums and art galleries* every year to view and interact with exhibits which give an insight into the culture and history of a destination.

The Louvre in central Paris houses, amongst 29,000 pieces of art and artefacts, the world's most famous painting, the *Mona Lisa,* and the statue *Venus de Milo*. Approximately six million people visit the Louvre each year. The building was first used to exhibit artefacts in 1793, making it one of the earliest European museums. The Louvre is easily recognised by its glass pyramid entrance.

The Museum of Modern Art (MoMA), New York, was founded in 1929 as an educational institution and dedicates itself to being the foremost museum of modern art in the world. Over 1.5 million people visit MoMA each year. It has over 135,000 paintings, sculptures, architectural models, drawings, prints, photographs and over 19,000 films and four million film stills.

The Louvre in Paris is one of the world's great museums and art galleries

Think about it

1 Why are museums and art galleries important tourist attractions?

2 What groups of visitors do museums and art galleries attract?

Key terms

Natural attractions The natural features of an area.

Built attractions These are human-built features or attractions for a particular purpose.

Theme park A human-built attraction with a particular theme including rides and other amusements.

Tourist facilities

There are many *tourist facilities* that are designed to meet the needs of visitors. These include:

✱ Accommodation

✱ Food and drink

✱ Entertainment

✱ Events.

Accommodation

The *range of accommodation* available at a tourist destination varies according to the quality and level of service on offer and also the price of stay. Some visitors prefer the independence of self-catering accommodation, whereas others like varying levels of service and luxury in the type of establishment they choose. Levels of service can be classified into bed and breakfast stays; half board, where an evening meal is provided in the cost; full board, which includes lunch and evening meal; and all-inclusive, which adds bar snacks and drinks to the full board option.

The main *types of accommodation* on offer can include: hotels, guesthouses, inns, holiday centres, hostels, villas, apartments, chalets, caravans, camping, and farm accommodation. Each of these appeals to different types of tourist and so many destinations will seek to provide a range of accommodation types to attract a cross-section of holidaymaker. Disabled groups and the elderly may seek accommodation that has good access. Young families may wish to have family rooms that are adjacent to the main bedroom and be in accommodation that welcomes family groups. Backpackers and students who are travelling tend to seek cheaper accommodation with fewer facilities.

A hotel tends to have five or more bedrooms that are available to let but not calling itself a guesthouse or a boarding house. A guesthouse is a modern name for a boarding house, a private house where the owner rents out rooms and may also provide meals. An inn or public house may have a small number of guest bedrooms that tend to be advertised on a bed-and-breakfast basis.

Farm accommodation has become a familiar sight in the countryside as farmers offer rooms and farm cottages to tourists. It is an attractive alternative for those who wish to stay in the countryside. Not only can they witness rural life at first hand but also stay in authentic farm accommodation.

Caravans and camping range from a basic farm field to purpose-built sites with restaurants, bars, shops, children's activities and other on-site services.

Think about it

What are the advantages and disadvantages of camping?

Holiday centres are often built for the purpose of catering for large numbers of tourists and have become resorts in their own right. They include an all-inclusive package of accommodation, food and entertainment.

The UK company Haven Europe operates 30 holiday parcs in France, Italy and Spain. In 22 locations they rent spaces in locally managed parcs to provide luxury mobile homes and camping facilities. In addition they own 8 French Siblu (pronounced 'see blue') holiday parcs in the popular tourist regions of Aquitaine, Brittany, Charente Maritime, Languedoc and Vendee.

Skills practice

Using a range of travel brochures and travel guides compare the variety, cost and standard of accommodation in an American city with a rural holiday in a European destination.

Food and drink

Food and drink can be associated with specific countries, regions and places. When we travel abroad we expect to see traditional foods on the menu. Eating locally prepared food is part of the tourist experience of visiting another country. Very often we are attracted to a particular country because we like the local food and drink. Many destinations choose to offer a range of international and local food and drink to meet the needs of a wide range of tourists.

Two areas of tourism that are growing in popularity are food and wine tourism. This includes tourists being offered experiences and visits which solely focus on the food or wine produced in a particular area.

CASE STUDY

Napa Valley, California

Napa Valley is 30 miles long and up to five miles wide and is famous for its wine production. It attracts 5 million visitors a year, with a peak in the number of visitors during the harvest months of September and October. There are over 200 wineries in Napa Valley and it has become one of California's most popular visitor destinations. The valley's warm climate and rich fertile soil has made the area perfect for growing vines. The region is famous for growing grape varieties that are traditionally found in the Bordeaux region of France, with a recent trend to growing Italian varieties. Many tourist industries have developed as a result of the vineyards; these include hot air balloon rides, private visits to wineries and wine tours by bicycle and by kayak along the river . There are many quality restaurants that are popular with visitors. For more information visit:
http://www.napavalley.com
http://www.nappavalleyonline.com

Wine tours are popular in France and Italy and also in other countries in central and southern Europe. What are the attractions in going to visit a winery? What type of tourist is attracted to these places?

Complete the following table, the first two have been done for you.

FOOD AND DRINK	COUNTRY OR REGION IT IS ASSOCIATED WITH
Pizza	Italy
Champagne	France
Pasta	
Black Forest Gateau	
Strudel	
Hamburger	
Paella	
Goulash	
Tapas	
Souvlaki	
Camembert	
Chowder	

Entertainment

Entertainment plays an important role in the attraction to visit a particular destination. Some tourists go to a particular place solely for the entertainment on offer; others seek amusement once they have arrived. The entertainment available can take on a variety of forms and will appeal to a range of ages and types of visitor. It can include: theatre, cinema, music, comedy, sport, street performers, nightclubs, pubs and bars. Each of these entertainment categories can also be divided into different aspects which will appeal to different visitors, for example music can mean experiencing live music such as classical, opera, musicals, pop and rock concerts; participating in music in karaoke sessions, and hearing recorded music in pubs and nightclubs.

Large cities will offer many types of entertainment as a focus for a range of tourists, and such entertainment can sometimes be found concentrated within particular areas, for example theatre districts. Tourist resorts can also offer a range of entertainment to visitors or specialise in certain types of entertainment, and hotels can also play their role in providing a programme of activities to keep guests entertained.

CASE STUDY
Broadway, New York

Broadway, the famous theatre district in New York, is located within a thin strip of Manhattan, called the Great White Way. There are 38 theatres packed into this small area of the city, most of which host world famous productions each night. Broadway theatres offer large-scale productions with professional and well-known actors and actresses.

Off-Broadway theatre offers a wider variety of styles, presenting work that mainstream Broadway is concerned will not make lots of money. Smaller venues with 100–500 seats are classified as Off-Broadway.

As well as the plays and musicals available on Broadway, visitors to New York can also apply for tickets to be part of the audience for the recording or broadcast of approximately 30 regular television shows.

CASE STUDY
Ibiza

The Mediterranean island of Ibiza has become increasingly popular as a holiday destination during the past ten years due to its reputation as being the centre of the world's clubbing scene, which dominates three months of the year.

Many clubs and resorts on the island have gained international status for the DJs and music on offer. Famous clubs include Café del

Mar, Pacha and Space. The island is advertised as the summer party capital of the world.

The island doesn't only offer clubs and music, it also provides the traditional Mediterranean attractions of warm climate, sandy beaches, history and a wide range of holiday accommodation, food and entertainment. Ibiza tourism officials have recognised that 65 per cent of visitors return for at least a second time, although they recognise the difficulty in trying to attract new tourists to the island because of its reputation as a summer party capital.

worn and jugglers, mime acts, acrobats and fire-eaters crowd the narrow streets.

Skills practice

1 Describe one major event in either Europe or North America.

2 Why does it attract large numbers of people?

3 How does a town or city benefit from hosting such an event?

Think about it

What entertainments and events interest you when you are going on holiday? Is this the same as your friends and family? How does a tourist destination try and cater for tourists with different needs?

Travel times to different destinations, the significance of time zones and the International Date Line

Think about it

Why is it important to know the departure time of a journey and also how long the journey will take?

Events

Events can provide the main attraction to a particular destination and appeal to a wide range of audiences. They are organised and designed to attract large numbers of people. They include sporting events, music festivals, art festivals and carnivals and may range from international ones to local ones:

* International events are important to the global community, for example the Olympic Games where athletes from across the globe compete against each other.

* National events are important to a whole country, for example the Celtic music festival, Dublin, to celebrate the musical history of Ireland.

* Regional events are important to the region of a country, for example the Texas Hot and Spicy festival celebrating the food of the region.

* Local events are important to a village, town or immediate locality, for example the Venice Carnival, Italy, where traditional masks are

Time zones

When we travel to different countries we may pass across different *time zones*, which means having to change our watches and clocks to local time as we pass through those countries.

Imagine that the earth is like an orange, where imaginary lines extend from the north to the south poles like segments of the orange. The most important line is the prime meridian that is used as the starting point; the most often used is the Greenwich Meridian that passes through London. Meridians are used to calculate distances west or east of the meridian and these are called longitudes. When the Sun is at its highest position at midday (noon), all places along the same line of longitude experience midday.

As the Earth turns from west to east, places on its surface turn from morning to noon, afternoon, evening and night. To the west it is before midday and east it is after midday. When it is midday in London it is 7 am in New York and 1 pm in Paris.

Countries like France and Great Britain have the same time zone for the entire country.

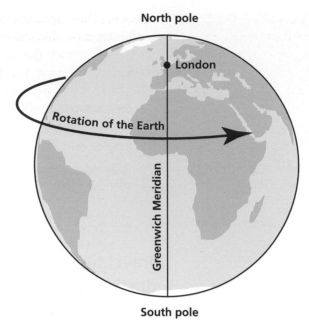

Figure 3.7 The Greenwich Meridian

However, larger countries like America and Canada extend across several time zones. When it is 7 am in New York it is 4am in California.

International Date Line

By moving further west along the map between the western edge of North America and Russia,

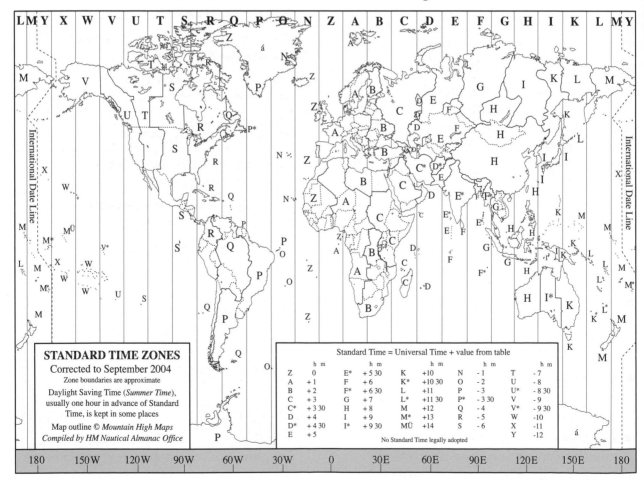

Figure 3.8 World time zones

there comes a point where places along this line of longitude are 12 hours behind the Greenwich Meridian. If it is midday along the Greenwich Meridian it is midnight along this other line, called the *International Date Line*. Moving further west would not only be an earlier time but also a different day.

The International Date Line avoids crossing through any country. It would create problems to be in the same country with parts of it in totally different days of the week.

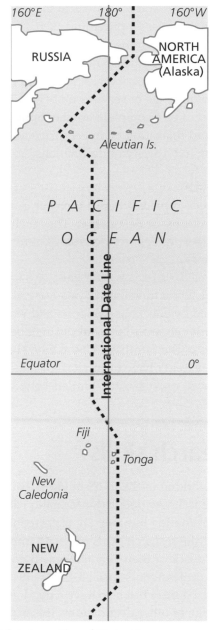

Figure 3.9 International Date Line
People travelling by air between long-haul destinations can cross several time zones before reaching their destination. They may lose or gain several hours. This interferes with their body clock and as such they may feel the need to sleep at odd hours of the day. This is called 'jet lag'. People are often tired after travelling and losing or gaining hours can often lead to temporary fatigue.

Skills practice

Complete the following table. You will need to refer to Figure 3.8 and an atlas. The first one has been done for you.

The time in London is 12 pm
The time in New York is 7 am

The time in Paris is 12 pm
The time in New York is _____

The time in Berlin is 8 pm
The time in Paris is _____

The time in Dallas is 2 am
The time in Boston is _____

The time in Los Angeles is 6 pm
The time in Montreal _____

The time in Washington DC is 10 am
The time in Reykjavik _____

The time in Madrid is 2 pm
The time in Athens is _____

The time in Budapest is 9 pm
The time in Vancouver is _____

The time in Amsterdam is 5 am
The time in Helsinki is _____

The time in Copenhagen is 8 am
The time in New York is_____

The time in Chicago is 4 pm
The time in Rome is _____

Key terms

Time zone The world is divided into zones of time, so that as you travel east you gain time and as you travel west you lose time.

International Date Line This is an imaginary line that runs north to south at 180° longitude, either side of which the time difference is 12 hours. So, if it is midday along the Greenwich Meridian it is midnight along the International Date Line.

The main travel routes and gateways to major destinations

Travel routes

Travel routes include road, rail, air and sea. Each of these are chosen depending on distance to travel, cost, convenience and availability, length of journey time and services available whilst travelling.

Road travel involves cars and coaches journeying along motorways, autobahns, freeways, trunk roads and through tunnels. Road travel tends to be mainly for domestic tourism and short visits over international borders. Using a car offers flexibility in terms of choosing route, time of departure and time of arrival. A driver can choose to break a journey with stops en-route or drive straight through to a destination. Coach travel tends to be less flexible as pick-up and drop-off points need to be established and there is a larger group of people to transfer to the final destination. Coaches and taxis can also be used to transport passengers from airports to their holiday destination – this is known as a *transfer*.

Rail travel offers high-speed links between major destinations as well as regional links and also some scenic railway routes. Rail companies can offer a range of services, including different seating accommodation, buffet cars and refreshment services, and a range of ticket types depending on the time and type of journey.

Air travel is the fastest method of travel available to a destination and can be used for domestic, short-haul and long-haul journeys. As a form of travel flying has increased in popularity over the past ten years with the result that there are now more airlines offering flights and there are price wars between airlines. Low-cost airlines, for example, offer cheaper seats with a reduced level of in-flight service.

There are two types of air travel, *scheduled flights*, which follow a particular timetable and fly whether or not the seats are all filled, and *charter flights*, which are linked with package holidays. These are when an aircraft is booked by tour operators for a certain destination at a certain time; they do not follow a regular timetable.

Travelling by air allows a quicker journey time and the opportunity to travel over long distances with relative ease; in addition there are in-flight services of refreshment and duty free sales on offer. As with rail travel the passengers are restricted to specific travel times for departure and arrival; they also have the disadvantage of having to check-in for their flight usually two hours before departure, which adds to journey time.

Sea travel subdivides into two types, ferries and cruises. *Ferry* transport takes travellers on foot, in cars, lorries and coaches across stretches of water and offers services such as shops, restaurants, cabins, lounges and play areas to the passengers. Other types of vessel providing such a service include sea catamarans.

Cruises on the other hand involve large ships, which are often described as floating hotels and offer a wide range of services on board. They tend to be part of or a complete holiday option offering luxury and relaxation all in one place while travelling to a variety of destinations.

Gateways

A *gateway* is a place where a traveller can enter or leave a country or destination. They include airports, seaports, border crossings, railway and bus stations.

Land border crossings offer gateways to other countries when travelling by road or rail and are monitored by checking passports and visas. Since 1995 border controls between the member countries of the European Union who signed the Schengen Treaty have been relaxed, causing unrestricted movement of tourists between these countries.

Research skills

People working in the tourism industry cannot be expected to know detailed information about every destination but they are expected to demonstrate research skills to obtain information for their work or their clients. Some travel and tourism professionals specialise in a particular region or country but also have a good general knowledge of other destinations. It is expected that you can identify important destinations and attractions but would need to research opening times or latest prices.

Researching involves:

* being clear about what you are trying to find out

* knowing how to search for information

* deciding what might be useful

* collecting and presenting relevant information

* drawing conclusions about your findings

* acknowledging your sources.

Being clear about what you are trying to find out

Setting clear aims and objectives is important when beginning any form of research, whether it be designing a questionnaire or finding information in a library or on the Internet. The *aim* is what you intend to find out or write about. The *objectives* are the steps you are going to take in order to meet your aim.

The following is an example:

Aim:

To discover information about the location of a destination, its landscape and climate.

Objectives:

* To select a suitable travel destination

* To research information on a selected travel destination

* To identify and describe its location

* To identify the main features of its landscape and identify major landscape features

* To identify main features of its climate using climate data.

Knowing how to search for information

It is important to get to know how a library is organised. There is usually a catalogue or a computer system that tells you what books are on the shelves and which ones are being borrowed. These computer systems are searchable using a title or author search or a key word search.

If you are using the Internet then knowing how to search for information will save you a lot of time.

It is best to start with one search engine such as Google although others are available.

A *Boolean search* allows you to use certain key words; they may differ between search engines although the basic principles are the same:

AND will let you add terms together (e.g. Spain AND Holiday).

OR widens the search to look for either word (e.g. Mallorca OR Majorca).

NOT allows you to exclude related words (e.g. Turkey AND Holiday NOT Birds).

Deciding what might be useful

It is easy to become interested in a topic and try to cover too much information. Find out who your audience is and remove information that is irrelevant no matter how interesting it may appear. Knowing who is likely to read or hear your work will tell you something about what level of information you require

Collecting and presenting relevant information

Try to collect information from a variety of different sources as this will help to make your findings more reliable. If possible support your evidence from another source. Information can change very quickly and as such you need to be sure that you have the most accurate and up-to-date information.

Drawing conclusions about your findings

If you have researched a lot of information and have many maps, tables and graphs in your report then it is useful to provide a summary and be able to draw conclusions about your findings.

Acknowledging your sources

Whatever books and resources you have been using always quote them in your writing. This is useful if you want to come back to a source to add more detail or to let the reader know where to find further information. It is also important if you are copying information to quote the source. You would feel cheated if someone copied your work without permission; copying other people's work without referencing it is called *plagiarism*.

After writing a quote in speech marks, place the author and date in brackets with the relevant page number separated by a comma. For example,

'Customer needs and expectations are constantly changing' (Marvell 2003, p. 53).

At the end of your assignments you need to include a list of references. They should be arranged alphabetically. If the same author is used then the most recent date is used first.

The correct way of acknowledging and referencing sources is to use the Harvard style of referencing:

> Author, Author initials. (Date) *Title*. Place of publication: Publisher.

The title should be underlined or placed in *italics*, for example:

> Marvell, A. (2003) *UK Travel Destinations*. Oxford: Heinemann Educational Publishers.

In journals or newspapers where there are many authors, the style is the following:

> Author, Author initials. (Date) Title of article. *Title of journal*, volume (part number) or date, page numbers.

An example is:

> Holden, W. (2005) Hidden gems of townhouse Paris. *The Mail on Sunday*, 1 May, pp. 92–93.

When using Internet sites try to quote the author and date of publication if at all possible, or the date accessed, for example:

> Little, M. (2004) Freelance Spain. A brief history of Spain, 17 November, http://www.spainview.com/history.html

Primary sources

Primary sources refer to reports or published first-hand information. For example, an airport requires information about the quality of services that are offered. It is only possible to gather this information by asking customers directly. The responses may then be analysed and presented in a report, which is then used to inform decision-making.

Secondary sources

It is an important skill to be able to gather information about destinations from a range of *secondary sources*, including gazetteers; the Internet; brochures; maps; guidebooks; newspapers and trade journals.

It is essential to know which source to select to develop research skills and also to recognise that the sources must be precise, valid and provide a suitable amount of detail. Knowing which sources to choose allows efficient information gathering that will save time.

Gazetteers are published geographical dictionaries or indexes, which contain a list of geographical features and descriptions organised in alphabetical order.

The *Internet* is a popular source for a huge range of information and many tourist boards and visitor attractions have dedicated websites to provide information to visitors.

Brochures are produced in order to promote a range of products and services including holidays and accommodation.

Maps provide the location of geographical features and can include road maps and other travel routes, street maps, and maps suitable for walking and hiking.

Guidebooks are produced to provide information about a particular destination or area and contain a variety of information on the main visitor attractions, history, places of interest to visit, culture, sport and accommodation in the locality.

Newspapers report information on destinations as items of news. Some national newspapers publish regular travel supplements that provide details about travel destinations.

Trade journals are publications devoted to news and features designed to inform members of the industry. Examples of trade journals for travel and tourism include *Travel Weekly* and *Travel Trade Gazette*.

Tourist generating and receiving areas

Tourist generating areas are countries where people travel from and *tourist receiving areas* are those areas where people travel to. People who visit travel destinations are described as *inbound tourists*. There were 400 million inbound tourists to European countries in 2002, representing 57 per cent of global travel. Asia and the Pacific received the second largest numbers of inbound tourists. The Americas received the third largest with 16 per cent of all inbound tourists.

Those tourists who leave their country to travel to another are described as *outbound tourists*.

Tourist appeal

There are many reasons why people visit principal destinations as inbound tourists. This is due to the appeal of the destination in meeting the needs of different types of tourists. The appeal of these destinations is reflected within holiday brochures and guidebooks. It is easy to see the differences when comparing an 18–30-year-old's holiday brochure with a summer sun brochure and a brochure specialising in holidays for mature couples and the retired.

Some destinations can appeal to a wide range of tourists and combine many different types of attractions. For example, in Austria walking holidays and Sound of Music tours are advertised alongside activity holidays, extreme sports, skiing holidays and city breaks.

Future popularity and appeal of tourist destinations

There are a number of factors that have a direct impact on the *future popularity and appeal of tourist destinations*. These are:

✱ Advances in technology

✱ Major events

✱ Security

✱ Exchange rates

✱ Promotional activity

✱ Fashion.

Advances in technology

The growth in home computers has revolutionised communication and access to information. Through developments in e-tourism people are able to book holidays using the Internet and use computers to research information regarding a visitor destination.

Tour operators, tourist boards, hotels, theme parks and local authorities are able to provide a great amount of information via the Internet. Details of events, attractions, accommodation, weather conditions and transport can help a tourist plan a holiday. Some Internet sites have

1 Using a range of holiday brochures that appeal to different types of tourists, compare the differences in expectation of a family group going on holiday, a recently retired couple and a group of university students by completing the following table:

FACTORS	NEEDS OF A FAMILY GROUP	NEEDS OF A RETIRED COUPLE	NEEDS OF A GROUP OF UNIVERSITY STUDENTS
Climate			
Topography			
Natural attractions			
Built attractions			
Events			
Food, drink and entertainment			
Accommodation available			
Accessibility and types or transport			

2 Identify the similarities and differences between the three groups.

become very sophisticated in offering virtual tours of destinations, attractions and hotels.

Advances in technology related to transport usually mean that more passengers are able to travel quicker and cheaper than before. The Airbus A380 is a brand new 'double decker' aircraft that seats 555 passengers. The wings were designed in the UK and the aeroplane is being assembled in France with assistance from Germany and Spain. As it is a wide-bodied aircraft it can be adapted to offer in-flight beds, and there is also dedicated space within the aircraft for a diverse range of uses, and could potentially include office space, shop, bar and even a mini-casino. It is expected to go into service in 2006.

1 Using the Internet take a virtual tour of a theme park, hotel or destination in Europe or North America.

2 What did you learn during your tour?

3 What advantage does a virtual tour have over a traditional guidebook or brochure?

Airbus 380

Major events

Major events such as international sporting events, festivals and exhibitions can attract tourists from all over the world. Not only does the event encourage people to visit but international media provides an opportunity to promote a country as a potential tourist destination and also to encourage repeat visits by tourists who have visited before.

The UEFA European Championship is the third-largest sporting event in the world, after the Football World Cup and the Olympics. The event held in 2000, called Euro 2000, was hosted by Holland and Belgium. It attracted 1.2 million football spectators and broadcast to a global television audience of 7 billion viewers.

Major events can also highlight less popular towns and cities. For example, the Barcelona Olympic Games in 1992 helped to provide an alternative tourist destination to the Spanish Costas and enabled the city to become one of the top European city-break destinations.

Think about it

What international sporting or music events have you watched on television? Did it encourage you to think about visiting the countries they were held in or travelling to see a similar event?

Security

Security is one of the key issues when considering the impact on the future popularity and appeal of a destination. Tourists need to feel safe and confident about visiting a destination; if they do not feel safe then it is unlikely that they will visit.

The terrorist attacks on the United States on September 11th 2001 had a dramatic effect on the numbers of inbound visitors. The terrorist attacks were particularly disturbing as passenger aircraft were used as weapons. This reduced the numbers of people wishing to travel long distances as people preferred to stay closer to home.

The wars in Afghanistan and Iraq and terrorist attacks in Bali and Egypt further reduced consumer confidence in long-haul travel and countries such as the United States experienced a decline in inbound tourists from the UK. The US Office of Travel and Tourism Industries and the Department of Commerce recorded 3.8 million arrivals from the UK in 2002. This represents a decline of 7 per cent on the 4.1 million UK visitors in 2001. The numbers of visitors include people travelling on business, visiting friends and relatives (VFR), as well as holidaymakers.

Further concerns over personal safety relating to the infectious disease SARS (Severe Acute Respiratory Syndrome) in 2002 and 2003 reduced the numbers of UK visitors travelling to the Far East and to Canada.

Governments and the travel industry have reassured tourists that they are doing their best to maximise security. Reduced fares and promotions have also helped consumer confidence to recover.

Outbound holiday visits by UK tourists between 1999 and 2002 saw a 29 per cent decline in visits to North America, an 11 per cent rise in the number of tourists to destinations of member countries of the European Union and a 16 per cent rise in the number of visits to European countries outside of the European Union.

Advice on travel safety and security is issued by the Foreign and Commonwealth Office via their website and is updated several times daily. For further information visit http://www.fco.gov.uk

Skills practice

1 Describe the impact of international security issues on passengers travelling from the UK.

2 Visit the Foreign and Commonwealth Office website and examine the advice given to UK residents travelling to destinations in Europe and North America.

Exchange rates

The *exchange rate* or value of the British pound in relation to other currencies can affect the popularity of tourist destinations. When the value of the British pound is higher than other currencies it makes travelling abroad less expensive as we are receiving more local currency for our money. When the value of the British pound is low compared to other currencies it makes travelling abroad more expensive as we are receiving less local currency for our money. Values of foreign currency are displayed in travel agents, where there is a bureau de change, in banks and newspapers.

Some countries within the European Union have replaced their traditional currency with the Euro. The Euro was launched in January 1999 and enables tourists and businesses to trade between countries using the same currency. There are twelve countries that have the single currency: Austria, Belgium, Finland, France, Germany, Greece, Ireland, Italy, Luxembourg, Netherlands, Portugal and Spain.

Each time money is exchanged, a bureau de change or bank charges a small commission fee. Although some offer commission-free exchanges where no charge is made, the amount of commission is usually hidden in the rate of exchange.

Exchange rates are not the only consideration when calculating the cost of goods and services abroad. The *rate of inflation* is an important factor as this shows how much prices have increased. If a holiday destination is seen to be expensive or offer poor value for money then cheaper alternative destinations are usually chosen.

Skills practice

1 Using today's exchange rates make a list of those currencies that have seen an increase in value and those that have seen a decrease in value.

2 To what extent does this have an impact on the popularity of the destinations?

3 Which of these currencies are in Europe and North America?

Promotional activity

How a destination is promoted can have a major impact on its popularity and appeal. Local authorities and national tourist boards spend thousands of pounds each year to market their destination to attract inbound tourism. It is important that potential visitors know what the destination can offer in terms of accommodation, facilities and attractions.

Most other countries have a national tourist board office in London in order to promote their country to the UK and to offer advice and travel

TOURIST CURRENCY RATES OF EXCHANGE	
Australia (dollar)	2.3514
Barbados (dollar)	3.3474
Canada (dollar)	2.2403
China (renminbi)	15.16
Czech (koruna)	40.94
Cyprus (pound)	0.8220
Egypt (pound)	9.7309
Euro	1.4119
Hong Kong (dollar)	14.15
India (rupee)	73.44
Indonesia (rupiah)	15702
Japan (yen)	199.41
Kenya (shilling)	129.90
Malta (lira)	0.6064
Mexico (peso)	19.00
Morocco (dirham)	15.30
New Zealand (dollar)	2.5115
South Africa (rand)	11.13
Sri Lanka (rupee)	176.49
Switzerland (franc)	2.2023
Thailand (bath)	68.31
Tunisia (dinar)	2.1626
Turkey (new lira)	2.4364
United States (dollar)	1.8277

One way of keeping in touch with the current tourist currency rates is through the business pages of daily newspapers. The above is a selection of rates for the British pound recorded in the press on 11 April 2005

services to UK residents who are interested in their country as a travel destination.

The European Union is the main tourist generating and receiving area for international tourism flows. On 1 May 2004 ten new countries joined the EU: Cyprus, Czech Republic, Estonia, Hungary, Latvia, Lithuania, Malta, Poland,

Slovakia and Slovenia. Further countries are set to join, including Bulgaria, Romania and Turkey. These provide new market opportunities to attract inbound tourists. Malta and Cyprus are already popular tourist destinations and countries like Hungary are working hard to promote themselves to attract tourists from the UK.

CASE STUDY

Hungary

The Hungarian Tourist Board recognises that Eastern Europeans are familiar with what Hungary has to offer, while Western Europeans know very little. The Tourist Board has to change the perception of Hungary as an Eastern European country to one that is recognised as a fellow European country. In the UK the Hungarian Tourist Board organised a series of promotions based on '2004 Year of Hungarian Culture'. City breaks to Budapest were promoted in Germany, the UK and Belgium. Current campaigns focus on health tourism, as Budapest is Europe's largest spa city with 80 thermal springs and 20 spa baths. Promotional channels include billboards, posters in travel agents, advertisements in the press and on television, including CNN, CNBC, Eurosport, National Geographic and the Travel Channel.

Source: Mintel (2004)

Skills practice

Using a range of newspapers, travel supplements and magazines provide examples of European and North American destinations that are advertising their country or destination in order to attract more visitors from the UK.

Fashion

Changing fashions will affect the popularity of destinations as one resort becomes increasingly popular in comparison to another. *Fashions* can be defined as a current style adopted by society. Fashions are affected by technological change, media influences, new developments and changing customer expectations, as well as employment trends and amount of personal income. Fashionable destinations tend to be visited more frequently than those that are not.

Fashions can be reflected in social trends and attitudes. New types of holidays are created by changes in fashion, which in turn creates changes in demand. A growing interest in health and sport has generated a rise in the number of specialist activity holidays, including underwater diving, golf, spa holidays, water sports, horse riding and mountain biking. Not only do these holidays offer a chance to relax but also to learn new skills, meet other people with similar interests and to further personal achievement.

Key terms

Tourist generating areas These are areas where tourists travel from.

Tourist receiving areas These are areas where tourists travel to.

Outbound travel Those who leave one country to travel to another country.

Inbound travel Those who arrive in one country from another country.

Exchange rate The value of one currency against other currencies.

Rate of inflation The rate at which prices increase in an economy.

Different types of transport

Tourists may have choices to make relating to the type of *transport*. For example, they may be able to choose between different departure airports if they are flying. They can also choose between different airlines, as many European destinations are accessible by both traditional airlines and 'low-cost' airlines, scheduled and charter services.

Tourists can also choose to travel by Eurostar and other high-speed rail networks. Alternatively, people can choose to drive to their destination using ferries or the Channel Tunnel and the autoroute or motorway system.

The methods by which tourists may choose to travel are:

* Road
* Rail
* Air
* Sea.

Road

When travelling by road, tourists can choose to travel by car or by coach. Travel by road is the most popular form of transport in Europe, carrying 78 per cent of passengers. Even when alternatives are presented, the car is the most accessible form of transport over short distances. Car use is more popular with domestic holidays but the use of ferry services and Eurotunnel have provided access to the European motorway system. Motorway networks are fast and efficient although drivers are sometimes discouraged from driving into major towns and cities. Concerns over pollution and congestion have meant that most city authorities have invested in other forms of public transport such as park-and-ride schemes.

Car hire is widely available and tourists can rent vehicles from airports, rail terminals, seaports and also through accommodation providers, as well as booking directly through a car hire company. Fly-drive holidays are very popular in North America, however many rental companies in North America require that drivers carry a major credit card, have a valid license and are over the age of 21.

European motorways display two numbers, a motorway or autoroute number and an E number, identified by green and white signs. The European International Network is a series of numbered routes across Europe and consists of a grid system of road numbers, with even numbers used for routes running east to west and odd numbers running north to south. The idea is to simplify the use of road numbers, which can change when crossing country borders. However, not all European countries have adopted the system as many major routes have been designated as E roads in the UK, but few, if any, are signposted using this system.

Most motorways or autoroutes in Europe and North America are toll roads and most bridges also demand payment in order to cross.

When driving abroad it is important to be aware of driving regulations as they differ from country to country. For example, in France the maximum speed permitted on a motorway is 130 km/hr (81 mph) and 110 km/hr (69 mph) when wet or for drivers holding a licence for less than two years. In towns the legal maximum is 50 km/hr (31 mph).

Skills practice

Using a European road atlas or a route planner on the Internet, identify the E roads used on the following journeys:

Paris to Amsterdam
Rome to Amsterdam
Paris to Munich
Bordeaux to Toulouse
Le Mans to Calais
Madrid to Valencia
Nancy to Salzburg
Hamburg to Berlin
Tromsø to Tornio
Budapest to Gdansk

Skills practice

You need to do research to answer the following questions.

1 What are the driving laws in the USA and Canada?

2 How do they compare to Europe and the UK?

Outbound *coach tourism* is dominated by UK trips to France, usually for four nights or more. The amount of coaches travelling between the UK and France is growing at a rate of 3.5 per cent each year. In 2002, 219,460 coaches travelled between the UK and France either using the Dover–Calais route or Eurotunnel. Other popular destinations that have seen a rise in the numbers of coaches from the UK include Belgium, Italy and Luxembourg, with Central and Eastern European destinations growing in importance.

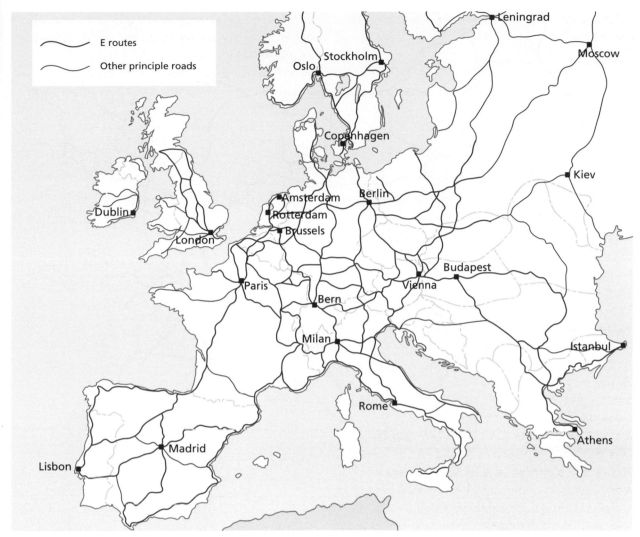

Figure 3.10 Key autoroutes of Europe

The top five coach holiday destinations in Europe as booked by UK tourists through Leger Holidays are:

1 France
2 Belgium
3 Italy
4 Austria
5 Holland.

Source: Travel Weekly (2002)

The two largest UK coach operators are Shearings and Wallace Arnold. Shearings carries approximately 575,000 passengers a year, owns 38 hotels and a fleet of 259 coaches. Wallace Arnold carries around 550,000 passengers a year with a fleet of 225 coaches and owns 8 hotels. The coach routes follow the autoroutes (Figure 3.10).

Travel within Europe is dominated by Eurolines, a European network of coach companies that was established to coordinate coach services across several countries. The company serves over 300 cities and 500 destinations.

In North America, Greyhound is the most established long-distance bus company, offering routes to all of the major cities in the USA as well as the Canadian cities of Montreal, Toronto and Vancouver. Bus routes follow the interstate highways (Figure 3.11) and stop every 100 miles to pick up passengers and to stop for comfort breaks and to change drivers. Buses are the cheapest way to travel long distance and are favoured by budget travellers.

Coaches are also used to *transfer* people between the destination and the resort. Tour operators hire local coach companies to pick up passengers at airports and drop them off en-route. Taxis can also be used to transport smaller numbers of people.

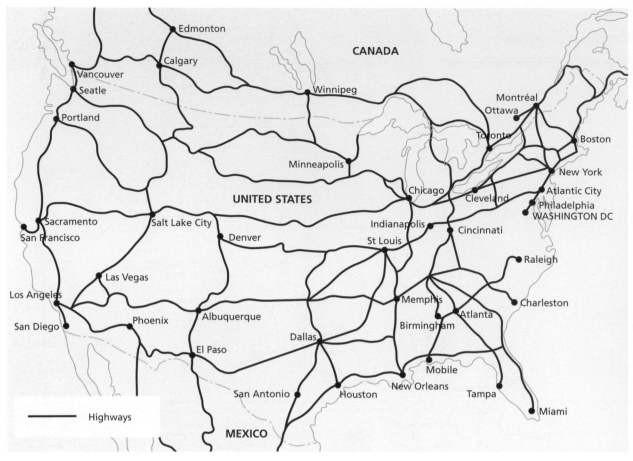

Figure 3.11 Key highways of North America

Rail

The *railway network* in Europe covers some 154,000 kilometres (95,500 miles) compared to the motorway network which covers 50,000 kilometres (31,000 miles). Despite such a vast network, rail passengers have fallen from a 10 per cent share of traffic in 1970 to 6 per cent in 2001. This is not surprising when between 1990 and 1999 Europe saw its motorway network *increase* by 25 per cent.

Railways offer the convenience of centrally located stations and relative ease of travel. However the UK has experienced a lack of investment in the railway network for many years compared to Europe. European services run faster and operate more frequently. Eurostar destinations from London Waterloo include Paris, Brussels, Lille, Disneyland and Avignon. By connecting with local services, Eurostar makes it

possible to travel to other destinations, including Amsterdam, Bordeaux, Bruges, Lyon, Nice and Tours. The service from London travels via Ashford International terminal in Kent. Eurostar carries 64 per cent of all UK passengers travelling to Paris. The main difference between Eurostar and Le Shuttle is that Eurostar is a train with passenger carriages whereas Le Shuttle can transport cars, coaches and motorcycles complete with their passengers.

The most famous railway company is the Orient Express. The Venice Simplon Orient Express offers luxurious travel between London, Paris, Venice, Rome, Budapest, Vienna, Prague, Bucharest and Istanbul. The service runs between March and November. The traditional service from London to Venice lasts for two days with one night on board. The carriages reflect a golden age of train travel from the 1920s, the original carriages still being used. The Orient Express offers a scenic view of Europe coupled with the highest level of customer service and luxury.

A luxury railway carriage on board the Venice Simplon Orient Express

Skills practice

In the United States Amtrak operates the national railway service. To travel from New York to Chicago takes 19 hours and to travel between New York and Los Angeles takes 66 hours. How does this compare with road and air travel? You will need to do research to answer this question.

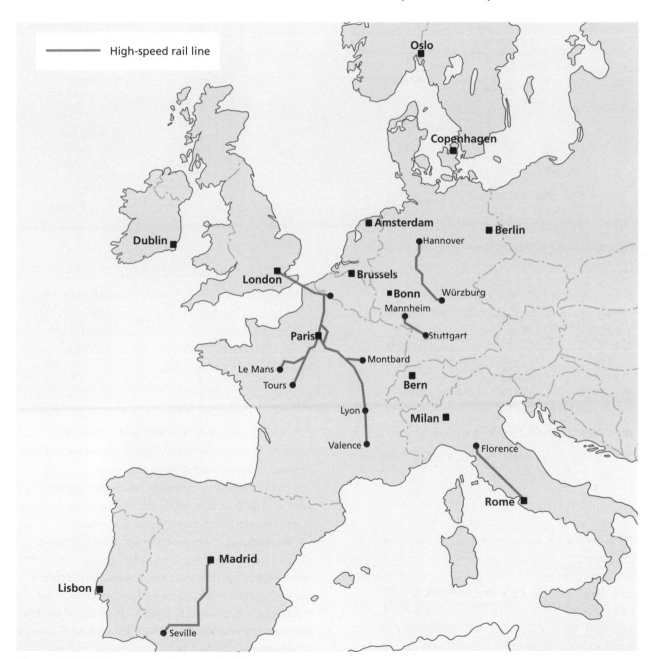

Figure 3.12 High-speed rail routes in Europe

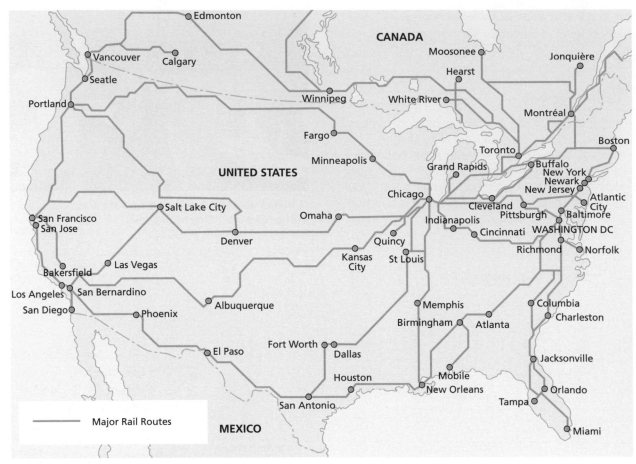

Figure 3.13 Major rail routes in North America

Scenic railways offer the tourist a unique experience of historic carriages and scenic beauty. Most only run during the summer months and are very popular, so booking is essential. In the United States examples include:

✱ Cass Scenic Railroad in the Appalachian Mountains, West Virginia

✱ Grand Canyon Railway, Colorado

✱ Cumbres and Toltec Scenic Railway, Rocky Mountains, Colorado.

Skills practice

Select one scenic railway in Europe and another in North America. Describe the route taken, the attractions that can be visited, levels of comfort and prices.

Underground railways provide a regular service with ease of transport below congested streets. Underground railways can be found in busy cities, including London, New York, Paris, Montreal and Amsterdam.

Air

Air travel is the preferred method of travel for most tourists. It offers relatively quick and direct access to short-haul and long-haul destinations. Half of the UK population makes at least one flight each year and 20 per cent of all international passengers begin or end their journey in a UK airport.

With the recent reductions in the number of people flying long haul and the highly competitive market that exists between airline operators, strategic alliances have been established between rival airlines to share routes and to cut costs. The major global airline alliances are shown in Table 3.2:

Table 3.2 Major global airline alliances

STAR ALLIANCE	ONEWORLD	SKY TEAM	KLM/NORTHWEST
Air Canada	Aer Lingus (Eire)	Aeromexico	KLM (Netherlands)
Air New Zealand	American Airlines	Air France	Northwest (USA)
All Nippon Airways	British Airways	Alitalia	
Asiana Airways	Cathay Pacific	Czech Airlines	
Austrian Airlines Group	Finnair	Delta Airlines	
bmi (British Midland)	Iberia	Korean Airlines	
Lufthansa	Lan-Chile		
Mexicana	Qantas		
Scandinavian Airlines (SAS)			

Budget airlines

There has been a tremendous growth in *budget airlines* during the last five years. Their success has been attributed to offering cheap regular flights to popular destinations. The recent success has been based on the following conditions:

* Using the most economical aircraft

* Not offering an in-flight service, reducing cabin staff and cleaning costs

* Reducing leg room whilst complying with government safety regulations

* Flying to popular destinations but avoiding routes dominated by major airlines

* Making efficient use of the aircraft flying several trips every day.

In the United States, Southwest Airlines is the largest budget airline, handling over 60 million passengers each year and flying to 60 US destinations. Other US budget airlines include AirTran Airways, JetBlue and Frontier. In Canada, WestJet and JetsGo offer budget flights.

In the UK, Ryanair and easyJet have dominated the market. Ryanair discovered that by reducing its ticket prices by half, compared to the major airlines, passenger numbers dramatically increased. Fares to some destinations in Germany are 80 per cent cheaper than those offered by Lufthansa and as a result the airline carries over 2 million passengers to Germany each year. Ryanair flies to 155 destinations in 17 European countries, including: Austria, Belgium, Denmark, England, Finland, France, Germany, Ireland, Italy, the Netherlands, Northern Ireland, Norway, Portugal, Scotland, Spain, Sweden and Wales. Of the 29 million passengers that fly with Ryanair, 43 per cent are leisure passengers, 36 per cent are visiting friends and relatives (VFR) and 21 per cent are travelling on business. France is the most popular destination for UK budget airlines. Ryanair flies more passengers to France than Air France.

In comparison easyJet operates from 55 airports, offering 180 routes. The airline carries 24 million passengers each year with 8.75 million of these originating from the UK. Other major UK budget airlines include: bmibaby, Flybe and MyTravelLite.

Skills practice

1 Using a selection of budget airline websites, identify the main routes taken by travellers from the UK.

2 Why have the budget airlines been so successful?

3 What strategies are being used by the major airlines in order to compete with the budget airlines?

Airports

UK airports handle approximately 190 million passengers each year; this figure is expected to grow to between 350 and 460 million by 2020. Heathrow is the busiest UK airport, handling over 63 million passengers each year, which accounts for approximately 40 per cent of air passengers in the UK. Gatwick Airport handles over 30 million passengers each year. However, the two largest airports are under increasing competition from the growth of regional airports. Airports offer a wide range of services, including retail, restaurants, ticketing, car parking and accommodation.

Airports also allow passengers to transfer between flights. Many airports are regarded as *hubs*, places that receive connecting flights from many destinations, allowing passengers a flexible combination of routes. Regional airports may not always offer a direct flight to a chosen destination, but instead offer a route that requires a transfer at another airport. These can be more expensive than travelling direct.

Due to the expansion of air travel in the UK the new Terminal 5 at Heathrow will add extra capacity. Stanstead Airport in Essex continues to expand and is the fastest growing airport in Europe; British Airports Authority (BAA), which owns the airport, is planning to double its capacity to 50 million passengers a year. There are plans to add a third runway at Heathrow between 2015 and 2020 with a second runway at Gatwick after 2019.

Regional airports offer local convenience with less congestion and cheaper car parking. Regional airports that continue to expand include the following:

Table 3.3 UK regional airports

REGION	AIRPORTS
The Midlands	Teeside, Birmingham
North of England	Manchester, Liverpool John Lennon, Carlisle, Newcastle
Northern Ireland	Belfast International, Belfast City, City of Derry
Scotland	Edinburgh, Aberdeen, Dundee
South-East	Luton, Norwich, Southampton, Southend, Kent International Airport, Lydd, Shoreham and Biggin Hill
South-West	Bournemouth International, Bristol International, Exeter, Newquay
Wales	Cardiff

Skills practice

1 Visit the British Airports Authority (BAA) website http://www.baa.co.uk and identify the services they offer to passengers.

2 Visit a regional airport website and identify the services that it offers to passengers.

3 Suggest why regional airports are handling increasing numbers of passengers.

In 2003 the world's busiest airports were the following:

Table 3.4 The world's busiest airports in 2003

RANK	AIRPORT (AIRPORT CODE)	LOCATION	TOTAL NUMBER OF PASSENGERS
1	Hartsfield-Jackson Atlanta International Airport (ATL)	Atlanta, Georgia	83,578,906
2	O'Hare International Airport (ORD)	Chicago, Illinois	75,373,888
3	London Heathrow Airport (LHR)	London	67,343,960
4	Tokyo International Airport (HND)	Tokyo	62,320,968
5	Los Angeles International Airport (LAX)	Los Angeles	60,710,830
6	Dallas-Fort Worth International Airport (DFW)	Dallas-Fort Worth, Texas	59,412,217
7	Frankfurt International Airport (FRA)	Frankfurt	51,098,271
8	Charles De Gaulle International Airport (CDG)	Paris	50,860,561
9	Schipol Airport (AMS)	Amsterdam	42,541,180
10	Denver International Airport (DEN)	Denver, Colorado	42,393,693
11	McCarran International Airport (LAS)	Las Vegas, Nevada	41,436,571
12	Sky Harbor International Airport (PHX)	Phoenix, Arizona	39,493,519
13	Barajas International Airport (MAD)	Madrid	38,525,899
14	Don Muang International Airport (BKK)	Bangkok	37,960,169
15	John F. Kennedy International Airport (JFK)	New York	37,362,010
16	Minneapolis Saint Paul International Airport (MSP)	Minneapolis Saint Paul, Minnesota	36,748,577
17	Hong Kong (HKG)	Hong Kong	36,713,000
18	George Bush Intercontinental Airport (IAH)	Houston, Texas	36,490,828
19	Detroit Metropolitan Wayne County Airport (DTW)	Detroit, Michigan	35,199,307
20	Beijing (Peking) (PEK)	Beijing, China	34,883,190

Source: Airports Council International (2005)

Skills practice

1 From the list of the world's busiest airports above identify those that are in Europe and North America and locate these on a map.

2 Suggest why most of the world's busiest airports are located in the United States.

Sea

Because the UK is an island it has many *seaports*. Ferry companies are facing increasing competition from the Channel Tunnel and the budget airlines. In the mid-1990s two out of three passengers who travelled across the English Channel did so by ferry, since the start of this century two out of every three passengers who travel across the English Channel do so by air. Nine out of 10 UK ferry passengers travelling outbound from the UK go to France, the rest travel to the Netherlands, Belgium and Scandinavia.

The ferry companies are looking to expand and the port of Dover invested £70 million in four new ferry berths to enable growth of the next generation of *ro-paxes*, passenger car ferries that also have large freight handling capabilities. Dover handles 60 per cent of passenger traffic across the English Channel. Dover Harbour Board have also invested in new check-in booths to allow passengers and freight to be processed more quickly.

Skills practice

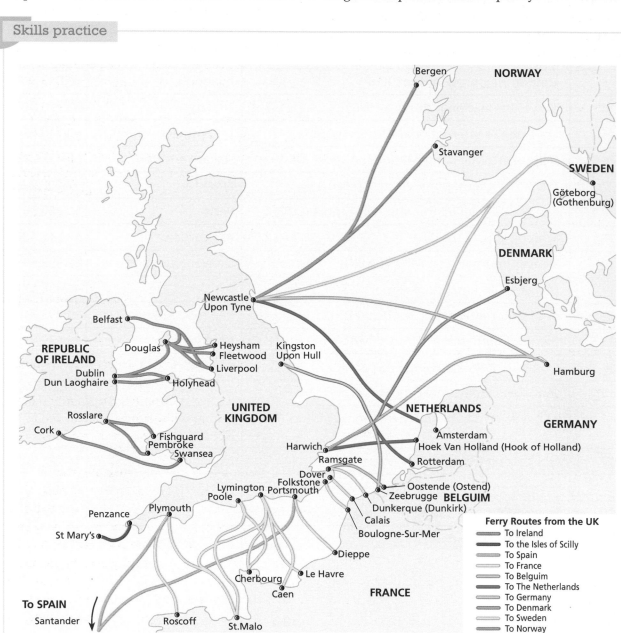

Figure 3.14 Ferry services routes from the UK

Using the map of ferry services from the UK, identify the routes taken by the following ferry companies:

- P & O Ferries
- Brittany Ferries
- Hoverspeed
- Sea France

Cruises

The UK is the second largest cruise market after the USA, with 940,000 cruise sales in 2003, a 14 per cent increase in sales on the previous year. The Mediterranean remains the most popular cruise destination in the world, although recently there has been growing interest in Northern European and Scandinavian cruises. The 55–65 age group dominates demand, with significant numbers in the 45–54 age group and the 65 plus. Older generations are attracted by the high quality of service and convenience of being aboard a luxury cruise ship whilst visiting a range of tourist destinations.

Skills practice

1 Using a range of cruise brochures identify the most popular itineraries in the Mediterranean.

2 Using the cruise brochures, identify the most popular itineraries in North America.

3 What are the main attractions of taking a cruise holiday?

Factors affecting tourist choice of travel method

There are several factors affecting tourist choice and the method of travel; the main considerations are:

* Cost of travel, including en-route costs
* Convenience for the nature of the group travelling
* Distance to be travelled, including journeys to airports
* Amount of time available for the journey, including check-in times at airports
* The purpose and duration of the visit
* Comfort, convenience and facilities offered.

Costs are an important factor to consider because in times of a recession spending on leisure and tourism is one of the first areas where savings can be made. The cost of a holiday is not just the cost displayed in the brochure. There are hidden costs such as entrance fees, food and drink, souvenirs and buying goods and clothes for a holiday.

Convenience can include date and time of travel and also the location of gateways. Airports and seaports that are at a long distance from home are less appealing than those that are closer to home and require less effort to get to.

The amount of time available for a holiday is also another important factor. A week's holiday might be better spent in a short-haul destination rather than a long-haul destination due to the amount of time spent travelling. This will also depend on the purpose of the visit. The three main purposes of visits are: leisure, business and visiting friends and family (VFR).

Levels of comfort and expectation may be reflected in the price, for example travelling on a budget airline compared to a traditional airline.

Tourists will often use a variety of types of transport to get from home to their final destination. This will depend on their preferred method of transport, on convenience, price, level of comfort and speed of travel. Examples include:

* Taxi
* Scheduled bus service
* Hire car
* Use of own car
* Accepting a lift from a friend or member of the family
* Rail.

Even within the destination tourists have a choice of transport available. They may prefer to stay within the destination and explore on foot. They may decide to use a hire car, taxi, local bus or train service or travel on the bus excursions chartered for the tourists.

Choices made by tourists may also change because the tourists themselves are changing. Increased travel and advances in technology bring about changes in expectation and level of service. Independent travellers, those not travelling as part of an organised package holiday, account for 55 per cent of the holiday bookings market. Between 1998 and 2004 the number of independently booked holidays increased by 60 per cent. This growth has been helped by the availability of low-cost travel and an increased use of the Internet in making bookings and researching potential destinations. UK tourists are not just seeking beach holidays but coupled with an increase in the short break market, they are increasingly seeking to experience different cultures and explore local heritage.

1 Why do people working in the travel and tourism industry need to know where major destinations are?

2 Can you name and locate the major continents and oceans on a map?

3 Can you name and locate the major tourist destinations and cities in Europe and North America?

4 Can you describe the climate of major destinations in Europe and North America?

5 Can you name some of the natural and built tourist attractions in Europe and North America?

6 Give examples of some of the tourist facilities found at major travel destinations.

7 Why are travel times and travel zones important to tourists?

8 What are some of the major travel routes across Europe and North America?

9 How would you go about researching information on a tourist destination? Give examples of primary and secondary sources that you would use.

10 Why do different types of people choose to visit different destinations as tourists?

11 What factors are significant in creating appeal to different types of tourists?

12 Describe the factors that affect future popularity and appeal of tourist destinations.

13 What are the different ways in which a tourist may travel to their destination?

14 Why is transport essential to the development of tourism?

15 Describe the factors affecting tourists' choice of travel.

UNIT ASSESSMENT

Portfolio practice

You have been asked to produce a portfolio of travel information for different types of customers travelling from the United Kingdom to two contrasting destinations: one in Europe and one in North America.

Your portfolio should contain:

- Information about the location of each destination, its landscape and climate.

- The script for a welcome meeting at each destination, linking the tourist facilities and major attractions to different customer types.

- Research into and analysis of the choice of methods of travel to each destination and travel while at the destinations, including appropriate maps.

- Recommendations to potential customers based on an evaluation of the appeal of each destination, and an evaluation of its likely future potential.

The welcome meeting

A holiday representative, or 'rep', delivers a welcome meeting to inform holidaymakers about local facilities and attractions. Part of the welcome meeting is for the holiday rep to make the attractions appear as exciting as possible so that the holidaymakers will want to visit them and get the most from their holiday. The holiday rep also acts as a sales person and will offer to arrange various visits and excursions to the most popular sites. The holiday rep must be able to identify what makes these attractions popular and understand which types of tourist they would attract by suggesting appropriate visits and excursions to the holidaymakers.

We have chosen Sorrento as an example of a European tourist destination and Los Angeles as an example of a North American tourist destination, and produced the following account of the areas, incorporating the sort of information that will be required for your portfolio. The same treatment will be required for whatever destinations you choose.

Sorrento, Italy

Information about the location of the destination, its landscape and climate

Sorrento has been a popular tourist destination since the 18th and 19th centuries and is located on the south-west coast of Italy in the Campania region, overlooking the Bay of Naples. The town is situated on a headland jutting out into the sea known as the Sorrento Peninsula, which forms part of the Amalfi coastline and is described in many guidebooks as one of Europe's most beautiful coastlines.

Here you could draw a location map of your destination and the surrounding area. In the case of Sorrento this includes the Amalfi coastline and the Bay of Naples.

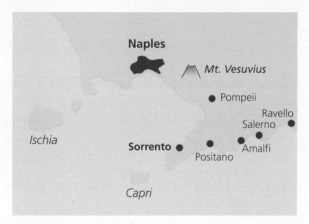

Figure 1 Location of Sorrento

Sorrento is a town built on a natural limestone cliff 60 metres (200 feet) above the sea. To the east are the limestone Lattari Mountains which rise steeply to heights of 1440 metres (5000 feet) and form the spine of the Sorrento Peninsula. The Amalfi coast is a dramatic landscape with a mix of steep mountains, forests and towns perched high on the cliffs. Amongst the mountains can be found olive groves, vines, almond and lemon orchards.

The northern side of the Bay of Naples, stretching round to the city of Naples, is a volcanic landscape dominated by the volcano Mount Vesuvius. The Bay of Naples itself provides a sheltered natural harbour with capes, bays, steep cliffs and tiny beaches.

Climate

Sorrento experiences a Mediterranean climate, the summers are long, hot and dry and the winter temperatures average at 10°C. Climate details for the nearest city of Naples (see table on page 128) demonstrate the average temperature, hours of sun and rainfall for the region:

Table 1 Climate information for Naples

Month	Average sunlight (hours)	Temperature (°C) Average		Record		Discomfort from heat and humidity	Relative humidity		Average precipitation	Wet days (+0.25 mm)
		Min	Max	Min	Max		am	pm	(mm)	(mm)
Jan	4	4	12	−4	20	−	77	68	116	11
Feb	4	5	13	−4	20	−	78	67	85	10
March	5	6	15	−4	25	−	77	62	73	9
April	7	9	18	1	27	−	79	61	62	8
May	8	12	22	3	32	−	85	63	44	7
June	9	16	26	7	35	Moderate	75	58	31	4
July	10	18	29	11	36	Medium	73	53	19	2
Aug	10	18	29	13	37	Medium	74	53	32	3
Sept	8	16	26	8	34	Moderate	78	59	64	5
Oct	6	12	22	3	29	−	79	63	107	9
Nov	4	9	17	−2	26	−	81	68	147	11
Dec	3	6	14	−4	20	−	80	70	135	12

Source: BBC Weather Centre (2004)

Italy is one hour ahead of Greenwich Mean Time; when the time is 4 pm in London it is 5 pm in Italy.

The following information will be useful to assist you in writing a script for a welcome meeting linking the tourist facilities and major attractions to different customer types

Attractions

With a wide choice of mountains, beaches, cities, historical sites and museums there is plenty to see and do. Staying in Sorrento itself offers a variety of activities and also a perfect base to travel to many other major attractions and sites, including the Amalfi Coastal Drive, the Roman ruins at Pompeii and Herculaneum, the city of Naples and the islands of Capri and Ischia.

Sorrento

Sorrento first began to find popularity as a tourist resort in the early nineteenth century and it still retains its small town charm. The resort attracts many English, German and Italian tourists. Although the town has no beach there are *stabilimenti*, which are piers that jut out into the sea upon which loungers and umbrellas can be hired for sunbathing and relaxing in the summer sun. The town comes alive at dusk for the daily *passeggiata* when visitors and locals stroll through the small streets browsing at the souvenirs and shops and stopping for a drink or meal in the bars, pubs and cafés. Sorrento is famous for intricate handcrafted woodwork gifts and also *limoncello*, an alcoholic drink made from lemons that are grown locally.

Sorrento

Amalfi coastal drive

This famous coastal road covers 80 kilometres (50 miles) and includes a series of hairpin bends and dramatic views. The coastal drive includes the historic towns of Salerno, Ravello, Amalfi, Positano and Sorrento that cling to the sides of the cliffs. From the coastal road beautiful gardens, vines, olive, almond and lemon trees can also be seen.

Pompeii, Mount Vesuvius and Herculaneum

For visitors who are interested in Roman history or are interested in finding out about the geology of the area, a visit to Pompeii, Herculaneum and Mount Vesuvius is recommended. Both Pompeii and Herculaneum can be accessed easily from Sorrento via the *Circumvesuviana* railway or by attending one of the many organised day excursions.

Situated in Ercolano, 12 kilometres (7.5 miles) south of the city of Naples, Herculaneum is much smaller but better preserved than Pompeii. The town was covered in 20 metres (6 feet) of mud after the eruption of Vesuvius in 79AD. A small area has been excavated allowing visitors to walk through the streets and see well-preserved houses and shops. Visitors can learn about the horrors of the eruption as people fled and were trapped between the hot gaseous mud and the sea.

Pompeii is the much larger and more famous of the two archaeological sites. Although the buildings are not as well preserved as at Herculaneum, Pompeii offers the visitor a wider view of Roman life, with shops, houses, streets, amphitheatres, the Forum, baths and a gladiator arena. The town was destroyed when a rain of ash buried it followed by the *pyroclastic flow*, a devastating collection of ash, rock and other material that flowed like an avalanche, covering the whole town. Pompeii first started to be excavated in 1748 and the finds of the excavations are on display in the National Archaeological Museum, *Museo Archeologico Nazionale*, in Naples.

If the towering volcano that dominates the skyline impresses the visitor then it is important to visit the source of the disasters, Mount Vesuvius. The volcano can be accessed from Pompeii by catching one of the buses outside of the *Circumvesuviana* railway station or by taking part in one of the

organised excursions. The volcano is 1281 metres (4200 feet) tall and the last eruption was in 1944. There are basic tourist services at the car park before embarking on the half-an-hour climb to the crater along a gravel path. The view from the top overlooking the Bay of Naples is breathtaking. The view of the crater is also dramatic as small clouds of vapour can often be seen escaping. The volcano is still active and potentially could erupt at any time, however the volcano is being monitored 24 hours a day by a team of scientists and their observatory is open to visitors during the morning. Mount Vesuvius and the surrounding countryside is recognised as a National Park, providing a unique environment for wildlife.

City of Naples with Mount Vesuvius in the background

Naples

The city of Naples contains many attractions. It is a bustling city that offers historians, shoppers, children and many other tourists something to view and enjoy. The city is the capital of the region of Campania and is an area of complete contrasts. One of the most important attractions is the *Museo Archeologico Nazionale*, which houses one of the most comprehensive collections of Greco-Roman artefacts in the world, including sculptures, mosaics and artefacts from Herculaneum and Pompeii.

There are also many religious buildings to visit. One of the largest and most fascinating is the grand cathedral, the *Duomo*, which has undergone many alterations since being first built in 1272 and experiencing disasters such as an earthquake in 1456.

For the shopper Naples boasts that anything can be bought within the city, with most of the shopping being centred around the *via Toledo*. For the children Naples offers several castles, Europe's oldest aquarium, the *acquario*, which contains 200 examples of sea life found in the Bay of Naples, and the *Edenlandia* funfair.

The city does have a reputation for street crime and care should be taken around the central station, *Stazione Centrale*. Naples can be accessed from Sorrento via the *Circumvesuviana* railway, by local bus service or on one of the organised coach excursions.

City of Naples

The Islands of Capri and Ischia

The two islands can be found off the Sorrento coast.

Capri has many picturesque towns and villages, quality restaurants, cafés, designer shops and narrow streets. It has been associated with rich and famous celebrities who visit the island. Many of the restaurants display pictures of their famous guests. If the weather is fine, boat trips using small rowing boats are available to the *Grotta Azzurra*, the Blue Grotto. This is where a refraction of light off the walls of the cave creates a magical blue glow, and the reflection of light off the sandy bottom creates a silver glow combining to create a spectacular scene.

Island of Capri

Ischia, the largest of the local islands, has a collection of thermal springs, as the island is volcanic in origin. Long sandy beaches and fishing villages can be found in combination with forested mountains. The visitor can enjoy the beaches, shop in the resort and drink the locally produced wine for which the island is renowned, or be pampered by spa treatments and take a dip in one of the thermal spas during the summer.

Activities

Events

Sorrento's patron saint *Sant'Antonio* is remembered on 5 February each year with processions and a large market. There are also a series of Easter processions that draw large crowds from neighbouring towns.

In July–August Sorrento hosts a series of classical music concerts, which is popular with tourists and local people.

The Sorrento Film Festival takes place in late November and early December and is regarded as one of the most important celebrations of Italian cinema in the country.

Food, drink and entertainment

The food is typically Italian with lots of pasta and pizza and famous Italian ice cream. *Limoncello* is a favourite drink with visitors. Local wine is also of good quality, the red wine *Lacryma Christi* being produced from grapes grown on the side of Mount Vesuvius. An evening stroll along the *via Cesareo* is part of local tradition as the town comes to life during the early evening into the night.

The *Teatro Tasso* theatre offers a range of local musical shows that appeal to visitors wishing to experience Italian music and culture. Local music is performed on a regular basis, which is considered to be more authentic than what is performed during Italian 'theme-nights' in tourist bars and hotels.

The popularity of Sorrento as a UK holiday destination is reflected in the presence of the *Circolo dei Forestieri*, the Foreigners' Club, where each night British people can be seen drinking British beer in an Italian setting with live music.

Accommodation

One of the most exclusive hotels that is a landmark in the centre of Sorrento is the *Grand Hotel Excelsior Vittoria*. Located on the site of an old Roman villa, it has been owned by the Fiorentino family since it opened in 1834 and has some of the best local gardens and terraces that overlook the Bay of Naples. There are plenty of 4-star and budget tourist hotels in Sorrento as well as a youth hostel, the *Ostello delle Sirene*. Campsites are also available to the west of Sorrento, which are easily reached via the SITA bus service from the railway station.

> *You will need to do research into and an analysis of the choice of methods of travel to the destination and travel while at the destination, including appropriate maps*

Travel to Sorrento

From the UK the most common method of travel to Sorrento is by air, arriving at Naples' *Capodichino* Airport. Flights can be taken from Aberdeen, Belfast, Birmingham, Blackpool, Bournemouth, Bristol, Cambridge, Cardiff, East Midlands, Edinburgh, Exeter, Gatwick, Glasgow, Heathrow, Humberside, Leeds/Bradford, Liverpool, London City Docklands, Luton, Manchester, Newcastle, Norwich, Southampton, Stansted and Teeside. Visitors on package holidays are usually transferred to Sorrento by coach; alternatives include using airport buses or the local *Circumvesuviana* railway service. Tourists can hire cars at the airport providing they have their driving license and insurance details.

A direct flight to Naples takes approximately two hours, with a coach or taxi transfer to Sorrento taking one hour, depending on traffic. Most of the scheduled flights that fly direct to Naples from the UK are dominated by the British Airways service from Gatwick. Recently other carriers such as Alitalia, easyJet and bmi have included scheduled services. As Sorrento is a popular package holiday destination many chartered airlines operate from regional airports across the UK.

Naples also has frequent rail connections with the rest of Italy via the *Stazione Centrale*, including hourly trains to Rome, a journey which takes between two and three hours. There are coach services to Naples from all other major cities in Europe and there is a London to Naples direct coach, run by National Express Eurolines.

Arrival by car in the region is possible via Italy's motorways, all of which are toll roads. From the north this would involve travel on the E45/A1 and then A3 or A16/A30 from the east.

Travel in and around Sorrento

The centre of Sorrento is easily accessible. There are local buses that operate along the Sorrento peninsula; these are orange in colour and run daily every 20 minutes until 8 pm. Longer distances can be made on SITA buses which are blue; these travel further along the Amalfi coastline. Tickets for SITA buses can be bought from places that display the SITA sign, including bars and shops near bus stops.

Trains run from Sorrento to Naples via stops such as Ercolano and Pompeii on the *Circumvesuviana* railway line. Tickets can be purchased at the railway station and the trains run approximately every 20 minutes from 5 am until 10.30 pm, and later at the weekend during the summer season.

Hydrofoil and ferry services operate between Sorrento, Naples, Ischia and Capri on a daily basis and timetables can be obtained from the port in Sorrento or from local hotels.

Taxis tend to be expensive in the region, so if travel by car is preferred then car hire from the airport or in resort would be advisable. However driving in Naples is not for the inexperienced.

The following are recommendations to potential customers based on an evaluation of the appeal of the destination and an evaluation of likely future popularity

Sorrento and its surrounding area is popular with honeymoon couples, the older traveller and family groups. Italian food and culture is popular in the UK, so to experience an authentic Napolitana pizza in Naples and surrounding areas is part of the attraction. The town has a romantic charm with small shops, cafés and views over the Bay of Naples. The area also has many designated coastal walks for the active holidaymaker.

The ruins at Pompeii are well known and give a chance to explore Roman history at first hand. Naples provides the visitor with the historic charm and the hustle and bustle of a busy city.

Over 2,500,000 UK tourists visit Italy each year and stay for an average of 4.3 days, with longer stays in the south of Italy. The southern region of Italy is also experiencing a modest growth in the number of tourists. The north of Italy, in particular cities offering art and cultural attractions, are doing less well, mainly due to a reduction in the number of German and American tourists.

Approximately 8 per cent of Italy's inbound tourists originate from the UK, 8 per cent from France, 22 per cent from Germany and 12 per cent from the USA. The Italian tourism industry makes an annual profit of approximately €13.1 billion (£9.49 billion).

The hotel sector has seen a decline in the number of people staying by 1.4 per cent, but alternative accommodation, including farmhouses, hostels, and guesthouse accommodation, has seen an increase of 3 per cent. However, visitors from the UK prefer hotel accommodation rather than other types of accommodation; Naples alone offers over 28,500 hotel rooms.

Italian tourism is facing increasing competition from other Mediterranean destinations, such as Turkey, Bulgaria and Croatia which offer beach and cultural holidays at a cheaper price. However, the warm climate and extensive coastline in the south of Italy offers a strong potential for future development. The tourism market may have reached a stage of maturity in Sorrento but the potential for future development in terms of business, cultural and historical attractions are favourable.

For the latest travel advice to Italy visit the Foreign and Commonwealth Office website http://www.fco.gov.uk.

For further information visit:

Italian State Tourist Board http://www.enit.it

Italian State Tourist Board in North America http://www.italiantourism.com

Visit Sorrento http://www.visitsorrento.com

Los Angeles, USA

Information about the location of the destination, its landscape and climate

Over 24 million people visit Los Angeles each year, known locally as LA or the City of Angels, after its Spanish ancestors. Los Angeles is home to approximately 17 million people. It is a sprawling metropolis, a mega-city, that has grown so large that it is made up of 5 districts and 88 towns. It is the second largest city in the USA.

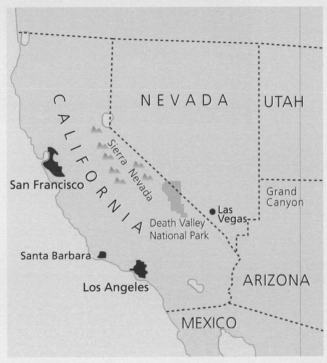

Figure 2 Location of Los Angeles

Los Angeles is in the state of California on the west coast of America. The state of California covers an area of 404,710 square kilometres (156,260 square miles), one-and-a-half times the size of Great Britain, and has 2000 kilometres (1250 miles) of coastline. The sandy beaches are located in the south with a more rocky and dramatic coastline towards the north. Inland the landscape is dominated by large mountain ranges that run north to south in line with the Pacific coast. In the east the Sierra Nevada mountain range reaches heights of 4000 metres (13,000 feet). The landscape features steep-sided valleys and large waterfalls.

Between the mountain ranges is Central Valley, which is 600 kilometres (372 miles) long and 60 kilometres (37 miles) wide. The San Joaquin and Sacramento rivers flow through the valley into the sea at San Francisco Bay. Further south are the desert valleys, including Death Valley, a dried salt lake that is 87 metres (286 feet) below sea level, the lowest point on the surface of the Earth.

Along the centre of California is where the two continental plates, the Pacific and the North American, are slowly moving past each other. These parts of the Earth's crust move around 3cm a year. When they rub together there is a shudder, which results in an earthquake. There are approximately 10,000 minor earthquakes each year. A large earthquake is likely to occur within the next one hundred years, but scientists are monitoring the movement of the ground so advanced warning may be given.

Climate

Los Angeles has a Mediterranean-like climate with warm dry summers and cool damp winters. The topography of the land affects the type of climate of California. The San Gabriel Mountains to the north of Los Angeles influence the weather. Moist air moves inland from the Pacific Ocean and is cooled as it rises over the mountains. This cooling effect produces heavy rainfall on the west side facing the sea. The east side of the mountain is in a rain shadow and receives less rain.

Central Los Angeles

The north of California is cooler than the south. The cooler conditions are perfect for wine production, especially in the vineyards of the Napa Valley near San Francisco. In the southern deserts, July and August can be unbearably hot as temperatures in Death Valley can reach 122°F (50°C).

Table 2 Climate information for Los Angeles

Month	Average sunlight (hours)	Temperature (°C) Average		Record		Discomfort from heat and humidity	Relative humidity		Average precipitation	Wet Days (+0.25 mm)
		Min	Max	Min	Max		am	pm	(mm)	(mm)
Jan	7	8	18	−2	32	–	67	47	79	6
Feb	8	8	19	−2	33	–	74	53	76	6
March	9	9	19	−1	37	–	77	51	71	6
April	9	10	21	2	38	–	82	55	25	4
May	9	12	22	4	39	–	86	59	10	2
June	10	13	24	8	41	Moderate	87	58	3	1
July	12	16	27	9	43	Medium	88	55	0	0
Aug	11	16	28	9	41	Medium	87	54	0	0
Sept	10	14	27	7	42	Medium	82	52	5	1
Oct	9	12	24	4	39	–	75	49	15	2
Nov	8	10	23	1	36	–	62	38	31	3
Dec	8	8	19	−1	33	–	60	44	66	6

Source: BBC Weather Centre

Los Angeles is located in a geographical basin. As cool air falls into the basin it prevents air pollution from escaping. This causes a mixture of foggy conditions and air pollution known as smog. Smog can irritate people suffering with asthma. It is estimated that 70 per cent of air pollution in Los Angeles is caused by vehicle emissions, as approximately 7 million vehicles are used daily. The sea fog only stretches inland for a few miles but it does reduce the temperature by several degrees.

California is set on Pacific Standard Time, which is 8 hours behind Greenwich Mean Time, 3 hours behind New York and 2 hours behind Chicago.

Attractions

Visiting Los Angeles is an exciting experience. This vibrant and diverse city is a collection of separate districts, each with its own identity. The financial and administrative heart of Los Angeles displays many skyscrapers, reflecting the economic wealth of the city. This wealth is based on the growth of the service sector, high-tech industries and leisure industries, which are mainly linked to film and the movies.

In Downtown Los Angeles, the Civic Center hosts a collection of governmental and federal buildings. Civic Hall is a large white tower 28 stories high that was made famous as the Daily Planet building in the film *Superman*.

Walt Disney Hall is an impressive metal structure that is shaped to resemble the opening of a rose and is the home of the Los Angeles Philharmonic Orchestra. The Museum of Contemporary Art (MoCA) contains a range of exhibits, including pop art, photography and multimedia shows. There are musical performances, which are usually free of charge. The Cathedral of Our Lady of the Angels (OLA) is a large modern Catholic cathedral set amongst a large plaza, gardens and a conference centre. It can hold up to 3000 worshippers with an interior larger than a football field.

El Pueblo de Los Angeles is a 44-acre historic park on the north-eastern edge of Downtown and includes many of Los Angeles' first buildings that date back as early as 1818. It is near to Union Station and provides access to Chinatown, which is home to over 200,000 Chinese Americans. Little Tokyo is the Japanese equivalent to Chinatown; although smaller in size it has traditional gardens, shops, cultural centres and Buddhist temples.

Exposition Park is located a few miles south of Downtown. It hosts a range of museums and sports facilities. The Rose Garden stretches for 7 acres and is popular for walks and is an escape from the busy city. Popular museums include the Natural History Museum of Los Angeles County with rare dinosaur skeletons and an insect zoo with live exhibits, the Californian African American Museum and the California Science Center with interactive exhibits and a 3D IMAX Theatre. The Los Angeles Memorial Coliseum is famous for hosting the first Super Bowl in 1967 and two Olympic Games in 1932 and 1984. It is now the home of the University of Southern California football team.

Hollywood is famous for its movie and film industries which began in the 1920s. The famous Hollywood sign is perched on the hillside of Mount Lee on the edge of Griffith Park. The original sign dates from 1923 and was used to promote a housing development by spelling out the word 'Hollywoodland'. The sign was shortened and became famous worldwide through its association with the entertainment industry.

Griffith Park is another large green open space where families can relax and explore the Los Angeles Zoo, the Autry Museum of Western Heritage and the Griffith Observatory and Planetarium.

Hollywood, Los Angeles

West Hollywood is home to some of the trendiest nightclubs, bars and restaurants. Sunset Strip is part of Sunset Boulevard where many famous music and film personalities have lived and entertained. There are many film and television studios, and some offer free tickets to live shows. Famous studios include: Walt Disney Studios, NBC Television Studios, Universal Studios, Warner Brothers Studios, Paramount Studios and Sony Pictures, which owns Columbia and TriStar Pictures.

Hollywood Boulevard is one of Los Angeles' most famous streets. Lining the sidewalks are the names of over 2500 celebrities engraved in bronze stars. The Hollywood Entertainment Museum is a celebration of the Hollywood film industry and offers a chance to see original film sets and costumes, including the command bridge of the *USS Enterprise* from Star Trek and the bar from the television comedy *Cheers*.

North of Sunset Boulevard is Beverly Hills, with large mansion houses, designer boutiques and expensive restaurants centred on Rodeo Drive. Visitors can find out where celebrities live

Rodeo Drive, Beverly Hills

by taking one of the guided tours. Other local attractions include the Museum of Television and Radio, the Museum of Tolerance and the Museum of Jurassic Technology, which includes some weird and bizarre exhibits.

West of Beverly Hills is Westwood, another wealthy neighbourhood that also has a large student population as it is the home of the University of California Los Angeles (UCLA). Visitors are allowed on campus to visit the library, sculpture gardens, art galleries, museums and film school. To the north of Westwood is the Getty Center. It was the home of the famous multi-millionaire John Paul Getty and includes a collection of lavish art works and a research centre. Entrance is free to the public.

The coastline of Los Angeles is dominated by the Santa Monica Bay, which escapes most of the smog and the heat associated with Los Angeles. The resort of Venice offers a mix of local people: street performers, musclemen and women, surfers and skaters. It is known locally as Muscle Beach.

Its bohemian reputation attracts students, artists and hippies. Originally designed to resemble the canals of Italy's Venice as part of a theme park, the original theme park has disappeared but visitors can explore what remains of the open waterways.

Further north along the coast is the famous resort of Malibu, 44 kilometres (27 miles) of coastline that is home to some world-famous A-list celebrities. Large mansions are hidden away from the roadside and patrolled by security guards. However, many celebrity spotters hang out at local stores and cafés in the hope of seeing someone famous. Away from the beach is Malibu Creek State Park, once owned by the 20th Century Fox studios and which provided the setting for many of the Tarzan movies and for the classic wartime television show M*A*S*H. The park is open to the public and includes a lake, waterfalls and hiking trails.

Muscle Beach, Los Angeles

A visit to Los Angeles would not be complete without a visit to Anaheim, the home of Disneyland. Disneyland opened in 1955 and has set the standard for theme parks across the world. Popular attractions include Main Street, Adventureland, Frontierland, Fantasyland, Tomorrowland, and the usual Disney characters. The California Adventure is adjacent to Disneyland and is regarded as a separate park. It contains a range of new attractions that include California Screamin' and The Twilight Zone Tower of Terror™ for the thrill seekers, family adventure with Jim Henson's Muppet Vision 3D and fun for the children with Jumpin' Jellyfish and Princess Dot Puddle Park.

For visitors who wish to experience a different theme park, Knott's Berry Farm park offers several themed lands, but it is the roller coasters that are the main attractions. Knott's Berry Farm has also been recently extended with the opening of an adjacent water park, Soak City USA.

Activities

Events

Los Angeles hosts a whole range of festivals throughout the year, which have national, regional and local significance. Below is a list of just one example from each month of the year. Many other festivals and events can be found listed in the guide books and brochures:

January	1 January is the Tournament of Roses in Pasedena when spectators can see a parade of floral floats and marching bands on Colorado Boulevard (http://www.tornamentofroses.com)
February	The Academy Awards happen at the end of February when the Oscars are presented at the Kodak Theater
March	St Patrick's Day with a parade along Colorado Boulevard in Old Town Pasadena
April	Long Beach Grand Prix with Indy car racing around Shoreline Drive
May	Mid-May allows visitors to view the work of popular and potential local artists during the Venice Art Walk
June	Late June includes the hosting of the carnival-like Gay Pride Celebration, with parades and street stalls
July	4 July is Independence Day in the United States and LA hosts huge fireworks displays and festivities in many communities within the city
August	Nisei Week in Little Tokyo with a celebration of Japanese America, including traditional martial arts demonstrations, karaoke and Japanese performances
September	5 September is Los Angeles' birthday; there is a civic ceremony and street entertainment to mark the founding of the city in 1781
October	31 October is the traditional Halloween Parade in West Hollywood
November	2 November is the Dia de los Muertos (Day of the Dead) celebrations throughout East Los Angeles, with many Mexican traditions being upheld
December	1 December is the annual Hollywood Christmas Parade, with a procession of brightly lit floats to launch the first of many Yuletide events

Food, drink and entertainment

Whatever a visitor to Los Angeles wants to eat and however much they want to spend can be accommodated in the city. For the customer who doesn't want to spend a lot on food there are a large number of budget food providers, including coffee shops, delis, diners and drive-ins offering soups, omelettes, sandwiches and burgers. Some are restaurants open 24 hours a day.

There are many establishments offering California cuisine, American dishes and also Cajun food. California cuisine is more widely found in Los Angeles than the traditional American cuisine of steaks, ribs, baked potatoes and salads. California cuisine offers local ingredients that are grilled rather than fried. Cajun cooking offers a range of inexpensive spicy fish-based dishes.

Being a cosmopolitan city Los Angeles also offers food from around the world, and has Mexican, Latin American, Italian, Spanish, Greek, Japanese, Chinese, Thai, Korean, Indian, Sri Lankan and Middle Eastern restaurants, examples of which can be found in each district. Vegetarian restaurants are to be found across the city but mostly in Westside.

Los Angeles has many bars available where you can get a drink. Each district of the city has its own types of establishment, ranging from beachside bars to cocktail lounges. Smoking is banned in most establishments under California law. If a traveller wants a bar-like atmosphere but no alcohol then one of the famous coffee houses is worth a visit.

Evening entertainment is widely available in Los Angeles, with a huge variety of pursuits available, ranging from clubs and discos, live music, comedy and theatre, to film. It is recommended when searching for entertainment and the trendiest nightclubs to look in local newspapers such as the *LA Weekly* or the *Los Angeles Times*.

Live music is extensively available, with a choice of music venues throughout the city. There is a lively rock and revived punk scene as well as hip-hop, country, jazz, salsa and reggae music on offer in venues such as the Hollywood Palladium, the Cat Club, the Blue Saloon and many others.

Classical music is not so widely available. Opera is performed by the LA Opera and the Orange County Opera Pacific, both of which stage productions between September and June.

The city boasts a wide range of comedy clubs, including the Comedy Store and the Improvisation, both of which host famous comics and open-mike sessions for the rising stars of comedy.

There are many theatres hosting musicals and classics with all-star casts, including the Alex Theater and Pantages Theater. There is also a collection of fringe theatres which host smaller productions and experimental shows, including the Cast-At-The-Circle theatre and the Open Fist Theater.

Most major feature films will be released in Los Angeles before anywhere else and shown in one of the many movie houses in Westwood or Santa Monica Parade.

Accommodation

Los Angeles has over 100,000 rooms available. Choices range from basic budget motels, hostels, bed and breakfast inns and camping sites to world-class hotels.

Each neighbourhood and district has its own range of accommodation available, apart from campsites which are mostly found on the edge of the urban area along the coast and in the San Gabriel Mountains.

Famous celebrity hotels include the Beverly Hills Hotel on Sunset Boulevard and the secluded Hotel Bel-Air on Stone Canyon Road.

> **You will need to do research into and analysis of the choice of methods of travel to the destination and travel while at the destination, including appropriate maps**

Travel to Los Angeles

The quickest and easiest way for the UK tourist to reach Los Angeles is by flying direct to Los Angeles International Airport. A non-stop flight from London to Los Angeles takes approximately 11 hours. Carriers that operate non-stop flights include Air New Zealand, American Airlines, British Airways and Virgin Atlantic.

There are flights to Los Angeles from the following UK airports: Gatwick, Heathrow, London City, Bristol, Cardiff, Newquay, Plymouth, Southampton, Birmingham, East Midlands, Norwich,

Humberside, Newcastle, Teesside, Isle of Man, Liverpool, Manchester, Leeds/Bradford, Aberdeen, Edinburgh, Glasgow, Inverness, Belfast City and Belfast International. Most of these airports offer a direct service.

On arrival at Los Angeles International Airport tourists can travel by the use of a courtesy bus to various hotels, or by taxi, car rental or a free bus to the Metropolitan Transportation Authority (MTA) bus terminal from where buses can be caught to different parts of the city.

If a visit to Los Angeles is part of a wider tour of the United States, the city can also be reached via one of the many domestic flights from around the country. The city can be arrived at by Amtrak train, which has private cabins and dining cars, by bus using the Greyhound bus service, by driving a hire car or as a part of a fly-drive package.

Travel in and around Los Angeles

When travelling in and around Los Angeles public transportation is operated by the Metropolitan Transportation Authority (MTA), which runs a widespread bus and rail system throughout the city. Downtown and some neighbourhoods are also served by DASH minibuses and Santa Monica and western Los Angeles is served by the Big Blue Bus.

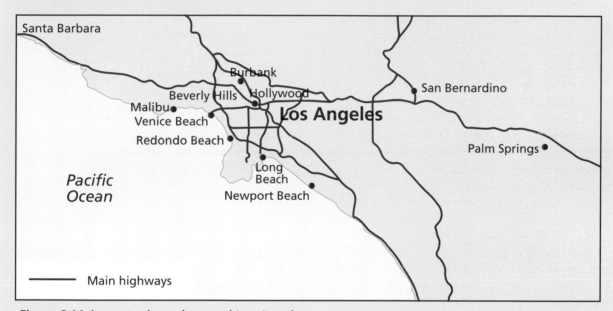

Figure 3 Main routes in and around Los Angeles

The following are recommendations to potential customers based on an evaluation of the appeal of the destination and an evaluation of likely future popularity

Los Angeles offers many attractions to families, student groups and independent travellers. Family groups will be attracted by the theme parks of Disneyland and Knott's Berry Farm and by the many film and television studios. Students will be attracted by the nightlife, the glamour of Hollywood and Malibu Beach.

Within any big city casual visitors are recommended to avoid certain neighbourhoods. Exploring Los Angeles by foot during the day is not a problem, but be extra cautious in East LA, Compton and Watts because of gang-related activity, and avoid them after dark. Poorly-lit side streets in Hollywood and Venice should also be avoided. Venice beach is notorious for criminal activities and as a result most areas of the beach are out of bounds after dark. However, areas such as Westwood and Beverley Hills and many of the other coastal resorts have lower rates of crime.

North America remains the most popular long-haul destination to be visited by UK residents. The threat of terrorist attacks has reduced the numbers of people travelling, although consumer confidence is returning, assisted by similarities in both culture and language. People in the UK are familiar with American culture through film, television, fashion and food.

Variations in economic performance and rising oil prices may affect the cost of holidays to the USA. Rising oil prices means that travel becomes more expensive. A slow down in economic growth means that people tend to spend less on their holiday and find cheaper alternatives, travelling to short-haul destinations rather than long-haul.

However, the exchange rate remains favourable for UK residents travelling to the USA. The average exchange rate for the US dollar in 1998 was $1.66 to the British pound and in 2002 the exchange rate was $1.50 to the British pound. This means that people travelling abroad can buy more for their money. Many consumer items in the USA are cheaper than in the UK.

For the latest travel advice to the USA, visit the Foreign and Commonwealth Office website http://www.fco.gov.uk.

For further information visit:

The Californian Division of Tourism http://www.visitcalifornia.com

LA Downtown visitors center http://www.lacvb.com

Santa Monica visitors center http://www.santamonica.com

Resources

Sorrento

Belford, R., Dunford, M. and Woolfrey, C. (2001) *The Rough Guide to Italy*. London: Rough Guides.

Hanley, A. (ed) (2000) *Time Out Guide: Naples Capri, Sorrento, and the Amalfi Coast*. London: Penguin Books.

Hatchwell, E. and Bell, B. (eds) (2002) *Insight Guides: Italy*. Singapore: APA Publications.

Leech, M. and Shales, M. (2001) *Globetrotter: Naples and Sorrento*. London: New Holland Publishers.

Simonis, D., Adams, F., Roddis, M., Webb, S. and Williams, N. (2002) *Lonely Planet: Italy*. London: Lonely Planet Publications.

Williams, R., Muscat, C. and Bell, B. (eds) (2001) *Insight Guide: Southern Italy*. Singapore: APA Publications.

Los Angeles

Campbell, J., Chilcoat, L., Derby, S., Greenfield, B., Heller, C.B., Martin, S., Miller, D., Morris, B., Ohlsen, B., Schulte-Peevers, A., Wolff, K. and Zimmermann, K. (2004) *Lonely Planet: USA*. London: Lonely Planet Publications.

Dickey, J.D., Edwards, N., Ellwood, M. and Whitfield, P. (2003) *The Rough Guide to California*. London: Rough Guides.

Lagrange-Leader, F. (ed) (2002) *Everyman Guides: California*. London: Everyman Publishing.

Teuschl, T. (2002) *Insight Compact Guide: California*. Singapore: APA Publications.

Wilcock, J., Zenfell, M.E. and Bell, B. (eds) (2001) *Insight Guide: Southern California*. Singapore: APA Publications.

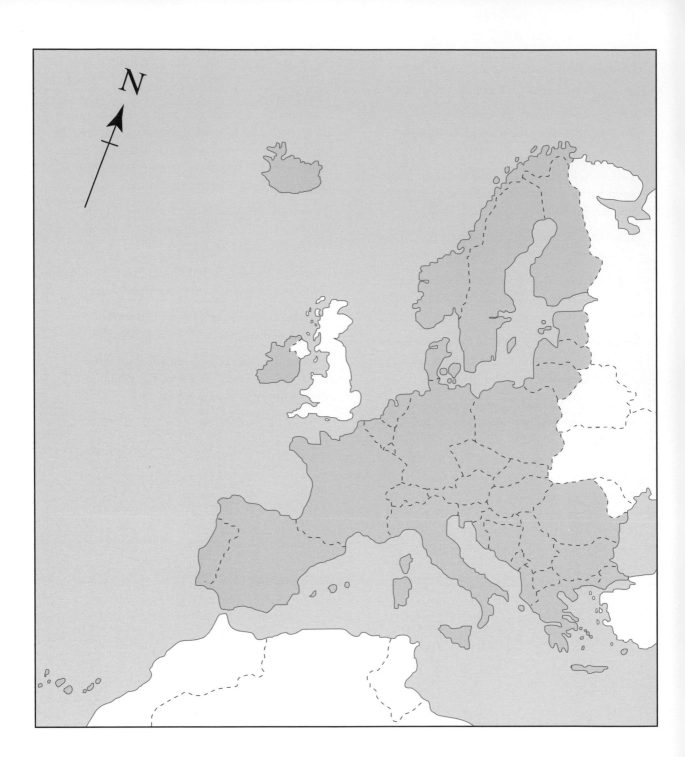

N

Working in travel and tourism

Introduction

This unit will provide you with an understanding of the employment opportunities available in the travel and tourism industry, the reality of working in travel and tourism and the personal and professional qualities needed in order to gain career success.

For this unit you will have to research the work involved in one job in the travel and tourism industry. The position you study will need firm links to the travel and tourism industry and can be in either the private or public sectors.

The unit provides you with a perfect opportunity for work-related learning. To research a job role thoroughly, you can work-shadow, observe or take part in a work experience placement. A combination of all three could be used to give you a detailed insight into the position. As well as conducting primary research, desk research should also be used to supplement your findings. The intention is that primary research should establish what the job entails and what the experience is really like.

By considering your own personal qualities and personal development, you should be able to develop your own values and attitudes.

How you will be assessed

For this unit you need to produce a portfolio based on an investigation into one job in the travel and tourism industry.

Your portfolio should include:

* A report on each of the seven key areas: duties, training, communication skills, professional skills, personal qualities, feedback and personal development

* Examples of how each of these skills and qualities interact with other people's roles to solve problems and deal with complex situations in the travel and tourism industry

* A detailed analysis of your sources of information, with commentary on both their availability and usefulness

* An evaluation of your own strengths and weaknesses against the requirements of the job studied.

The assessment for this unit aims to test your level of knowledge, the way you apply this knowledge and your skills of analysis and evaluation.

To access the highest marks and grade possible for this unit your report must contain the following:

* Well-developed detail of the seven key areas of the job role you are investigating, relating desk research to any practical experience of the job you have with appropriate comparisons. You will also need to show an appreciation of the unwritten demands of the job and the need to respond to unfamiliar situations.

* A balanced conclusion on how various skills are used in the industry to solve problems effectively by mixing and matching appropriate sources of information. You need to develop the information you have collected to show the application of skills in your investigated job role to the industry as a whole.

* In the analysis of your sources of information you must provide evidence of desk and field research from a wide range of sources. Comments on validity and reliability need to be well developed and you must show an appreciation of source limitation. Your report will include specialist vocabulary to analyse information and reach valid conclusions.

* In evaluating your own strengths and weaknesses you need to assess yourself in a wide variety of contexts and evaluate these against the demands of the job role you are investigating.

After studying this unit you need to have learned about:

* The range and nature of employment opportunities in the travel and tourism industry

* The duties involved in particular jobs within the travel and tourism industry

* The purposes of providing training for jobs within the travel and tourism industry and the type of training that is offered to people doing jobs within the industry

* Communication skills needed in travel and tourism jobs

* Professional skills needed in travel and tourism jobs

* Identifying the characteristics and personal qualities needed by travel and tourism professionals to succeed in their work

* The importance of feedback in maintaining and improving standards

* The ability to honestly evaluate your own strengths and weaknesses in relation to the standards, skills and qualities you have seen in action and to assess how and where you would fit into the travel and tourism industry.

The range and nature of employment opportunities in the travel and tourism industry

Travel and tourism is one of the fastest growing sectors of the UK economy and provides approximately two million jobs. Recognised by both local and central governments as a major employer and contributor to the wealth and economic stability of the country, the travel and tourism industry offers a wide range of career opportunities. The opportunities arise in the commercial sector (tour operators, hotels, theme parks, airlines etc.), the public sector (national government departments and agencies, local government, regulatory bodies) and the voluntary sector. Rewarding career opportunities are offered by the travel and tourism industry at a variety of different levels. For the most ambitious to those who work part-time, the travel and tourism industry has something to offer just about everyone in terms of jobs.

The range of levels at which travel and tourism employment can be found is vast. This range extends from 'front-line' staff (reception, travel agency consultants, call centre operatives, catering staff), through middle management roles (day-to-day supervision of front-line operations) to senior management, strategic planning and decision-making roles at a high level in both public and private organisations.

Skills practice

Working with a partner or in small groups, create a list of twenty different job roles in the travel and tourism industry.

Once you have completed this task, compare your ideas with other groups and try to create a whole class list of different job roles.

Think about it

In groups of three or four, discuss what you think it would be like to work in the travel and tourism industry.

Interdependency

Have you ever worked as part of a team and relied on others to complete a task? Have you ever had a classmate or colleague call upon your skills and knowledge to help them get a job done? If the answer is yes, then you have been *interdependent* on others and others have been interdependent on you. Very few people are skilled at absolutely everything and at times we rely upon or are interdependent on the specialist knowledge of others to complete tasks and projects. Many job roles in the travel and tourism industry are interdependent on other job roles. For example, a member of an air-cabin crew for a chartered airline relies upon travel agents and tour operators to successfully promote and sell holidays. Without tour operators and travel agents promoting and selling holidays, there would be less demand for chartered flights and fewer job opportunities and vacancies for members of air-cabin crew.

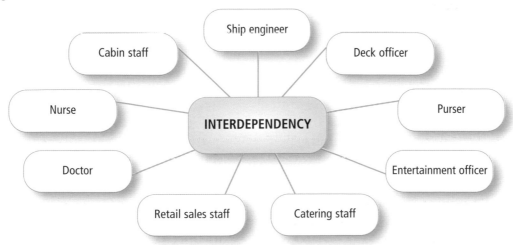

Figure 4.1 In the travel and tourism industry people depend on one another for any operation to succeed, as shown in this example of the interdependency of cruise ship staff

Interdependency therefore means that people with different job roles within the travel and tourism industry rely on each other to provide them with specialist skills and knowledge, customers and information.

Think about it

As well as the example given in Figure 4.1, can you identify five different job roles within the travel and tourism industry and describe their relationship with or interdependency on other job roles within the industry.

If working nine to five, Monday to Friday, appeals to you then perhaps a career in the travel and tourism industry isn't for you. Travellers and tourists demand products and services twenty-four hours a day, seven days a week and many career opportunities in the travel and tourism industry require staff to work seasonally, part-time, shifts and unsociable hours. Consider the travel representative in a Mediterranean resort. Holidaymakers arrive from UK airports at all hours of the day and night and once a week you would be expected to be on airport duty during the night. In an emergency you might be the only person holidaymakers know and trust and be called upon to assist even if it is your day off. The plus side though means that you work in warmth and sunshine all year round!

As the travel and tourism industry centres around offering customers value for money and quality services, the customer is always right and every job in the travel and tourism industry seeks to ensure the happiness and well-being of customers. Therefore jobs in this industry tend to have a real customer focus and employees need the necessary skills to be able to deal with the general public.

CASE STUDY

Saffy and her awkward customers

Saffy, at twenty-one years old, had thought she had found the perfect job. She had been employed by Aegean Dreams, a tour operator specialising in holidays to Greece and its enduringly popular islands, as a resort representative. Saffy had been placed on the island of Zakynthos, an island rich in history, which attracts a broad cross-section of holidaymakers, from families enjoying the safe beaches on the island, retired couples taking it easier in the quieter resorts, to the twenty-somethings looking for long lazy days in the sun and even longer nights spent dancing in the island's night clubs.

Saffy was resort representative for Lagana, a vibrant resort attracting both families and the twenty-something set. Every Thursday was Saffy's day off and even though she loved her job, she enjoyed this precious day off and looked forward to it all week. After her weekly welcome meeting on a Wednesday evening at 8 pm at the Princess Apartments and Studios for new arrivals to the resort, Saffy was off duty until 8 am on Friday. That was the theory, but in practice it could be very different. Below is the tale of one incident involving awkward customers and the time it took Saffy to deal with them.

One particular Wednesday, Saffy had completed her welcome meeting and was clearing up the shot glasses from the complimentary ouzo given to guests to get them into the holiday mood, when guests who had been particularly awkward during the meeting, chatting and asking irrelevant questions, approached Saffy to complain about their accommodation. The family complained to Saffy about their accommodation being too small and that they wanted a sea view rather than a poolside view. Saffy was reluctant to help guests who had been rude and talked over her during the welcome meeting, but it was after all the mission statement of Aegean Dreams 'to exceed the dreams of our customers on every holiday', so she duly went to speak with the manager of the apartment complex. It was customers like this paying for holidays that kept Saffy in a job.

Saffy arranged for the family to be moved to a room more to their liking and at 9 pm left the Princess Apartments and Studios happy in the knowledge that she had the next twenty-four hours at least to herself.

By 10.30 pm that evening, Saffy was relaxed and getting ready to go out for a night on the tiles. Her work mobile telephone rang and Saffy in two minds whether to answer the call, reluctantly answered the phone, as the number was that of her boss. Nicky, the resort manager, was calling to let Saffy know she was in the local hospital emergency department waiting for the leg she had broken two hours earlier to be put into plaster. This meant that Saffy would need to be on call for the evening and the next day, her day off. Being on call meant that Saffy was the point of contact for all guests of Aegean Dreams in the resort, in the case of emergency. Saffy kicked off her dancing shoes, as there was no way she could go out now. With any luck she thought nobody would require her services and she should still be able to enjoy her time off to some extent.

Awkward customers need to be handled with tact and patience

Two-thirty in the morning and the phone starts ringing! Saffy jumped out of bed and answered her phone. It was the family from the Princess Apartments and Studios whom she had dealt with after the welcome meeting. The family were complaining about their new accommodation, that it was infested with insects and there was no way the family could possibly stay there. The family had contacted reception and apparently the night porter was unwilling to help them in their hour of need. Saffy assured them she would be with them as soon as possible and put on her uniform and grabbed her car keys.

She arrived at the apartments fearful of what she would find. The family were waiting outside; the night porter was shrugging his shoulders and speaking at great speed about cockroaches. With the father of the family, Saffy entered the room expecting to see bugs and creepy crawlies everywhere. In the living area of the apartment there was nothing. The father of the family opened the bathroom door and told Saffy to brace herself. With a deep breath Saffy looked into the bathroom to see one solitary cockroach in the bath!

This was the first of three calls Saffy received whilst on call that Friday. She was called out to

a young man with a hangover from over-indulging the night before who wanted some headache tablets, and a family who had all got sunburnt! None of these were real emergencies, but all in a day's work (or a day's off work in this case) and Saffy at all times had to be the smiling, helping face of Aegean Dreams.

1 **What skills and personal qualities do you think are needed to be a successful resort representative?**
2 **Holidaymakers are the customers of the tour operators. What do you think most holidaymakers are looking for in their resort representatives?**
3 **From reading the case study, what do you think are the high points of working as a resort representative and what are the downsides of such a role?**
4 **Why in your opinion was it important for Saffy to do all she could for the family who had almost ruined her welcome party when they asked for her help?**
5 **If you were Saffy, how would you have dealt with the situation with the cockroach? Think about how you would have reacted and what impact this would have on this family's perception of Aegean Dreams.**
6 **Saffy was called out to what were pretty trivial problems on her day off. Why was it important for Saffy to still attend to these holidaymakers?**

One great way to practise dealing with awkward and difficult customers is to simulate situations and role-play how you would deal with such customers. Working in pairs, take it in turns to be a resort representative and a complaining customer. Role-play how you would deal with these situations:

- Customer is unhappy with the food being served in the hotel in which they are staying.
- Customer feels that their hotel room is too noisy as they are facing the main street of the resort they are staying in.
- Customer has fallen out with the friend they are holidaying with and wants to go home.

As the resort representative remember to be professional and deal with customers in an efficient manner, trying to offer solutions to the perceived problems of customers.

Due to the demanding environment of pleasing customers at all times of day and night, a strong sense of camaraderie and teamwork is essential. Being able to cooperate with others and work as part of a team are essential to any job role in the travel and tourism industry.

Think about it

Why do you think teamwork is essential to many jobs in the travel and tourism industry?

CASE STUDY

UK residents' visits abroad up by 4% to 63.5 million

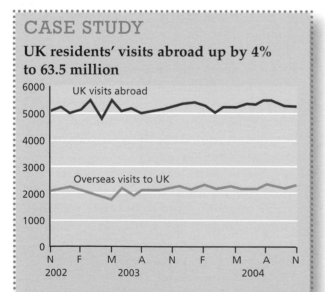

Figure 4.2 Overseas residents' visits to the UK and UK residents' visits abroad (seasonally adjusted)

UK residents' visits abroad continued to rise, up 4 per cent when compared with a year ago, to 63.5 million. This showed a continued increase in visits to areas that are further afield. Although the number of visits to Western Europe remained broadly unchanged at 49.2 million, visits to North America rose by 15 per cent (to 4.8 million) and to other parts of the world by 22 per cent (to 9.6 million) over the same period.

Over the same period, visits by overseas residents to the UK rose by 11 per cent to 27.2 million. There was an increase in visits from residents of Western Europe by 8 per cent (to 17.5 million), from North America by 11 per cent (to 4.4 million), and from other parts of the world by 20 per cent (to 5.4 million).

During September to November 2004, the number of visits to the UK by overseas residents was 6.8 million – an increase of 2 per cent when compared with the previous three months. However, spending fell by 1 per cent to £3.2 billion.

Over the same period, the number of visits overseas by UK residents fell by 1 per cent to 15.8 million, while the associated spending increased by 2 per cent to £7.6 billion.

Source: Office for National Statistics, February 2005

1   **What is the above data showing? Consider both the travelling habits of tourists and their spending.**
2   **The above data shows that many UK tourists visit overseas destinations for their holidays. Identify as many jobs in the travel and tourism industry as possible connected with providing UK tourists to overseas destinations with a quality service that provides value for money.**
3   **Many overseas visitors to the UK are received at airports in this country. Identify at least ten job opportunities which are available in UK airports.**
4   **One important and topical area of work in the travel and tourism industry is that of working for the Home Office dealing with immigration issues. Why do you think**

that immigration officers have such an important role to play in forming opinions overseas visitors have of the UK?

5 After studying the data above, what do you think will happen to the number of jobs in the travel and tourism industry in the UK over the next ten years? Remember to fully explain and justify your answer.

Skills practice

Locate the Camelot web pages and find out:
- What jobs they currently have available
- What age you need to be in order to apply for any of the posts
- Whether any of the posts appeal to you
- The skills and abilities required for one of the posts you can choose from the organisational chart.

CASE STUDY

Camelot Theme Park

Camelot Theme Park opened in 1983 and was originally owned by a local businessman before it became home to Park Hall Hotel's 119 acres. Camelot Theme Park is now owned by the Bank of Scotland and a Venture Capital Company called Close Brothers, and operates under the registered name of Prime Resorts Ltd. The following organisational chart shows the wide variety of employment opportunities available at Camelot, from the Operations Director to seasonal staff. There are a further three areas (known as support functions) not shown on the chart: these are Sales and Marketing, Human Resources and Maintenance.

Camelot employs nearly 200 seasonal staff each year. These staff are usually employed between Easter and the end of October. If the company is happy with their work they may be recalled for a further season. There is also an opportunity to impress the company and apply for the permanent and full-time positions.

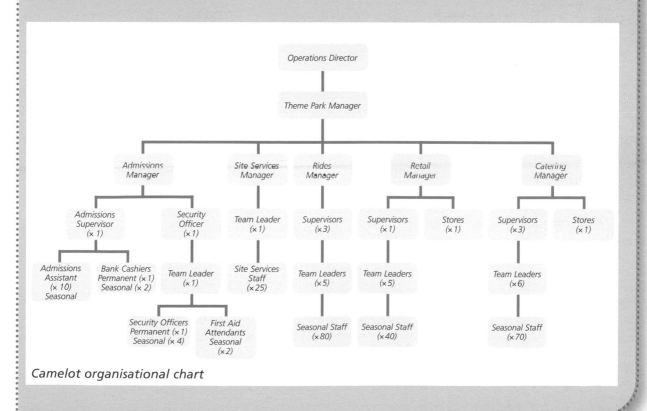

Camelot organisational chart

Not all organisations in the travel and tourism industry are as large as Camelot. In fact, the industry consists of many more small and medium-sized companies. As it is a service industry many of the job roles will involve dealing directly with customers in a variety of tasks. As you will find, there are many different types of jobs in the travel and tourism industry and not all involve glamour and overseas travel!

The following section gives an insight into some of these jobs:

Working in visitor attractions

Visitor attractions are often the main reason why people travel to destinations. Of course there are a wide range of attractions, from zoos, museums, theme parks to sport and recreational grounds. There are, therefore, a wide variety of job roles available. These include:

Figure 4.3 Job roles in visitor attractions

Skills practice

In pairs, choose a local visitor attraction. Try and work out which jobs are involved in order to make it a successful attraction. Select one group member to telephone or visit the attraction and ask the manager for a copy of their organisational chart. Compare with your original ideas.

Skills practice

Check out the website for the Association of Leading Visitor Attractions (ALVA) list of the properties involved in the ALVA and choose one of them you might like to work for, giving your reasons.

Business tourism

Business tourism is one of the fastest growing areas within the travel and tourism industry. It includes conferences, meetings, corporate hospitality, incentive travel and working at exhibitions. The job roles can be very demanding and varied. Positions available include: administrators, interpreters and translators. Some larger organisations, such as Shell, have their own in-house travel agency, where staff are employed to work as a travel agent solely for the other company employees. The role involves organising travel arrangements for the staff by organising trips, booking tickets and planning detailed itineraries.

Activity/sports-related tourism

Many people travel to watch or play sports. Activity holidays are very popular with people from all walks of life. Today, we are all encouraged to take more exercise and live a healthier lifestyle. Activity holidays can be taken in hundreds of sports, for example golf, skiing, sailing, tennis, cricket, to name a few.

Activity holidays is a growing sector in travel and tourism

Such is the growth in this area of tourism that in 2001 and 2002 VisitBritian sponsored an additional set of questions aimed at the sports tourism market to be included in the International Passenger Survey (IPS). The following four questions were added:

* Did you go and watch a sporting event during your visit?
* Was this the main reason for your visit?
* Did you take part in any amateur sport or physical activity during your visit?
* Was this the main reason for your visit?

The results of the summary revealed that a total of 1.6 million overseas visitors to the UK either watched a sporting event or participated in amateur sport during their stay. This equates to almost 7 per cent of the total of 24.2 million overseas visitors to the UK in 2002. It was found that these visitors spent considerably higher than the average whilst in the UK, they also appear to stay longer, in fact nearly twice as long as the average overseas visitor. The most popular visitors to the UK for either watching or playing sport were from the Irish Republic, USA, Germany, France and the Netherlands.

Activity-style holidays can be marketed to families, the 50-plus, couples, individuals and groups such as schools and colleges. There are currently hundreds of operators who offer sport/activity-style holidays.

Job roles within this sector will include:

* Working face to face with the public through coaching for each different type of sport, e.g. sailing, horse riding, canoeing, football, and acting as tour manager, guide and tour representative
* Working behind the scenes planning and organising the activities, such as administration, product development and marketing.

There may also be opportunities to work at major events such as Wimbledon, horse racing and motor racing, the Commonwealth Games (Manchester in 2002) or the 2012 London Olympic Games and Paralympic Games.

Skills practice

Investigate other major sporting events in the UK where there may be opportunities to find employment.

National and regional tourist boards

The role of the national and regional tourist boards is to promote and develop tourism to and within their regions. They all have members such as hoteliers, visitor attractions, ground handlers, tour operators, guest house and B&B owners. Each board will work hard to represent their members and promote and develop tourism in that region through a number of initiatives. Employment opportunities cover marketing and promotions staff, PR managers, development officers, administration, finance and membership officers. Some boards also offer in-house trainers. The marketing and promotions staff will have the opportunity to travel around the UK and overseas to exhibitions and on sales missions to 'sell' their destinations in order to encourage more people to visit.

Skills practice

Find out how your regional tourist board markets to domestic and overseas visitors. Try and find a list of all the current jobs at the board.

Make a list of all of the regional tourist boards in the country, plot them onto a map showing the extent of their regions.

Tourist information centres (TICs)

There are approximately 560 tourist information centres in England, 150 in Scotland, 62 in Wales and 26 in Northern Ireland. They can be owned and operated in a variety of ways, such as:

* Local authorities

A tourist information centre

* National parks
* National tourist boards
* Private companies (such as the Convention Bureaux and public/private initiatives, e.g. marketing Birmingham).

Tourist information centre staff offer assistance with accommodation bookings (also known as BABAs – Book A Bed Ahead scheme), transport and sightseeing information for domestic and overseas visitors. Staff must be able to deal with vast numbers of customers asking challenging questions. Tourist information centres are also used by the local community for booking tickets to local events and shows.

Skills practice

In pairs, visit your local tourist information centre. Make a list of all the personal qualities you think are necessary to be a good information assistant.

Working for a tour operator

Whilst studying travel and tourism you will be aware of the hundreds of tour operators who work within the UK. These operators are divided into three categories: outgoing, incoming or domestic.

You are probably well aware of the large international tour operators such as Thomson and the types of packages and products they sell. You will have seen and heard plenty about working as an overseas representative for these kinds of companies. However, you may not be aware of some of the different types of roles which are also available whilst working for a large tour operator. These include:

Figure 4.4 Tour operator roles

* *Negotiators or contractors* They put together the holiday packages. The role involves negotiating with local suppliers, carriers, car hire companies and hoteliers to put together the package holiday at an affordable price.

* *Researchers and developers* They look for new ideas and places for the company to sell. These are then transferred into the new brochures and sold to the general public.

* *Reservation clerks* They receive and make calls to travel agents and the general public, keeping everyone up to date with the new packages and making reservations on the computer.

* *Marketing and sales* They conduct market research, analyse market trends and sell and promote the holiday packages. Training, courses and events may be run for the travel agents in order that they can learn about the new products and services on offer, ready to be sold to the general public.

* *Tour managers* They travel with holiday groups, ensuring everything runs smoothly en route. Tour managers must ensure that everything runs to time; if there are any delays they must notify local hoteliers and suppliers. Good communication skills are vital at all times.

Travel agencies

If you walk down your high street you will come across several well-known travel agencies. You may also see one or two independent agencies (not attached to the larger multiple organisations). Many of the large agencies will have links with tour operators, airlines and call centres. A travel agent will offer a full holiday service to all potential holidaymakers, from booking separate parts of the holiday to offering currency exchange, car hire and insurance deals (known as ancillary services). Agents will also be involved in researching tailor-made holidays, day trips to theatres, city or weekend breaks, and organising bookings for coach tickets.

CASE STUDY

Thomas Cook

German-owned Thomas Cook AG operates travel agencies, airlines and hotels as well as various tour operator brands, including JMC, Thomas Cook Holidays and Club 18-30. They offer a 12–16 month 'Challenge' programme to university graduates and internal applicants, giving them the opportunity to enter a national and international management training programme.

Visit the website www.thomascook.info and find out more about the training programme.

Travel transport operators

For some people travelling to a destination is as important as the holiday itself, for example an interesting train journey, an overnight ferry trip, or even a cruise. Whilst for others, for example business people, it is vital to get to a destination as quickly as possible and the method of travel is secondary to the experience at the destination.

Travel and tourism jobs can be found with the following types of transport operators:

* Airline
* Ferry
* Coach
* Train
* Cruise ship.

Naturally, there are many different employment roles available for each of the above. The most well known is probably the role of a cabin crew member.

Skills practice

Read the following advertisement for cabin crew. Draw up a list of pros and cons for working as a cabin crew member.

EasyJet Airline Company Ltd

CABIN CREW – PERMANENT CONTRACTS   **This is an ongoing vacancy**
GATWICK, STANSTED, LUTON

Our Cabin Crew must ensure that our customers' safety and comfort come first and that they create a memorable experience by providing a friendly, enthusiastic, courteous and fun service at all times. The job is busy and can be physically demanding. Cabin Crew must be prepared to work on any day of the year, at any time of the day.

To be considered for a position as Cabin Crew you must meet all of our minimum requirements. If you do please visit www.easyjet.com/en/jobs to complete an application form.

You should be:
• Friendly and personable.
• Mature in attitude and outlook.
• Able to remain calm and efficient under pressure.
• An excellent communicator with people of all ages and cultures.
• A team player.
• Flexible and adaptable.
• Able to take direction and accept feedback.

Minimum requirements
– Age 19+.
– Height 5'2" (1.58m) to 6'3" (1.90m) with weight in proportion to height.
– Physically fit and able to pass a medical assessment.
– Fluent in English, both spoken and written.
– Able to swim 25m.
– Possession of right to live and work in the UK.
– Possession of passport allowing unrestricted travel within Europe.
– Educated to at least GCSE level grade C in English and Maths.

All successful applicants must pass the four-week new entrant training course which is held at London Luton Airport. Our standards and expectations are very high and exam pass marks of at least 90% must be achieved throughout the course before new entrants can graduate as easyJet Cabin Crew.

Cabin Crew earn on average £18,000pa and Senior Cabin Crew £22,000pa. Our contracts are permanent and our Cabin Crew enjoy a range of additional benefits, such as 36 days annual leave, a non-contributory pension and staff travel.

Source: Easyjet

There are of course many job roles available at an airport and these include: passenger service agents (airline check-in staff), administrators, receptionists, shop and retail staff, air-traffic controllers, immigration officers, customs and excise workers.

Coach and ferry employment is, perhaps, not seen to be as glamorous as working for a cruise line or an airline. Nevertheless, there are interesting roles available, such as:

* *Coaches*: drivers, guides, tour managers, traffic managers, administrators

* *Trains*: drivers, retail staff, customer service agents, conductors

* *Ferry*: catering, retail and pursers.

Skills practice

1 Take an example of a coach company, for example Shearings, and find out if they use on-board guides. Also find out where they travel to.

2 Find out the Eurostar routes. What qualities do you think would be required to work on a train?

Cruise ships

Cruising is the fastest growing sector of the tourist industry. There are now over a thousand cruise liners afloat, with new ships being launched each year. They carry millions of passengers to a huge range of destinations. The ships themselves are like floating cities with everything on board you could possibly need, from hairdressers to swimming pools. Naturally there are a wide range of roles available, including:

* Deck and engineering officers and ratings

* Assistant pursers (hotel department, responsible for catering, administration of the ship, dealing with accounts, paying the crew, and passenger welfare and entertainment)

* Youth staff are responsible to the purser. They look after children on board by supervising games, childcare, play and youth work.

* Entertainment officer/cruise director/social host or hostess – depending on the ship this will usually involve general passenger entertainment, which may be singing, dancing, joke telling etc.

* Catering and bar staff

* Hairdresser/beauty therapist

* Retail sales staff

* Medical staff – doctors, nurses, pharmacists

* Croupier – working in the different casinos

* Cabin staff – room stewards, keeping passengers supplied with linen and dealing with housekeeping.

Skills practice

Visit the website www.cunard.com for information about recruitment of deck and technical officers. Find out what qualifications, personal qualities and training opportunities are available.

Holiday centres

Holiday centres play an important role in the tourism industry. They currently provide holidays for over three million people and cater for all kinds of tourist types, from families to OAPs. Examples of holiday centres include:

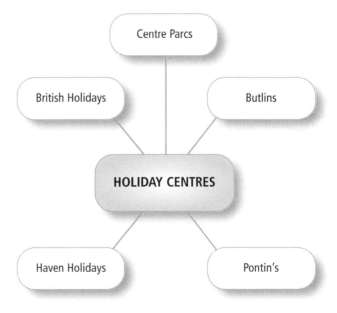

Figure 4.5 Holiday centres

Holiday centre

Holiday centres aim to provide all the facilities a holidaymaker would require without having to leave the site. This usually includes accommodation, restaurants, cafés/snack bars, pubs, entertainment including kids clubs, shops, swimming pools, gyms, spas and sports facilities.

Seasonal employment

There are many kinds of seasonal jobs available in travel and tourism. Naturally employment of this kind is restricted for a set time period and the salaries vary. Roles vary from sports coaching at PGL to couriers at Eurocamp. However, the experience of working and living overseas often offsets the rates of pay. The following are examples of TUI seasonal posts.

Resort representatives/ski escorts/walking guides (winter/summer)

These are roles that involves a great deal of customer contact. You must be friendly, outgoing and excellent at communicating with the public. Ideally, you will have a background in customer service or sales. For the ski escort posts you should have at least 10 weeks' skiing or snowboarding experience and be confident in all types of terrain. Walking guides are responsible for setting up walking programmes for customers which include full and half-day walks two or three times per week.

Specialist sun representatives (summer)

This role involves providing the highest level of customer service in a resort and ensuring that guests have an enjoyable holiday. Representatives must have a detailed local knowledge and a passion for both travel and local culture. They must hold a current, clean driving licence and be fluent in either French, Italian, Spanish, Portuguese or Greek.

Chalet hosts (winter/summer)

There is the opportunity for individuals, couples or friends to act as chalet hosts. The role involves keeping everything running smoothly and efficiently. In addition to cooking, chalet staff are responsible for the daily cleaning and housekeeping duties, shopping, stock control, budgeting and hosting. All chalet hosts must be outgoing and friendly.

Hotel managers/assistant managers (winter/summer)

These posts are based in the TUI club hotels. The main roles involve being responsible, approachable, diplomatic and working on initiative. Ideally, you will have a working knowledge of the local language, plus sound IT skills.

Kitchen porter/night porter (winter/summer)

This is a combined role in which work is done on a rota basis. Assistance is given to preparation, cleaning, stock rotation and washing up. As a night porter you will complete regular security and fire checks, in addition to cleaning public areas and helping to set up breakfast.

Nannies and family nannies (winter/summer)

Nannies will need an NNEB, BTEC or NVQ level 3 in Childcare, a Diploma in Nursery Nursing or an equivalent UK qualification. All nannies work in well-equipped resort crèches and clubs, looking after children from 6 months to 12 years.

Whizz Kids leaders/Arctic rangers (winter)

Whizz Kid leaders will look after children from the ages of 4 to 10 and will manage full and half-day activity programmes, which include lunch and lunchtime supervision, plus a drop-off/pick-up service from ski school and activities three evenings per week. All leaders must have experience of working with children, combined with lots of energy, a good imagination and creativity.

Watersports instructors (summer)

RYA dinghy and windsurf instructors are required for the watersports centres in Corsica and Turkey. Working in a small team, the staff are responsible for the safe and efficient beach operation, which includes delivering private lessons and intensive courses to guests. The role demands a high level of customer service and enthusiasm.

Skills practice

Look at three other tour operators and compare the seasonal jobs that they are currently offering. Try and compare rates of pay if available. You might choose these operators: Eurocamp, Sunsites, Keycamp Holidays.

Seasonal work in the travel and tourism industry

Duties of jobs in the travel and tourism industry

The duties of a job are all the different tasks and responsibilities that you are expected to perform as part of your job role. In the travel and tourism industry your duties will be different, depending on which type of job you have, the number of hours you work and the level at which you are working.

As in any sphere of work, there are duties and tasks that are common to many jobs. Many large organisations have staff who work in separate departments:

* Health and safety
* Physical resources
* Personnel or Human Resources
* Finance and Administration.

Smaller organisations may have staff who must fulfil several of these functions, for example an administrative assistant in a small activity centre may be responsible for organising the staff pay as well as liaising with the fire officer for regular checks of the building.

There are also some duties which may be common to many jobs, such as:

* Completing paperwork
* Answering questions (external and internal)
* Being able to know where to find relevant information
* Knowing what you are responsible for and to whom you are responsible to
* Prioritising work tasks
* Dealing with customers.

Providing leisure facilities

Mudasser Alahan works as Operations Director for a private sector organisation providing leisure facilities for the residents of and visitors to the Hastings and Bexhill-on-Sea areas of East Sussex. The company Mudasser works for runs leisure centres and swimming pools on behalf of the local authority and has a commitment to not only provide good quality services for local residents but to also provide entertainment for the many visitors to the area.

A leisure centre

Hastings and Bexhill-on-Sea are located on the south-eastern coast of England and for many years this has been a popular domestic tourist resort for people who live in the south-east of England. Due to the resort's proximity to ferry ports and the Euro tunnel terminus at Ashford, Kent, the area also attracts many visitors from continental Europe. During the summer months, the towns play host to many foreign students, particularly French, German and Austrian students who visit the area to attend language schools to learn English. These students stay with local families and an entertainments programme is put together to help them enjoy their free time outside of language school. Mudasser's organisation plays a large role in providing activities for the visiting students. Below is a transcript of an interview conducted with Mudasser about the duties of his job and how the organisation he works for provides products and services for visitors to the area.

Hayley: Being an Operations Director makes you sound very important. Are you?

Mudasser: Of course I am! No, I agree it sounds very grand but unfortunately it isn't as glamorous as it sounds. Basically, it means I oversee the day-to-day running of all the leisure centres we run on behalf of the local authority, Rother District Council.

Hayley: Does that mean you have lots of staff to look after?

Mudasser: Yeah – we have lots of staff but the numbers change depending on the season. When we have more visitors to the area in the summer months of June, July and August, we need more staff. For example, we need more lifeguards/pool attendants, more people who work in our kitchens, dining areas and bars, and more cleaners.

Hayley: What facilities does your organisation offer to tourists and local residents?

Mudasser: We offer lots of different facilities in our different centres. One of our centres in Bexhill is a leisure pool complex. This has proved to be really popular with the students who visit the area to learn English in the summer. The organisers of the language schools work with us quite closely as they think the leisure pool is a great place for their students to visit. We have special themed nights where inflatables are put in the pool and current chart music is played. The students love this. I meet with the organisers of the language schools about three times a year to negotiate special prices for the students and sometimes to organise and plan parties for students' birthdays or leaving celebrations.

Hayley: What about the other centres you are responsible for?

Mudasser: We run a large centre in Hastings, which has a host of different facilities. It has a swimming pool, a state-of-the-art gymnasium, a sauna, solaria, restaurant, bars and conference facilities.

Hayley: Who uses this facility then Mudasser?

Mudasser: It's about a fifty-fifty split between locals and visitors to the area. We cater for a wide range of people at this facility. We get our regulars who live locally who use the gym and sauna etc. and we also get local business people who hire out our conference rooms for meetings. Tourists also use our swimming pool more than anything else and eat in our restaurant and drink in our two bars. Because of the weather in this country being unpredictable and very often wet, we find many tourists use our swimming pool.

Hayley: It sounds as though you must be very busy overseeing the running of such large and popular facilities, but what does a normal day entail for you?

Mudasser: On the whole no two days are the same. That's why I really love the job – the variety. However, there are things that I have to do every day. I usually start work at about 8 am and can finish at 11 at night on a bad day, so the hours are long. I start in my office at the Bexhill leisure pool and talk with the duty manager there as to the plans for the day. I also then telephone the duty manager at our Hastings centre to make sure everything is okay there. By doing this I get an idea of how busy the day will be and if there are any staff shortages that need sorting out. Staffing can be a major issue for us as we need to have certain levels of staff for health and safety reasons and to meet the conditions of our contracts with the local council. After I've done my daily briefings and telephoning, the day can take all sorts of different shapes depending on what needs to be done.

Hayley: So, what might you do?

Mudasser: Staying on the subject of staffing, I like to be involved in the recruitment of all staff who will work in our centres, regardless of what level the job is for. I think it's really important as we need to project a certain image to our regular customers and visiting tourists. Therefore, I want to ensure that all our staff are of a good quality. On the quality issue, I also get involved in training our staff. I believe that it's important for all new recruits to the business to know that senior management are approachable and interested in the development of staff. I also become involved in the continuing professional development of our existing staff as I think that trained workers are much better workers and ongoing training shows our commitment to our staff.

As Operations Director, the way the centres are run is my ultimate responsibility, so I visit both of the centres unannounced to carry out quality checks. I also organise our mystery visitors, who use the facilities and observe and record details on the way they were treated by staff, the cleanliness of the facilities and the overall quality of their experience.

An important part of my job is to liaise with external agencies. I meet with the council regularly to tell them how well we are doing! I meet with environmental health officers, local business organisations and the local tourist board.

Hayley: As Operations Director who do you report to?

Mudasser: I report directly to the owner and Managing Director of the business. He has several other business interests, so for all intents and purposes I run everything to do with the leisure centres.

Hayley: That's an awful lot of responsibility, do you enjoy the job?

Mudasser: When I've done a fourteen- or sixteen-hour shift, the answer would have to be no. But on the whole, I find the job very rewarding. I love working with people, both our staff and the general public, and to be honest I like the responsibility. It's what I've worked and studied for. Since being sixteen I have worked in the leisure and tourism industry and have worked my way up to where I am today.

1   Mudasser is part of the senior management team of an organisation that provides products and services for locals and tourists. Mudasser is in charge of many members of staff. What job opportunities do you think are available in the organisation Mudasser works for?
2   Mudasser stated that he has to work with many different outside agencies. What role do you think Mudasser can play in shaping

tourist provision in the Hastings and Bexhill-on-Sea area?
3   As Operations Director, Mudasser has to take overall responsibility for health and safety at the leisure centres. What pieces of current legislation do you think Mudasser's organisation must adhere to and why is this important?
4   Mudasser's job is very demanding. What do you consider to be Mudasser's key duties?
5   Mudasser revealed that he has to often work long hours and has much responsibility. How do you think Mudasser contributes to the success of the organisation?
6   For Mudasser's job role, write a job description. Identify what you believe to be the main duties and responsibilities of an Operations Director.

Training in the travel and tourism industry

Happier workers are better workers. Better workers are those who feel confident to perform the duties of their job description. Confident workers are those workers who have the necessary skills to do a job properly. Skilled workers are those workers who have received training.

Figure 4.6 Flow chart showing the relationship between training and motivation in the workplace

Skilled workers are more confident that they have the necessary skills to do a job properly. This allays fear, which makes workers happier. Workers who are happy are generally more motivated and productive and are therefore better workers.

Today many organisations in the travel and tourism industry see training as integral to satisfying the needs and wants of customers and of recruiting and retaining staff of the highest quality.

The number of job roles within the travel and tourism industry is vast and many of the different professions which make up the job opportunities available within the industry have professional bodies and organisations who are committed to developing the skills of members and improving the face of the industry. Some of these organisations arrange training events for members and are genuinely concerned with the initial training and continuing professional development of employees in the industry. One such organisation is the Institute of Tourist Guiding.

The Blue Badge

The coveted Blue Badge for tourist guiding is the British national standard guiding qualification and internationally recognised benchmark of excellence.

The Blue Badge qualification course is held in London and successful candidates are awarded the Badge by the Institute of Tourist Guiding. The course is detailed and comprehensive, the examinations rigorous and registration an achievement.

Outside London courses are run in response to demand for guides in particular areas, usually by local and regional tourist bodies or colleges and institutions.

As well as acquiring knowledge, Blue Badge guides are trained in the selection and presentation of material. This has been so successful that English trainers have trained guides all over the world, and the Blue Badge is recognised internationally.

Blue Badge guides have a wide range of languages, specialities and interests, and can guide on foot, in cars, on coaches, on trains and on boats.

They have a wealth of experience which is respected by discriminating tour operators and travel agents throughout the world.

They take pride in constantly updating their knowledge to enable their visitors to enjoy Britain's immense, unique and varied heritage.

They are practical, punctual, and reliable and thrive on the unexpected, welcoming individuals or groups, here on business or for pleasure.

What do you perceive to be the benefits of being a member of such an organisation for tourist guides?

Training, either in-house or externally, is always offered to employees by a good employer. It helps to provide guidance on the skills required to be an effective member of staff. Most employers will give new staff a full induction upon starting their job. This helps the new member of staff to familiarise themselves with their role, the environment, people they will work with, who they are responsible to and all aspects of health and safety.

Training is vital for continuing good practice within an organisation and also helps staff to

* keep well informed of new systems such as paper-based and computer-based ones

* stay well motivated

* keep up to date with industry practice, e.g. know about new Acts and regulations such as the Data Protection Act, Working Time Directive, Disability Discrimination Act, etc.

* help to give excellent customer service

* keep within the law on practices concerning health and safety

* enhance performance and personal development

* increase productivity.

Many organisations will conduct a *training needs analysis*. This is a system where staff training is identified, introduced or improved upon. Some employers will implement training in house. This means training is developed whilst an employee carries out their normal duties, for example in a travel agency the manager may train a new employee on the use of their computer and booking systems.

Many employers today prefer to take on employees who have had some form of experience – therefore it is always a good idea to gain experience in dealing with customers (customer service, retail or marketing) on a part-time basis, such as working in a restaurant, café or hotel. Volunteering for work is also considered a good idea. Working for nothing doesn't sound brilliant. However, it will give excellent work experience which might be invaluable for future employment.

Travel and tourism courses are available in many colleges across the country. Examining boards will offer full-time travel and tourism courses from degree, AS, A2, to first diploma level. However, it is also possible to train and become qualified whilst working. NVQ/SVQs are available for travel agency, tour operations and tourist information centre work. The Association of British Travel Agents also offers a Certificate known as ABTAC (Association of British Travel Agents Certificate) and a Tour Operators Certificate (ABTOC). Qualifications are offered in business travel by the Guild of Business Travel Agents and in airfares and ticketing by the Travel Training Company (TTC). The TTC is the largest training provider for the industry. Trainees receive structured training whilst learning on the job in, for example, travel agencies. They also work towards NVQs in travel services. A two-year Modern Apprenticeship is now available for working in travel agencies.

Skills practice

1 Contact a local travel agency and see if they offer a Modern Apprenticeship – find out what is involved and how long it takes to complete.

2 Look up the web pages for the Travel Training Company. Find out what is involved if you want to study for an ABTAC or ABTOC.

Key terms

NVQ National Vocational Qualifications

SNVQ Scottish National Vocational Qualifications

Both of these qualifications offer individuals an opportunity to develop a career within a chosen part of the industry. They help improve job competence for staff at different levels within an organisation.

Communication skills

Speaking, listening and the use of body language are all ways we communicate with others. In the majority of jobs the ability to communicate with a variety of people at different levels is essential and the travel and tourism industry is no exception. In such a people-focused environment as the travel and tourism industry, workers have to be able to communicate with:

* Other staff
* Suppliers
* Customers
* Anyone else who can influence travel and tourism operations. For example, central and local government, the media and consumer associations.

Skills practice

Write a list of ten methods of communication you use to interact with others. Consider the advantages and disadvantages of each method you have identified.

Successful organisations use a variety of different communication methods to effectively organise themselves. Communication takes place in many different ways and can be put into many different categories.

Key terms

Internal communication Communication between all employees in the same organisation.

External communication Communication with all people outside of the organisation you work for. For example, customers, suppliers and local and central government.

Open communication This is where information is communicated to a wide group of people in an organisation and is not limited to who can receive or access that information.

Restricted communication Information that is communicated to only one person or a selected group of people.

Lateral communication This type of communication takes place between employees on the same level of an organisation's hierarchical structure, for example between one sales consultant in a travel agent to another sales consultant.

Vertical communication Communication up and down an organisation's hierarchical structure, that is communication between employees and supervisors/managers.

Good communication within any organisation is often the key to its success or failure. Travel and tourism organisations use a mixture of different communication systems. One-way communication involves information being passed in one direction, such as displays and signs in a restaurant or point-of-sale material in a tourist information centre. Two-way communication involves the sending and receiving of information, for example through telephone conversations, video conferencing and meeting face to face with clients.

In business, written communication is still used by many organisations as a more formal form of dealing with clients, for example letters, reports, memos, advertisements, press releases, etc. Written communication allows detailed or complex information to be sent and retained. It also provides evidence of a previous engagement or discussion. Signatures are still required in formal business dealings and this is still very important in the travel and tourism industry.

Think about it

With a partner think of five examples from the travel and tourism industry where a signature would be required.

As you will be aware, travel and tourism is a service industry and as such verbal communication is used as a vital tool for both formal and informal dealings. Verbal communication can take various forms:

* Meetings
* Giving presentations, speaking to the public
* Giving directions to the public at a tourist information centre
* Training, interviewing and appraising staff
* Managing and supervising staff
* Dealing with customers
* Dealing with complaints.

Impact of ICT

Today, the impact of ICT on the travel and tourist industry is enormous. These are some of the ways in which the industry has been affected by the development of information technology:

* *Intranet* This is a system through which information is transmitted electronically for sharing among all those who work in an organisation.

* *Email* This is an electronic mailing system which makes it possible to contact many different people at one time, instantly. It is quick and cheap, can be sent instantly to people in other countries and can be used for sending photos and diagrams.

* *EPOS (electric point of sale)* This is used, for example, in bars and restaurants where computer-based systems help with easy payment details and allows finance managers to track payments.

* *Global distribution system (GDS)* Examples are Galileo, Worldspan, etc. This is a complete information and booking system used by travel agents and tour operators around the world.

* *Video conferencing* This is the use of video technology to hold meetings between people who are at some distance from one another, in some cases at other ends of the world.

* *Swipe cards* These are used for gaining entry to theme parks.

* *Central reservation system (CRS)* This is used for making travel and accommodation bookings, for example to hotels and on trains.

Skills practice

The following is the mission statement of Galileo:

'Our mission is to be the leading provider of travel information and transaction processing worldwide by deploying solutions that drive measurable results for our customers.'

Visit Galileo's website and find out how it tries to achieve its mission.

Professional skills

Many jobs require more skills than are actually called for in the job description. These skills are professional skills and it is often assumed that workers have these skills when they are recruited to a particular type of work. This is especially true of workers at a supervisory or management level in the travel and tourism industry.

For the completion of your portfolio, you should observe and report on how your chosen jobholder exercises skills such as:

* Prioritising tasks – i.e. organising time
* The ability to 'read between the lines'
* The ability to discriminate between the trivial and the crucial
* Knowing what resources to use and when to use them
* Working with a diary
* Report writing.

Prioritising tasks in a travel and tourism organisation is vital. It is imperative that you can plan and organise your own work effectively. It is useful to divide daily tasks into different categories such as:

* Non-routine tasks which are done occasionally and are not important
* Routine tasks which should be done on a regular basis
* Urgent tasks which need to be done straight away.

Prioritising skills can take a little while to learn, however it is something which will develop after a short period of time and with practice! The best way to start a task is to check whether or not it is important and how urgent it is.

As a general rule the more organised you are the easier it is to plan your time and deal with routine tasks; this will leave time for those urgent interruptions. Remember, it will probably take you longer to complete a task the first time you are given it.

Using the most appropriate resources will also help to complete tasks quickly and efficiently. Every organisation has its own procedures for obtaining and storing information. It is important

that all employees understand where to find the correct resources and how to use them. Travel and tourism organisations will use a variety of information resources, such as:

* Telephone directories
* Timetables
* Journals
* Maps
* Brochures and guides to destinations
* Dictionaries
* Internet searches.

Skills practice

Plan and organise a trip away for a small group of you and your friends. Organise the trip and make sure that you prioritise all the necessary points before the holiday takes place. You may wish to devise a grid, such as the one below, to help you:

Date	Activity	By who	To be completed by (date)

Points you may wish to include:
* Choosing the holiday
* Booking transport
* Choosing and booking hotel(s)
* Booking and organising ancillary services – insurance, car hire, etc.
* Planning inoculations
* Budgets and payments.

One way to help you develop good organisational skills is to incorporate work planners, diaries, schedules and lists. These will all help by giving a visual prompt to all activities which need to be undertaken. Even whilst at college, you can make a clear list of all the tasks you need to do and then tick them off as you complete each one.

Skills practice

Make a clear list of all your outstanding college tasks. Compare your list with other group members. See how many tasks you can complete by the end of the day/week/month.

A computer diary is useful for organising your tasks and time

There are many diaries in use in travel and tourism organisations, for example a page to a day, a week to a view, two weeks to a view. Some organisations use computer-based diaries where details of events and dates can be typed into a grid. The system will warn you if you have a clash of appointments and it will also give you reminders of important events. Events which re-occur can be programmed in, saving extra time. Using a computer diary can also be useful for finding and linking data such as telephone numbers, postal addresses and email addresses. They are also useful for reducing the amount of paperwork used in an office.

The main advantages of using paper-based or computer-based diaries include:

* Keeping timed appointments
* Taking forward jobs to be done at a future date
* Highlighting jobs which need to be done on a specific date
* Booking out events
* Reminders for important events
* Making provisional dates and notes.

How to write reports

Reports are different to essays. A report usually follows a recognised format to make it easy for the reader to follow each point and be able to track points from previous reports. A recognised format is as follows:

* **Title page**
* **Table of contents**
  This will be arranged in sections and subsections which will have page numbers in a neat column on the right-hand side.
* **Introduction**
  This will contain a brief outline of what is in the report with a background to why the report has been written. This may also include the main sources of information used.
* **Sections**
  The main sections of the report will now follow. Usually subheadings are used identified with numbered points, for example:
  2.1 Methodology
  2.2 Purpose
  2.3 Evidence
  Further subheadings may be used:
  2.1.1 Aims
  2.1.2 Objectives
* **Conclusion**
  This section must answer the purpose of the report as covered in the introduction. It should summarise the research (if any was carried out) and provide a concluding statement.
* **References**
  These are a list of sources that were accessed to help in compiling the report.
* **Glossary**
  This is compiled if new and different terms or jargon have been used in the report.
* **Appendices**
  All appendices must be linked to the text, for example the information gathered in questionnaires.

Personal qualities

Success at work is dependent upon the characteristics displayed by the individuals completing the task in hand. For your portfolio, you will need to be able to identify the characteristics which make travel and tourism professionals succeed at their work. Good practitioners in the travel and tourism industry need to demonstrate a variety of qualities and skills. These include:

Figure 4.7 Some of the qualities and skills needed in the travel and tourism industry

These skills will also reflect the underlying values and attitudes of travel and tourism professionals.

In order to succeed in their work, tourism professionals must be able to deal with a variety of complex and involved situations, such as an overseas representative having to deal with several unhappy holidaymakers. You will probably have seen popular TV programmes showing airports and airline staff dealing with a variety of different scenarios. No two problems appear to be the same. What is clear, however, is that whilst dealing with the general public a vast amount of patience is required. You must never lose your temper and you should attempt to stay as calm as possible. Other important personal characteristics include:

＊ Maintaining a corporate image both in attitude and appearance. Many travel and tourism organisations require their staff to wear a uniform. They may also have a policy on how hair should be worn, if make-up is allowed and if body piercing and tattoos are acceptable. Retaining a good corporate image is vital as it helps to promote the organisation, provide a

good image and give excellent customer service, which in turn will see repeat visitors.

＊ Remaining loyal to an organisation.

＊ Using correct language at all time. It is essential that customers do not overhear bad language or gossip.

＊ Having a confident and approachable manner.

＊ Being assertive, which is particularly useful with difficult customers or challenging situations.

＊ Having the ability to work as part of a team and follow instructions.

＊ Being able to deal with stressful situations, e.g. air rage.

＊ Having good administrative skills – completing forms and reports using legible handwriting.

＊ Having good IT skills.

＊ Having the ability to use a public address system, and adopting a clear tone and not speaking too quickly.

＊ Being able to solve problems on a daily basis.

＊ Having the ability to ask the correct question.

In order to win and retain customers within a travel and tourism organisation, it is important to identify and meet all the different needs of customers. As a general rule, a 'need' is the reason why a customer is buying a travel or tourism product/service. Using a variety of questioning techniques, it is possible to assess whether or not a customer is happy and has all of their needs met.

There are different examples of questions, such as:

＊ Information questions, e.g. How, What, Where, When and Why?

＊ Probing questions, e.g. 'Could you give more information?'

＊ Group processing questions, e.g. 'How can we help you?'

On many occasions good negotiating skills will also be required. This will involve discussing something with the aim of reaching a joint agreement. Travel agents will sell holidays and will need to offer options in order that customers can make the most appropriate decision. Agents will also attempt to sell a variety of 'extras', such as insurance deals, car hire and currency exchange.

Conduct research into the uniforms and name badges worn by the staff in your local travel agencies.

CASE STUDY

Charlie the air cabin crew member – where did it all go wrong?

Charlie was ecstatic when he landed his dream job of working for one of the major chartered flight carriers. Since being a small boy and travelling to Tenerife for the first time, Charlie had been able to envisage himself working up and down the aisles of an aircraft and carrying out the safety demonstration, complete with life jacket and whistle!

As soon as he was old enough, Charlie started to apply for jobs as a member of air cabin crew and had worked hard to impress at interview and initial training. Unfortunately, twelve months on Charlie has not had his seasonal contract renewed and has been told he will not be required for the next high season. The reasons Charlie's superiors gave for his dismissal included:

- Being late to work on more than three occasions and causing staffing problems and potential delays to flights
- Not responding to customers when they called for assistance when on board the aircraft
- Being more interested in looking good than attending team briefings
- Failure to take on board comments and suggestions made by management on how to improve.

1. Charlie was obviously so pleased that he had been recruited to the job of his dreams that he did not pay much attention to actually fulfilling the responsibilities of his job role. What do you consider to be the main responsibilities of air cabin crew?
2. What personal qualities should Charlie have displayed to be successful in his chosen career?

3. Travel and tourism careers require workers to be able to communicate effectively with customers. Why do you think communication with customers is so important in the travel and tourism industry?

Listening

One of the most important yet underused skills when dealing with people is that of listening. You have to really concentrate when someone is speaking to you to fully understand the points that are being made to you. You must also resist the temptation to interrupt as this puts people off what they were going to say.

Think about it

In which job roles in the travel and tourism industry do you think listening is a vital part of the job and satisfying customers?

Most people love to talk about their favourite subject – their children, themselves, their job, the football team they support. Given half the chance, many of your customers will tell you their life story before they actually tell you what you really need to know to be able to help them. This example sums up the point: 'He was one of the most brilliant conversationalists I've ever met. He stood and listened to everything I said the whole night.'

The most important point about listening carefully to customers is that you will find out exactly what they want.

Think about it

Imagine you are working in your local tourist information centre during the busiest summer months. What would be the consequences if you did not listen properly to visitors requiring information about the local area?

Feedback

To constantly improve the products and services that they offer and to gain a competitive edge over rivals, organisations in the travel and tourism industry place a great deal of importance on feedback from their customers. Without constructive feedback, travel and tourism organisations would find it very difficult to move forward and satisfy the needs and wants of their customers.

Tourism professionals are very aware of the importance of what their customers, colleagues and superiors think about them and will often go to extraordinary lengths in order to meet the required standards.

For your portfolio, you have to describe the standards which your chosen jobholder is expected to meet and whether these standards are set by the jobholder or by management. The key points are:

* How the standards set compare with the competition and the industry
* Methods of evaluation – by numbers, by responses, by profitability
* Methods of rewarding targets met
* Incentives for setting and reaching new targets.

Methods of collecting and measuring feedback

There are many recognised methods of collecting and measuring feedback. Tourism professionals are very aware of the importance of what customers, colleagues, suppliers and other organisations think of them. They will, therefore, adopt a variety of methods to ensure that their work and conduct is effective and not wasteful of time and effort. Some methods for measurement include:

* Mystery customers
* Focus groups
* Questionnaires
* Telephone surveys
* Email surveys
* Benchmarking (comparing with other similar organisations).

Such research can provide data which is then used to improve the organisation. This may look at the number of visitors to a theme park. Should numbers fall significantly, action will need to be taken to improve visitor numbers through a variety of schemes such as improved marketing and product development.

Many organisations believe in rewarding their staff who do well, achieving high sales targets. This helps to motivate staff and encourage them to continue to improve and perform well for the company. Reward schemes can vary according to the organisation. Incentive travel is one way that staff are rewarded. They may be given a free holiday to an exotic destination or tickets to an event or show of their choice, for example the FA Cup Final, Wimbledon, etc. Other organisations may simply give their staff a financial bonus.

Personal development

Researching the job roles of others and the duties and skills needed to be able to successfully fulfil a job's requirements, takes an enormous amount of skill and analytical ability. But how do you measure up to the demands of a job in the travel and tourism industry? Honestly appraising your own skills and identifying further areas of development will enable you to access the highest marks for this unit and hopefully will give you the best start to any career you wish to follow.

Tools for personal development

Competition in today's labour market is fierce and the quality of applicants for jobs is of a high standard as students are leaving education with a host of qualifications. To be able to critically evaluate one's own performance is of enormous benefit and can give candidates an advantage when applying for jobs, as you tend to be more realistic and have greater confidence in your own abilities.

Identifying our strengths can be easy as we all have an idea of what we are good at. Identifying our weaknesses may not be so easy as nobody likes to think that they are under-performing or failing in a particular area. One way of objectively looking at our strengths and weaknesses, the opportunities that are open to us and the possible constraints or threats that may impede our success, is to produce a SWOT analysis. SWOT (strengths, weaknesses, opportunities and threats) analyses are used by many organisations in both the commercial and not-for-profit sectors to assess an organisation's current position and to plan for the future. Individuals can also produce a SWOT analysis to help them with their own career development. Potential employers realise that nobody is perfect and like to recruit people who are positive and have an idea of how they can develop further. A SWOT analysis of yourself will allow you to better understand your own capabilities.

CASE STUDY

Life after graduation

Janey Holland has recently graduated from Bournemouth University with a degree in tourism. After enjoying her degree immensely and spending the third year of her studies working for a large international hotel chain as an assistant to the sales and marketing manager, Janey is looking to venture into management herself, but is finding it very difficult, as competition for jobs in this sector is fierce.

Janey has attended several interviews and has received some positive feedback from organisations. But she has lost out on two jobs to people who are more experienced. As you can imagine Janey is feeling despondent and wants to start earning money to pay back student loans and buy a car.

Below is a quadrant showing Janey's strengths and weaknesses as identified by the interviewers at her last two job interviews. Complete the quadrant concentrating on the opportunities and threats, which could help or hinder Janey in her quest to find the job of her dreams.

Strengths	Weaknesses
• Good knowledge of the hotel industry • Good qualifications • Good communication skills	
Opportunities	**Threats**

Analysis of sources of information

For your portfolio you need to be able to comment on and evaluate the sources of information you have used to complete all the tasks required. You will need to consider the availability, validity and reliability of the data you have used. You will also be expected to use a variety of both primary and secondary data in the completion of your portfolio.

Availability of information may in some cases prove to be restricted. Some organisations are reluctant to release information to those external to the organisation as the information is sensitive or may be of interest to competitors.

When collecting information the reliability and validity of that information must be considered. For data collected to be reliable, you must consider what you are trying to achieve and set clear objectives. If you are unclear about the information you need to collect for your portfolio, then the resulting information you collect will be unclear. When using information collected by somebody else (secondary data), you need to be aware that this information was collected for a specific purpose that might not be the same as your purpose and that the information might be dated.

To assess the validity of the information you collect, you need to ensure that the information provides you with the data and results you want and not something else.

Finally, with any information collected, you need to be able to interpret this information and draw conclusions from it. In this case, if the information you collect is both reliable and valid, then you can successfully complete your portfolio work.

Knowledge check

1 Describe what you think interdependency means in a travel and tourism context and give an example of how it works.

2 What sort of job roles would you find in business tourism?

3 What sort of jobs would you find in activity or sports-related tourism?

4 What are the functions of tourist boards and tourist information centres?

5 Name some of the roles that are required by a tour operator and say what they involve.

6 What is the function of a travel agent?

7 Name some of the jobs involved in the running of a cruise ship.

8 Name the facilities provided by holiday centres.

9 What are some of the seasonal jobs available in the travel and tourism industry?

10 What personal qualities are required for working in the travel and tourism industry? Describe what some of these involve.

UNIT ASSESSMENT

Portfolio practice

For this unit you need to produce a portfolio based on an investigation into one job in the travel and tourism industry.

Task 1

To investigate the duties of a worker in the travel and tourism industry, devise a questionnaire and list of interview questions to find out the main roles and responsibilities of their job. Both your questionnaire and interview should try and draw out information on the following:

- The tasks that need to be carried out in an average day
- The duration of tasks in an average day
- The number of people involved in carrying out those tasks
- The contribution made by the worker to the success of the organisation they work for
- The demands these tasks place upon the worker
- Interaction of the worker with other staff in completing their duties.

Task 2

Interview somebody who works in the travel and tourism industry about the communication methods they use to be able to do their job effectively and whom they have to communicate with. Using the key terms above, identify the types methods of communication that fall into each category.

Task 3

Complete a SWOT analysis for yourself. Perhaps ask others you know (peers, family, employer) for their opinions to help you complete a quadrant reviewing your skills and areas that need further development.

Task 4

Hopefully, to help you complete your portfolio you will have completed a period of work experience or work shadowing in an organisation to get a real feel of the job role of your chosen worker. If you have done this, ask a member of management at the organisation to give you an interview. Ask them to imagine you are applying for a job in the organisation and go through all the official recruitment channels. If you are lucky enough to get an interview, ask for written feedback to assist you in identifying your own strengths and weaknesses in relation to a job role within the travel and tourism industry.

Task 5

Consult the careers department in your college. It may be able to help you in identifying your strengths and weaknesses and suitability for a job role in the travel and tourism industry. Many careers departments can help you to access career planning software and questionnaires.

UNIT
5

Marketing in travel and tourism

Introduction

This unit introduces you to how travel and tourism organisations use various marketing techniques in order to increase their customer base. Basically, effective marketing leads to an increase in profits and contributes to the overall success of the organisation.

So what is marketing and how can it help? Marketing is a continuous process that embraces everything travel and tourism organisations do to identify, anticipate and satisfy customer needs and expectations. These organisations can then provide the right products and services for their customers. Remember, customers only buy what they need and want. Organisations that do not carry out effective marketing are leaving their success to chance, which is not the way to survive in business.

This unit will also enable you to gain a greater insight into the travel and tourism industry and builds on the activities and learning from Unit 1 Inside Travel and Tourism.

You need to know and understand the key stages of the marketing process and realise the importance of marketing in an industry which is characterised by fierce competition and constantly changing customer needs and expectations. You also need to investigate how travel and tourism organisations apply the marketing process to their business.

How you will be assessed

This unit is assessed by portfolio evidence based on an investigation into travel and tourism organisations and their marketing activities.

Your portfolio should include:

✳ A report on the significance of market segmentation to the travel and tourism industry

* An assessment of the most appropriate promotions mix for a specialist tour operator and a multiple travel agent
* An evaluation of the key marketing activities of a chosen travel or tourism organisation
* An analysis of the internal and external business environment of a chosen travel and tourism organisation.

The unit is organised into four sections all of which form the basis of the key stages of the marketing process.

After studying this unit you need to have learned about:

* Marketing objectives
* Market research
* Market segmentation
* Analysing the internal and external business environment
* Developing a marketing mix.

What is marketing?

According to the Chartered Institute of Marketing, 'Marketing is the management process for identifying and satisfying customer needs profitably.' More simply, 'Marketing is finding out what customers need and want, then providing them with it at a profit.'

Any organisation's marketing should put the customer at the centre of decision making. Marketing aims to attract customers and keep them. No travel and tourism organisation will survive for long unless it has an effective marketing policy. This means that all of an organisation's policies are based on meeting customer needs and creating satisfied customers who will return to purchase the products of the organisation.

The basic function of marketing is to ensure that the right product is delivered to the right person at the right price. If achieved, this should lead to a thriving and successful organisation.

CASE STUDY

The mystery of marketing

Daniel Wilcock studies travel and tourism at college. As part of the course, his tutor asked him to find out what the 'man in the street' knew about marketing. He went about this by conducting market research among members of the public. He began by introducing himself and asking people if they would answer one question.

'Good morning, my name is Daniel and I am a student at Rushmore College. I am doing a project for my course. Would you mind answering one quick question for me please? Thank you.

'My question is: What do you think the term marketing means?'

Daniel asked one hundred adults. These were the results:

* 10% said it was connected with advertising
* 7% said it was something to do with selling
* 83% didn't know.

Daniel concluded that marketing is a mystery to most people.

Let us look at the concept of marketing in more detail.

* Is it just about advertising?

    No. Advertising is only one part of the marketing process. The confusion arises probably because we are subjected to many types of advertising attempting to persuade us what products we should buy.

* Is it just about selling?

    No. Again, like advertising, selling is only one part of marketing.

* Is it only used by big, international organisations?

    No. Marketing is carried out by organisations big and small alike. It should not just be restricted to the private sector either. Public and voluntary sector organisations should place a high priority on marketing as they too have customers.

* Is it used only for one-off projects?

    No. Marketing should be a continuous process, which involves keeping up to date with changing customer needs and expectations.

* Is it carried out by high-flying, energetic people in their twenties?

    No. It does help to have a natural, warm personality, however appropriate training provides the basis for anyone to work in marketing.

The marketing function is a crucial part of an organisation and is vital to its success:

* Forward thinking organisations recognise that marketing is part of the management process and rank it alongside other functions, such as research and development, customer service and finance.

* Failure to find out what customers want is to court disaster. It is of paramount importance to identify what existing and potential customers want. One of the marketing function's main tasks is to carry out extensive market research to determine whether an organisation is meeting customer needs.

* Market research enables travel and tourism organisations to keep up to date with existing and future fashions and trends. New products and services can be developed to meet future expectations. This keeps an organisation ahead of the competition.

* Travel and tourism organisations may have different aims and objectives. For example, a tour operator's main aim is to make a profit whereas a local authority tourist information office's main aim may be to encourage as many visitors to the area as possible. Either way, an organisation's marketing objectives must be geared towards its aims and objectives.

Skills practice

Provide your own definition of marketing, making it easy to understand and easy to remember.

The marketing process

The following are the steps in the marketing process:

Figure 5.1 The marketing process

* *Get to know your customer* To do this you need to find out:
    * What they want

- How much are they willing to spend
- Where they come from
- What they feel is value for money
- How they want to be treated.

The information you obtain about your customers can help define exactly what they want.

✳ *Develop your product* Once you know what customers want, products and services can be tailored to suit their needs at the right price.

✳ *Promoting your product* Making customers aware of the products and services on offer will ensure they have the opportunity of buying what they want.

✳ *Evaluating your product* Marketing is a continuous process and as customers' needs may change, it is essential to evaluate each stage of the marketing process in terms of the following questions:

- Have customers' needs changed?
- What are competitors selling?
- Are promotion campaigns reaching customers effectively?

Think about it

Choose a travel and tourism organisation you are familiar with. What benefits would it accrue if it developed an effective marketing policy?

The key stages of the marketing process

Marketing aims and objectives

Travel and tourism organisations need to have aims and objectives which define what they want to achieve and how they are going to achieve them.

Some organisations adopt a mission statement, which is a brief statement about their purpose. For example, the mission statement of the Disney Corporation is 'We are in the business of making

people happy', and the British Airways mission statement is 'We aim to be the world's favourite airline'. A travel agent's mission statement could be 'To sell dreams'.

Some management consultants think that mission statements are nothing more than a public relations exercise to promote a positive image of the organisation. However, what a mission statement can do is set out the general direction an organisation wants to take. The aims and objectives give a more specific framework for an organisation developing its mission statement.

Skills practice

Produce a mission statement for the following organisations making sure the statements have impact and are easy to remember.

- Thomas Cook
- Virgin Airlines
- The English Tourism Council
- Alton Towers
- National Express.

Aims and objectives

Having produced a mission statement as part of its marketing objectives, an organisation should then produce more specific aims and objectives.

The aim of an organisation sets out the overall purpose, for example to provide excellent customer service or to develop new products. The objectives are what is specifically needed to achieve the aim.

To be effective, objectives must be 'SMART':

Specific	It must be well defined
Measurable	It must quantify the objectives
Achievable	The objectives must be achieved with the resources available
Realistic	They must achieve the desired goal
Timed	They must be achieved within a certain timescale.

The following example illustrates an organisation's mission, aims and marketing objectives.

Happy Valley Holidays

Mission statement

> We are in the business of making dreams come true for all our customers.

Aim   **To ensure all staff are fully proficient in selling these dreams by:**

Objective **Ensuring that all staff undergo customer service training and gain the Welcome Host award by the end of the year**

Aim   **To promote exclusive products and raise customer awareness by:**

Objective **Distributing 10,000 high-quality brochures to existing and potential customers over the next three months**

Aim   **To provide first class-holidays by:**

Objective **Ensuring that all holiday destinations are thoroughly researched and approved by tour operators**

Skills practice

Devise a series of aims and objectives for a travel and tourism organisation of your choice, using the format above.

Market research

Market research enables travel and tourism organisations to provide the right products to their customers.

It provides information on customers' attitudes and wants. It helps organisations plan for future development, identify new markets and find solutions to any problems that have been identified from analysis of the research data.

Market research helps managers make effective marketing decisions based on facts, not guesswork. Feedback from market research may show why some people may prefer a competitor's products. It may also show why some products are more popular than others, or it may identify the very latest trends in customer spending.

A careful analysis of market research data will show whether or not an organisation's aims and objectives are being met.

A structured marketing research approach can help travel and tourism organisations do the following:

* Provide the right products for their customers

* Identify any problems and work out solutions

* Demonstrate to customers that their views are acted upon

* Plan future development in the knowledge there is a market for their products

* Identify new market opportunities based on customer needs.

Think about it

Why is it important that travel and tourism organisations produce a set of aims and objectives? Under what circumstances do you think these aims and objectives could change?

Types of research

Qualitative research

This method of research asks people to express their opinions and feelings. It uses open questions such as 'Why do you travel with us?' or 'What type of accommodation do you prefer?'

This type of research can produce very useful information that can be extracted, analysed and used by an organisation to provide customers with what they want.

The data can include what people think and feel about an organisation's products and services, their suggestions for improvements and their general impressions of the organisation.

However, there will be many different opinions given by many different people. This makes the analysis of the information gathered more complicated. An example could be research into what people think and feel about Disneyland Paris. They may be asked about what makes them go there (motivation), how they feel about its location, and what they think about the customer service (attitudes).

Quantitative research

Quantitative research produces factual information by asking closed questions, which only require a simple 'yes' or 'no' answer. This makes any analysis relatively easy.

This kind of research involves compiling statistics and records what customers do at Disneyland Paris, for example gathering information on the number of rides they went on, the number of times they went on them, the number of people they were with and the number of times they have been there.

Market research methods

Travel and tourism organisations need basic information about their customers, so that they know what groups to target and what products to provide.

The information on customer characteristics should include:

If there is sufficient accurate knowledge about customers, the right decisions can be made about pricing, the type of product to provide and the most effective advertising to adopt.

Market research involves collecting and analysing information. There are two types of research for doing this: primary research and secondary research.

Primary research, also known as field research, involves collecting and analysing information first hand, by using face-to-face interviews and surveys. The information collected is known as primary data.

This kind of research has several *advantages*: the data is original and up to date; it focuses on the population in question, and it is specific on what needs to be researched.

There are however certain *disadvantages* to this method of research. It can be expensive, in terms of payment to interviewers or the postage costs of thousands of questionnaires. It can also take a long time to collect and has to be managed and monitored throughout.

Secondary research is also known as desk research. It uses second-hand data, that is using material that has already been published. Examples include books, newspaper articles, annual reports, company accounts and government reports.

Figure 5.2 Market research is used to compile details of customers for marketing products to them

The *advantages* of using secondary research include the wide range of data available, which is usually free, as in the case of obtaining it from the resources of a public library.

There are however certain *disadvantages* to using secondary research. It can become out of date quickly, which may mean that statistics and facts are not relevant to the research being undertaken. The information may not specifically refer to the issue you are investigating, so you may have to make do with something that is similar rather than exact. Also there are questions whether this kind of research is reliable, whether the information has been analysed properly and whether the research methods used were valid.

Skills practice

Using your own research skills (either using the Internet or reports), try and find out how one major travel and tourism organisation carries out its primary and secondary research.

Let us now look in more detail at the **primary research methods** used in marketing.
Travel and tourism organisations may use the following primary research methods for collecting market research data:

* Surveys, by using face-to-face, postal and telephone methods
* Focus groups
* Observation
* Internet.

Surveys

For surveys to be effective you need to find out what or who the target market or sample is. It could be people over a certain age, individuals between the ages of twenty and thirty years, women, or business people.

A sample is the total number of people to be interviewed. For example, if Disneyland Paris decided to interview a 10 per cent sample of visitors and the total 'population' on the day of sampling was 10,000, then one thousand interviews would need to be carried out. This would be very time-consuming and expensive, in terms of paying the interviewers. However, it is more practical and more cost-effective than interviewing ten thousand people.

There are different ways of conducting a survey.

Personal surveys

Personal surveys involve face-to-face interviews with either individuals or groups of people. An interviewer puts questions to members of the public, whose answers and responses are recorded.

As well as using a formal set of questions, an interviewer may also raise certain relevant topics to encourage further discussion and to elicit more information. Further questions can be asked as the discussion progresses.

Personal surveys can produce valuable quantitative data, such as the occupation of the respondent, age, income and spending habits.

Using structured questionnaires to gather information from customers enables an organisation to find out what their customers want and gives customers the opportunity to air their views about the organisation.

Questionnaires need to be designed so that the required information is obtained. There are a number of basic rules to follow:

* Questions must be kept simple and easy to understand
* Questions about age and marital status should be asked at the end of the interview when a relationship has been built up with the interviewee
* Questions should be relevant and specific to the subject you want to find out about
* Ask no more than eight questions, otherwise the interviewee may get bored, and probably has very little time to spend answering questions
* Ask open questions in order to elicit more information by using the form of questions which ask 'What?', 'Why?', 'How?' or 'When?' For example, 'What do you look for when booking a holiday?'
* Make sure the sample is large enough so that your results are valid
* Do not ask questions that turn out to be a memory test, for example 'During your first week on holiday how many times did your holiday representative visit you and tell you about the local area and the excursions on offer?'

* Always greet and introduce yourself to the interviewee and explain to them what your survey is about. And don't forget to thank them at the end of the interview!

Always test or 'pilot' a questionnaire to check that the right questions are being asked and that they are easily understood.

There are two types of questions to be asked on questionnaires: closed and open questions.

* *Closed questions* are used mainly for quantitative research and require only a 'yes' or 'no' answer. They can therefore be answered quickly and the responses ticked against tick boxes. An analysis of the responses is then relatively easy.

* *Open questions* are asked when respondents are required to express an opinion and show their feelings about what they are being asked. These are examples of open questions:

'What did you think about your accommodation?'
'What improvements could we make to ensure your holiday is even better next time?'
'How good was your holiday representative?'

Skills practice

1 Below is an example of an ineffective questionnaire. Analyse it and explain why you think it is ineffective. Discuss your findings with your group.

Travel and Tourism Questionnaire

I am doing a survey. Can I ask you some questions?

1 Are you married?
2 How old are you?
3 How many children have you got?
4 Do you smoke?
5 How much would you pay for a holiday in Spain?
6 How much did you spend on food on the first day of your holiday?
7 Don't you agree that air travel nowadays is far more cost effective than travelling by train?
8 Who decides where you go on holiday?
9 How much do you earn per year?
10 Why do you think holidays abroad are better than those in the UK?

---

2 Now devise an effective questionnaire related to travel and tourism, using the guidelines on questionnaire design.

The *advantages* of a personal survey are:

* The interviewer can explain anything the interviewee is not sure of

* The pace of questioning can encourage spontaneous responses

* Good response rates are possible

* Uniformity of interview technique and questions makes quantitative analysis of the data possible

* Unlike a postal survey, there is no uncertainty over who actually answers the questions.

The *disadvantages* of a personal survey are:

* The interview is expensive in that interviewers have to be paid, as well as having to be fully trained, which is an additional expense

* Personal surveys are time-consuming, which can result in only a small, unrepresentative sample being obtained in the time available

* Respondents may be limited by closed questions, and not have the opportunity to express their feelings

* Respondents may be wary of being interviewed and may not have much time to spend, so they quickly answer the questions just to escape

* The interaction between respondent and interviewer may influence the answers interviewees give, which may distort the data collected.

Postal surveys

Market research is often conducted through the post. This is done by selecting people identified as a target market and posting questionnaires to them which they are asked to fill in. A stamped-addressed envelope is included, to encourage the targeted people to respond; otherwise the response level is likely to be low.

Postal surveys are used to target many people in a very short time. No interviewers are needed and no training is required, so there are no wages to pay for interviewers and less time is spent than doing face-to-face interviews.

Those targeted by the survey can be encouraged to respond by being offered incentives, such as the opportunity to win a free holiday in America if they complete the questionnaire.

Many travel and tourism organisations use this method of market research to find out if customers were satisfied with the level of service they received whilst on holiday or if the accommodation, transfers and resort were satisfactory.

Postal surveys can be distributed in a number of ways:

* Travel and tourism organisations, such as travel agents or tour operators, post them to their customers as soon as they have returned from holiday

* Facilities, such as hotels or tourist attractions like theme parks, may have questionnaires on site at the reception area, where they can be picked up, filled in and posted back

* Air cabin crew or couriers may hand out questionnaires to holidaymakers or travellers at the end of a holiday or journey for them to be filled in by the customers and posted back to the organisation.

The *advantages* of postal surveys are:

* A large number of people can be targeted

* It is relatively cheap to collect the data

* There is no interviewer to influence the results

* They are easy to set up and administer

* The respondents have time to consider their answers and consult others if necessary.

The *disadvantages* of postal surveys are:

* The response rate is very low, even with the offer of incentives

* There is no control over who actually completes the questionnaire

* There is no way to find out if respondents have understood the questions

* The sample of responses may be unrepresentative of the total market, that is responses may be largely from people who have strong opinions on the topic

* You do not get spontaneous responses to the questions.

Skills practice

Devise a postal questionnaire that will give you the information you want and will motivate people to complete it.

One problem with postal surveys is that they may not provide genuine responses

Telephone surveys

There are travel and tourism organisations which conduct telephone surveys in order to get quick responses to the questions they need to ask existing and potential customers.

One of the problems with telephone surveys is that the targeted person may suspect that the organisation is trying to sell something. To solve this the telephone survey might be introduced in this way:

'Good morning, my name is Peter Hayward and I am a student at the Dukeries College. I am conducting a survey as part of my course on the type of holidays people in the area take. Would you mind answering a few simple questions? I won't take up too much of your time.'

The request is simple and has been asked in a very polite manner without applying pressure. However, remember that the respondent may not have much time to answer the questions, so the responses may be ill-considered.

The *advantages* of telephone surveys are:

✳ Good response rates are possible

✳ Many interviews covering a vast geographical area can be carried out in a short space of time

✳ There are no transport costs for sending interviewers to locations to conduct interviews

✳ The costs per interview are relatively low.

The *disadvantages* of telephone surveys are:

✳ People distrust being interviewed on the phone by someone they don't know

✳ Telephone interviewers may be discouraged by a high level of negative responses, and lose enthusiasm and willingness to make further calls

✳ Interviewers must be trained in the skills of conducting telephone surveys, which adds to the cost.

Skills practice

Devise a script for a telephone survey interview that avoids giving people the impression that you are trying to sell them something. Then phone someone you know, who is not so familiar with your voice to recognise you, and test out the script on them. Once you have had a response, tell them who you are and the reason you were making the call.

Trying to conduct a survey over the phone can arouse suspicion among respondents

Focus groups

Travel and tourism organisations use focus groups of customers to find out what they think and feel about their organisation. This is qualitative research and it works in the following way. A group of no more than twelve people are selected, they meet together and are interviewed for about an hour by an experienced interviewer. Each of them is asked to talk about their thoughts and feelings about a particular topic, such as an existing or future product an organisation is developing and promoting. These responses are analysed and a report is written on the conclusions that may have a bearing on an organisation's decision making.

You may doubt whether a relatively small group of people can provide an organisation with sufficient feedback to base its decisions on. However, focus groups are known to work and can influence organisations when it comes to improving customer service or dealing with specific issues like pricing policies.

The *advantages* of focus groups:

* People have the time to reflect and to interact with one another, revealing what they really think and feel about certain things

* They are the source of very useful qualitative information.

The *disadvantages* of focus groups are:
* It is an expensive way of gathering information, in terms of the costs of an interviewer and analysing the information gathered

* The high costs of using this method means it is used mainly by large organisations, however it can be a worthwhile investment for organisations of any size.

Skills practice

Many travel and tourism organisations use focus groups to find out what their customers expect and want from them. Talk to your tutor or make enquiries at travel and tourism organisations in your area to find out if they are organising a focus group in the near future and whether you can attend to observe what goes on.

Observation

Observation is a method of primary research used by many travel and tourism organisations. Theme parks, exhibition centres and tourist attractions use it to observe customer behaviour, traffic flow or to monitor events.

There are two types of observation: direct observation and participant observation.

Direct observation

Direct observation is carried out by a researcher who observes and records the behaviour of individuals and groups as they go about their business. In travel and tourism this can involve:

* Watching and listening to the receptionist at a tourist information centre

* Observing a holiday representative giving a welcome speech.

Direct observation can also be carried out through accessing closed circuit television (CCTV), for example in shopping centres, hotels and theme parks.

Participant observation

In using this method a researcher becomes part of the group being studied in order to find out how a group works. In the case of travel and tourism staff, part of their job may be to 'eavesdrop' on customers' conversations to find out what they think and feel about the products and services being delivered. The value of this is that you are more likely to find out more from these open and honest responses than from a formal interview.

Observation plays a part in discovering what the competition is offering. One way of doing this is to buy a competitor's products or services. For example, a travel agent may book a holiday through another travel agent or a hotelier may stay at a competitor's hotel to find out more about what they are offering. They may discover that there are certain features of the products or services that they can incorporate into their own business or they may need to strengthen certain ones in their own in order to compete.

The *advantages* of observation are:

* You can observe what people actually do, not what they say they do

Overhearing what customers are saying about a company's holiday products can provide useful feedback

✱ People are observed in their own environment and so act as they normally do

✱ Observation can take place over a period of time, which allows for any changes in groups or situations to be observed.

Think about it

As a group, think about any disadvantages of using observation as a method of market research.

The Internet

Market researchers use the Internet to find out what customers' views are about organisations. Travel and tourism organisations use it to access the vast amounts of useful information on the industry, for example what products and services competitors are offering. One advantage is that it is easy to access the relevant site, ask questions and analyse the responses.

A huge amount of secondary information is available on the Internet and it is easy to access it. It is certainly less time-consuming than researching books and reports in the library.

Many travel and tourism organisations also sell their products on the Internet. They do this by accessing their own database of customers who order catalogues and purchase the products and services of the organisation. The database also provides an opportunity to target customers for doing market research on existing or new products. This can be a valuable source of research.

Think about it

The Internet has made communication so much easier and is a vast source of information which can be used for your studies.

How do you use the Internet for research purposes? How could you use it when finding out about market research or marketing in general?

Mission statement This is a statement made by an organisation about the purpose behind what they do. For example, an organisation's purpose may be to bring low-cost holidays to greater numbers of people.

Aims An aim is the overall plan an organisation has for its business.

Objectives These are the specific actions that are to be taken to achieve the aims.

Saga specialises in holidays for the over-50s

Market segmentation

A particular market, such as travel and tourism, can be segmented into different groups of customers according to certain interests and characteristics. In doing this the industry identifies the types of people who have a need for certain products and services. In this way a travel and tourism organisation can more clearly identify what certain customers want and need and so make the effort to satisfy them. By identifying customers and their wants and needs, the organisations can advertise and promote their products more effectively to particular groups of people, rather than use the 'hit and hope' advertising strategy.

There are several ways of dividing, or segmenting, the market:

* Age
* Life cycle
* Social group
* Lifestyle.

This enables organisations to build up a profile of their customers.

Age

Different age groups tend to have different interests, wants and needs. For example, many senior citizens want to take day trips to the seaside and enjoy the company of others on the trip. Many want to spend winter in warmer climates, such as in Spain. In recognition of this tour operators promote six-week stays in Majorca at reduced prices in January and February.

Saga Holidays is one organisation which specialises in holidays for people over the age of

fifty. From its beginnings in 1952, Saga Holidays has grown to become an international organisation, offering all types of holidays for older people with varying levels of income. A magazine, car insurance and a radio station have all been established as part of the organisation.

Younger people, aged between 18 and 30, tend to prefer a different type of holiday. They want to meet people, dance and party every night, and generally have a fun-packed time. An organisation called Club 18–30 targets this market with holidays to places such as Malia in Crete. Beach barbecues, wet 'T' shirt competitions and all-night parties are the format for this type of holiday.

Club 18–30 specialises in holidays for young people

This age group may also enjoy adventure holidays which include trekking in the Himalayas or scuba diving in the Caribbean.

Skills practice

Find examples of travel and tourism organisations that specifically target their products and services to specific age groups.

Life cycle

Travel and tourism organisations can focus on their customers by targeting the life cycle categories of a market. This involves segmenting or categorising customers into one of nine stages of their life. The life-cycle categories of customers can be determined through market research, so that travel and tourism organisations target the appropriate products and services to the customers at whatever point in the life cycle they are at.

The life-cycle categories, along with their likely preferences, are shown below:

1 **Bachelors/spinsters** Young single people with a reasonable level of disposable income. They enjoy lots of nightlife, music and package holidays to Spain and Greece.

2 **Newlyweds, partners living together** They have a higher disposable income. Their interests include eating out regularly and holidays in Florida, the Far East and India.

3 **Full nest 1** Young couple/married/living together, youngest child less than six years old. They enjoy family trips to the zoo and self-catering holidays.

4 **Full nest 2** Young couples with children, youngest over six years. Lower disposable income therefore less money to spend on holidays.

5 **Full nest 3** Older couple with older children who are still dependent, probably studying. Lower disposable income. Leisure activities are centred on the home.

6 **Empty nest 1** Older couples, no children or children have left home and independent. Disposable income less restricted. Weekend breaks to London, Edinburgh or Paris. Holidays abroad, perhaps twice a year.

7 **Empty nest 2** Older couples, chief earner retired. Income becomes restricted once again. Leisure activities centred around home.

8 **Solitary survivor 1** Single/widowed person. Restricted income. Home-based leisure activities.

9 **Solitary survivor 2** Single person retired. Little spare cash. Little to spend on leisure time activities.

Skills practice

How can travel and tourism organisations use the life-cycle category method of research to target their markets? Give examples.

Of course there are exceptions to the above. Many people are now taking early retirement with a reasonable pension and income that enables them to afford holidays abroad after retirement.

Social group

This method of researching the market according to the social group is also known as socio-economic grouping. It categorises people according to occupation and income. In general, people who have similar jobs and similar incomes tend to have similar lifestyles and tastes.

The social group classification and type of holidays is as follows:

* **Group A** Lawyers, chief executives, directors. Expensive holidays, exclusive golf clubs.

* **Group B** Doctors, teachers, managers. All-inclusive holidays.

* **Group C1** Supervisors, junior managers. Fly/drive holidays.

* **Group C2** Plumbers, electricians. Package holidays.

* **Group D** Drivers, postal workers, porters. Cheaper package holidays.

* **Group E** Casual workers, students, people who are unemployed. Coach holidays, day trips.

It is assumed that those who belong to particular categories have similar amounts of disposable income and spending habits. It is also assumed that people in Group A have the highest level of disposable income. However, this is not always the case. There are always anomalies in making generalisations and classifying groups. For example, people in Groups C1 and C2 may have a higher disposal income than those in A and B, a larger part of whose income may be spent on private education for their children or private health care for the family.

Some of those in Group A may not always remain in that group, for example there may be cases of some falling into other groups, even into Group E if, for example, they are made redundant.

This classification system is for marketing purposes only. Travel and tourism organisations use it to select the market segments that match their products and services.

Lifestyle

Another method of segmenting the market is to categorise people according to their lifestyles, that is the way they live, their interests, opinions and leisure activities.

An example of this occurred in the 1980s when groups were categorised in distinctive ways using terms that became catchphrases. For example, in the 1980s the term 'Yuppie' stood for 'Young urban professional', that is a highly successful single person earning a large salary and who could afford to buy luxury goods and services such as upmarket cars and exotic holidays. Another was the designation of 'Dinkies', who were 'Double income no kids', that is young couples between the age of twenty-five and thirty with no children and a high level of disposable income.

Travel and tourism organisations take the lifestyles of their customers into account when developing their advertising campaigns, so that these are aimed at the right target market. Banks

promoting credit cards and insurance companies promoting car insurance do the same thing.

A lifestyle classification was developed in the 1980s called ACORN –'A Classification of Residential Neighbourhoods – which classified people into the following categories:

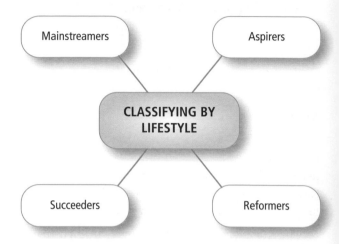

Figure 5.3 This is the ACORN classification of people into lifestyles that can be used by tourist organisations for targeting products to appropriate customers

* **Mainstreamers** These are people who lead a conventional lifestyle, who buy well-known product brands such as Adidas sportswear. They are the biggest of the four categories, accounting for about 40 per cent of the population. Their interests include watching television, walking, gardening.

* **Aspirers** They tend to be entrepreneurs who take risks and spend their money on exclusive and expensive products like holidays in the Caribbean or fast cars. Their hobbies include power-boat racing, wind surfing and scuba diving.

* **Succeeders** They have succeeded in achieving their ambitions and can afford a lifestyle that matches their success.

* **Reformers** They are concerned with the quality of life and the environment. Probably the most educated of the four groups, they may, for example, join 'pressure groups' to influence

decision-making when it comes to issues like planning permission and housing development that may affect the environment.

Skills practice

What type of products and services could travel and tourism organisations promote to the people in each of these lifestyle categories?

Analysing the internal and external business environment

SWOT analysis

Travel and tourism organisations need to know how well they are performing. One way they can do this is through a SWOT analysis. They can use this method of analysis to examine the internal factors that may affect an organisation's success. The main purpose of the analysis is to discover what factors cause success or failure in the market in which the organisation is competing. What emerges from the analysis can help the organisation to focus on what it needs to do to improve performance.

A SWOT analysis involves examining an organisation's internal and external environment:

* **Strengths** These are the things that an organisation does well. An organisation needs to maintain and build on these strengths to make sure its products and services are competitive.

* **Weaknesses** These are the problems in an organisation that affect its performance in providing the appropriate products and services and competing effectively. An organisation needs to find ways of overcoming these weaknesses.

* **Opportunities** An organisation needs to work out how it can capitalise on new opportunities to develop new products and attract new customers.

* **Threats** These are anything that may damage the performance or competitive position of an organisation. An organisation needs to limit these threats to avoid damaging effects to its financial success.

An organisation needs to do something about its strengths and weaknesses, which are internal factors; for example, it can employ experienced and qualified staff (strengths) and improve poor facilities (weaknesses).

Opportunities and threats are external factors outside the control of the organisation, such as the development of new markets (opportunities) and the lack of finance (threats).

An organisation that examines itself through a SWOT should discover the following:

* The strengths that can be built on

* The weaknesses that can be overcome

* The opportunities that can be taken advantage of

* The threats to be aware of and eliminated.

The SWOT analysis should tell an organisation what action it needs to take to improve its performance and increase its share of the market.

CASE STUDY

SWOT analysis: Sunshine Holidays

Based in York, Sunshine Holidays has been in business as a tour operator for ten years. During that time it has built up a reputation for providing package tours, mainly for family groups to places like Italy, Spain and France.

However, with the advent of low-cost flights and the trend towards more and more people booking holidays via the Internet, business has slowed down, and as a result profits have slumped.

Sunshine Holidays are worried because, as a family business, cutbacks may have to be made.

Carry out a SWOT analysis for Sunshine Holidays. Draw conclusions from the analysis about what action the company needs to take to become a successful business again.

Skills practice

Carry out a SWOT analysis of a travel and tourism organisation of your choice and prepare a report based on your findings that will determine future policy and strategies for your chosen organisation.

PEST analysis

The external influences on a business environment are analysed by using a PEST analysis (also known as a STEP analysis). This form of analysis takes into account the political, economic, social and technological factors that may affect an organisation's business activities. The main purpose is to analyse the external pressures of an organisation which may affect its opportunities and threats and from that to work out future strategies and policies.

The following are the aspects of the external environment that an organisation needs to consider in making a PEST analysis.

✱ **Political** This includes government legislation, taxation, EU rules and regulations, interest rates, funding levels, licensing laws.

✱ **Economic** This takes into account inflation, employment levels, disposable income, exchange rates, recession.

✱ **Social** This takes account of early retirement, changes in lifestyle, shorter working week, education, demographic changes, holiday entitlement, changes in working practices.

✱ **Technological** This looks at computerised reservation systems, the Internet, developments in transport systems, global communications, mobile phones, Internet banking.

Developing a marketing mix

The 'marketing mix' comprises the key elements of products an organisation offers to meet customer needs and expectations. Two groups make up a market: existing and potential customers who want to buy the products and services on offer; organisations that want to sell the products and services to meet the buyers' needs and expectations.

Four factors are involved in the marketing mix: product, price, place and promotion; these are known as the 4 Ps. Travel and tourism organisations need to take these into account when meeting the needs and expectations of their customers.

Figure 5.4 The marketing mix

Getting the marketing mix right can help increase business and boost sales. This involves getting the right product in the right place at the right price using the right type of promotion. A successful marketing mix gains more customers and increases the likelihood of success.

Product

A product can be described as the goods and services provided by organisations. The customers' needs are satisfied by buying the product. In the travel and tourism industry products include weekend breaks, theme parks, package holidays, hotels, museums, souvenirs, food and drink.

The products in travel and tourism are both tangible and intangible. A tangible product is one you can see, such as a hotel; an intangible product is one you cannot see, such as a package holiday, which is something you experience. Travel and tourism products are also perishable; for example, a ticket for a journey to Paris on Eurostar on a particular day that is not sold on that day cannot be resold the next day.

There is also no guarantee that travel and tourism products will give you the same experience every time. A holiday in Majorca one year when the weather is superb may be completely different the next because the weather is so poor.

What travel and tourism organisations need to get right every time is the way they treat their customers, otherwise they will lose them.

When selling their products, travel and tourism organisations must know what their customers want and hope to experience. A family holiday abroad should be enjoyable and excellent value for money. There should be a variety of activities for all the family to take part in a safe and secure environment. The experience should be happy, relaxed, and even exciting.

Organisations also need to be continuously developing their products to offer more options and improvements on existing ones, in order to retain their customers. They need to make sure their customers do not lose interest in what they have to offer. Travel and tourism is a highly competitive industry, and if organisations don't develop new products to meet customers' changing needs, many of those customers will look elsewhere for what they want – i.e. to a rival.

Customer satisfaction

There are a several ways travel and tourism customers can be satisfied:

* *Quality of customer service* If a travel agent treats a customer badly, the customer might complain, not return or do both. This emphasises the importance of customer-service training for all staff.

* *Standard of facilities* Nowadays people expect value for money not poor quality goods or outdated facilities.

* *Atmosphere* Facilities should be bright, warm and welcoming. This should be matched by the attitude and appearance of staff.

Positioning

An organisation can *position* itself in a particular market by targeting specific types of customers. For example, Alton Towers has strongly positioned itself in the theme park and entertainments market, and easyJet has positioned itself very favourably in the low-cost airline market.

If travel and tourism organisations can establish a strong market position it means their products and services can be easily identified as meeting the needs of customers in that market.

Organisations position themselves in the market according to their product and customers, as in the case of a theme park

Identify five travel and tourism organisations that have positioned themselves in certain markets and describe the markets in which they operate.

The Boston Matrix

Travel and tourism managers use the Boston Matrix method to analyse strategies to ensure future survival and expansion. It is done by judging how the organisation's current products and services are performing. It also helps identify any changes that have to be made to ensure future success.

The Boston Matrix, developed by the Boston Consulting Group in the United States, breaks products down into four categories.

* **Star products** These are products with a large share of a high-growth market and they have the greatest future potential. Already successful, they are in the growth phase of the product life cycle. When the market matures, they will be the 'cash cows' of the business. Although they are not likely to contribute much to current cash flow due to the heavy investment required to develop them, they need to be encouraged. The appropriate strategy is therefore to build the brand or product. Sales must be increased. If possible, so too should market share. Competition needs to be fought off. If possible, the product should have the largest share of the market since this will be the most profitable position in the long term.

* **Problem children products** This group might have future potential as they are in growth markets, but their sales are not particularly good.

  Managers have to make difficult decisions about 'problem children' products. They have three main choices.

  1 *Build the product or brand* In putting extra resources into the product, managers are gambling that the product will increase its market share and its growth.
  2 *Harvesting* This means maximising profit and cash flow, probably by raising prices and cutting market spending. Sales are likely to fall, but the profit per unit sold will increase by a larger percentage, giving the rise in profit.
  3 *Divestment* This means either dropping the product or selling it to another business.

* **Cash cow products** Those products which are able to generate funds, possibly to support other products. They are mature products with a stable market share.

  Cash cows are highly valuable to an organisation. They are likely to be in the maturity phase or saturation phase of the product life cycle. With little need for investment, the product can be milked for cash. This provides the finance for investment in other products of the organisation, in particular 'star' products. Some problem children products also need investment. In some industries, cash cows provide the funds for large research and development budgets for products of the future.

  Cash cows still need defending from competition, however. So promotion is an important part of the defensive strategy for a cash cow. Some investment may also be needed to finance extension strategies for the product. Overall though, the most appropriate strategy for cash cows is holding – i.e. spending just enough on promotion and product development to maintain sales and market share.

* **Dog products** These are products in decline. They provide little or no cash flow or profit to an organisation. In many cases the most appropriate strategy to adopt is divestment, either selling it to another business or dropping the product altogether. However, some dogs are worth harvesting if they are still profitable. This means maximising profit and cash flow, probably by raising prices and cutting marketing spending.

Travel and tourism organisations must avoid their product mix having too many products within each category. Obviously, organisations do not want lots of 'dogs' but they should also avoid having too many 'stars' and 'problem children'. Products on the left-hand side of Figure 5.5 are in the early stages of the product life cycle and are in growing markets, but the cost of developing and promoting them will not yet have been recovered.

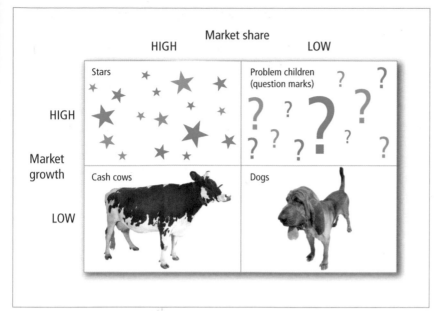

Market share

HIGH   LOW

Stars

Problem children
(question marks)

HIGH

Market
growth

LOW

Cash cows

Dogs

Figure 5.5 The Boston Matrix

This will drain the organisation's resources. Balancing these with 'cash cows' will mean that the revenue from the 'cash cows' can be used to support products in a growing market.

The development cost of 'cash cows' is likely to have already been recovered and promotional costs should be low relative to sales. This does not mean, though, that organisations would want lots of 'cash cows' and few 'problem children' and 'stars'. This is because many of the 'stars' and perhaps some 'problem children' might become the 'cash cows' of the future.

Product life cycle

The product life cycle shows the different stages in the life of a product and the sales that can be expected at each stage.

Some products and services may be very popular and sell very well for a short while. Eventually however they will lose their popularity as all products tend to do, unless the organisation can revamp the product's image and possibly find a new market. For example, the Butlins holiday camps before and after the Second World War were extremely popular until competition from overseas package holidays in the 1960s led to declining sales. As a result they were revamped into holiday centres with new and more modern facilities. There was even a name change from Butlins holiday camps to a more exciting and

modern 'Funcoast World'. The following are the stages in the product life cycle:

1 **Development** This is when the product is in the design stage and is not yet on the market. No sales are made at this stage. Ideas are tested, market research is carried out and a decision to launch the product is taken. Travel and tourism organisations invest a huge amount of money on research and development in the hope that this investment will lead to a popular and profitable product. Many new products never get beyond the developmental stage if it is felt that they won't sell sufficiently well to make a profit.

2 **Introduction** This is when the product is launched. Organisations like to ensure this stage lasts as little as possible because costs are still being incurred on activities such as advertising and promotion. What's more, it also takes time for customers to gain confidence in new products.

3 **Growth** Rapid growth is likely as the product becomes established in the market. This should lead to profits being made although at this stage competitors may launch their own version of the product, so a fall in sales could take place.

4 **Maturity** Sales tend to level off as the product becomes established. In addition, competitors may charge less for their product as they didn't have to cover developmental costs – these were borne by the original manufacturer. Travel and tourism organisations at this stage need to decide either to let the product die or re-model it (as in the case of Butlins holiday camps).

5 **Saturation** Sales have reached a plateau and at this stage more and more competitors have entered the market, which means there is no longer room for growth.

6 **Decline** When new products appear, the original market goes into decline. This is usually due to new technology, a change in customers'

tastes or increased competition. The product will be eventually withdrawn from the market.

There are however various techniques that travel and tourism organisations can introduce in order to extend the life cycle of a product.

These include special offers on price, extra promotion and re-modelling the product so that it appeals to more people. For example, holidays in Scotland were once only geared to walking in the Orkney and Shetland Isles. A far bigger market was tapped when city breaks to Edinburgh and Glasgow were developed, skiing in the Cairngorms was promoted and even wedding weekends to Gretna Green were introduced!

Place

The place refers to the location where travel and tourism activities take place and how the products and services are distributed to the customer. This is the chain of distribution.

If facilities such as hotels, tourist information centres or travel agencies are not easily accessible to customers, they will not be successful. It is essential that facilities in the travel and tourism industry are located near to well-populated areas where customers and potential customers live or work. That's why restaurants, travel agents, concert halls and museums usually have a town or city centre location.

Good signposting and sufficient car parking spaces are also important, along with transport links to facilities.

Location

The location of facilities in the travel and tourism industry is vital for the success of the products and services being sold. An example are hotels. These are located in various places: city centres, the outskirts of town, at the seaside, next to airports or near motorways.

This is because they serve the needs of many different types of customers, such as holidaymakers, business people, sales representatives and people visiting friends and relatives. The following lists the location of hotels and the type of customers who use them according to their needs:

* City centre hotels   Business people, tourists
* Seaside hotels   Holidaymakers
* Motorway hotels   Travelling sales representatives
* Airport hotels   'Early fliers', that is people who have to catch early morning flights.

An example of a location with many visitor attractions is Blackpool Pleasure Beach. This is located in a town which has various other attractions, such as:

* Blackpool Tower
* Illuminations
* Promenade
* Seven miles of golden sands
* Zoo.

Blackpool beach

Blackpool is well served by the motorway network and has accommodation that includes hotels, guesthouses and bed and breakfasts. You can even use it as a stopping off place before moving on to the Lake District or Scotland. Accessibility to a location also refers to the facilities provided for people with disabilities.

Chain of distribution

Travel and tourism products and services need to be available to customers when they want them. Some products and services are delivered and paid for at the point of distribution, for example a meal in a restaurant.

However, some products and services are produced at a distance from the point of distribution, so a channel of distribution for making them available to customers is created. The channel includes:

✳ *Communication* This involves giving advice on ticket availability, information on flight times, directions to destinations. For example, booking a holiday in Great Yarmouth can be done through a travel agent or information about accommodation can be provided by tourist information centres. This distribution of information enables customers to book holidays and reach destinations with little effort. These are examples of communication channels for booking a hotel:

  • Use the phone to make a reservation
  • Use the same hotel chain or book a room through a tourist information centre
  • Use the Internet.

✳ *Stockholding* There needs to be sufficient products available for the customer to buy, for example a sufficient number of airline seats or hotel rooms.

✳ *Transportation* The product needs to be delivered to the right place at the right time.

✳ *Packaging and display* The product should be displayed to look attractive to customers, for example a display of holiday posters and brochures in a travel agency.

Many products are sold through third parties when it is not possible to sell direct. These intermediaries are usually retailers and wholesalers who deliver the product to the customer.

The chart below shows the distribution channel for a holiday.

Figure 5.6 Flow chart of the holiday distribution channel

This system of distribution has advantages and disadvantages:

The advantages of using a travel agent are a good location and loyal customers and a good image and a strong brand name. One of the disadvantages for a travel agent is high overheads for renting a high street location.

In the case of a tour operator the advantage is the organisation being reputable and well-known. A disadvantage is the lack of face-to-face contact with customers.

Price

When people pay for a product or service they want three things:

✳ A product that will satisfy their needs

✳ Value for money

✳ Quality goods.

There are certain factors that determine the price of a product.

✳ *Competition* The travel and tourism industry is highly competitive and in order to compete successfully a travel and tourism organisation will either have to lower the price or improve the product so that customers want to buy it.

* *Costs* Travel and tourism organisations have to cover the costs of providing products and services, otherwise they would make a loss. They will only stay in business if customers are prepared to pay the asking price of the products, so they have to arrive at a selling price which will ensure profits yet not put customers off.

  Price is the only part of the marketing mix that generates income; place, promotion and product all create costs. These costs can be covered if the right price is charged.

* *Supply and demand* The pricing of any product is governed by the laws of supply and demand.

  The law of supply is applicable to organisations, such as tour operators, that need to charge a certain price to make a profit. The smaller the profit the less prepared the tour operator is to supply the product.
  The law of demand states that the higher the price the less people will buy the product. Thus low prices mean more demand, but if prices go up sales go down. Arriving at the right price is far more complicated than just adding up all the costs then adding extra to create a profit margin. To complicate things even more, the travel and tourism industry charges different amounts for the same product at different times of year. For example, a holiday in France in August may be twice as much as the same holiday in March because of seasonal pricing policies.

* *The state of the economy* If the economy is going through a recession there will be less demand for products and services, particularly in the travel and tourism industry. This is because people will have less disposable income to spend on things like holidays. At the same time if the economy is booming, holiday sales usually rise because people have more money and can afford 'luxury' goods.

* *Organisation objectives* Private sector travel and tourism organisations aim to make a profit and gear their prices to achieve this. In contrast, public sector organisations, such as tourist information offices, mainly aim to provide a service.

Pricing strategies

Organisations need to be aware of the value customers put on a product or service. They have to find out what the customer is willing to pay. One way of doing this is to use market research to get a better idea of what prices to set for products and services. Once the organisation establishes this, there are certain pricing strategies they can implement to sell their products and services.

* *Market-led pricing* This is sometimes referred to as the 'going rate', whereby an organisation will match the prices the competition is charging. Obviously people shop around for the best deals, especially for holidays, and if they find a two-week holiday in Cyprus £200 cheaper in one travel agent than another, it is highly likely they will go for the cheaper price. However most organisations offer the same products at a similar price; this is market-led pricing.

  One risk with this pricing strategy is that profit margins are low, leading to lower overall profits.

* *One-off pricing* A travel and tourism organisation may have to work out a special price for a customer because there is no standard price for the product. Take as an example a businessman who wants to fly to China for a week, move on to Hong Kong for three days, and finally spend two days in Bombay to complete his business before flying back to England. This is a one-off trip for which the price cannot be worked out as if it was a package holiday. This is called one-off pricing as the product being provided is unique and cannot be provided 'off-the-shelf'.

* *Cost-plus pricing* Another method of arriving at a price is cost-plus pricing. An example is a hotel owner working out the costs of operating the business taking into account wages, heating, electricity, business rates and any loans. He then adds a flat rate or percentage for accommodation in order to arrive at a 'selling price' which will cover his costs and create a profit.

* *Peak and off-peak pricing (also known as variable pricing)* Many travel and tourism organisations adjust their prices for the same product at different times of the year, week or even day. For example, a ferry operator might halve its summer prices for trips between January and March.

Rail fares are varied according to the time of day people travel, for travelling the same distance. For example, a single rail ticket from Newark to London is £40 before nine o 'clock and £26 after nine o 'clock. The higher price is for peak-time travel, the lower price for off-peak travel.

* *Group discounts* Discounts are used to increase sales by making prices more attractive. One example is to offer groups of ten or more people going on holiday one free place. In the case of a school party of ten the teacher is allowed to travel free. Other examples are travel cards for students, concessions for senior citizens, and in some cases free travel for children under three years of age.

Discounting is a way of increasing business and boosting income.

* *Special offers* This is a popular device for attracting customers into shops and tempting them not only to buy the product on special offer, but also to buy products that are not on special offer.

An example is special discounts on late bookings, such as a flight-only £99 holiday to Majorca departing in two days time on Saturday, or two weeks in Crete, self-catering, £199 per person, departing next week. These discounts are aimed at filling the plane, commonly known as putting 'bums on seats'. Someone on such a discount may find themselves on the plane sitting next to someone who has paid twice as much, because they booked before the special offer was made.

* *Market penetration pricing* Another pricing strategy is that of using products as 'loss leaders'. The idea is to set a low price for a new product to tempt customers to switch from an existing competing brand. This is a long-term pricing policy, in that the low price has to be maintained for a sufficient period of time before adjusting it upwards, as to adjust it too soon risks upsetting customers.

Market penetration should not be seen as a one-off promotion, simply aimed at increasing business in the short term.

* *Market skimming* This takes place when relatively high prices are charged for products in order to retain their exclusivity, for example afternoon tea at the Ritz hotel or holidays in Bermuda. This strategy of pricing is aimed at customers willing to pay high prices for products and services such as first-class travel, expensive meals and exclusive 5-star hotels, perhaps as a reflection of their status or their desire for comfort and privacy.

Various methods can be used by travel and tourism organisations to determine the prices for their products. However, what they always have to keep in mind when setting prices are: how much the customers can afford to pay; what the competition is charging; and what is value for money for the customer.

Special holiday offers attract customers into travel agents

Promotion

Promotion is the means by which a travel and tourism organisation informs its customers about its products and services, and persuades them to make a purchase.

When the right product has been developed at the right price and distributed in the right place, then the organisation needs to tell people about it – i.e. promote the product to the market. The promotional activities of a hotel, for example, are geared towards filling its rooms, and those of an airline towards filling all its available seats.

Promotion is the most recognised aspect of marketing. It involves communicating with existing and potential customers to make them aware of a product and to persuade them to buy that product.

Promotion aims to:

* Make customers aware of the product
* Promote understanding of the product
* Persuade customers to buy the product – to increase sales
* Encourage customers to return – to generate repeat business.

Travel and tourism organisations use different promotional techniques, known as the promotions mix, to promote their products. These include:

Advertising

Advertising may be *informative* – i.e. designed to increase customer awareness of a product and help them make rational decisions, for example classified advertising in newspapers – or *persuasive* – i.e. containing a message which offers its receivers desirable and believable benefits. It is often argued that this type of advertising distorts customer buying. It may employ humour, sex appeal, sophistication, success and popularity to persuade.

However, advertising can be expensive and costs vary according to space, frequency and how long the advertisements run.

One method of advertising is to use the 'shotgun approach', which involves 'spraying' as many potential customers as possible in the hope that some of them will be persuaded to buy the product. Local radio is an example of local shotgun advertising aimed at attracting and influencing local people. However, the cost of advertising will be wasted if it does not reach its target audience and the message is not communicated effectively.

There are two kinds of promotions: *above-the-line promotions* and *below-the-line promotions*. The first uses independent media such as newspapers and television and the second does not depend upon the media and so the organisations have

Figure 5.7 Various ways of promoting travel and tourism products

some control over them. These promotion methods allow organisations to aim their marketing campaigns at customers they know are interested in a product.

However there are problems with below-the-line promotions:

* As with advertising, they are expensive and their outcome is difficult to predict

* They are often 'one-off' events, which have an impact for a limited period only

* Some types of promotion, such as direct mail and personal selling, are disliked by customers.

Let us look at *above-the-line promotions* in more detail.

Television advertising This is probably the most expensive form of advertising. A 30-second commercial during a break in *The Bill* costs thousands of pounds. This timeslot is classed as peak-time viewing, when there is an audience of millions. The advertising costs would reflect this. Production costs in making the commercial would also have to be taken into account.

Advertising on television is usually restricted to the larger travel and tourism organisations such as Thomas Cook and British Airways.

Newspaper advertising This can also be an expensive form of advertising. A full-page advertisement in a national newspaper would cost thousands of pounds, whereas an advertisement in a local paper may cost only £100. Over 60 per cent of the adult population regularly read a daily newspaper. Newspapers can be important in reaching a target audience, for example the readerships of the *Financial Times* and the *Independent* are mainly from social classes A and B.

Radio In recent years there has been a growth in the number of independent radio stations (local and national) in the UK and there has also been an increase in the numbers listening to the radio. These trends have been beneficial in terms of advertising to both small and medium-sized travel and tourism organisations.

Posters Posters are displayed in a variety of locations and tend to carry short messages. You will see them on billboards, around stadia, on buses and at bus stops. If they catch your attention and if you have time to read them, they can communicate a very effective message, which stays in the mind. This is especially true if the poster carries an image or photograph as well.

Shop windows are commonly used to display posters; travel agents in particular use their shop windows to promote their products, especially special holiday offers.

There are certain drawbacks with posters: full-colour printing on large sheets can be expensive and it is difficult to evaluate a poster's effectiveness.

Posters can be an effective way of communicating with customers

Let us now look at *below-the-line promotions* in more detail.

Direct marketing

Direct marketing, which is also known as direct mail advertising, involves the production of leaflets which are posted to households to promote products and services. One way of distributing leaflets is as inserts in magazines and newspapers.

Direct mail, or 'junk mail', is the fastest growing area of promotion and is very effective for organisations trying to reach a target audience. One form of direct mail is the personalised letter, which is sent directly to individuals by organisations with whom they have had no previous contact. Organisations using direct mailing as a selling technique target consumers by accessing a consumer database that provides information such as name and address, age group, past purchasing tendencies. They can use this information to send promotional materials, such as mailing special offers of holidays.

The most common direct marketing techniques used in travel and tourism are:

* Direct mail

* Telemarketing – i.e. contact by phone

* Door-to-door distribution – i.e. contact by post

* Direct response advertising – i.e. where the customer responds by phoning to collect a gift.

Public relations

Public relations can be defined as 'the deliberate, planned and sustained effort to establish and maintain mutual understanding between an organisation and its public'. The organisation attempts to communicate with its customers with the aim of increasing sales by improving the image of the organisation and its products. Public relations also aims to show the organisation in a good light and publicise what it has to offer. This involves contacting the media to inform them of forthcoming events and interesting stories. Holiday programmes on television, such as *The Travel Show* on the BBC, are good public relations for the destinations featured. They create a favourable image of the places which encourages people to holiday there.

Travel articles and stories in newspapers and magazines are another good source of public relations for destinations. Travel journalists are often given free holidays by travel companies and overseas tourist boards in the hope that their published articles will give a favourable impression of the area.

Personal selling

An organisation may promote a product through personal contact by its sales people. This involves face-to-face communication, with the salesperson trying to persuade the customer to buy the product. Selling products of course generates income, covers costs and makes profits.

It also involves promoting the organisation, for example by creating a good impression of that organisation, whether a travel agency or a tourist information office promoting an area.

The salesperson's main aim is to sell the product. He or she also has to search for new clients and offer additional after-sales backup. The advantage of personal selling is that the salesperson can gear his or her sales presentation to suit the individual. They can immediately answer any queries customers have. However, a disadvantage of personal selling is the high cost of selecting, training and operating sales personnel.

Exhibitions and trade fairs

Organisations promote their products and services at trade exhibitions or fairs. Examples are the British Travel Trade Fair, the International Group Leisure and Travel Show and the World Travel Market. Staff are on hand to answer any queries from potential customers.

The most effective displays of products and services are those that make people stop and look. Other incentives are the offers of free food and drink, or maybe the chance to win a fabulous prize in a competition.

In some cases there may be hands-on displays which entice people to 'have a go', such as skiing on a video simulator or using new technology to create a balloon flight across Africa.

If you ever have to run a display at an exhibition you will find that there are three types of visitors: customers, potential customers and time-wasters. It is crucial to identify prospective customers and encourage them to buy.

Customers tend to visit exhibitions and fairs looking for something new: new ideas, new products, new services. How long they spend at a display may vary from a few seconds to a few hours – it depends on what interests them. People tend to be drawn to displays by noise, music, crowds and demonstrations.

Exhibition display stands need to stand out as special in order to attract attention – after all there will be hundreds of other displays vying for people's attention. And staff need to be friendly, knowledgeable and informative.

A typical travel and trade exhibition would have the following incentives to attract passing trade:

* Scottish Highlands – a free glass of whisky

* Melton Mowbray – a free pork pie

* Bahamas – a chance to win a two-week break in the Bahamas

* Alton Towers – free family tickets

* Blackpool – a free stick of rock.

Sponsorship

Sponsorship can be an effective way for an organisation to promote itself to the public.

Sponsorship in football is used to promote a sponsor's business

Organisations sponsor teams or events by providing them with financial assistance, for example the Emirates airline sponsors Arsenal Football Club. In return, sponsors expect to receive plenty of good publicity and increased business. Other examples of sponsorship include Thomson Holidays, which sponsors Tottenham Hotspur Football Club, and the Air Miles Travel Company, which has sponsored exhibitions at the National Portrait Gallery.

Sponsorship needs to be beneficial to the sponsor and the sponsored organisation. The sponsors will want maximum publicity and increased sales. Whether this is their name on a premier league football shirt or at the beginning and end of a television programme, the main aim is to raise maximum awareness of the organisation.

Sponsorship deals can be very complex and legally binding, especially when millions of pounds are involved. Compliance and co-operation are crucial if both parties are to benefit from the deal.

Demonstrations

An organisation may demonstrate a product to potential buyers so that they can see what it is and involves. It could be a video of a holiday destination or the latest hotel reservation system. The purpose of the demonstration is to show what a product can do and how it can benefit the customer if they buy it.

Take the manager of a holiday centre that has decided to buy a state-of-the-art reservations system. A demonstration of the product would show the manager the speed at which reservations can be taken, the simplicity of the system, the number of staff training needed and the customer database it automatically creates.

Every demonstration should be clear, simple and informative. The benefits of the product to the buyer should be shown throughout the demonstration.

Sales promotions

In such a highly competitive industry, travel and tourism organisations need to do their best to win business. One way of achieving this is through sales promotions. These aim to persuade nonusers to try the product and to persuade regular customers to increase their purchases by offering some inducement to buy the product now rather than delay or not buy at all. Sales promotions are used to give a short-term boost to sales.

There are a variety of sales promotions to choose from:

* Coupons and refunds

* Competitions – to enter, you first have to buy the product

* Product endorsements, for example famous people using a product on television or celebrities opening new facilities

* Product placing – this involves an organisation paying for product brands to be placed on the sets of films and television programmes

* Free offers – free gifts with certain products

* Special credit terms, for example interest-free credit or ' buy now pay later' schemes

* Free samples.

Sales promotions can help motivate staff by getting them involved with the promotion and even offering them bonuses on the amount of products they sell.

Point-of-sale materials attract the attention of customers, as in the case of tourist information centres

customer's attention and interest; this is especially valuable in the case of travel agent shops. Once interest has been gained, a sales consultant should take over and try to convert the interest into a sale!

Point of sale (POS)

This involves creating an eye-catching display of the product, or information about the service. The display is positioned at the point at which the product is sold to customers. The point of sale is the actual place where the products are sold, for example the sale of souvenirs at the counter of a tourist information centre.

When customers arrive at the point of sale they are usually in a position to buy. If they have doubts about certain products, then there are special offers, promotions and discounts to encourage them to buy those products.

Point-of-sale materials in a shop window are created to entice customers inside. Posters, leaflets and brochures can be used to attract a

1 What is involved in marketing products in the travel and tourism industry?

2 Why is it important for an organisation to state what its mission, aims and objectives are?

3 In what ways does market research increase an organisation's chances of being successful?

4 What are the advantages and disadvantages of telephone surveys?

5 How important are focus groups and observation in discovering what consumers want or don't want?

6 What are the advantages of segmenting the travel and tourism market?

7 What is meant by the life cycle in the context of marketing and what are the different categories of the cycle?

8 List the lifestyle categories under the ACORN classification of consumers and say why this classification is useful in marketing products.

9 What is a SWOT analysis and how can it be useful to an organisation as well as to individuals?

10 What do you understand by the marketing mix?

11 Say what a product life cycle is and what the stages of it are.

12 How does a product chain of distribution work in the travel and tourism industry?

13 What are the factors that determine the price of a product?

14 Say what the different ways are by which an organisation can promote its products.

UNIT ASSESSMENT

Portfolio practice

For this unit you have to produce a portfolio based on an investigation into organisations in travel and tourism and their marketing activities.
It is assessed by your centre and moderated externally. You need to ensure you attempt all four components of the assessment requirements for this unit.

Part A

You need to produce a report on the significance of market segmentation to the travel and tourism industry.

You will need to explain the concept of market segmentation and describe the classification systems available to marketers. Your report should be detailed and make reference to the variables influencing consumer behaviour. You should include appropriate examples showing how named travel and tourism organisations segment their market and give an overall assessment of the significance of segmentation.

Part B

Here you will give an assessment of the most appropriate promotions mix for a specialist tour operator and a multiple travel agent.
Making reference to above-the-line and below-the-line promotions, you need to assess how and why the promotions mix for a specialist tour operator and multiple travel agent may differ. You must substantiate your conclusions with evidence gathered from named organisations.

Part C

You will make an evaluation of the key marketing activities of a chosen travel *or* tourism organisation. You should carefully select one travel and tourism organisation and research its marketing activities. It does not have to be the same organisation as studied previously.

You need to identify and describe the key marketing activities carried out by the organisation and then evaluate the success of this marketing.

Part D

You will produce an analysis of the internal and external business environment of a chosen travel and tourism organisation.

You need to produce SWOT and PEST analyses of a chosen organisation. These should be detailed and you need to explain how each influence identified affects the organisation.

Scenario

Imagine you have had ten years in the travel and tourism industry working and specialising in marketing travel and tourism organisations. You are now ready to apply for the position of Head of Marketing for the English Tourism Council. This is a top job with a salary of around £40,000 per year plus car.

Part of the selection process is to submit a report to your potential employers proving you have the necessary knowledge and expertise in marketing to do the job successfully. This is what you have to do.

Task 1

Produce a thorough and detailed report on the significance of market segmentation using relevant real-life examples which clearly demonstrate the range of classification systems. You should also show an excellent understanding of all the variables that influence consumer behaviour. (up to 12 marks)

Task 2

You have to give an assessment of the most appropriate promotions mix for a specialist tour operator and a multiple travel agent. You have to be able to apply knowledge to both organisations and ensure the promotions mixes are appropriate. You also need to show a full appreciation of the different needs of both organisations. Make sure that the full range of above-the-line and below-the-line promotions are considered and that conclusions are fully substantiated with appropriate evidence. (up to 18 marks)

Task 3

Give a critical evaluation of the marketing activities within the organisation, using appropriate information. Ensure that the evidence gathered is used to draw substantiated conclusions and that well-reasoned recommendations are made. (up to 18 marks)

Task 4

Produce in-depth SWOT and PEST analyses that are focused on your chosen organisation and demonstrate the ability to apply your knowledge. Show a competent use of technical language throughout your report. Finally make sure your information is relevant and presented to a high standard. (up to 12 marks)

UNIT 6

Tourism in the UK

Introduction

In this unit we are going to research and investigate the factors affecting the popularity of tourism in the UK. First we are going to look at the UK on a national scale and explore why it is a popular destination for domestic and incoming tourists. Then we will look at a local tourist board region, explore its main attractions and suggest possibilities for future improvements.

How you will be assessed

You will be assessed by producing a portfolio based on an investigation into tourism within the UK at national level. This will involve writing a report on the factors affecting the popularity of tourism. You will also be asked to produce another report based on your research into visitor numbers within the UK over recent years. Your findings should be supported by graphs and a bibliography of the sources that you have used.

You will then be asked to investigate tourism within a local tourist board region and give an oral presentation supported with visual aids such as slides, overheads or PowerPoint. The presentation will need to be recorded as evidence on either audio or videotape. In your presentation you will need to identify the main attractions and developments in tourism within your chosen region and to discuss these in the context of your UK study. The state of current provision in the tourist board region will need to be evaluated, highlighting any gaps in provision and suggesting possibilities for future improvements.

After studying this unit you need to have learned about:

✻ Factors affecting the popularity of tourism in the UK
✻ Statistics on tourism
✻ Tourism in a local tourist board region.

Factors affecting the popularity of tourism in the UK

Tourism is one of the largest industries in the UK generating 3.5 per cent of the UK economy. In 2004 27.7 million overseas visitors visited the UK and spent £13 billion. The UK is ranked sixth in the *international tourism* earnings league behind the USA, Spain, France, Italy and Germany.

The UK has many popular tourist destinations that attract visitors both from within the UK and from the rest of the world. The majority of overseas visitors to the UK travel from the USA, France, Germany, the Irish Republic and the Netherlands.

The UK has many tourist attractions that require an entrance fee whilst others are free of charge.

Edinburgh is one of the most popular urban tourist destinations in the UK

Skills practice

1 Using Table 6.1 (page 207) and the Internet or guidebooks, describe what makes each of the top ten paid admission attractions popular with visitors.

2 Using Table 6.2 (page 207) and the Internet or guidebooks, describe what makes each of the top ten free admission attractions popular with visitors.

3 Using Tables 6.1 and 6.2 suggest reasons why some attractions gained more visitors and some received fewer visitors between 2000 and 2003.

Within the UK as a whole, and in tourist board regions, tourists are attracted to both rural and urban destinations, and to areas where rural and urban features are combined.

Urban areas

Urban areas attract many domestic and international visitors. Towns and cities offer a rich variety of urban-based attractions, which include:

* Historic
* Cultural
* Retail
* Entertainment.

London receives the majority of overseas visitors to the UK, approximately 60 per cent, whilst other cities that are popular with incoming tourists include Bath, Stratford upon Avon, York and Edinburgh, all of which have many historic and cultural attractions.

Think about it

What are the main reasons why tourists visit towns and cities in the UK?

Historic attractions

Many inbound visitors come to see the *historic attractions* that the UK has to offer, as do domestic tourists who wish to learn more about their country's history.

Historic attractions are popular as travel destinations as they provide a link to the past. They include historic houses, castles, sites where important events took place and places associated with famous people. Historical attractions can also include heritage centres and places of worship such as churches and cathedrals.

Table 6.1 Top 10 paid admission attractions in the UK 2003 (by number of visitors)

ATTRACTION	REGION	2000	2001	2002	2003	PERCENTAGE CHANGE 2002/2003
British Airways London Eye	London	3,300,000*	3,850,000*	4,100,000	3,700,000	−9.8
Tower of London	London	2,303,167	2,019,183	1,940,856	1,972,263	+1.6
Eden Project	South West	498,000	1,700,000	1,832,482*	1,404,372	−23.4
Flamingo Land Theme Park and Zoo	Yorkshire and Humberside	1,301,000*	1,322,000*	1,393,300*	1,398,800*	+0.4
Windermere Lake Cruises	North West	1,172,219	1,241,918	1,266,027	1,337,879	+5.7
Legoland Windsor	South East	1,490,000	1,632,000	1,453,000	1,321,128	−9.1
New Metroland	North East	650,000*	650,000*	810,000*	1,200,000*	+48.2
Chester Zoo	North West	1,118,000	1,060,433	1,134,949	1,160,234	+2.2
Kew Gardens	London	860,340	989,352	987,266	1,079,424	+9.3
Canterbury Cathedral	South East	1,263,140*	1,151,099*	1,110,529*	1,060,166*	−4.5

* − estimate

Source: VisitBritain (2004)

Table 6.2 Top 10 free admission attractions in the UK 2003 (by number of visitors)

ATTRACTION	REGION	2000	2001	2002	2003	PERCENTAGE CHANGE 2002/2003
Blackpool Pleasure Beach	North West	6,800,000	6,500,000	6,200,000	6,200,000	0.0
British Museum	London	5,466,246*	4,800,938	4,607,311	4,584,000	−5.0
National Gallery	London	4,897,690*	4,918,985*	4,130,973*	4,360,461*	+5.6
Tate Modern	London	3,873,887	3,551,885	4,661,449	3,895,746*	−16.4
Natural History Museum	London	1,576,048	1,696,176	2,957,501	2,894,005	−2.2
Science Museum	London	1,337,432	1,352,649	2,722,154	2,886,850	+6.1
Victoria and Albert Museum	London	933,150	1,060,235	2,210,302	2,257,325	+2.1
Pleasureland Theme Park	North West	2,100,000*	2,000,000*	2,000,000*	2,100,000	+5.0
Eastbourne Pier	South East	N/a	2,000,000*	1,900,000*	1,600,000	−15.8
Great Yarmouth Pleasure Beach	East	1,500,000*	1,500,000*	1,500,000*	1,500,000*	0.0

* = estimate

Source: VisitBritain (2004)

Heritage centres have become popular, as many museums have adopted this title in order to appeal more to visitors. A heritage centre interprets the past in a variety of ways, including cultural and social accounts of the past using themed displays and interactive media. Examples include the Jorvik Centre in York, which has reconstructions of Viking life and animated figures. Industrial heritage can also be popular with visitors, including Cadbury World in Birmingham and Ironbridge Gorge in Shropshire.

Many *historic buildings* have been adapted to allow tourists to visit by incorporating additional facilities such as toilets and souvenir shops. Historic buildings may be described as being *listed* or *graded*. This means that strict regulations apply in order to protect them from inappropriate development or change. The gradings are:

* Grade I buildings are of exceptional interest
* Grade II* are particularly important buildings of more than special interest (rural locations)
* Grade II are of special of interest.

Currently 500,000 buildings are listed, of which the majority (over 90 per cent) are grade II.

Cultural attractions

Urban areas have more *museums and art galleries* than rural areas. Museums and art galleries contain artefacts, tourist facilities and special exhibitions to meet the changing needs of customers. Once thought of as merely being collections of exhibits, they have become centres of education and entertainment.

Skills practice

Complete the following table of the top five most visited historic properties in the UK in 2003:

MOST VISITED HISTORIC PROPERTIES IN THE UK	MAIN ATTRACTIONS OR REASONS TO VISIT
1 Tower of London	
2 Windsor Castle	
3 Roman Baths	
4 Stonehenge	
5 Tatton Park	

Source: VisitBritain (2004)

Skills practice

Complete the following table of the top five most visited museums and art galleries in the UK in 2003:

MOST VISITED MUSEUMS AND ART GALLERIES IN THE UK	MAIN ATTRACTIONS OR REASONS TO VISIT
1 British Museum	
2 National Gallery	
3 Tate Modern	
4 Natural History Museum	
5 Science Museum	

Source: VisitBritain (2004)

The top five museums and art galleries in the UK are all located in London. Other museums of national importance include the National Railway Museum (York), National Museum of Photography, Film and Television (Bradford), National Waterways Museum (Gloucester), Royal Armouries (Leeds), Museum of Scotland (Edinburgh) and the National Museum of Wales (Cardiff).

Cultural diversity in major cities such as London, Birmingham, Leicester and Bradford provide opportunities for cultural attractions and celebrations, including festivals, events and carnivals. Carnivals are a celebration of culture and can attract large numbers of tourists.

In 2004 the Notting Hill Carnival in London celebrated its 40th anniversary. The carnival is a celebration of Caribbean tradition through song, dance and costume. It is Europe's largest street party and regularly attracts over a million visitors. In 2003 316,000 visitors travelled from around the UK to London to see the carnival, and 90,000 visited from abroad. The large numbers of people who attend the carnival spend a total of around £45 million, which in turn supports 3000 jobs.

Retail

Shopping has become an important leisure and tourism activity. Tourists not only visit attractions they also visit shops and restaurants. For many this is the main reason for visiting a destination, which has led to a growth in the development of specialised shopping centres. Covent Garden in London is famous for its shops, boutiques and cafés and also for its street entertainers. Over 33 per cent of visitors to Covent Garden are tourists.

Out-of-town retail complexes and factory outlets are increasingly popular with domestic visitors. Over a quarter of them visit for the purpose of leisure and tourism. The five largest out-of-town retail centres each attract over 20 million shopper visits per year: these are Bluewater (Kent), Lakeside (Essex), the Trafford Centre (Manchester), Metro Centre (Gateshead) and Merry Hill (West Midlands). Over a quarter of visitors are in search of a day out rather than to make a specific purchase.

Entertainment

Entertainment can be an attraction in itself or be part of the visitor experience. It can include:

* Music
* Comedy
* Cinema
* Sport
* Theatre
* Nightclubs
* Club bars
* Pubs and bars.

Entertainment can vary from large theatrical events and performances to music concerts, street performers, talent contests and karaoke. Different types of entertainment will appeal to different types of visitor. For example, a family will require a range of entertainment that may include young children, teenagers, young couples and grandparents.

Nightclubs and theme bars are becoming increasingly competitive, not just in the type of music they play but also in terms of the price of drinks and the range of experiences and events offered.

Large cities will have many forms of entertainment to attract visitors. In London the West End is the main focus of entertainment facilities. It extends for approximately one square mile around Shaftsbury Avenue, Piccadilly, Covent Garden and The Strand. It is also known as 'theatreland' because of the numerous world-class theatres and entertainment venues situated there. Outside this area but included in the definition of the West End are the Royal National Theatre on the South Bank and the Barbican Theatre in the City. Other areas offering entertainment are becoming fashionable alternatives: examples are North London (Islington and Camden Town); East London (Clerkenwell, Farringdon and Old Street); West London (Portobello Road and Westbourne Grove); South London (Brixton). Soho is also fashionable for late night entertainment, clubs and restaurants.

Liverpool, European Capital City of Culture 2008

Liverpool has been awarded the European Capital City of Culture in 2008. It is estimated that it will bring an extra 1.7 million visitors to Liverpool, generating extra spending of over £50 million a year. Leading up to 2008 the city is spending over £2 billion on cultural and tourism projects, including city centre regeneration and the building

Liverpool, European Capital City of Culture

of a new arena and exhibition venue. Three distinctive buildings – the Liver, the Cunard and the Port of Liverpool, known as the 'three graces' – dominate Liverpool's skyline. In 2008 a new building, a 'fourth grace', will open; it will be a futuristic design to house the World Discovery Centre and will be called 'The Cloud'.

Currently Liverpool has the largest collection of modern art in the UK outside of London and has eight national museums and galleries and four theatres. It has 2500 listed buildings, 250 public monuments and the largest collection of grade II listed buildings after London. It has well known links to sport, music, film, festivals and events, offering a wide variety of history, culture, retail and entertainment.

Adapted from BBC, *Capital of Culture*

Think about it

1 Why was Liverpool selected as the City of Culture 2008?
2 How does Liverpool benefit from being awarded the title City of Culture?

Skills practice

Select a popular urban visitor destination in the UK and provide examples of the following types of attractions that can be found there:

- History
- Culture
- Retail
- Entertainment.

Rural areas

People visit the *countryside* for many reasons. Some want to relax, enjoy a picnic or admire the landscape, others want to experience sporting activities such as hiking, mountain climbing, mountain biking or fishing. Others may simply wish to walk the dog, to visit friends or relatives in rural towns and villages or to escape the hustle and bustle of major towns and cities.

The UK has a rich variety of rural attractions, which include:

* Wild areas
* Coastal areas
* Lakes and rivers
* Villages.

Tourists sightseeing in the Lake District

Wild areas

Wild or *wilderness areas* are remote parts of the countryside, places of unspoilt beauty and relatively few visitors. These areas include mountainous regions. A mountain has steep sides rising to more than 300 metres (980 feet). Although located at a distance from large urban areas, most mountainous regions in the UK are accessible by road, with car parks and lay-bys to enable drivers to stop and admire the views. For those wishing to walk or climb, footpaths are usually signposted, however sensible precautions need to be taken as the weather can change suddenly at higher altitudes. Most of the mountain areas in the UK are located within national parks. The best known ones include: Ben Nevis (1343 metres/4400 feet) in Scotland, Snowdon (1085 metres/3560 feet) in Wales, Scafell Pike (987 metres/3240 feet) in England and Slieve Donard (852 metres/2800 feet) in Northern Ireland.

Coastal areas

The *coastline* of mainland Great Britain extends for over 17,820 kilometres (11,073 miles), not including the many islands that lie offshore. Most people live no more than 125 kilometres (78 miles) from the sea. For the last 150 years the most popular form of holiday has been by the seaside. A beach can offer golden sands, a chance to sit in the sun or take part in activities such as water sports, beach sports, arcades, amusements and children's entertainment.

Areas of coastline vary in character: some have beaches, some have cliffs and some have mud flats and salt marshes. Beaches also vary: some may be made of sand and others made of pebbles or shingle.

Not all areas of the coastline have been developed for tourism. The main seaside resorts are urban in appearance with entertainment, amusements, bars and restaurants. Beyond the resorts are rural coastal areas.

Lakes and rivers

Lakes are popular with tourists, an example being the Lake District in Cumbria. At the heart of the Lake District is Lake Windermere, which is 17 kilometres (10.5 miles) long. Many visitors are attracted to the lake and the nearby picturesque towns of Ambleside, Windermere and Bowness. The lake has a long history of sailing and sailing boats are available for hire. Power-boating and water-skiing are also popular, but there are now restrictions on the speed of the most powerful motor boats to improve the safety of other water users and the quality of the environment.

Rivers also provide a wide range of tourist activities. Among them are riverside walks, watching boats, ferry trips and fishing, as well as more physical activities like canoeing, rowing and boating.

Think about it

1 Why are lakes and rivers appealing for visitors?

2 What are some of the problems associated with visitor pressure in these environments?

Villages

Rural villages offer an alternative to urban life. Cottages, small local shops, a village pub and a community spirit often appeal to those who wish to leave the hustle and bustle of busy towns and cities behind.

Farm-based tourism has become popular throughout the countryside with farmers offering rooms and farm cottages to tourists. Farm tourism provides an authentic location in which visitors can witness rural life first hand, particularly in the case of working farms. The range of rural pursuits in villages or in farm-based accommodation includes horse riding, fishing, cycling or golf.

CASE STUDY

UK National Parks

There are twelve national parks in England and Wales. Ten were established by the National Parks and Access to Countryside Act (1949) and the Norfolk Broads was established under a separate Act in 1981. The latest national park to be officially recognised in England is the New Forest, which became a national park in 2005.

A national park's purpose is to preserve wildlife and conserve areas of the countryside, as well as providing opportunities for recreation. The most visited national park in the UK is the Lake District with 22 million day visits per year.

In Scotland the National Parks (Scotland) Act was passed in July 2000. The first Scottish national park, Loch Lomond and the Trossachs, was established in July 2002, and the Cairngorms National Park was established in March 2003.

National parks currently cover 9 per cent of the land area of England and Wales. This represents 8 per cent of England, and 20 per cent of Wales. The two Scottish

Figure 6.1 National parks of England and Wales

national parks cover 7 per cent of the land area of Scotland.

Source: Office for National Statistics

Investigate a range of national parks in the UK and complete the following table:

	EXAMPLES OF RURAL ATTRACTIONS IN NATIONAL PARKS
Wild areas	
Coastal areas	
Lakes and rivers	
Villages	

Think about it

Why do national parks attract large numbers of visitors?

There is a wide range of factors affecting tourists' decisions to visit a destination that apply to both rural and urban areas. These include:

* Attractions, events and entertainment
* Food, drink and accommodation
* Transport and accessibility
* Social and political factors
* Economic factors
* Environmental factors.

Let's look at each one in turn to see how they affect the popularity of tourism in the UK.

Attractions, events and entertainment

A tourist destination needs to have a variety of attractions, events and entertainment that are value for money and meet the needs of its visitors. A wide range of choice needs to be available to suit the particular tastes and circumstances of visitors. This applies to urban and rural destinations. A visitor attraction must be clear as to what its 'product' offers and make sure that it meets customers' expectations. This can be determined through doing market research into needs and expectations of customers.

Many visitors are attracted to a destination for a particular reason. For example, they will travel to try out a new ride at Alton Towers or to see a concert or to attend a music festival. Other factors as to why people visit destinations are discussed next.

Skills practice

Using the VisitBritain website (http://www.visitbritain.com) or a collection of guidebooks, complete the following table:

MAJOR ATTRACTIONS, EVENTS AND ENTERTAINMENT IN THE UK THAT ARE POPULAR WITH OVERSEAS VISITORS		
Attractions	Events	Entertainment

Food, drink and accommodation

Hospitality and *accommodation* are important factors of any holiday. Different types of food and drink appeal to different groups of visitors. Visitor expectations will also vary in terms of:

* Cost
* Value for money
* Quality of service
* Quality of food and drink
* Range of choice.

Visitors may prefer different places to eat and drink, for example in a busy restaurant, a quiet café or a bustling bar.

Think about it

Name as many types of places as you can where food and drink can be made available to visitors.

Destinations need to provide visitors with a range of cafés, restaurants, pubs and bars to choose from and to make sure they suit the right types of visitors. For example, a family resort will need to place a greater emphasis on child-orientated cafés and restaurants that are value for money.

The availability of locally produced *food and drink* is increasingly important, particularly for visitors expecting to taste food and drink they would not experience at home. Local produce is also perceived to be fresh, high quality and authentic. Examples are whisky in Scotland, pasties in Cornwall and cheese in Cheddar.

Skills practice

1 What are the benefits in reducing the amount of 'food miles' or distance food has travelled from the farmers to the breakfast table?
2 Identify the following places or parts of the UK by their food or drink:
   * Haggis
   * Cheddar cheese
   * Cider
   * Jellied eels
   * Pasty
   * Lava bread
   * Brown ale
   * Black pudding.

CASE STUDY
The Real Bath Breakfast

A range of farmers' markets and food trails are promoted throughout the UK in order to satisfy the growing number of visitors who wish to taste regional food and drink. This has been part of a successful marketing strategy in the South West of England where food trails have been developed for Cornwall, Somerset, Wiltshire, South Devon, North Devon, Dorset and Gloucestershire.

The Real Bath Breakfast aims to provide visitors to the city of Bath with a taste of local produce at breakfast time. Hotels are allowed to display The Real Bath Breakfast logo if they serve breakfast using produce from within 40 miles of Bath.

Although the Real Bath Breakfast costs 5 per cent more than breakfast using ingredients bought from a supermarket, the benefits to the visitor and to local businesses outweigh the increase in price.

The Real Bath Breakfast

The range, quality, availability and price of *accommodation* can affect the popularity of a destination. It is important that the range of accommodation reflects the needs of the visitor.

Tourist boards in the UK have developed standards for grading the quality of tourist accommodation. Stars are awarded for hotels, self-catering and caravan parks, and diamonds are awarded for guesthouses and university accommodation. The higher the number of stars and diamonds the higher the quality of accommodation. However, accommodation at a lower star rating can also provide facilities found at a higher rating.

Transport and accessibility

Visitor attractions need to be accessible. The successful ones have transport services that make travelling to and from the attraction or destination as easy and as comfortable as possible.

Transport may also include organised services for transporting visitors to or around a destination, such as:

* Bus/coach services, including Park and Ride
* Taxi
* Train services
* Air services
* Riverboat, ferry and Seacat services.

On arriving at a destination visitors expect to receive clear information on car parking, bus times and routes, directions to main attractions and to organised information points such as a tourist information centre. If attractions are difficult to locate or if transport routes or services are congested, unreliable or expensive, then potential visitors may go elsewhere.

Car and coach access to destinations is of growing importance to tourists. Given that most tourists within the UK travel to their destinations by road, the signposting to the destination needs to be clear and there needs to be adequate parking. The motor car offers freedom of choice, however with increased usage and congestion, alternatives for tourism travel need to be offered. The volume of tourism trips by car has increased by 58 per cent in the last ten years, compared with 30 per cent growth in bus/coach travel and 48 per cent in rail travel. Inbound tourists often transfer to their holiday destinations by coach.

One possible way to cut the cost of congestion is for motorists and coach companies to pay for using a particular road through a system of tolls and payments. In 2003 a congestion charge was introduced in London, which suffers the worst traffic congestion in the UK and some of the worst in Europe. The charge is currently fixed at a £5 fee for a vehicle entering the centre of London. Over 40,000 cars enter central London during the morning rush hour and average traffic speeds have dropped below 10 mph. It is estimated that the congestion charge will cut delays by between 20–30 per cent by encouraging people to use public transport.

Access to transport services can depend on weather conditions, industrial action, mechanical failure or security threats.

CASE STUDY

Airport delays hit summer season

Chaos spread across UK airports yesterday as the start of another summer season was hit by delays and cancellations.

It comes as the public service union GMB announced that its 1000 members who work for Aviance could strike in the third week of June if pay talks between the two sides fail.

Aviance staff work in baggage handling and check-in at 17 airports across the UK. The Transport and General Workers' Union members who work for Aviance are also in the first stages of a ballot on whether to strike.

Meanwhile, thousands of passengers were left on the ground as airlines were forced to cancel scores of flights because of the air traffic control system failure at West Drayton, near Heathrow.

Heathrow, Gatwick and Stansted were all hit by the failure, while regional airports, including Glasgow, Birmingham, Bristol and Manchester, also struggled to get aircraft in the air. British Airways scrapped 27 flights, easyJet 40 and bmi 16, while Ryanair cancelled around 10 services. Hundreds more flights were delayed by up to five hours as airlines tried to clear the backlog.

Travel Weekly (Friday 4 June 2004)

Think about it

1 Using the above case study what were the two main issues affecting airport delays?

2 To what extent does this have an affect on the popularity of both domestic and inbound tourism in the UK?

Access is also important for groups of visitors with special needs. There are approximately 8.5 million disabled people in the UK and 2.5 million disabled people travel on a regular basis. However, only 2 per cent of accommodation in the UK has been assessed as being accessible for disabled users. The National Accessibility Scheme assesses the degree of accessibility for wheelchair users and those who have difficulty walking. The scheme forms part of the Tourism for All campaign that is promoted by national and regional tourist boards. As a result of the Disability Discrimination Act (1995), all accommodation providers, including small hotels and guesthouses, have to make reasonable adjustments so they do not discriminate against disabled people and are better able to meet their requirements. By law all service providers,

including visitor attractions and accommodation and entertainment venues, must take reasonable measures to remove, alter or provide a reasonable means of avoiding any physical barriers to accessing and using their premises.

For further information visit the Tourism for All website: http://www.tourismforall.org.uk

Think about it

Are urban tourism attractions more accessible to disabled visitors than rural tourism attractions?

CASE STUDY

The Eden Project

The Eden Project in Cornwall attracts approximately 1.8 million people each year. There are facilities for 1000 cars and 40 coaches. As part of a sustainable policy to lower the environmental impacts of travelling to the site, the Eden Project encourages 20 per cent of its visitors to travel by alternative means. One way is to buy a ticket to the Eden Project at a railway station which includes transport to the Project, entrance fee and a bus transfer service.

The Eden Project

Social and political factors

Social and political factors influencing the popularity of a destination include personal safety, the development of short-break holidays, government policy and consumer interests. These can be summarised as:

* Crime
* Growth of particular holiday types
* Fashion.

Crime

People will travel to destinations that they perceive to be safe and have low levels of crime. Towns and cities attract higher amounts of crime than rural areas. However, it only takes a few highly publicised crime incidents to persuade tourists to choose an alternative destination.

Major cities like London, Manchester, Leeds, Newcastle upon Tyne and Birmingham are increasing their attraction to visitors as 24-hour cities, offering a wide range of nightlife, culture, restaurants and bars. However, threats to personal safety can be an issue in discouraging people to visit. Many towns and cities within the UK have invested in private security, closed-circuit television (CCTV) and liaison between the police, businesses and local people in order to reduce the levels of crime. Tourists are affected by levels of crime and by the threat of terrorism.

time at work to allow for long weekends and to take advantage of price cutting and other financial incentives by hotel groups, such as paying for two nights and getting one free or special rates for dinner, bed and breakfast.

Popular destinations include coastal resorts, particularly in the West and South West of England. In addition, major cities are competing to attract short-break holidaymakers with an array of high-quality shows, events and package deals. This trend means that holidaymakers can enjoy the best of both worlds, combining a holiday abroad with one or two short-break holidays in the UK.

As the holiday industry continues to develop, special interest holidays are becoming more popular. These include:

* Activity and sporting holidays
* Themed holidays, including cookery, wine tasting, arts and education
* Rural and forest-based holidays such as Center Parcs
* Theme park holidays.

Special interest holidays appeal to those who wish to share their holiday experiences with people of similar interests. These holidays can also provide a sense of personal achievement and the development of new skills.

Growth of particular holiday types

More people are taking *short-break holidays* in the UK. Resorts, hotels and holiday parks are therefore changing their focus towards shorter-stay holidays.

Short-break holidays are increasingly popular because they enable people to more easily manage

Holidaying in the UK is not just for those with lower incomes or the older person who has neither the finances nor the desire to travel abroad. Young affluent domestic tourists take holidays in the UK, particularly those with small children, for whom travelling abroad is not an option.

Visiting friends or relatives (VFR) has stimulated growth in domestic tourism as many young people move away from home to find work or stay away after attending university. Career-orientated individuals and couples also often move to other parts of the country in order to take promotions at work. In many of these cases holiday time is an opportunity to visit and catch up with family and friends.

Increasing car ownership enables easy and flexible travel arrangements to allow some or all of the family members to travel.

Longer working hours have also caused a rise in the demand for short-break holidays in order to relax and get away from the pressures of work.

However it is the lifestage people are at that influences the choice of holiday the most. Different groups of people have different needs, which reflect the type of holiday that they take. A family with older children will make different holiday choices than a mature couple whose children have left home.

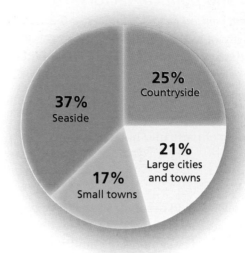

Figure 6.2 The most popular tourist destinations in the UK

Source: UK Tourism Survey

by the seaside, 25 per cent in the countryside, 21 per cent in large cities and large towns and 17 per cent in small towns.

Complete the following table:

LIFESTAGE	EXAMPLE OF A HOLIDAY DESTINATION IN THE UK
Young adults	
Families with small children	
Families with older children and younger teenagers	
Empty nesters – mature couples whose children have left home	

Think about it

Why is the seaside the most popular destination for holidaymakers in the UK?

Destinations can become popular and fashionable through what they can offer the tourist, successful advertising, media coverage and appropriate management.

The top ten paid admission attractions in the UK and the top ten free admission attractions in the UK (see page 207) can be considered fashionable because of the large numbers of people who visit them. Fashions for tourist destinations of course change as their popularity changes.

Fashion can be defined as a current style adopted by society. Fashions change with changes in technology, media influences, new developments and changing expectations, as well as employment trends and levels of disposable income.

Advertising and media coverage are crucial in raising public awareness and promoting certain holiday destinations. VisitBritain and the regional tourist boards have promotion programmes to ensure that destinations are well promoted.

Fashion

The seaside is the most popular of all tourist destinations in the UK. According to the UK Tourism Survey, 37 per cent of holidays are taken

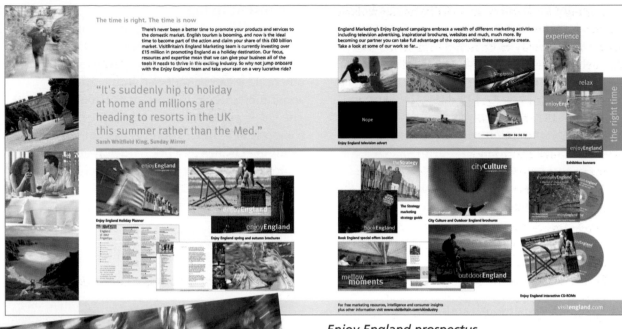

Enjoy England prospectus

Skills practice

1 Use the Internet to search the VisitBritain website and discover five fashionable destinations for each of the following headings:
   - Seaside
   - Countryside
   - Cities and large towns
   - Small towns.

2 Suggest what makes one destination fashionable compared to another.

Fashions can be reflected in social trends and attitudes. One such trend is gambling. The rise in gambling has had an affect on the development of UK tourist destinations. In 2002 the government relaxed restrictions on gambling, including:

✴ Ease of rules on where casinos can open

✴ 24-hour licensing with food, drink and live entertainment

✴ No upper limits on casino jackpots.

This has encouraged travel destinations and other leisure-based operations to consider the possibility of opening American-style casinos.

In 2004 the government relaxed the restrictions on licensing hours for pubs and bars allowing them to apply for 24-hour licences. Although most landlords were not in favour of opening 24 hours a day, it provides the opportunity to stay open longer for special events and to allow for the development of 24-hour entertainment venues.

Economic factors

The *cost* of a holiday is an important factor in the popularity and appeal of UK travel destinations, especially as high street travel agents can offer deals that make going abroad cheaper than staying in the UK. Potential visitors to the UK also take into account the relative cost of spending a holiday in the UK and whether it offers value for money. If the UK is perceived to be too expensive, then alternative cheaper destinations may receive more visitors.

The average cost of a holiday in England includes 31 per cent spent on accommodation, 6 per cent on entertainment, 18 per cent on travel and 26 per cent on eating and drinking. Other costs are also incurred.

The main economic factors that determine the popularity of the UK as a travel destination are:

* The cost of visiting attractions
* The cost of living
* The exchange rate.

The cost of visiting attractions

The *cost* of visiting an attraction depends on whether the visitor attraction charges an admission fee; see page 207. Visiting attractions can be expensive for large families. Some entrance fees can be expensive but provide good value for money. A theme park, for example, offers entertainment for a whole day and is therefore priced accordingly.

To attract more visitors many attractions offer a range of discounts. For example, groups and family tickets offer savings on the cost of tickets bought individually.

Another saving is to buy a combined entrance ticket for several attractions rather than buying tickets for each attraction. A prepayment system also allows visitors to save money and time by buying just one ticket or pass for a range of attractions, however they are only available in some destinations.

The cost of living

The *cost of living* is the cost of goods and services needed for an average standard of living. Some parts of the UK are more expensive to live than others. This can be reflected in the price of accommodation, transport, petrol, food and drink. The UK is perceived to be expensive in comparison to other countries within Europe. As a result the UK has to work harder at attracting visitors who may be tempted to travel to cheaper destinations.

Think about it

1 Which parts of the UK are more expensive and which are perceived to be cheaper?

2 Does this affect the appeal of these areas as tourist destinations?

The exchange rate

The *exchange rate* also affects the popularity of the UK as a destination. When the value of the British pound is high compared to other currencies, it makes travelling abroad cheaper; in turn other currencies which are lower in value will buy fewer British pounds, therefore making the UK more expensive for inbound tourists.

When the value of the British pound is low compared to other currencies it makes travelling abroad more expensive; in turn, it makes the UK less expensive for inbound tourists. See exchange rates in Unit 3 Travel Destinations, pages 113–114.

All these factors affect the spending power of the money in our pockets – our disposable income, which is what we have left after

CASE STUDY

London Pass

The London Pass is a prepayment card that allows free entry to over 50 attractions in London. A pass can be purchased for one day or up to a week. The benefits are that families and groups can pay in advance and know how much they will be spending on the attractions during their holiday. The pass costs from £12 a day and includes a free guidebook and other discounts. London Pass holders can also buy a Travel Card at the same time, giving unlimited travel on London's buses, Underground, train services, Docklands Light Railway and Tramlink.

Source: The London Pass

household bills and other expenses are accounted for. When the UK economy is growing more money is generated, so we tend to have more disposable income to spend on holidays and other leisure products.

Environmental factors

Tourists prefer clean and safe environments and will tend to avoid those areas perceived to be polluted or unsafe. They are also attracted by warm sunny conditions rather than cold damp conditions. The two main *environmental factors* that influence the popularity of a destination are climate and pollution.

Climate

The climate of a destination is a natural asset, depending on the type of holiday visitors are looking for. The British climate is one with warm wet summers and mild winters. This suits those visitors in pursuit of cultural and historic interests and those who are seeking the peace and beauty of the countryside. However, it is hard for the UK to compete for those in search of beach holidays in warm, dry sunny destinations. Climate nevertheless plays an important part in where people go on holiday in the UK. The south, which has the warmest, driest and sunniest climate, caters for 40 per cent of all British holidays.

Pollution

Pollution can exist in many forms, including:

* Water pollution – contamination of rivers, streams and coastal areas

* Air pollution – atmospheric contamination

* Land pollution – contamination of soil and landscapes.

The quality of the environment is an important factor in attracting tourists, for example to a coastal resort or a national park.

Beaches in the UK can be given awards for their environmental quality. Those that meet European standards of water quality – the Bathing Water Directive – may be given the Seaside Award, which is in recognition for the management and environmental quality of resort and rural beaches. Resort beaches that meet European standards of water quality, are well managed and promote environmental education are recognised by the Blue Flag award – see Unit 3 Travel Destinations. Tour operators will tend to favour beaches that are recognised for their clean water and high environmental quality rather than those that are not. The UK has many outstanding coastlines, however some of the beaches suffer from pollution, a problem highlighted by campaign groups such as Surfers Against Sewage.

CASE STUDY

Scotland

Scotland receives approximately 6.5 million visitors each year. It is famous for its culture, history and landscapes. The main attractions are historic monuments and museums, mountain climbing and hill walking, water sports, golf and winter skiing.

Skiing in Scotland is a specialised tourist industry that attracts approximately 100,000 skiing trips each year, contributing over £16 million to the rural communities of highland Scotland. The industry of course depends on an abundance of snow. There are five main ski areas in Scotland: Glencoe, Glenshee, The Lecht, Cairngorms and the Nevis range.

Golf is another activity sensitive to changes in climate, the putting greens have to be watered regularly during summer to avoid them drying out, particularly as extremes of temperature can damage the playing surface. There are over 550 golf courses in Scotland, the most famous being the Old Course at St Andrews.

Source: Climatic Research Unit, University of East Anglia

Think about it

Would you prefer to visit a beach that has been given a Blue Flag or a Seaside Award rather than one that has not? Give reasons for your answer.

Atmospheric pollution is a problem mainly in towns and cities and is caused by vehicle emissions and industrial processes. On hot sunny days air pollution can build up and cause breathing difficulties for people who suffer from asthma. To keep people informed who may experience problems with high pollution, weather forecasts sometimes include air quality indexes or pollution warnings to indicate the level of air pollution.

Land pollution can be caused by industrial waste spilling on to the land. Litter is the most obvious form of land pollution. It is unsightly and can cause health hazards if allowed to build up. Travel destinations invest large sums of money in keeping streets and beaches free of litter, however there still is a need to educate people to respect the environment by taking their litter home or disposing of it appropriately.

Tourism infrastructure

The existence of a *tourism infrastructure* can make a significant difference to the environment. It is needed to provide for people's basic needs and to transport tourists to their destinations.

Public and private organisations provide tourism infrastructure that affects the environment where tourism takes place. Public organisations include local councils and national government; private organisations include businesses and companies that make profit by providing a service. Both can be described as *stakeholders*. To balance the needs of tourists, local people, local businesses and the environment, careful management is required.

Roads

The *road network* is important to deliver tourists to a destination and provide a means of access to local services. The upkeep of local roads is the responsibility of local authorities and local councils, with national routes and motorways being looked after by the Highways Agency. The Highways Agency is an executive agency of the Department for Transport and is responsible for operating, maintaining and improving the road network in England on behalf of the government. The network is important to domestic tourism, especially in delivering tourists to popular destinations during holiday times. It is also important for bringing tourists to remote destinations away from the major towns and cities.

Motorways and trunk roads, or 'A roads', carry large numbers of passengers. Trunk roads carry one-third of all road traffic in the UK although they represent only 2.6 per cent of the total road network. Motorways and trunk roads can become congested at peak times, especially during bank holidays.

Think about it

1 How important are motorways and trunk roads to the popularity of tourism destinations?

2 How can visitors avoid traffic jams during peak times?

Figure 6.3 Tourism infrastructure

Railways

The *railway network* in the UK is owned by Network Rail, a private sector organisation that operates as a commercial business. All of Network Rail's profits are reinvested into maintaining and upgrading the railway infrastructure. It owns and maintains 21,000 miles of track and 2500 stations across Britain. It provides access to the tracks and stations and its main customers are the train and freight companies that operate the nation's train services.

A fast and efficient rail service is important for all businesses, not just tourism. Historically, the rail network has led to the development of many English seaside resorts, including Brighton and Blackpool. The future of the railway is important for the development of tourism in that it enables visitors to travel to the heart of major towns and cities, to remote rural locations and also abroad. Every year 7 million passengers travel by Eurostar between England and France through the Channel Tunnel. A fast, efficient, safe and reasonably priced rail service is required if people are to be persuaded to travel by public transport rather than by private motor car.

Airports

Airports provide access to domestic as well as international destinations. The growth in the use of regional airports has added to a recent growth in air travel. New routes bring new opportunities to attract visitors from different countries. For example, a new route between Bristol International Airport and New York operated by Continental Airlines opens up new possibilities for attracting visitors to destinations in the South West of England. At present most visitors from America fly into London Heathrow and Gatwick airports. New routes between England, Scotland and Northern Ireland also provide new opportunities, especially with the increase in the number of low-cost airlines.

The *British Airports Authority* (BAA) is a private company that owns and manages seven major airports in the UK. These include: Heathrow, Gatwick, Stansted, Glasgow, Edinburgh, Aberdeen and Southampton. An airport not only provides a means to travel to another destination but also provides a range of shopping and leisure facilities, as well as ensuring the needs and safety of its passengers.

The *Civil Aviation Authority* (CAA) is an independent organisation that is responsible for the airline industry in the UK. It does not receive any funding direct from the government but is responsible for policy, regulation, safety and consumer protection.

Think about it

Why is it important that tourism stakeholders (transport operators, private companies, government organisations and local councils) cooperate to provide an efficient and reliable transport service in the UK?

Water and power

Water, gas and electricity are needed when developing new destinations or increasing demand within existing destinations. These services are provided by private companies and are regulated by independent organisations funded by the government. Water services in the UK are regulated by Ofwat (Office of Water Services) and power is regulated by Ofgem (Office of Gas and Electricity Markets).

People require efficient, reliable and cheap sources of water and power and these are necessary in the continuing popularity of tourism in the UK. Some camping and caravan sites in remote locations may only provide basic services but increasingly consumers are demanding easier access to water supplies and electricity.

Sewage and rubbish disposal

The sewerage system in the UK is the responsibility of private water companies. The system needs to be efficient to deal with large numbers of people who visit popular destinations.

Rubbish disposal is the responsibility of local councils but visitors and local people also have a responsibility to dispose of their litter appropriately. Local authorities and visitors need to work together to ensure that areas are kept clean and to encourage people to recycle their rubbish in order to minimise the amount of waste.

Policing

The *police force* of a destination ensures the safety of visitors and local residents, provides security and advice, and monitors traffic by alerting road agencies and the media about delays, diversions or incidents.

Maintenance of public open spaces

People are attracted by *parks*, *gardens* and *public open spaces*. In busy cities there are green areas where people can relax, play, jog, sunbathe, have lunch or enjoy a few minutes away from work. Local authorities and councils maintain these areas. Maintenance includes the planting of trees and flowers, grass cutting, litter picking, design and safety. Some parks, such as St James's Park in London, which is located between Buckingham Palace and Downing Street, have become popular with visitors.

Management of national parks

National parks are managed by their own board or committee, known as a National Park Authority, which includes local councillors and government representatives. A national park officer and staff manage a national park according to the policy of the National Park Authority. The national park officer monitors tourism activities, employs rangers and decides on the best way in which to manage tourism in the park.

For a popular travel destination in the UK or a national park design a diagram to show how public and private organisations provide a range of services that affect the quality of the environment and the experience of the visitor.

Statistics on tourism

UK tourism can be divided into *domestic* tourists, UK residents taking tourism trips at home, and *incoming* tourists, those arriving from a variety of other countries.

Incoming tourism

Travel Trends is a government survey on travel to and from the UK based on results from the International Passenger Survey. The results are based on face-to-face interviews with a random sample of passengers as they enter or leave the UK. It is the main source of information to show international travel patterns: why people travel, where they stay and how much they spend.

International travel increases
Travel Trends 2003

Overseas residents' visits to the UK increased by 2 per cent in 2003, and their spending grew by 1 per cent according to Travel Trends, published by the Office for National Statistics. In 2003, overseas residents made 24.7 million visits to the UK, 0.5 million more than in 2002. They spent £11.9 billion while in the UK, £0.1 billion more than in 2002. UK residents made a record 61.4 million visits abroad, an increase of 3 per cent on the previous year. UK residents also spent record amounts abroad: £28.6 billion – an increase of nearly 6 per cent.

As a result, spending by UK residents on visits abroad was higher than spending by overseas residents visiting the UK in 2003. The difference (£16.7 billion) was £1.5 billion more than in 2002, making it a record deficit.

Source: Office for National Statistics, 17 December 2004

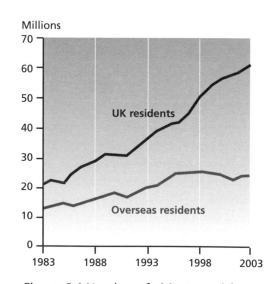

Figure 6.4 Number of visits to and from the UK

1 How many more overseas residents visited the UK in 2003 compared to 1983?

2 Suggest why more overseas residents visited the UK in 2003 compared to 1983.

3 Why was there a decline in overseas residents to the UK in 2001?

4 Suggest why the amount of UK residents travelling overseas has increased since 1983.

5 UK residents spend more money abroad than overseas residents visiting the UK. Discuss the problems associated with this deficit in terms of the UK economy.

How did the foot and mouth disease outbreak and the terrorist attacks in the United States affect the number of visitors to the UK in 2001?

Overseas residents' visits to the UK
Travel Trends 2003

In 2003, overseas residents made 24.7 million visits to the UK, 0.5 million more than were made in 2002. The number of visits had been decreasing since a peak in visits in 1998 and there was a particularly large fall of more than 9 per cent in 2001 when there was a foot and mouth disease outbreak between February and September and the terrorist attacks in the United States on 11 September. Visits from overseas residents have increased by 8 per cent since 2001, but despite the recovery the UK still had 1.0 million fewer visits from overseas residents in 2003 than in the peak year of 1998.

Spending by overseas residents on visits to the UK increased by 1 per cent in 2003 to £11.9 billion, but was still below the level reached in 2000.

Source: Office for National Statistics, 17 December 2004

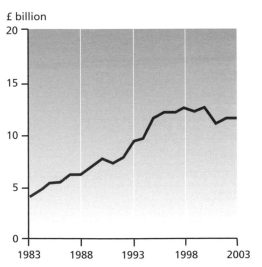

Figure 6.5 Overseas residents' spending in the UK 1983–2003

Purpose of visit
Travel Trends 2003

In 2003, as in previous years, holiday visits were the most popular reason for overseas residents to come to the UK and accounted for almost a third of all visits (32 per cent). This was followed by business visits and visits to friends or relatives, each accounting for 28 per cent of visits. Overseas holiday travellers spent the most in the UK, spending £3.7 billion in total or an average of £453 per visit, but business travellers tended to spend more per visit (£493 on average) and £3.4 billion in total.

Between 1999 and 2003, the number of holiday visits overseas residents made to the UK fell by 1.9 million, a decrease of 19 per cent. As might be expected, the number of holiday visits suffered the largest fall between 2000 and 2001 (18 per cent). A small recovery was seen in 2002 and 2003 but the number of holidays overseas residents took in the UK during 2003 was still 1.9 million below the figure for 1999.

Visits to friends or relatives were the only visits that continued to increase between 1999 and 2003. The number of overseas residents travelling to the UK to visit friends or relatives increased by 24 per cent during this period. The number of miscellaneous visits (such as shopping, study and medical visits) fell in most years between 1999 and 2003.

Source: National Statistics, 17 December 2004

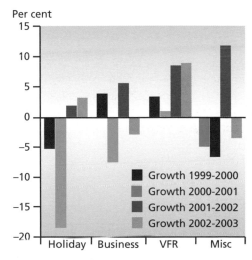

Figure 6.6 Growth of overseas residents' visits by purpose of visit

1 Using Figure 6.6, suggest why holiday visits are the most popular reason for overseas residents to come to the UK.

2 How do visitor destinations in the UK benefit by encouraging business delegates and conferences?

3 What impact might a fall in the number of overseas residents visiting the UK have on the economy?

4 Suggest why the number of visits by overseas residents to see friends or relatives increased between 1999 and 2003.

5 Using the graph showing growth in visits by purpose of visit, describe the changes in 1999–2000, 2000–2001, 2001–2002 and 2002–2003.

Country of residence

Travel Trends 2003

The majority of visits by overseas residents were from the European Union (EU) (60 per cent). Visits from this region increased by 5 per cent from 14.1 million in 2002 to 14.8 million in 2003, reversing the downward trend in visits in recent years and, in particular, the large fall in 2001.

In 2003, North Americans made 4.0 million visits to the UK, making North America the region with the second largest share of visits. However, the number of visits from residents of North America was 6 per cent down on the previous year and 18 per cent down on the number of visits made in 2000. Up until 2001, visits by North American residents had been steadily increasing in number.

Visits from residents of non-EU Europe have recovered from the fall in visits in 2001, with the number of visits rising from 2.2 million visits in 1999 to 2.4 million in 2003.

Residents of the United States continued to account for the largest share of visits to the UK (3.3 million) and to spend the most money (£2.3 billion). The residents of France and Germany made the second and third largest numbers of visits to the UK (3.1 million and 2.6 million visits respectively).

Residents of the United States made more leisure trips to the UK than did residents of any other country (2.6 million) and spent £1.6 billion on such visits, which was almost as much as the combined spending on leisure trips by residents of France, Germany, the Irish Republic and the Netherlands.

Source: Office for National Statistics, 17 December 2004

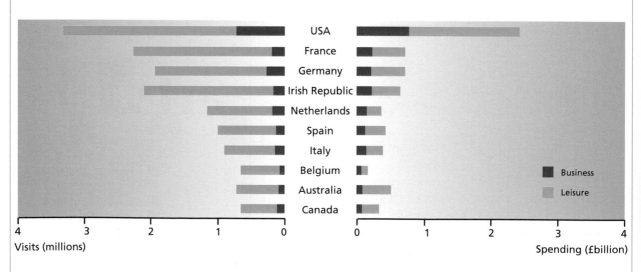

Figure 6.7 Visiting and spending for the top 10 visiting countries by purpose of visit

Area of stay in the UK
Travel Trends 2003

London was the most popular region of stay, with half of all overnight visits to the UK, including a stay of at least one night there, accounting for 11.7 million overnight stays. Such stays in the capital were associated with spending of £5.9 billion. The number of overnight visits to London was over seven times greater than those made to Scotland and thirteen times more than visits made to Wales.

The next most popular place of visit was Edinburgh, which hosted 0.8 million visits, followed by Manchester and Birmingham.

Source: Office for National Statistics,
17 December 2004

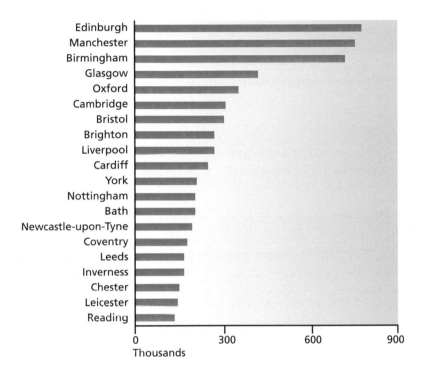

Figure 6.8 Top cities visited (excluding London) by number of overnight visits 2003

Skills practice

1 Using Figure 6.7, suggest why the majority of visits by overseas residents in 2003 were from the European Union?

2 Why are the figures of visits from residents of non-EU Europe in 2003 not directly comparable to today?

3 If you were to organise a series of advertising campaigns to attract overseas residents, which countries would you select and why?

4 Using the graph in Figure 6.7, describe the differences in the number of visits, the country of origin, the amount spent and the purpose of visit.

Skills practice

1 Using Figure 6.8, suggest why London is the most popular destination for overseas residents visiting the UK?

2 Suggest why Edinburgh is the second most popular place of visit.

3 What are the main reasons for overseas residents to visit Leicester and Reading?

4 How can the cities of Leicester and Reading encourage more overseas residents to visit?

Domestic tourism

In 2004 one thousand people took part in a survey called Destination England, organised by VisitBritain, to determine what domestic tourists think about their own country. The British take over 70 million holidays in England each year, spending an average of £12 billion. Some of these visits are purely for leisure, others may be combined with visiting friends or relatives (VFR). The survey discovered what tourists perceived as being a strength, a priority, an opportunity and a saving. It revealed that England's strengths lie in heritage and unspoilt countryside, whilst the biggest priorities and opportunities lie in developing its outdoor activities.

Table 6.3 Destination England: How well does it deliver?

STRENGTHS	OPPORTUNITIES
Factors which are very important to visitors, and at which England is already recognised as excelling at: • Unspoilt countryside • Quality of food and drink • Interesting villages, market towns and cities • Facilities for walking, rambling or hiking • History and heritage.	Factors which visitors recognise England performing very well at but could further develop: • Range of local produce, arts and crafts • Choice of camping and caravanning facilities • Activities for children • Myths, legends and folklores.
PRIORITIES	**SAVINGS**
Factors that are very important to visitors, but which England is not currently seen as excelling at: • Beaches and coastline • Chance to see wildlife in its natural habitat. In some cases this may simply be an education issue, where visitors are not aware of how good the English product actually is.	Factors which the majority of our visitors see as neither particularly important nor relevant to England as a short-break destination: • Golfing • Theme parks • Locations which are connected with books, films or rock and pop. For some sub-groups, these aspects of the English holiday product may have a greater influence.

Source: VisitBritain (2004)

Skills practice

Based on the results of the Destination England survey, provide a response to VisitBritain suggesting how tourism in England could develop during the next five years.

Day visits and excursions

An excursion is a short journey taken for pleasure – it includes day visits. These include visiting the cinema, going shopping or going out for a drink. There were 5.2 billion day visits taken for the purposes of leisure and tourism in 2003: 71 per cent to towns and cities, 24 per cent to the countryside and 5 per cent to the seaside or coast. This figure includes 1.1 billion day visits for the purposes of tourism, which accounts for 21 per cent of all day visits. Tourism *day visitors* are defined as 'people staying in places outside of their usual environment within any day, on visits lasting three or more hours and not made on a regular basis'.

The most popular leisure activities are going out for a meal or drinking (18 per cent), walking (15 per cent), visiting friends or relatives (14 per cent) and going shopping (11 per cent).

The most popular form of transport for those taking day visits is the private motor car, which accounts for nearly 60 per cent of all day visits. The average distance travelled for day trips depends on the destination. Those visiting towns and cities travel an average of 21 kilometres (13 miles), those visiting the countryside travel an average of 31 kilometres (19 miles) and those visiting the seaside or coast travel on average 48 kilometres (30 miles).

Between 1998 and 2003 the number of day visits decreased from 5.9 billion to 5.2 billion. During this time the number of visits to towns and cities decreased by 14 per cent, the number of visits to the countryside decreased by 12 per cent, whilst visits to the seaside or coast increased by 11 per cent.

Skills practice

1 Suggest why towns and cities are popular destinations for day visitors.

2 How would you encourage more day visitors to use public transport? Outline the benefits of your suggestions.

3 Suggest why visits to the seaside and the coast increased between 1998 and 2003.

4 Should the tourism industry be promoting day trips or longer visits that include one or two overnight stays?

The most recent tourism statistics can be found on the following websites:

Statistics on Tourism and Research (STARUK)
http://www.staruk.org.uk

Department for Culture, Media and Sport (DCMS)
http://www.culture.gov.uk

Office for National Statistics (ONS)
http://www.ons.gov.uk

Tourism figures are also available from each national tourist board. These national tourist boards have websites for the tourism industry as well as providing information for visitors:

England (VisitBritain)
http://www.visitbritain.org/ukindustry (see research and statistics)

Scotland (ScotExchange)
http://www.scotexchange.net

Wales (Wales Tourist Board)
http://www.wtbonline.gov.uk

Northern Ireland (Northern Ireland Tourist Board)
http://www.nitb.com

Tourist board regions

After considering the features and appeal of holidaying in the UK on a national basis we will now consider holidaying within a tourist board region.

In this second study, you will be able to apply the knowledge, understanding and research skills developed in your general study of UK tourism. In addition, you will be able to produce a more detailed and specific study of the attractions in a local region. You will then be in a position to evaluate the provision at present in order to identify gaps in the local region's tourist provision. Having identified gaps, you can suggest what could be done to fill these gaps to meet the needs of tourists and to help development of the industry in the region.

Each country in the UK has its own national tourist board which is responsible for encouraging visitors and helping to ensure that tourism businesses maintain high levels of quality to provide visitors with a memorable visit.

The UK has four *national tourist boards*. Their websites provide information for visitors:

England (VisitBritain)
http://www.visitbritain.org

Scotland (VisitScotland)
http://www.visitscotland.com

Wales (VisitWales)
http://www.visitwales.com

Northern Ireland (Discover Northern Ireland)
http://www.discovernorthernireland.com

Each of these national tourist boards coordinates a series of regional tourist boards.

Tourism in the UK is organised through a hierarchical structure with different organisations taking on different roles at a variety of different scales.

National level	**UK Government – Department for Culture Media and Sport (DCMS)** Role: To help the tourism industry improve what it has to offer for all visitors, to develop tourism policy and promote a positive image abroad.

VisitBritain
Role: To promote Britain overseas as a tourist destination and to lead and coordinate the marketing of England.

Regional level	**Regional Tourist Boards** Role: To bring economic, social and environmental benefits to the people who live and work in the region and to provide a rewarding and enjoyable experience for visitors. **Regional Development Agencies** Role: To coordinate economic development and regeneration strategies in the regions by working with the Regional Tourist Boards and other stakeholders.

County/District/ Local levels	**Local Authority Tourism Departments** Role: To plan at the county/district/local levels by representing the needs of residents and businesses and to bring the benefits of tourism to local areas whilst reducing any negative effects.

Tourist Information Centres
Role: To provide a service for visitors and local residents by giving information about visitor attractions and provide a booking service for those seeking accommodation.

Figure 6.9 The structure of tourism in the UK

Skills practice

1 Identify the tourist board region for your home area.

2 Select the tourist board region for the area you have chosen to study and investigate the extent of information contained on its website.

South West tourism

We are going to study one tourist board region; the example given here is from South West Tourism, however for the purposes of assessment you can select any tourist board region from the UK.

South West Tourism is a partnership of private enterprise and both local and central government. They work together to encourage the promotion and development of tourism in Bath and Bristol, Cornwall and the Isles of Scilly, Devon, Dorset, Somerset, Gloucestershire and Wiltshire. The region is also known as the West Country. The region has many contrasting features that attract a wide range of visitors.

The West Country has an extensive coastline that has played an important part in the culture and history of the region: Charles Darwin, Captain Scott of the Antarctic and Sir Francis Drake, who defeated the Spanish Armada, all

Figure 6.10 South West tourist board region

sailed from Plymouth. John Cabot, who discovered the mainland of North America, sailed from Bristol.

The coastline is also famous for its most southerly point, Land's End, which is the most southerly point in the UK, and the bustling seaside resorts of Torquay, Newquay, Weymouth and Bournemouth. Other parts of the coastline contain coastal walks, remote sandy beaches, dramatic cliffs, secluded coves and picturesque fishing villages. The resort of Newquay is famous for its surfing with eleven sandy beaches and seven miles of sand.

Inland from the coast is a rich variety of countryside from the national parks of Exmoor and Dartmoor to the flat landscape of the Somerset Levels and the rolling hills of Wiltshire. Farm and local produce is popular with visitors,

Surfers at Newquay

especially cider, wines, beef, lamb, fish, clotted cream, the Bath bun and Cornish pasties. Towns and cities include the cathedral cities of Salisbury, Wells, Truro and Exeter. The city of Bath is famous for its Roman remains and Georgian buildings whilst Bristol is the largest city in the West Country and has a thriving range of contemporary arts and live music.

Skills practice

Working in groups, each person is given the task to research a range of visitor attractions in each of the areas within the South West. Using a range of guidebooks, brochures and Internet sources, research examples of urban and rural attractions. Present your information as a poster and reveal your findings to the rest of the group.

The purpose of South West Tourism

The purpose of South West Tourism can be found in the organisation's mission statement and aims.

Mission Statement of South West Tourism

To act as the leader and voice of tourism in the region, and assist in the sustainable development of a profitable and growing quality tourism industry, contributing to the overall prosperity of the South West of England.

Aims of South West Tourism

To support and assist a competitive, growing, profitable and sustainable tourism industry in the South West by:

- Generating new and repeat customers through professionally researched and executed marketing campaigns.

- Steering the development of tourism in the region through key strategic development projects.

- Representing and lobbying for a fair economic and public policy position which will enable the industry to develop and grow.

- Saving tourism businesses money through membership benefits, discounted purchasing and cost-saving opportunities.

- Providing high-quality relevant business support services to tourism operators.

Skills practice

Visit the South West Tourism industry website http://www.swtourism.co.uk and find examples to complete the following table:

	EVIDENCE
What marketing campaigns does South West Tourism produce?	
What key development projects does South West Tourism get involved with?	
Is there any evidence of lobbying through press releases and membership of other tourism organisations?	
What are the benefits for businesses to become a member of South West Tourism?	
What business support does South West Tourism offer?	

Table 6.4 Key trends in South West tourism 2003

	UK RESIDENTS		OVERSEAS RESIDENTS	
	Trips (millions)	Spending (£ millions)	Visits (millions)	Spending (£ millions)
Holiday	16.7	3326	0.67	199
Business	1.7	432	0.34	135
Visiting friends or relatives	3.9	329	0.67	172
Other	0.4	177	0.2	157
Total	22.8	4265	1.9	663

Source: South West Tourism/United Kingdom Tourism Survey (UKTS)/International Passenger Survey (IPS)

Tourism in the South West attracts 26 million visitors each year. The industry is worth more than £8 billion annually to the South West economy, supporting over 300,000 jobs. Future prospects look good for the South West as more people in the UK are taking short-break holidays and choosing to stay at the seaside or on the coast. The table above shows the key trends in South West tourism.

These visits generate an average spend of £187 per trip by UK residents and an average spend of £353 per visit by overseas residents. Overseas residents spend more money because they stay longer, an average of 8.6 nights.

Skills practice

You have been asked by South West Tourism to organise a marketing campaign to increase visitor numbers and the amount spent within the region. Which group of visitors do you consider to be the most important to the South West? Which group would you decide to target to increase visitor numbers? Give reasons to justify your decision.

Think about it

Why do more UK residents visit the South West than overseas visitors?

Day visits

The South West accounts for 13 per cent of tourism day trips within England. There are more day trips to the coast and the countryside in the South West than in other tourist board regions. However these visits attract less spending compared to city and town visits.

Tourism day visits are expected to increase from an estimated 148.5 million in 2001 to 177.5 million in 2011, with expenditure rising from £3771 million to £4528 million in 2011.

Numbers of visitors are not evenly spread throughout the South West region as some areas of the region receive more visitors than others. As a result some areas receive more economic benefits than others, based on the amounts that visitors spend. The areas with the highest numbers of spending visitors are Devon and Cornwall and the areas with the lowest numbers are Gloucestershire and Wiltshire.

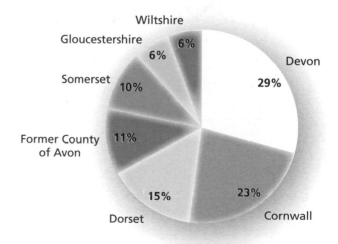

Figure 6.11 Visitor spending by county

Source: South West Tourism

Think about it

Is the future development of the South West dependent on the pattern of visitor spend across the region?

Visitor attractions

There are approximately 1000 visitor attractions in the South West region. Some of these have an international reputation, including Stonehenge, the Eden Project (see page 216), the Roman Bath and Pump Rooms in Bath. Over half (55 per cent) of visitor attractions are related to historic and cultural heritage, including museums and historic houses, which are concentrated in the north of the region around Bath and Bristol. Gardens are popular visitor attractions in Devon and Cornwall, including the Eden Project and the Lost Gardens of Heligan.

Think about it

Does the distribution of visitor attractions across the South West have an impact in terms of the numbers of visitors and the amount of spend?

Devon has the highest concentration of visitor attractions in the South West. It has 30 per cent of the region's farm attractions and its other attractions include steam/heritage railways, natural heritage attractions, historic houses, castles and wildlife attractions and zoos. Cornwall has the highest concentration (32 per cent) of historic and archaeological sites and the highest number of leisure and theme parks in the region.

CASE STUDY

Stonehenge

The most famous ancient monument in the UK is Stonehenge in Wiltshire. Built between 3000 and 5000 years ago this imposing circle of stone pillars is recognised as a World Heritage Site. The stones weigh between 4 and 50 tons each and are arranged in a series of circles.

Their geometric pattern has baffled archaeologists as to whether Stonehenge is a temple or an astrological observatory.

Stonehenge receives nearly 800,000 paying visitors every year, with approximately another 200,000 who stand on the roadside to view and photograph the stones.

Stonehenge is the most famous ancient monument in the UK

Table 6.5 Top 10 paid admission attractions in the South West of England 2003

ATTRACTION	LOCATION	VISITS
Eden Project	St Austell, Cornwall	1,404,372
Roman Baths	Bath	837,457
Stonehenge	Amesbury, Wiltshire	745,229
Longleat Estate	Warminster, Wiltshire	518,121
Land's End	Cornwall	500,000*
Paignton Zoo	Torbay, Cornwall	457,539
Tamar Cruising	Cornwall	375,000*
Westonbirt Arboretum	Gloucestershire	355,054*
Stourhead House and Garden	Wiltshire	328,526
Lynton and Lynmouth Cliff Railway	Devon	300,000*

*=estimate

Source: VisitBritain (2004)

Table 6.6 Top 10 free admission attractions in the South West of England 2003

ATTRACTION	LOCATION	VISITS
Lulworth Cove Heritage Centre	Dorset	441,776*
Bath Abbey	Bath and North East Somerset	350,000*
Cornish Cyder Farm	Cornwall	340,000
Gloucester Cathedral	Gloucestershire	293,354*
Truro Cathedral	Cornwall	200,000*
Teign Valley Glass and House of Marbles	Devon	200,000*
Cardew Design Tea Pottery	Devon	150,000*
Pump Room	Bath and North East Somerset	146,546*
Bristol Industrial Museum	Bristol	130,000*
Otterton Mill Centre	Devon	109,000*

*=estimate

Source: VisitBritain (2004)

Skills practice

1 Using the top 10 paid admission attractions and the top 10 free admission attractions in the South West of England identify which are urban-based attractions and which are rural attractions.

2 Produce a map of the South West showing the location of important visitor attractions.

Use a colour code to distinguish between urban-based attractions and rural attractions.

3 Investigate why the top 10 paid admission attractions and the top 10 free admission attractions in the South West of England are popular with large numbers of visitors.

Accommodation

There are nearly 17,000 commercial accommodation providers in the South West region. Hotels and inns account for 40 per cent of businesses offering serviced accommodation with 60 per cent being bed and breakfasts and guesthouses.

However, there is more self-catering accommodation than serviced accommodation in the South West, in terms of the number of businesses and the number of bed spaces. Devon has the highest number of hotels and guesthouses in terms of the number of bed spaces available.

Bed-and-breakfast accommodation is more equally divided across the region but with slightly higher numbers in Dorset and Devon. Devon has twice as many farms offering accommodation than the other counties and there is less farm accommodation available in Dorset and Wiltshire. Caravan parks are found across the region but most are in Cornwall. There are many small self-catering cottages across the region with the majority in Devon and Cornwall.

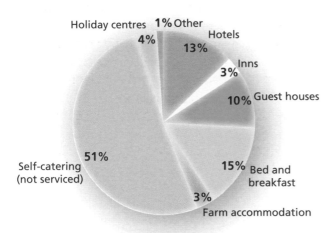

Figure 6.12 Percentage of accommodation businesses in the South West

Source: South West Tourism

Think about it

To what extent does the pattern of accommodation reflect the popularity and type of visitor destinations?

Events and entertainment

The South West hosts many live performances, shows, events and festivals. These attract visitors who often stay overnight, which increases the economic benefits to the region. Popular events include:

* Bath International Music Festival
* Bath and West Agricultural Show
* Bude Jazz Festival
* Bristol Balloon Festival
* Cheltenham International Jazz Festival
* Greenbelt Festival
* Glastonbury Festival of Contemporary Performing Arts
* Plymouth Folk Music Festival.

CASE STUDY

Glastonbury Festival of Contemporary Performing Arts

The Glastonbury Festival of Contemporary Performing Arts is the largest green field music and performing arts festival in the world. The festival is set amongst 900 acres, nearly a mile and a half across. It hosts some of the biggest names in music and attracts over 1200 acts and over 150,000 visitors.

Source: Glastonbury Festivals

Glastonbury Festival

Food and drink

Locally produced food and drink is an important asset to the South West. It is famous for its Cornish pasties, Devon cream teas, Somerset cider, Cheddar cheese and Wiltshire ham. It is estimated that up to 69 per cent of visitors regard the provision of quality food as making a positive contribution to their holiday: approximately 66 per cent of tourists purchase or eat local foods during their visit. The most popular venues for eating out are: pubs (64 per cent), tea-rooms (43 per cent), cafés and snack bars (32 per cent) and fish and chip shops (31 per cent). Also see pages 214–215.

Transport and accessibility

The south of the region is situated on a peninsula that juts out into the Atlantic Ocean. It is one of the extremities of the British Isles, with Lands End being the most southerly point. This presents a challenge for travellers and for tourism in the area, as regions in extreme or peripheral locations take longer to travel to. The longer it takes to complete a journey, the fewer people who will be prepared to travel.

Most visitors to the South West travel by car. The M5 motorway provides easy access from the north and those from London travelling along the M4 can join with the M5 at Bristol to travel to the South West. At Exeter travel to Cornwall is by a series of A-roads following the A38 via Plymouth and across the Tamar River at the toll bridge.

Visitors can fly direct to the region by air via Bristol International, Exeter, Plymouth, Newquay and Bournemouth International airports from a range of domestic and international destinations. However most visitors who travel by air do so via Gatwick and Heathrow and then proceed by rail, coach or hire car to the South West.

Sea travel is also possible. There are ferry services to Plymouth and Poole from France, from the Channel Islands to Poole and Weymouth and from the Isle of Scilly to Penzance.

There are frequent rail services to the South West, the most frequent being found in the north of the region, but there are trains that run direct to Plymouth and Exeter and connect with local services.

Comparing the South West region with the UK

During the 1990s the South West region increased its share of the UK tourism market. It was successful in attracting large numbers of short-break domestic visitors, however its share of longer holidays has not dramatically increased. UK residents visiting the South West have consistently spent more in the region each year. In 2000, they spent on average £162 per visit to the South West compared to a UK average of £160 per visit. However, the figure is much lower than the average for Scotland, which was £195 per visit in 2000. In 2003, UK residents spent £187 per visit, much higher than the average for Wales, which was £152 per visit.

Recently there has been a decline in the number of overseas residents visiting the South West. They spent an average of £489 per visit to the UK in 2000, but those visiting the South West only spent an average of £334 per visit. In 2003 overseas residents spent an average of £475 per visit to the UK.

The South West is dependent on holiday visits, as it has not been as successful as other parts of the UK in attracting visitors travelling on business. The South West is, however, successful in attracting more VFR (visiting friends or relatives) visits than any other rural area in the UK.

The region has more visitors staying longer than in other parts of the UK. They stay for four nights or longer, and generate 64 per cent of the spending in the region compared with 52 per cent for the UK as a whole.

The region receives a similar social profile of visitor compared with the rest of the UK. It attracts a slightly lower proportion of AB/C1 visitors (professional, managerial and skilled office workers) than other regions, although more C2 (skilled manual workers) visit this region compared to other regions in the UK.

Think about it

Why does the South West have more staying visitors than other regions in the UK?

The quality of accommodation in the South West is similar to the UK average in terms of the number of stars and diamonds awarded to hotels, guesthouses and self-catering accommodation. However, the South West region has more 1 and 2 star hotels (58 per cent) compared to the rest of England (47 per cent). At the luxury end of the market the South West has fewer 4- and 5-star hotels: 6 per cent of all hotels in the South West have 4- and 5-stars, compared to 9 per cent in England, 17 per cent in Wales and 24 per cent in Scotland. In comparison, the South West has many more high-quality guesthouses and bed-and-breakfast businesses: 49 per cent are awarded a 4- and 5-diamond rating, compared with 15 per cent in Wales and 23 per cent in Scotland.

Occupancy levels for serviced accommodation, which includes hotels, guesthouses and bed-and-breakfasts, is, however, below the national average. Room occupancy in the UK is on average 57 per cent compared with the South West region at 53 per cent.

Think about it

To what extent does the quality of accommodation reflect the type of visitor to the region?

Although seasonality is an important factor with higher numbers of visits being made in the peak summer season, the trend is similar to that of the UK as a whole. However, fewer attractions in the South West are open all year compared to the national average.

Most of the visitors to the South West are domestic visitors, accounting for 92.7 per cent of all visitors, with only 7.3 per cent from overseas. This compares with a UK average of 87.2 per cent of domestic visitors and 12.3 per cent of overseas visitors. The proportion of overseas visitors in the South West is lower than England and Scotland but is equal to Wales.

Overseas visitors to the South West originate from a wide range of countries, which shows that the region is not dependent on visitors from a single country. The top five overseas originating countries are:

* USA
* France
* Germany
* Ireland
* Australia.

In comparison, Scotland is more dependent on visitors from the USA and Ireland is more dependent on visitors from the UK.

Most of the domestic visitors to the South West follow a similar age profile to the rest of the UK, however the South West has a higher proportion of domestic visitors aged over 55. The average age of visitors from overseas to the South West is slightly younger than those visiting the UK as a whole, which suggests that the South West is recognised as a family destination. The South West attracts less overseas visitors aged 16–54 compared to the UK as a whole but attracts more overseas visitors aged over 55.

Think about it

Suggest why the South West receives more visitors over the age of 55 than any other region in the UK.

Evaluate provision

It is important to evaluate the provision of tourism in the South West in order to identify any gaps and to suggest how the industry can develop further. Comparing current trends in the South West with the rest of the UK has already revealed several gaps. There may be historical, social, economic, geographical or environmental reasons why the level of tourism provision differs from one region to another.

It is important for destinations and visitor attractions to maintain their popularity and appeal and the tourism industry in the region has to identify the needs of both domestic and incoming tourists, including those that are on holiday, visiting friends or relatives (VFR) or on business. By reviewing current provision and making improvements the tourism industry can help meet the needs of visitors both now and in the future.

In order to identify gaps in provision we need to establish what visitor attractions exist in the local tourist board region. This can be achieved by researching examples from brochures, Internet sites and guidebooks. It is also useful to compare examples from other similar tourist board regions to see what attractions and new developments are taking place. If a successful tourist attraction has been developed in one region it may be suitable for it to be developed in another.

Certain types of attractions that appear to be under-represented may suggest a gap in provision. For example, it is necessary to recognise that different tourist regions have their own particular mix of attractions. It would not be feasible for a major theme park like Alton Towers to exist in every county or region. Some attractions may have local rather than national appeal but could have the potential to expand and be developed to appeal to a larger number of tourists.

A successful tourist destination will have a diversity of attractions to appeal to different types of tourist, including young, old, family and groups. If a tourist board region relies on many visitors from overseas then visitor information is often made available in languages other than English. A tourist destination will also be able to provide a range of attractions and entertainment when the weather is hot and sunny as well as cold and wet.

CASE STUDY

Towards 2015

South West Tourism has carried out a review of its current provision as part of a new tourism strategy, **Towards 2015**.

A tourism strategy provides a policy for managing the future development of tourism. In order for the strategy to be written the present position needs to be evaluated. Only then can gaps in provision be identified. A strategy looks forward to the future and its aims depend on the agreements reached between the various public and private stakeholders.

There is a concern amongst tourism managers that without careful management, any future growth in tourism in the South West could threaten the long-term prospects of the industry. Some of the concerns are:

- While there will be more new jobs, they would be seasonal, forcing people to find alternative sources of work in the off-peak season, and of low quality, requiring few skills which may be reflected in poor quality of service.

- While there will be more new visitors, they would be in parts of the region and at times of the year which are already at capacity in the established resorts and attractions.

- Where now the local community supports tourism, increased traffic and damage to the environment could create feelings of alienation and resentment, which may cause local people to oppose any future growth in the industry.

In response to these concerns South West Tourism devised Towards 2015. The plan aims to:

• Protect the environment

• Improve the quality of life of local people

• Take advantage of the region's existing strengths

• Create a long-term and sustainable industry.

It is expected that the industry will benefit financially from this strategy with the estimated income from tourism increasing by £1.2 billion.

One of the ways it hopes to achieve this is to move away from the traditional way in which tourist destinations are marketed. Rather than simply promoting an area to attract visitors the strategy is to market 'customer experiences'. People choose the holiday that they want rather than its location, for example a customer is more likely to decide that they want a 'weekend of sheer indulgence' or an 'adventure activity break'.

This will be made possible by establishing destinations and experiences around a collection of different marketing brands.

For further information visit the Towards 2015 and South West Tourism websites.

Source:
South West Tourism

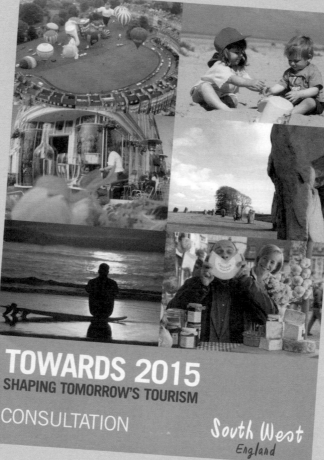

Towards 2015 tourist strategy for the South West

Think about it

Why is it important for a tourist board region to

• protect the environment;

• improve the quality of life of local people;

• take advantage of the region's existing strengths; and

• create a long-term and sustainable industry?

1 Using the Visit South West website, give examples of the destinations, experiences and attractions that are being promoted under the following brands:

SOUTH WEST TOURISM MARKETING BRANDS	EXISTING PROVISION, DESTINATIONS, ATTRACTIONS AND EXPERIENCES
Sheer indulgence	
Close to nature	
Traditional beach holiday	
Its adventure	
Discovery	
Romance	
Living heritage	
Easy pre-school	
It's cool	
Relax and recharge	

2 How useful are these marketing brands in promoting the South West?
3 Are there any attractions that are not represented?
4 How will Towards 2015 benefit local businesses?

The following are the number of the types of tourist attractions in the South West region.

Table 6.7 Tourist attractions in the South West region

	Devon	Cornwall	Glos.	Somerset	Wiltshire	Dorset	Avon	Total
Museums/art galleries	53	38	37	31	25	35	23	242
Historic houses/castles	47	24	27	17	16	27	5	163
Other historical/archaeological sites	12	30	17	14	19	11	8	111
Gardens	20	43	10	10	11	15	5	114
Workplaces	24	13	13	18	0	13	3	84
Wildlife attractions/zoos	18	13	6	10	0	10	2	59
Natural heritage visitor attractions	14	5	8	4	5	3	5	44
Visitor/heritage centres	11	7	9	7	2	3	5	44
Farms	13	5	9	5	3	4	1	40
Places of worship	8	2	7	4	3	5	6	35
Leisure/theme parks and attractions	8	10	3	4	1	5	2	33
Steam/heritage railways	8	5	6	3	1	1	0	24
Boat trip	7	2	0	1	1	0	2	13
Total	243	197	152	128	87	132	67	1006

Source: South West Tourism

1 Using the information in Table 6.7, describe the provision of tourist attractions in the South West.

2 What types of tourist attractions are largely represented and which types are under-represented?

3 How do the different counties of the South West region compare in terms of their mix of visitor attractions?

4 Is the number of visitor attractions useful in evaluating provision? Suggest other information that you would wish to investigate.

5 The number of tourist attractions is based on information held on the South West Tourism database. Why might some tourist attractions not appear in this database?

6 What gaps in the provision of tourism attractions can you identify?

7 Suggest how South West Tourism can fill the gaps you have identified.

Once you have established the gaps in the provision of tourist attractions you then need to consider gaps in the other factors that affect a tourist's decision to visit an area. Look back at pages 213–224. Some of the headings to consider include:

* Events and entertainment

* Food and drink

* Accommodation

* Social, economic and environmental factors

* Amount of tourism infrastructure.

The benefits to local businesses can be extensive. Major tourist attractions such as the Eden Project encourage visitors to stay overnight rather than just spend a day in the region. Visitors staying longer spend more money, which benefits local shops, hotels, restaurants, bars and other attractions. In turn these businesses spend money in the local economy by paying staff and local suppliers, which widens the benefits of tourism to other businesses. If an area is seen to benefit from having large numbers of visitors then other businesses will be attracted to the area to provide a range of services in order to further enhance the range of tourism provision.

Knowledge check

1 Why is the tourism industry important to the UK?

2 What is the difference between a domestic and an incoming tourist?

3 Name ten examples of urban-based attractions.

4 Name ten examples of attractions in rural areas.

5 What are the factors affecting tourists' decisions to visit a destination?

6 What is meant by the term 'tourism infrastructure'? Give examples from both public and private organisations.

7 Which sources would you use to find statistics on tourism trends in the UK?

8 What are the main current trends in UK tourism?

9 What is the purpose of a regional tourist board?

10 Identify the tourist board regions in England and Wales.

UNIT ASSESSMENT

Portfolio practice

You need to produce a portfolio based on an investigation into tourism within the UK on a national basis and in a local tourist board region.

A written report on factors affecting the popularity of tourism in the UK

You need to demonstrate developed knowledge of a wide variety of factors affecting the popularity of the UK as a tourist destination.

Look back at pages 213–224 and consider why the following affect the popularity of the UK as a tourist destination:

- Attractions, events and entertainment
- Food, drink and accommodation
- Transport and accessibility
- Social and political factors
- Economic factors
- Environmental factors
- Tourism infrastructure.

You need to show how these factors interact together. For example, transport and accessibility is related to the level of tourism infrastructure as road builders, developers, railway companies, airports and airline companies work together to provide an integrated transport system. The range of attractions that are available in a tourist region will affect the provision of food, drink and accommodation depending on the needs of visitors.

Tourism can create a range of consequences in the form of social, political, economic and environmental factors. Increasing numbers of tourists do not always produce automatic benefits as they can put pressure on the availability of existing tourism infrastructure and local environments. Tourism produces a range of social consequences, some of which may be positive in terms of job creation and increasing the range of local facilities, but they can also be negative, leading to resentment and tension between local people and visitors.

It is a good idea to include examples in this section as you are then able to discuss the factors that affect the popularity of the UK as a tourist destination. Consider the information presented on the VisitBritain industry and tourist websites and the DCMS website, to get a sense of how the tourism industry in the UK is represented.

A written report into research into visitor numbers within the UK over recent years, graphical analysis of those figures and a bibliography of your sources

In this section you will need to show a variety of well-developed research skills, using a variety of sources. Consider using the most up-to-date sources available, and compare them to using the statistics presented in this book. Do not be surprised if last year's information is not available as it can take months for the information to be collected, analysed and presented to the industry.

A selection of appropriate sources has been suggested on page 229, which include several on the Internet. STAR UK is the main source of published data on tourism trends in the UK. The DCMS and the VisitBritain industry websites also contain information on tourism trends. For detailed information visit the Office for National Statistics website which publishes results on international travel trends. It also publishes a quarterly Business Monitor for overseas travel and tourism, detailing results from the International Passenger Survey. The Business Monitor contains data on visits to and from the UK by overseas residents and visits abroad by UK residents. The information is presented as tables with little or no analysis. Data that has been analysed appears in the annual Travel Trends report.

Rather than quote a range of data from these sources you are expected to present it using a variety of appropriate graphical techniques. If you are representing data that contains values, for example the number of people visiting a destination, then a bar chart is often used.

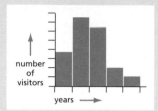

Figure 1 A bar chart

If you are representing data over a series of several years, then a line graph is normally used.

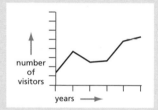

Figure 2 A line graph

If you are representing data using percentages, then a pie chart is normally used.

Figure 3 A pie chart

If you are representing classes of data, for example you are using age categories 10–19, 20–29, 30–39, 40–49 etc., then a histogram is normally used.

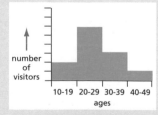

Figure 4 A histogram

Once the data is represented graphically there needs to be a thorough analysis of the trends shown by the data. Describe what you see and account for any variation in visitor numbers by describing events, incidents or changes in the tourism industry. Use appropriate vocabulary to analyse information where possible. Remember to quote examples from your graph, using actual data and dates to support your analysis.

You will need to produce a bibliography, so it is always useful to accurately record your sources as you use them. For information on writing a bibliography see Unit 3 pages 109–110.

Evidence of an oral presentation about tourism in a local tourist board region putting it in the context of the UK study

You are expected to present well-developed information about tourism in a tourist board region. The tourist board region can be chosen from the list on page 248. Make sure you identify where your tourist board region is located in relation to the rest of the UK. Map evidence is always useful to display the location of important urban-based and rural tourist attractions. You may be asked to justify your choice of tourist board region; this can easily be done with reference to major tourist attractions and statistics.

You need to become familiar with the trends and issues affecting your chosen region. Rather than present a descriptive account of what you have discovered about your tourist board region you are required to analyse the information thoroughly and set it in context by comparing it with the UK as a whole. After describing trends in the number of visitors for your region, compare them to national trends. If your region is performing better or worse than the rest of the UK then suggest reasons for this. It is important to give an insight as to why particular trends emerge and to describe the impacts of those trends.

You are asked to convey this information in the form of a presentation. The presentation should be well structured and supported with a range of relevant visual material. It may be useful to consider the use of PowerPoint software, handouts, brochures, posters and other display material. The next section will discuss how to prepare and deliver a positive presentation.

How to deliver a presentation

Careful planning is important when preparing for a presentation. It is important that a presentation should be structured so that information flows in a logical and easy-to-follow sequence.

Think about it

What makes a good presentation?

You may wish to follow the IDC model:
- Introduction
- Development
- Conclusion.

Introduction
The opening is very important as it gives the audience a clear indication of what is to follow.

I	Interest	This may be achieved by asking questions, using visual aids such as OHPs, video, maps and diagrams, anything that stimulates audience interest in the subject matter to be covered.
N	Need	Tell the audience what they are going to gain from listening. We are always interested in what we will gain from a situation.
T	Title	Tell the audience exactly what you are going to cover.
R	Range	Give the audience an idea of the contents, their degree of involvement, for example when they can ask questions and how long the presentation will last.
O	Objective	State your objective or outcome of the presentation.

The whole of the introduction should only take a few minutes.

Development

The development section cannot be planned until a clear objective has been set. The objective in this case will be contained within the assessment briefing. The information during the development section should reflect what is to be achieved during the presentation.

In order to do this it is necessary to analyse your research on the subject. This can be done using a list of ideas, a concept map or spider diagram. From this information you can then extract what Must, Should and Could be included in your presentation.

Musts   Vital information that must be given to the audience if the objective is to be reached.

Shoulds   Important information that should be given to the audience to assist in the understanding of the Musts.

Coulds   Information that is not vital to achieving the objective but is useful in enhancing the presentation, providing it does not distract the audience.

Conclusion

Check that the objective has been reached. It can be achieved by the use of a short summary or a set of questions.

Following the conclusion it is usual to thank the audience for listening.

Preparation is the key to success. If you are prepared then it means that you are well organised and rehearsed. Enjoy telling people about your research.

Characteristics of a good speaker

Your voice
- Your voice should be clear and audible
- Do not read from a script or note cards but tell the audience your information
- Vary your pace, not too fast and not too slow
- Pause occasionally to collect your thoughts and to gain attention.

Appearance
It is important to dress to impress and complement what you have to say. What impression will your appearance give to the audience?

Body language
You should be upright, alert and relaxed. Avoid crossing arms or placing hands in pockets.

Eye contact
Maintain eye contact at all times to check that people are listening and to show the audience that you are talking to them.

Interest and enthusiasm
Be positive and enthusiastic about your presentation. Establish yourself as someone worth listening to. If you are interested in the subject matter then other people will be too.

Visual aids
Visual aids are there to support your presentation not to distract from it. They should be simple and bold.

Video camera

Be prepared to make the presentation in front of a camera or an audio recorder. Your tutor may need to keep a record of your presentation. Make your words clear and avoid fidgeting. If you think you have made a mistake keep going. Be confident and enthusiastic, this will help you to deliver a successful presentation.

A presentation

Skills practice

Complete the following table:

BENEFITS AND PROBLEMS OF USING VISUAL AIDS IN PRESENTATIONS		
Visual aid	**Benefits**	**Problems**
Whiteboards/chalkboards		
Flipchart		
Overhead projector (OHP)		
Handouts		
Video and film		
PowerPoint		
Posters		

Evidence of an oral evaluation of the current provision in the tourist board region, making reference to gaps in the provision and suggesting possibilities for future improvements

Following on from the first part of your presentation you are to provide a well-developed evaluation of provision in the tourist board region. You need to evaluate the range of attractions, accommodation, services and infrastructure by using relevant examples.

You need to establish a way of identifying gaps in provision either by adding references from national trends, comparing provision to other similar tourist board regions or by identifying gaps within different parts of the region. This is then used to make a detailed analysis of the gaps in provision. Then, make a series of detailed and realistic suggestions for appropriate improvements. Make sure to fully justify your recommendations by saying how the region will benefit by your recommendations.

During your presentation you will be expected to use words and expressions which convey appropriate meaning. This includes the use of technical words and phrases found within the tourism literature. However, it is best to convey the information clearly and to avoid using unnecessary jargon or terms that you may not be confident with. Above all, enjoy telling other people about the findings of your research.

Resources

AA (2003) *The Days Out Guide 2004*. Basingstoke: AA Publishing.

AA (2004) *Motorist's Atlas Britain 2005*. Basingstoke: AA Publishing.

Andrews, R., Brown, J., Humphreys, R., Lee, P. and Reid, D. (2002) *The Rough Guide to Britain*. London: Rough Guides Ltd.

Berkmoes, R.V., Bedford, N., Callan, L., Davenport, F. and Ray, N. (2001) *Lonely Planet England*. London: Lonely Planet Publications Ltd.

Fullman, J. (2001) *Britain's Top Tourist Attractions*. Norfolk: Navigator Guides.

King, J. (2001) *Lonely Planet Wales*. London: Lonely Planet Publications Ltd.

National Statistics (2004) *Travel Trends 2003: A report on the International Passenger Survey*. London: Her Majesty's Stationery Office.

Parker, M. and Whitfield, P. (2003) *The Rough Guide to Wales*. London: Rough Guides Ltd.

Reid, D. and Humphreys, R. (2004) *The Rough Guide to Scotland*. London: Rough Guides Ltd.

Smallman, T., Cornwallis, G. and Wilson, N. (2002) *Lonely Planet Scotland*. London: Lonely Planet Publications Ltd.

Websites

There are 9 regional tourist boards in England, 3 in Wales and 13 in Scotland. Some of the regional tourist boards have their own website providing information specifically for the tourism industry.

England
Cumbria Tourist Board
http://www.cumbria-the-lake-district.co.uk and http://www.cumbriatourism.info
East of England Tourist Board
http://www.visiteastofengland.com and http://www.eetb.org.uk
Heart of England Tourist Board
http://www.visitheartofengland.com and http://www.heartofenglandtourism.com
Northumbria Tourist Board
http://www.visitnorthumbria.com and http://www.tourismnortheast.co.uk
North West Tourist Board
http://www.visitnorthwest.com and http://www.nwtourism.net

South West Tourism
http://www.swtourism.co.uk, http://visitsouthwest.co.uk and
Tourism South East (South East and Southern Tourist Boards)
http://www.industry.visitsoutheasternengland.com
Visit London
http://www.visitlondon.com
Yorkshire Tourist Board
http://www.yorkshiretouristboard.net and http://www.yorkshirevisitor.com

Scotland
Aberdeen and Grampian Tourist Board
http://www.agtb.org
Angus and Dundee Tourist Board
http://www.angusanddundee.co.uk and http://www.angusanddundeeexchange.net
Argyll, The Isles, Loch Lomond, Stirling and the Trossachs Tourist Board
http://www.scottish.heartlands.org
Ayrshire and Arran Tourist Board
http://www.ayrshire-arran.com
Dumfries and Galloway Tourist Board
http://www.galloway.co.uk
Edinburgh and Lothians Tourist Board
http://www.edinburgh.org
Greater Glasgow and Clyde Valley Tourist Board
http://www.seeglasgow.com
Highlands of Scotland Tourist Board
http://www.visithighlands.com
Kingdom of Fife Tourist Board
http://www.standrews.com/fife
Orkney Tourist Board
http://www.visitorkney.com and http://www.orkneyexchange.net
Perthshire Tourist Board
http://www.perthshire.co.uk and http://www.perthshireexchange.net
Scottish Borders Tourist Board
http://www.scot-borders.co.uk
Shetland Islands Tourist Board
http://www.visitshetland.com

Wales
North Wales
http://www.nwt.co.uk
Mid Wales
http://www.mid-wales-tourism.org.uk
South Wales
http://www.southandwestwales.roomcheck.co.uk

UNIT 7

Overseas destinations study

Introduction

In this unit, you will develop your knowledge of travel and tourism geography within the southern hemisphere. Through detailed investigation and research, you will learn about two countries, and the regions and tourist areas within them.

You should assume you are working for a consultancy advising UK tour operators looking to expand their programmes in the southern hemisphere. You will prepare a destination profile on two countries and through analysing appeal, popularity and access, justify your recommendation for UK tour operators.

At the outset of your investigation you need to make sure you are able to find sufficient data and appropriate statistics to show visitor trends in each of your chosen countries over recent years, and that your two chosen countries are sufficiently contrasting to allow you to evaluate the tourism potential of each and then make clear recommendations as to which should be included in tour operators' future programmes.

How you will be assessed

You will be asked to produce a portfolio based on an investigation into the tourism potential of two countries in the southern hemisphere for inclusion in tour operators' programmes.

Your portfolio will contain a destination profile for the two countries, including information about locations, features, facilities and amenities. You will be asked to provide a comparison of costs and options for travel to the two countries. Your portfolio should contain research and analysis of the appeal of the countries for UK tourists, drawing on data showing visitor trends over recent years, including analysis of current coverage by UK tour operators. Finally, your portfolio will include an evaluative report for tour operators, recommending which of the two countries to include in their future programme.

After studying this unit you need to have learned about:

* Destination profiles for two countries
* Costs and options for travel
* Destination popularity
* Evaluating destination profiles and making recommendations for tour operators.

Destination profile

You need to identify two countries within the southern hemisphere for your research and provide an overview of the regions and tourist destinations within them in the form of a destination profile. Each profile should include:

* Locations of the regions and the tourism destinations and availability of internal transportation within each country

* Features (climate, topography, accessibility, attractions)

* Facilities and amenities available to tourists

* The role of the countries' governments in planning for the development of tourism, helping to provide the infrastructure and environment within which tourism can develop, and promoting the tourist industry.

Locations of the regions and the tourism destinations

A *hemisphere* is one half of the Earth when it is divided along the Equator. The *Equator* is a line around the middle of the Earth at 0° latitude. The earth has two *hemispheres*, one north and one south of the Equator. In Unit 3 Travel Destinations and Unit 6 Tourism in the UK we looked at a range of tourist destinations in countries found in the northern hemisphere, including the UK, Europe and North America. In this unit we are going to look at countries in the southern hemisphere.

Countries in the southern hemisphere are considered *long-haul* destinations (see page 251 and definition in Unit 3) as they take more than five hours to fly to from the UK. However not all long-haul destinations are found in the southern hemisphere.

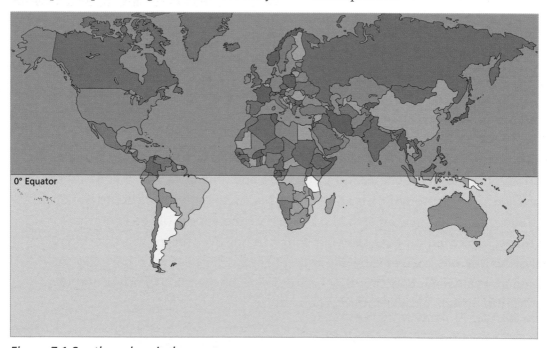

Figure 7.1 Southern hemisphere

Table 7.1 Top 10 long-haul destinations visited from the UK 2004

RANK ORDER	COUNTRY	NUMBER OF VISITS ABROAD BY UK RESIDENTS (IN 000s)
1	USA	4000
2	Canada	780
3	Australia	650
4	Thailand	600
5	Singapore	650
6	Hong Kong	400
7	South Africa	360
8	Egypt	355
9	Dubai	350
10	India	340

Source: ABTA (2005)

Skills practice

1 From the table showing the top ten long-haul destinations visited from the UK in 2004, identify the most popular holiday destinations in the southern hemisphere.

2 Using an atlas locate these countries on a blank outline map of the world (on page 144).

3 For each of the countries located, identify a popular tourist attraction.

It is important to know the locations of the main tourist regions and destinations within the popular tourist countries in the southern hemisphere and to know the availability of internal transportation. You will need to identify different ways of travelling to the main tourist regions and destinations.

Tourism regions within each country are important, as they will tend to cater for the needs of most visitors. In these regions many western food outlets and hotels are to be found, similar to those we experience in the UK. However, for some people this does not represent the true identity of the country and a hotel or hostel in an area a short distance away from the tourist region may provide a more authentic experience of the country.

Internal transport is an important factor in any tourist destination. On arriving at an airport, railway station or seaport, tourists will wish to seek efficient ways of getting to their accommodation. After a long journey tourists do not wish for a complicated set of internal transfers but to arrive at their accommodation safely, quickly and comfortably. Internal transfers may be by taxi, coach, or by public transport. In an unfamiliar country it is important to plan ahead and establish where key locations are and the route by which one needs to travel to the destination.

Main features

We will now look at some of the main features of overseas destinations in the southern hemisphere. The main features of any destination are:

* Climate
* Accessibility
* Topography
* Attractions.

Climate

Climate is important for any destination, as it can be very different to what is experienced in the UK. When the UK is experiencing winter, the northern hemisphere is tilted away from the Sun, at the same time the southern hemisphere is tilted towards the Sun and experiences summer. Many tourists from the UK travel to the southern hemisphere during the winter months in order to escape the cold, to spend time in countries that are experiencing summer. For example, between December and February in the UK it is often cold and wet whereas in the southern hemisphere Australia is experiencing a hot summer. Australia experiences winter months between June and August.

CASE STUDY

The four seasons in Australia

The seasons in Australia are:

Spring	September–November
Summer	December–February
Autumn	March–May
Winter	June–August

The nearer countries are located to the Equator the warmer they are. This is because the Equator receives the most energy from the Sun all year round. The closer the country is to the South Pole the colder it is as there is less energy from the Sun.

Australia

Some countries are so large that they experience a variety of different types of climate. Australia has a total landmass of 7.7 million square kilometres (4.8 million square miles) and extends from 2623 kilometres (1626 miles) north to south and 3278 kilometres (2032 miles) east to west. The area is so vast that Australia is larger than all of the countries in Europe put together (see Figure 7.2).

Australia experiences four distinct climatic zones:

1   The tropical north
2   Subtropical east coast and the Great Dividing Range
3   Mediterranean southwest
4   Desert and semi-desert of the centre.
(See Figure 7.3.)

The tropical north has a wet tropical climate and can be uncomfortably hot during the summer months. The best time to visit is during the cooler winter months. One of the key tourist attractions found in this climatic zone is the Kakadu National Park, which is famous for its coastal swamps and crocodiles.

The east coast is a subtropical region with the Great Barrier Reef to the north. The city of Brisbane is a famous tourist area, with the Gold Coast to the south and the Sunshine Coast to the north, both offering a surfer's paradise. To the

south the cities of Sydney and Melbourne have wetter winters and drier summers and are where most of Australia's population live.

The Great Dividing Range is Australia's mountain range, its highest point being Mount Kosciusko at 2228 metres (7310 feet), high enough for winter sports, including skiing and snowboarding.

The southwest is drier than the east coast. The summers are long and dry and are similar to the conditions found in southern Spain and Italy. The area around Perth has been developed as a tourist region but many unspoilt beaches remain along the coast outside this area.

The arid desert and semi-desert conditions found in the centre of Australia receive less than 225 millimetres of rainfall each year. The area is red and dusty and very hot. The most famous landmark is Uluru, or Ayers Rock, situated in the Uluru-Kata Tjuta National Park.

Skills practice

Choose two different climate regions in Australia.

1   Explain how each region appeals to tourists.
2   How does the climate affect the activities in these regions?

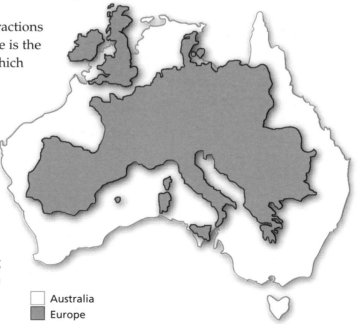

Australia
Europe

Figure 7.2 A comparison of the sizes of Australia and Europe

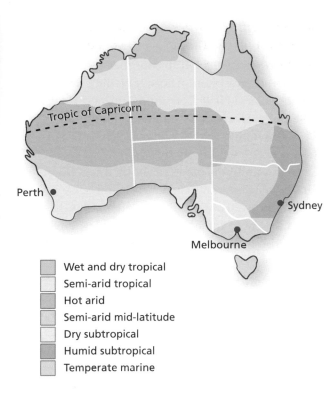

Figure 7.3 Climatic zones of Australia

Key:
- Wet and dry tropical
- Semi-arid tropical
- Hot arid
- Semi-arid mid-latitude
- Dry subtropical
- Humid subtropical
- Temperate marine

Topography

Topography means the shape of the land. Highland areas consist of hills and mountains whereas lowland areas include valleys and coastlines. Mountainous regions can be cold and hostile and have little in the way of facilities for the tourist, except those areas that have been developed for skiing and winter sports. Lowland areas are more heavily developed for tourism as the topography is flatter, allowing easier access by road and river. The coastal areas provide attractions for tourists in terms of beaches and access to the sea.

New Zealand

New Zealand consists of two main islands, the North Island and the South Island. Both islands have a central spine of mountain ranges leading to rolling valleys and the coast. Approximately 20 per cent of North Island is mountainous whilst the South Island is over 60 per cent mountainous. The highest mountain is Mount Cook on South Island (3764 metres/12,346 feet) which is situated in the Mount Cook National Park. A volcanic plateau with hot springs, mud pools and geysers dominates the centre of North Island. New Zealand

has over 15,000 kilometres (9300 miles) of coastline, with sandy beaches to the north and the east. The capital city of Wellington is located on the coast on the southern tip of North Island and is the most southerly capital city in the world.

The unique topography of New Zealand inspired Peter Jackson, director of the film trilogy *Lord of the Rings*, to recreate J.R. Tolkien's 'Middle Earth' using the stunning scenery.

Figure 7.4 The physical geography of New Zealand

Key:
- Mountain areas
- ▲ Mount Cook
- ● Capital city

Skills practice

1 Using Figure 7.4, describe the topography of New Zealand.

2 Explain how the topography of New Zealand can provide many natural attractions for tourists and visitors.

3 Consider why Peter Jackson was inspired by the scenery of New Zealand for the making of *Lord of the Rings* and what impact this may have had for tourism.

CASE STUDY

Tsunami

On Boxing Day morning 2004, the second biggest earthquake in recorded history caused a devastating tidal wave, called a *tsunami*. The earthquake took place in the Indian Ocean and caused the deaths of over 300,000 people. It affected many tourist resorts in the northern hemisphere, including resorts in Sri Lanka, India, Thailand, Maldives and Malaysia. It also affected countries in the southern hemisphere and those that lie on the Equator, including Indonesia, Seychelles and the African countries of Kenya and Tanzania.

The worst affected area was Banda Aceh on the island of Sumatra in Indonesia. Here the entire city was destroyed with the loss of over 200,000 lives. Although the city is located just north of the Equator, the island straddles the Equator with towns and cities in both hemispheres.

Many of the areas hit by the tsunami rely on tourism. A report by the World Tourism Organisation suggests that 30 per cent of tourists cancelled their holidays to the affected areas and chose alternative destinations. The reduction in the number of tourists caused a loss of earnings of approximately $3 billion.

In March 2005 the island of Sumatra in Indonesia suffered another earthquake; fortunately it did not cause another tsunami, however it claimed over 1000 lives.

Source: BBC Online

Skills practice

1 Investigate the effects of earthquakes and tsunami on the tourism industry in the southern hemisphere.

2 To what extent is the topography and the location of tourist facilities a cause for concern for the countries involved?

Accessibility

Accessibility is an important factor for those travelling from the UK to countries located in the southern hemisphere. Those travelling to Australia and New Zealand by air tend to include a stopover in either Singapore or Hong Kong; those travelling to destinations such as Brazil or South Africa tend to fly direct.

Accessibility is made easier by direct flights from major international airports in the UK, such as Heathrow, Gatwick, Birmingham, Manchester and Glasgow. Not all airports in the UK offer direct routes to all countries within the southern hemisphere.

The southern hemisphere can also be accessed by sea. However, the considerable distances involved encourage many tourists to combine air and sea travel, that is they fly to a certain destination where they then board a cruise ship to travel around the southern hemisphere oceans visiting places of interest. Both Australia and South America are popular cruise destinations with tourists travelling from the northern hemisphere during the winter to the summer conditions of the southern hemisphere.

Think about it

Why do many people who travel to Australia and New Zealand arrange to break their journey and stopover?

Skills practice

1 Using the Internet or a selection of travel brochures, research a cruise to South America, Australia or South Africa.

2 What are some of the main attractions that make up the itinerary of a cruise?

3 Can passengers join or leave the cruise during its voyage? If so, where?

Access to a tourist destination is not just about arriving at an airport or seaport, it also includes internal transfers. These can include: coach, taxi, hire car or public transport.

Access is important for those with special needs, such as wheelchair users. Most major airports and seaports have wheelchair access. An increasing number of hotels and tourist attractions have made provision for wheelchair access, however the degree of wheelchair access and special needs provision varies between countries.

Accessibility can also include access to culture and language. The top three long-haul destinations from the UK have one thing in common, they are all English-speaking nations.

English is spoken in Australia and is one of the main languages of South Africa. Also some of the languages spoken within the southern hemisphere are familiar to other European countries, for example Spanish is spoken in Peru and French is spoken in Tahiti. In Bali, which is part of Indonesia, the languages of Bahasa Indonesia and Balinese are spoken, although English is understood in some of the major tourist hotels and attractions. For many tourists access to language is an important consideration, for others it is less important; however it is useful to learn some popular words and phrases before travelling.

Attractions

It is important for a destination to have a range of different attractions for the visitor. We have already identified in Unit 3 Travel Destinations (pages 86–101) and Unit 6 Tourism in the UK (pages 206–213) that there are different types of tourist attractions. They include:

✳ Natural attractions

✳ Built attractions.

To encourage visitors from the UK, it is necessary for destinations in the southern hemisphere to have attractions that encourage people to travel large distances in order to visit them. Such attractions are unique and tend to reflect the history, culture and natural beauty of the host country.

Think about it

1 To what extent does Machu Picchu combine both elements of natural and built attractions?

2 Why is Machu Picchu such a popular tourist attraction?

CASE STUDY

Machu Picchu, Peru

Machu Picchu is an ancient settlement built by the Incas around 1400 AD. It is popular with tourists visiting Peru. It was a sacred place built high above the Urubamba River valley. The deserted city is located between two mountain peaks. The site contains the ruins of nearly 200 buildings surrounded by terraces that were used to grow food and were watered by natural springs. The buildings were so carefully made that even a knife blade cannot be inserted between the building blocks, which weigh over 50 tons each. Machu Picchu is steeped in mystery, as the city was designed as an astronomical observatory, and was eventually abandoned; mummified bodies have also been discovered there.

The ancient settlement of Machu Picchu

1 Select a destination that would suit a mature couple whose children have just left home to go to university and who wish to travel to a country in the southern hemisphere. What would attract them to the destination you have chosen?

2 Select a destination that would suit an independent backpacker wishing to travel to a country in the southern hemisphere. What would attract them to the destination you have chosen?

Facilities and amenities available to tourists

We have already identified in Unit 3 Travel Destinations, pages 102–105, and Unit 6 Tourism in the UK, pages 213–215, that there are different facilities and amenities available to tourists. They include:

* Accommodation

* Food and drink

* Entertainment and events.

When promoting a destination in a travel brochure a tour operator has to consider whether to emphasise the availability of food and drink, entertainment and accommodation that visitors from the UK are familiar with. If the tour operator is seeking to promote a destination to backpackers, explorers and other independent travellers, they are more likely to emphasise local foods, traditional customs and local accommodation.

Different countries offer a range of facilities and amenities to tourists. Some destinations have developed an extensive range of tourist facilities whilst others offer more traditional facilities and amenities.

CASE STUDY

Botswana, Africa

Tourism in Botswana has been slow in developing. It was largely ignored until the early 1960s and became a destination for hunters. Today much of the wildlife is protected as 17 per cent of the country is devoted to national parks and game reserves. Outside of these areas much of the land is controlled as Wildlife Management Areas. Famous natural attractions include the Chobe National Park, the Tsodilo Hills, Botswana's first World Heritage Site, and the Kalahari Desert. Botswana has become a leading safari destination. Wildlife highlights include elephants, rhinos, cheetahs, wildebeest, zebra, lions, springboks and brown hyena.

Accommodation is available in the many campsites, mid-range hotels and high-quality lodges found in the national parks and game reserves. Campsites and lodges are best accessed by a flight in a small aircraft lasting half an hour. Landing is at a local landing strip

timeless
BOTSWANA
YOUR GUIDE TO AFRICA'S MOST EXCITING SAFARI DESTINATION

WHY BOTSWANA IS UNIQUE
We explore the key aspects that make the country so popular

SPOILT FOR CHOICE
An overview of the country's diverse attractions and a summary of the activities offered

YOUR QUESTIONS ANSWERED
A practical guide to help you prepare for the safari of your life!

Botswana has many attractions for tourists, including organised safaris

rather than an airport with transfer to the accommodation by four-wheeled-drive vehicle. Larger hotels are found in the major cities of Gaborone, Kasane, Maun and Francistown.

Food and drink is usually served in the lodges on an all-inclusive basis, although budget safaris and campsites are self-catered. Many lodges employ qualified chefs. Meals are standard European fare with an emphasis on African fruits. Visitors are not asked to eat strange creepy-crawlies (except as an experiment!) or food that they are unfamiliar with.

Botswana has developed many activities and events that make use of its natural resources. These include:

- Walking safaris
- Horseback riding
- Quad biking
- Elephant-back safaris
- Mountain biking
- Mokoro (dugout canoe) safaris
- Night drives.

National events are based around the capital city of Gaborone. Local events are more frequent and widespread. The Maitisong Festival is a celebration of local music, dance and drama held in March–April. The Gaborone Showgrounds host the Industry and Technology Fair in May and the International Trade Fair in August.

For more information visit: http://www.botswanatourism.org.uk

Skills practice

1 What are the attractions in visiting Botswana?

2 How does the standard and type of accommodation in Botswana compare to accommodation in the UK?

3 Suggest why European menus are popular in lodges and hotels.

4 To what extent could the range of facilities and amenities be extended? Suggest some alternatives that would be popular with visitors from the UK. You will be required to carry out further research in order to answer this question.

Role of the government

The role of government is necessary in planning for the development of tourism and helping to provide the infrastructure and environment within which tourism can develop. Governments also help to promote the tourism industry.

Tourism infrastructure provides transport networks, including roads, railways, airports and seaports. It also includes the regulation and/or provision of utilities such as electricity, gas, water and the disposal of sewage and waste. Governments also help in the development of tourist facilities and amenities by allocating areas of land for development and by offering incentives and assistance to companies who wish to build there. However, in some areas tourism development may not be suitable due to environmental concerns or the existence of rare species of plants and animals that require protection.

Most governments have a department or minister dedicated to the development and promotion of tourism. Government tourism departments support the development of the tourism industry by providing policy and guidance, encouraging investment and financial support, giving advice on quality standards, publishing tourism statistics and market information, giving advice on responsible and sustainable tourism, and planning tourism infrastructure such as transport networks.

Most countries that receive visitors from the UK have an office based near London to promote their destination. Some offices provide an enquiry service to the public whilst others provide a brochure service and deal almost exclusively with tour operators and event organisers. Most government tourism departments have a website providing a range of tourist-related information.

Australia to take centre stage in the UK this week

Australia will take centre stage in the United Kingdom this week with new tourism promotions being rolled out in the market to boost awareness of Australia as a tourist destination.

The new tourism promotions are timed to coincide with Australia Day celebrations in Australia's largest long-haul tourism market, the UK. In the past year there were around 670,000 visitors from the UK to Australia, making it the biggest source of overseas tourists to Australia, after New Zealand and Japan.

The Minister for Small Business and Tourism, Fran Bailey, is in the UK this week for the launch of the Australia Week campaigns and to meet with key travel trade partners in the UK, to promote Australia.

'Australia has long been a highly desirable destination for British tourists. The challenge is to inspire more British travellers to holiday in Australia and experience the country beyond the major gateways,' Fran Bailey said.

'Tourism Australia's marketing activities in the UK show aspects of Australia to complement existing perceptions. This is designed to compel tourists to want to experience the destination first hand.

'Australia Week celebrations in particular provide an excellent opportunity to capture consumer awareness, helping to generate record levels of interest and desire for Australia in this major tourist market.'

A key activity during Australia Week celebrations will be the official opening of the Destination Australia Partnership's new premises in Australia House in London. The move to Australia House will see Tourism Australia and all State and Territory tourism organisations operations in Europe co-located for the first time.

Source: Australian Government, Department of Industry, Tourism and Resources (2005)

Skills practice

1 What is the role of national government in planning for the development of tourism?

2 Why did the Australian Minister for Small Businesses and Tourism travel to the UK?

3 How is the Australian government promoting Australia as a tourist destination?

4 Using the Australian government website, http://www.industry.gov.au provide a range of examples of how the government is supporting the development of tourism in Australia.

5 Select another country within the southern hemisphere. Using the Internet, research the government website for your selected country and compare the ways in which they support the development of the tourism industry.

Costs and options for travel

Journeys made from the UK may be charged at different prices by different tour operators, transport principals and travel agents, including online bookers. It is therefore important to know:

* The range of travel costs charged by the market

* The different options for travel.

When researching a travel destination it is useful to receive quotes from more than one tour operator. In the UK there are approximately 700 tour operators, although four large companies dominate the market.

A travel agent can usually search for a competitive price on your behalf. The major tour operators own some of the high street travel agencies and therefore you may wish to select more than one travel agency in order to compare prices. The major companies and their respective travel agents are:

* Thomson (Lunn Poly)
* MyTravel (Going Places)
* Thomas Cook (Thomas Cook, Worldchoice)
* First Choice (Travel Choice, Bakers Dolphin).

The high street is a very competitive place and often the best holiday and travel deals are found there, as travel agents openly compete with each other.

Bookings can be made direct with some tour operators. Although they claim to offer cheaper prices than travel agencies, very often the prices are comparable. Small independent tour operators offer a more specialised and personal service for special interest holidays. Their brochures may not appear in all high street travel agencies.

Travel principals are the main travel companies that provide air, sea, rail and road transport. In terms of the southern hemisphere the main travel principals are airlines, although some companies operate round-the-world cruises.

Travel principals can also offer a range of travel products in addition to transport, and can even offer a whole travel package. For example, British Airways offers flights, hotel bookings, car hire, insurance and foreign currency.

Online bookers can provide telephone or Internet booking services, acting as an agent for tour operators and travel agents. Many specialise in late availability and last-minute deals offered at reduced prices.

Comparing prices between tour operators is not always straightforward as they can charge a variety of different costs. Some tour operator costs are based on six nights rather than seven nights and sometimes airport taxes, supplements and transfers are hidden in the small print, separate from the eye-catching special deal price.

The price of a holiday depends not only on where you are travelling to, what accommodation you are staying in, but also when you wish to travel. The costs are higher during the summer peak season compared to the off-peak season.

CASE STUDY

Mauritius

The island of Mauritius is located in the Indian Ocean. The island is typical of many paradise islands, with palm trees, clear blue waters and white sandy beaches. Most visitors stay in luxury resort hotels and venture out to shop or to go on sightseeing trips. Mauritius is a popular honeymoon destination and offers beauty spas, fishing and diving trips, and championship golf courses. The island is also famous for its extinct flightless bird, the dodo. The island has received much attention from UK tour operators during the last five years. There are 139 tour operators in the UK that feature Mauritius in their programmes. The island has grown in popularity with visitors from the UK; in 2004 92,652 visitors from the UK travelled to Mauritius, compared with 58,683 visitors in 1999.

For more information visit: http://www.mauritiustourism.co.uk

Mauritius is a popular destination with tourists, especially honeymooners

Costs

The following example is based on one 5-star luxury resort hotel on the island of Mauritius. The hotel has a mixture of deluxe rooms and junior suites. There are four restaurants and bars, two swimming pools, beaches, a spa and fitness centre, water sports and a golf course.

The following costs are based on two adults for 7 nights in a deluxe room on a half-board basis (dinner, bed and breakfast) with return flights.

Table 7.2 Cost of staying at a 5-star luxury resort hotel on the island of Mauritius

Tour operator A	Prices start from £1763 per person plus taxes for 7 nights
Tour operator B	Prices start from £1698 per person for 6 nights, extra nights start at £173, plus taxes (Honeymoon couples can receive a discount of up to £940 per week)
Half-board deluxe room rate booked direct with the hotel	£215 to £500 per person per night depending on the time of year
Return flight booked direct with an airline	£761 plus £80 taxes per person depending on the date and time of flight and route taken

Different options for travel

There is a range of options available for travel to countries in the southern hemisphere from the UK. These include:

* The possibilities offered by UK regional airports
* Different air routes and transport principals
* Stopovers.

Regional airports provide the convenience to fly to many destinations but are restricted in the number of destinations in the southern hemisphere. Several tour operators offer discounted or free flights from regional airports in the UK to meet with the connecting flight. For example, direct flights to Mauritius depart from London Heathrow airport and Paris Charles de Gaulle airport. Both British Airways and Air France offer incentives to fly from regional airports in the UK and to connect with these flights. This increases the options for travel; previously it would have been necessary to travel by road or rail to Heathrow or to pay for a connecting flight to Paris.

Direct routes tend to cost less and be more convenient to the passenger. However some long-haul destinations in the southern hemisphere require a stopover to refuel and replenish the aircraft. It also provides an opportunity for passengers to relax in the comfort of a hotel and explore another destination.

In addition to travelling by air it is also possible to travel by cruise ship to the southern hemisphere from the UK. Passengers can embark on a cruise at seaports such as Southampton. Alternatively, passengers can fly from the UK to a destination in the southern hemisphere and join a cruise. Cruise ships are large floating hotels accommodating over 500 people, and have high standards of luxury. They provide a range of services, such as restaurants and bars, theatres, cinemas, casinos, shops, beauty treatments and sports activities. Some of the main travel principals offering round-the-world trips include Cunard, with its flagships *Queen Mary 2* and the *Queen Elizabeth 2*, Fred Olsen, with the flagship *The Black Watch*, and P & O, with cruise liners *Artemis* and the *Oriana*.

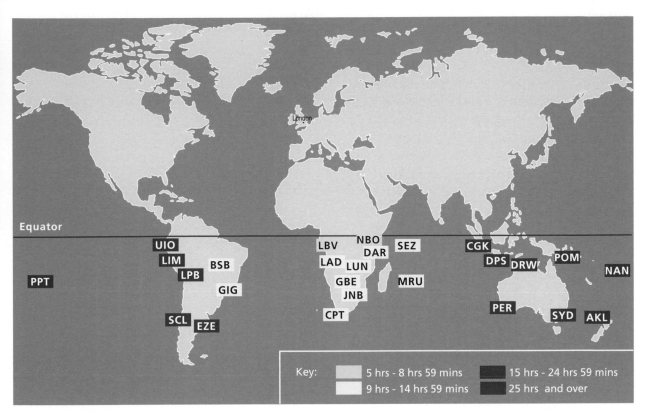

Figure 7.5 Flight times to the southern hemisphere from London

1 Match the major airports in the southern hemisphere listed below to their international three-letter code. The code corresponds to the international airports in Figure 7.5, the map of flight times from London to the southern hemisphere:

INTERNATIONAL AIRPORTS IN THE SOUTHERN HEMISPHERE	
Auckland, New Zealand	La Paz, Bolivia
Brasilia, Brazil	Luanda, Angola
Jakarta, Indonesia	Lusaka, Zambia
Cape Town, South Africa	Mauritius
Dar es Salaam, Tanzania	Nadi, Fiji
Denpasar, Bali, Indonesia	Nairobi, Kenya
Darwin, Australia	Perth, Australia
Buenos Aires, Argentina	Port Moresby, Papua New Guinea
Gaborone, Botswana	Papeete, Tahiti, French Polynesia
Rio de Janeiro, Brazil	Santiago, Chile
Johannesburg, South Africa	Mahé, Seychelles
Libreville, Gabon	Sydney, Australia
Lima, Peru	Quito, Ecuador

2 Does a long journey deter people from travelling? Explain your answer using relevant examples.

3 Using Figure 7.5, the map of flight times from London, for which destinations would you recommend a stopover?

CASE STUDY

Saga Rose World Cruise

The *Saga Rose* follows a Southern Cross route from Southampton in the UK taking in South America, Antarctica, Australasia, the Indian Ocean and Africa. The cruise lasts for 108 nights before returning to the UK.

For more information visit:
http://www.saga.co.uk

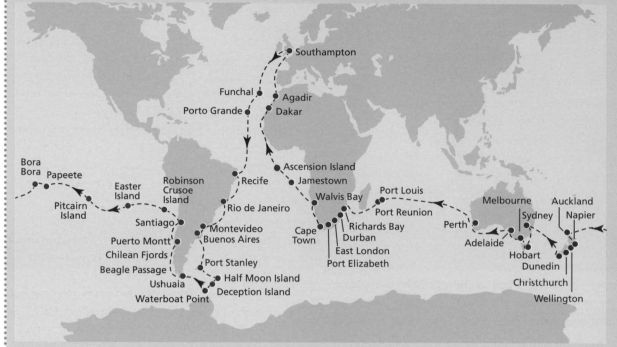

Figure 7.6 The Saga Rose cruise route to the southern hemisphere

Source: Saga

Skills practice

1 Describe some of the main attractions that passengers will experience on the Saga Rose World Cruise.

2 How much does a world cruise cost and what does this cost include?

3 What types of passengers are attracted by world cruises?

Destination popularity

The popularity of countries as tourism destinations for UK visitors depends on these factors:

* The appeal of the country to tourists from the UK

* The degree of coverage provided by UK tour operators.

The appeal of a country to tourists from the UK

Tourists from the UK are attracted to countries that offer good weather and a favourable climate compared to our own. Tourists also are attracted by destinations that offer sun and beach resorts to relax in after a long journey. However, UK tourists wish to do more than just lie on a beach, they also are interested in touring holidays, sightseeing, visiting cities, and visiting places of cultural significance. They also appreciate having a variety of attractions and places to visit, and the flexibility to decide where they want to visit. Tourists from the UK tend to make spontaneous decisions about what they want to see and do.

UK tourists aged between 25 and 34 years are most likely to travel further. On long-haul visits young people spend less than older people but they take longer trips than people from older age groups. For example, the average trip to Australia is 86 days for 16 to 24 year olds compared with 40 days for those aged 25 and over.

Holiday tourism may be one reason for visiting a destination. Many visitors from the UK are attracted to Australia and New Zealand because they have friends or relatives who live there.

The appeal of long-haul destinations has grown considerably. The top holiday destinations for UK tourists are short-haul, but after experiencing several short-haul destinations there is an increasing desire among people to explore less familiar countries and regions. Education has broadened people's awareness of other places and cultures, creating a further demand for long-haul travel.

Changing *demographics*, or population trends, have resulted in more people living longer and saving more for their retirement and for a holiday of a lifetime. This is reflected in the increase in the popularity of cruise holidays; in 2003 the number of passengers from the UK on cruise holidays exceeded one million for the first time. Round-the-world cruises have also seen an increase in popularity. Being the fourth-largest economy in the world means that the UK has more people with higher levels of disposable income than many other countries. Tourists from the UK tend to spend more than most countries on visits to long-haul destinations and stay longer than most other countries. More tourists from the UK travel to long-haul destinations than tourists from Germany, Japan or America.

Think about it

1 Why do some countries have more appeal to UK tourists than others?

2 What would you expect from a holiday in the southern hemisphere?

3 Why are demographics important in the appeal of a country to tourists from the UK?

The appeal of a destination can be measured by the number of holidays that are sold, the number of repeat bookings, the satisfaction of visitors through customer satisfaction questionnaires and market research surveys. These provide an indicator to the tour operator as to whether the destination is growing or losing appeal. An explanation of these trends is important, as the tour operator needs to know whether the current trend will continue and to decide on what appropriate action to take.

The appeal of a country to tourists from the UK is reflected in the number of visitors who travel there. This is recorded in the UK as outbound travel and in the receiving destination as inbound travel. For details regarding UK outbound tourism statistics visit the Office for National Statistics website: http://www.ons.gov.uk and search for a publication called *Travel Trends*.

Inbound travel data for specific countries in the southern hemisphere can be found on relevant government and national tourist organisation websites. It is useful to receive travel data that covers several years for trends to be identified. Data for the previous year may not always be available as tourism statistics can take a while to be collected, analysed and published.

Once the data has been researched you need to explain any trends in popularity and draw conclusions from interpreting the data, giving an account of the destination's likely future popularity. The data can easily be presented as a graph and the shape of the graph can be an indication of future growth or decline.

Think about it

What are the factors that can influence the popularity of a tourist destination?

CASE STUDY

Indonesia

Indonesia is a collection of islands located across 3000 miles of ocean. The four main islands that are popular tourist destinations are Bali, Java, Sumatra and Sulawesi. The most popular island for UK tourists is Bali, as it combines white sandy beaches with volcanic landscapes and rice terraces with traditional culture and religious temples. Tourism is a vital part of the economy as it is estimated that 85 per cent of the population of Bali benefit economically as a result of the tourist industry.

Bali, Indonesia

Table 7.3 Indonesia tourism statistics

	1999	2000	2001	2002	2003
Number of visitor arrivals from the UK	138,296	161,662	189,027	160,077	98,916
Total number of overseas visitor arrivals	4,727,520	5,064,217	5,153,620	5,033,400	4,467,021
Average expenditure per visit by UK resident (US$)	1452.55	1350.13	1504.78	1067.03	1087.22
Average expenditure per visit by overseas residents (US$)	996.34	1135.18	1053.36	893.26	903.74
Average length of stay by UK residents (days)	14.52	14.60	13.46	12.55	14.27
Average length of stay by overseas residents (days)	10.51	12.26	10.49	9.79	9.69

Source: BPS-Statistics Indonesia

Skills practice

1 Using the tourism statistics for Indonesia, produce two graphs, one showing the number of visitors from the UK between 1999 and 2003 and another showing the total number of overseas arrivals.

2 Describe the trend in the number of visitors from the UK between 1999 and 2003.

3 How does this trend compare to the total number of overseas arrivals?

4 A nightclub in Bali was the target of a terrorist bomb in October 2002 which killed over 200 people. How might this have affected the number of visitors to the region?

5 Compare the average expenditure per visit by UK residents with the average expenditure by overseas visitors.

6 Compare the average length of stay per visit by UK residents with the average length of stay per visit by overseas visitors.

7 What are the likely future prospects for tourism in Indonesia? Use evidence to support your answer.

The degree of coverage provided by UK tour operators

Tour operators are very influential in the way in which we buy our holidays. Although there is an increasing trend for people to book their own flights and accommodation on the Internet, the majority still prefer to choose their holidays from brochures that are produced by tour operators.

Tour operators have to make a series of decisions on which destinations to include in a holiday brochure: which country, which resort and which hotels to promote. Clearly not all destinations can be included, so to be included in a holiday brochure is the successful result of a highly selective process.

Think about it

What are the benefits for a tourist destination to be included in a tour operator's brochure?

A holiday brochure promotes destinations based on images, a brief written description and price. The way in which a tour operator represents a particular destination is crucial in terms of encouraging people to book a holiday. The tour operator will try to represent the destination in the best possible way in order to maximise bookings.

A holiday brochure may devote one or two pages to a particular destination or a destination may be represented over several pages. Destinations in the southern hemisphere are typically found in 'worldwide' brochures and brochures promoting individual countries, such as Australia and South Africa.

Tour operators may also promote selected destinations through travel agencies. There are approximately 7000 travel agencies in the UK, and they are an important source of promoting and selling holiday destinations. The window displays and special deals of a travel agent may encourage people to choose one destination over another. Tour operators may also market certain destinations through television, newspaper and radio advertisements. This raises awareness of the tour operator but also promotes a range of travel destinations.

Skills practice

Identify the most popular countries in the southern hemisphere by researching a range of brochures produced by UK tour operators.

1 Select a range of worldwide holiday brochures and dedicated holiday brochures for countries in the southern hemisphere.
2 Which countries receive more coverage than others?
   Coverage can be measured by
   • the number of pages devoted to a particular country
   • the size of photographs and use of appealing images
   • the order of countries within the brochure.
   Analyse your findings by identifying which countries receive the most coverage.

Values and attitudes of visitors and stakeholders

A *stakeholder* is a person or a group of people who have an interest in an issue being discussed. In tourism stakeholders include the various sectors of the industry as well as people directly and indirectly affected. The development of tourism in a destination involves many stakeholders, including government, commercial tour operators, transport principals, providers of local excursions, local businesses, residents, pressure groups and tourism associations. Government is a major stakeholder. Governments create tourism policy that gives a sense of direction to the tourism industry, they influence planning regulations, work on behalf of local people and businesses, support development projects and also liaise with other governments and organisations.

Think about it

How does a government help to provide facilities and amenities for tourists?

Different values and attitudes of visitors and other stakeholders in the industry affect the development of tourism in a destination. Visitors play an important part in the development of tourism. Visitors who are attracted to a destination will ultimately demand a certain level of resources, facilities and attractions. Tourism businesses are only too aware of the need to meet customer expectations and to make profit on meeting those demands. A destination where there is a strong demand for budget accommodation may ultimately lead to more budget accommodation being made available.

Visitors are attracted to safe and clean environments. Destinations are becoming more sustainable in their approach by taking action to preserve and enhance their natural and built environments. *Sustainable tourism* is about managing tourism's impacts on the environment, communities and the economy, to make sure that the effects are positive rather than negative, for the benefit of future generations.

The natural environment for some tourists is just a backdrop, whereas for others it is a place to explore, to experience sport and leisure, and to interact with local people. Travelling to areas to see natural attractions or to engage with local culture is an example of *ecotourism*.

CASE STUDY

The Travel Foundation

The Travel Foundation works with tour operators, governments and local people to promote sustainable tourism. Sustainable tourism is about making a positive difference when we travel to and spend time in destinations. This is what it involves:

- Enjoying ourselves and taking responsibility for our actions – respecting local cultures and the natural environment
- Giving fair economic returns to local families – helping to spread the benefit of our visit to those who need it most
- Recognising that often water and energy are precious resources that we need to use carefully
- Helping to protect endangered wildlife and preserve the natural and cultural heritage of the places we visit
- Protecting and enhancing favourite destinations for the future enjoyment of visitors and the people who live there.

Source: The Travel Foundation

CASE STUDY

The Tahune Forest AirWalk, Tasmania, Australia

The Tahune Forest Reserve is famous for its Huon pine trees which are native to Tasmania. Tasmania is an island state of Australia and attracts approximately 580,000 visitors each year. The Tahune Forest provides visitors with short walks, viewing platforms, information sites, a visitor's centre, function room, camping, picnic and barbecue areas. The AirWalk extends for more than half a kilometre (approximately 0.3 of a mile) and allows visitors to walk above the forest canopy at heights of between 22 and 37.5 metres. This gives visitors a chance to look down upon the forest and view forest life in the treetops that they would not normally see, as well as being able to enjoy spectacular views to nearby rivers and mountains. AirWalk was opened in 2002 and attracted nearly 155,000 visitors in its first year. It is accessible by wheelchair.

AirWalk has been recognised for its achievements in promoting sustainable tourism by winning the international Green Globe 21 award and the Ecotourism Australia Award for Excellence. By allowing people to walk above the forest, the AirWalk has meant that visitors have had a minimal impact on the life of the forest below.

For further information visit:

Green Globe 21
   http://www.GreenGlobe21.com
Forestry Tasmania
   http://www.forestrytas.com.au

Skills practice

1 Why has the Tahune Forest AirWalk become one of Tasmania's most visited tourist attractions?

2 To what extent is the Tahune Forest AirWalk a good example of sustainable tourism?

Many island destinations in the southern hemisphere, such as the Seychelles and Mauritius, have small numbers of luxury hotels to attract high-spending tourists in order to minimise impact on the local environment and at the same time maximise the benefits to the local economy and local people. Government strictly controls the development of hotels and other tourist facilities. This is to ensure that the natural beauty visitors come to see is not spoilt by unplanned development. These islands are popular honeymoon and wedding destinations.

Think about it

Why are exclusive island resorts a popular choice for honeymoon couples?

Skills practice

1 For one destination in the southern hemisphere, identify its natural attractions.

2 What evidence is there that the destination is promoting sustainable tourism?

3 To what extent does this affect the appeal of the country to tourists from the UK?

4 How might sustainable tourism affect the future development of tourism at your selected destination?

Recommendations for tour operators

Tour operators often employ tourism consultants for specific research projects, including the preparation of destination profiles. Tourism consultancies and market research organisations can provide independent research and sell the information to tour operators and other tourism organisations. Accurate and reliable information helps tour operators to make decisions and plan for the future.

Before destinations are presented in a brochure, research is carried out to assess whether the destination has the potential to generate the sales of holidays expected. Destination profiles are also used to uncover new market opportunities as well as identifying the changing needs of visitors. Tour operators will attempt to predict the needs of holidaymakers in terms of the type of destination, the type and standard of accommodation, how long people want to stay and how much money they are prepared to pay. The information is used to help decide whether to expand the programme of activities in a certain destination or to look for new destinations elsewhere.

Knowledge check

1 Name the main countries in the southern hemisphere that receive tourists from the UK.

2 Describe the main tourist attractions in the southern hemisphere.

3 Identify the main features of a tourist destination.

4 Identify the main facilities and amenities available to tourists.

5 What is the role of government in planning for the development of tourism?

6 Identify the different options for travel in the southern hemisphere, including the use of regional airports, different air routes and the possibility to include a stopover.

7 What are the different costs charged by tour operators, transport principals, travel agents and online bookers?

8 Explain which countries in the southern hemisphere are popular with tourists from the UK.

9 Which destinations in the southern hemisphere receive the most coverage by UK tour operators?

10 Reflect on the information and knowledge that you have researched and provide advice to a tour operator on which destination to include in their future programmes.

UNIT ASSESSMENT

Portfolio practice

You need to produce a portfolio based on an investigation into the tourism potential for inclusion in tour operators' programmes of two countries in the southern hemisphere.

You need to check that the places chosen are indeed countries, using an up-to-date atlas or other reference source such as the Foreign and Commonwealth Office website http://www.fco.gov.uk

Bali, for example, is not a country, it is part of the country of Indonesia. Antarctica is a continent bound by international treaty and is also not a country.

The southern hemisphere is the world south of the Equator, so any country completely south of 0° latitude is permissible. However, some countries that you may consider choosing straddle the Equator, for example Ecuador, Brazil, Kenya and Indonesia. Those countries that straddle the Equator and are in substantial part the southern hemisphere are permissible. Further details on which countries are permissible and which are not:

- **Permissible countries**: Any country entirely within the southern hemisphere, plus: Ecuador, Brazil, Gabon, Congo, Zaire, Kenya, Indonesia and Kiribati.

- **Countries that are not permissible**: Any country entirely within the northern hemisphere, plus: Colombia, Uganda, Somalia and the Maldives.

Your portfolio should include:

- A destination profile for two countries in the southern hemisphere, including information about locations, features, facilities and amenities

- A comparison of costs and options for travel to the two countries

- Research and analysis of the appeal of the countries for UK tourists, drawing on data showing visitor trends over recent years, including analysis of current coverage by UK tour operators

- An evaluative report for tour operators, recommending which of the two countries to include in their future programme.

Destinations in this unit are at the national scale, therefore they will appear as countries. Some destinations are easier to research than others, having more user-friendly information in the public domain. Make sure that you have access to sufficient resources that meet the demands of the assessment. It is best to think about the resources that you need and check availability before committing yourself to producing a destination profile. Do not underestimate the time it will take to research your selected destinations.

When selecting your two destinations it is advisable that they are sufficiently contrasting to allow you to make a recommendation to the tour operator. You may find less to say about countries that have many similarities.

Useful resources for this assessment are:

- An up-to-date atlas

- Travel brochures from a selection of tour operators

- Travel guidebooks

- TV and radio broadcasts

- Destination promotional materials

- The World Travel Guide

- Access to the Internet to search for

  ○ Government tourism related websites

  ○ National tourism organisation websites

  ○ Commercial tourism websites

  ○ Transport principals' websites

  ○ Hotel websites

  ○ Tour operators' websites

  ○ Online guidebooks, e.g. the *World Travel Guide* http//www.columbusguides.com

  ○ News items and industry-related news, e.g. *Travel Trade Gazette* http://www.ttglive.com and *Travel Weekly* http://www.travelweekly.co.uk

- Country profiles and news items that occasionally feature in travel supplements published in some of the Sunday broadsheet newspapers

- People are a valuable source of information, for example a travel agency or tour operator contact may be an appropriate resource for destination profiling and comparing costs and options. But remember that these people are there to sell travel products and have a job to do, so they may not always be available to assist with your enquiry.

It is useful to check with the Foreign and Commonwealth Office's website to obtain travel advice on your selected destinations http://www.fco.gov.uk

You will have a hard time persuading a tour operator, and your tutor, why you have made a recommendation to include a destination in the tour operators' programmes of activities if the Foreign and Commonwealth Office is advising British nationals not to travel to your selected country.

Once you have your resources you need to think about the structure of your profiles. It is best to follow the structure that is suggested. When writing your destination profiles remember that you are producing these as a tourism consultant advising UK tour operators looking to expand their programmes in the southern hemisphere. Your use of written language and presentation style should reflect this.

You will find that once you begin your research you will find lots of information. It is necessary for a researcher to consider which information is important and which is not. If you find an interesting piece of information, you need to assess whether it is relevant to the destination profile. It is always best to use several sources to compare information. Information sourced from the Internet should always be treated with caution as anyone can publish information on a website and often there are no independent checks to see if the information is accurate and up-to-date. It is best to use Internet resources related to government agencies, known companies, publishers and news agencies. It is good practice to represent the sources of information that you have used in your report in a list of references or a bibliography, see Unit 3 Travel Destinations, pages 109–111.

The aim of the destination profiles is to help a tour operator decide which country to include in a future programme of activities. You are the person providing the advice. Make sure that you do not just describe the destination but you also discuss the importance of the main features and amenities, that you analyse the tourism data, evaluate the information and provide recommendations.

A destination profile for South Africa

Location

The Republic of South Africa is located in the southern hemisphere in the African continent. The country covers an area of 1,221,037 square kilometres (757,043 square miles) and has a population of 43.1 million. South Africa extends 2000 kilometres (1240 miles) from the Limpopo River in the north to Cape Agulhas in the south and 1500 kilometres (930 miles) from Port Nolloth in the west to Durban in the east. It has the Indian Ocean on its eastern coast and the Atlantic Ocean on its western coast. The country shares its borders with Namibia, Botswana, Zimbabwe, Mozambique, Swaziland and Lesotho. There are three capital cities: Pretoria is the administrative capital, Cape Town is the legislative capital and Bloemfontein is the judicial capital.

Figure 1 Location and key features of South Africa

Features

Climate

South Africa has a varied climate but most of the popular tourist areas are dry and sunny. The south coast experiences a temperate climate with maximum temperatures around 26 °C, falling to a minimum of 18 °C. The east coast experiences a tropical climate, with heavy summer thunderstorms. However the climate becomes increasingly drier and hotter towards the north. Cape Town has an average of between 6–11 hours of sunlight per day compared to London, which has an average of between 1 and 7 hours of sunlight per day.

Topography

South Africa is divided up into three regions: the Kalahari Desert, the coastal regions (low veld) and the mountain uplands (high veld). Mountain ranges run along the coastline from the Cape of Good Hope towards the northeast, including the Drakensberg Ranges. The most famous mountain in South Africa is Table Mountain near Cape Town. It is 1086 metres tall (3564 feet) and is a high plateau, the top being flat like a table. This attracts many visitors who can take a cable car to the summit and go for walks, admire the view or use the tourist facilities, including a shop and restaurant.

Accessibility

Internal tourism infrastructure is well developed with daily internal flights between the major airports and provincial areas, including: Bloemfontein, Cape Town, Durban, East London, Johannesburg, Kimberley, Port Elizabeth and Pretoria. Small airlines operate between other airports and landing strips and air charter services are available.

Table 1 Climate of Cape Town

Month	Average sunlight (hours)	Temperature (°C) Average		Temperature (°C) Record		Discomfort from heat and humidity	Relative humidity		Average precipitation	Wet days (+0.25 mm)
		Min	Max	Min	Max		am	pm	(mm)	(mm)
Jan	11	16	26	7	37	Moderate	72	54	15	3
Feb	10	16	26	5	38	Moderate	77	54	8	2
March	9	14	25	6	39	Moderate	85	57	18	3
April	8	12	22	3	39	–	90	60	48	6
May	6	9	19	–1	35	–	91	65	79	9
June	6	8	18	–2	29	–	91	64	84	9
July	6	7	17	–2	29	–	91	67	89	10
Aug	7	8	18	–1	32	–	90	65	66	9
Sept	8	9	18	1	34	–	87	62	43	7
Oct	9	11	21	1	32	–	79	58	31	5
Nov	10	13	23	4	34	–	74	56	18	3
Dec	11	14	24	5	38	Moderate	71	54	10	3

Source: BBC Weather Centre

Sea travel operates on a scheduled service between the major ports of Cape Town, Durban, East London and Port Elizabeth.

The railway network is extensive, with a variety of train companies offering inter-city services. Several luxury express services operate between the major cities as well as providing scenic excursions to the Transvaal on board steam train safaris.

The road network provides easy access to the rest of the country, with motorways linking major cities. Bus and coach operators provide a frequent service through operators such as Greyhound and Intercape. Taxis operate in all major areas and car hire is available from airports and city centres. Traffic drives on the left-hand side and an international driving permit is required for visitors, although a UK driving licence with photo-identification is acceptable. The minimum age to hire a car is 23, although some car-hire firms will accept 21-year-olds at a premium cost. The maximum speed limit on major routes is 120 kilometres per hour (75 miles per hour).

Travel times

The following table gives approximate travel times in hours and minutes from Cape Town to other major towns and cities in South Africa.

Table 2 Approximate travel times from Cape Town in hours and minutes

	AIR	ROAD	RAIL
Johannesburg	2.00	15.00	24.00
Durban	2.00	18.00	38.00
Pretoria	2.00	16.00	26.00
Port Elizabeth	1.00	7.00	–
Bloemfontein	1.30	10.00	20.00

Source: Columbus Guides

Language

There are 11 official languages including Afrikaans, English, Zulu and Xhosa. Most people speak English and Afrikaans as well as another official language.

Disabled travellers

It is worth noting the advice to disabled visitors. Although most international hotel groups are aware of the need for disabled access and most businesses will try and accommodate wheelchair users, access is restricted. The following is the general information for disabled visitors:

'Generally speaking, our facilities for disabled visitors can be improved, and this is an area our government is working on. An increasing number of accommodation establishments have wheelchair ramps and bathroom facilities for the disabled. Almost every national park has at least one accessible chalet and many accommodation establishments have one or two wheelchair-friendly rooms. Most of our sports stadiums have accessible suites, stands or areas for wheelchairs near accessible parking as well as special toilet facilities. Most public buildings also cater for wheelchair access.'

Source: South African Tourism

Attractions

The top ten visitor attractions in South Africa are:

1 Cape Town Waterfront
2 Cape Point
3 Table Mountain
4 Wine Route
5 Garden Route
6 Kruger National Park
7 Durban Beachfront
8 Whale Watching
9 Blyde River Canyon
10 Tour of Soweto.

The Kruger National Park

South Africa has an abundance of natural attractions, with 19 national parks and a variety of wildlife, including elephants, giraffes, crocodiles, buffalo and lions.

One of the most famous national parks is the Kruger National Park, which is located in the northeast of the country and extends for over 100,000 square kilometres (62,000 square miles). The Kruger Park accommodates approximately 5000 visitors at any one time, with only 3 per cent of the Park having been developed to provide facilities and amenities for tourists, leaving the rest for the wildlife. Serviced accommodation is available in the Park in the form of camps and private lodges. The Kruger National Park has a large diversity of species, for example there are at least 500 species of birds. Animal populations include more than 300,000 zebra, 5000 giraffes and 7500 elephants.

The Blyde River Canyon Nature Reserve is located south of the Kruger National Park. It is the third largest gorge in the world, after the Grand Canyon (USA) and Fish River Canyon (Namibia). Popular activities include wildlife watching, safaris, fishing and hiking. Pilgrim's Rest is popular with visitors to the area, as it is a former gold-mining town with many original buildings remaining, including the Royal Hotel.

Cape Town is South Africa's oldest city, founded by Dutch settlers in 1652. One of the most famous features, and a leading attraction in South Africa, is the Victoria and Alfred Waterfront. This area has been extensively redeveloped and provides a range of restaurants, bars, speciality shops, boutiques and hotels, as well as an Imax cinema and the Two Oceans oceanarium set alongside the picturesque harbour. A canal is being developed to link the Waterfront with the city centre.

Victoria and Alfred Waterfront in Cape Town

Another popular attraction is Robben Island, 12 kilometres (7 miles) offshore, which is the former prison where political prisoners were held, including Nelson Mandela, for campaigning against apartheid. The island was first opened to the public in 1997 and has been declared a UNESCO World Heritage Site. Today it attracts over 300,000 visitors each year. Approximately 31 per cent of visitors are from South Africa and 11 per cent from the UK.

Visits from Cape Town include Hout Bay, a fishing village that offers trips to see nearby seal colonies. Another attraction is Cape Point, part of the Cape of Good Hope Nature Reserve, with spectacular views across the Atlantic Ocean and the Indian Ocean.

Travelling east from Cape Town along the Western Cape visitors can explore the Garden Route, a coastal drive that includes views of bays, beaches, high cliffs, waterfalls, woodland and lakes. From the Garden Route whales and dolphins can often be seen swimming close to the shore. Further inland, villages and nature reserves can be explored.

Travelling inland visitors can also visit the wine regions of Stellenbosch and Constantia, known as the Wine Route, to the north-east of Cape Town. Many wineries offer tours, tastings, restaurants and gift shops. South African wine is increasingly popular in the UK.

KwaZulu-Natal is located in the north-east of the country and is known as the 'garden province'; it leads down to the Indian Ocean. Plantations of sugar cane, tropical fruits and maize can be seen. The area is famous for its military heritage as it was the area of conflict between the Zulus, Boers and British in the 19th century. The tourist board has devised a battlefield route for those interested in military history.

As this is a subtropical region visitors are made aware that the coastal areas are hot and humid during the summer season. The coast around Durban is famous for its surf beaches, sailing and scuba diving, which attract many local people as well as tourists. The most popular beach is the Golden Mile, which extends for 6 kilometres (4 miles) along the coast. Anti-shark nets protect most of the beaches, as the area is home to the Great White shark. Shark-cage diving has become popular with adventurous divers. South Africa

The Golden Mile in Durban

has also gained an international reputation for whale watching as the whales attract great interest as they swim close to the western coast.

Durban is a bustling city and the third largest in South Africa. It offers museums, art galleries, parks, gardens and a wide range of shops and entertainment. The Sea World Aquarium and Dolphinarium is popular with tourists, as is the Victoria Street Market, displaying a range of Indian and African produce, crafts and food.

Sports tourism is a growing industry in South Africa. The country has over 500 golf courses, with the cooler months of May to September being popular with golfers. For those seeking more extreme sports, South Africa has the world's longest bungee jump, from the bridge overlooking the Blaukrans River in Western Cape, with a drop of 216 metres (709 feet).

Visitors seeking a greater cultural and historical understanding of South Africa often visit the township of Soweto, near Johannesburg. Soweto is the largest black township in South Africa and became a symbol of resistance against apartheid. Personal tours of the township are available and widely promoted in local hotels. Visitors are advised to book an organised tour if they wish to visit the township.

Facilities and amenities available to tourists

Accommodation

South Africa offers a wide range of accommodation from 5-star luxury hotels to accommodation in thatched huts (*rondavels*), which are usually found in game reserves. Traditionally these huts have provided basic accommodation, but most have now been converted into luxury air-conditioned suites. Many of the luxury hotels are found in the major cities and tend to be owned by international hotel groups, including Holiday Inn and Sun International.

There has been a recent growth in the provision of basic accommodation to meet the growing demand of backpacker holidays; many national parks provide backpacker hostels.

Accommodation is graded by a national voluntary scheme from 1 to 5 stars, similar to the scheme that exists in the UK. The grading scheme also applies to guesthouses, bed-and-breakfasts and self-catering accommodation. Camping and caravan sites are also included. There are more than 800 camping and caravan sites in the country.

Food and drink

South Africa produces an excellent range of meat, seafood and garden produce. Local meats are offered as well as a selection of seafood, including rock lobster. Much of the cuisine is a reflection of the various groups that have come to South Africa. Durban has an Indian influence with curries and other spicy foods, while more traditional food with Malay and Dutch influences can be found in Western Cape, with Karoo lamb and venison. A typical dish is a *potjiekos*, a stew cooked on an open fire in an iron pot with layers of meat, vegetables and potatoes that is allowed to simmer for several hours. Often these turn into social occasions involving family and friends. Traditional African cooking does not usually appear on menus in restaurants, as it is often a basic meal of maize and vegetables with some stewed meats. South African wine, however, has an international reputation for quality. Local beers are also good and are reasonably priced.

Entertainment and events

One of the most famous entertainment and event venues in South Africa is Sun City, a luxury resort north-west of Pretoria. It is a collection of four world-class hotels, including the Palace of the Lost City, built in the heart of an ancient volcano next to the Pilanesberg National Park. The resort has attracted many visiting rock stars and international shows and has hosted events such as Miss South Africa, the FIM Motocross World Championship and international golf tournaments. It is also a major business and conference venue.

Sun City, South Africa

The capital cities and major towns in South Africa have a wide selection of bars, restaurants, theatres, cinemas and nightclubs. The country hosts a variety of national and international events each year:

January	South African Open Golf Tournament
	Cape Fest World Music Festival
February	Alfred Dunhill PGA Golf Tournament
March	Klein Karoo National Arts Festival
April	Bosveld Marathon
May	National Hot Air Ballooning Championship
	Cape Times Waterfront Wine Festival
June	National Arts Festival
July	Oyster Festival
August	Oppikoppie Rock Festival
September	Formula One Powerboat Grand Prix
	Cape Town International Opera Festival
October	Oktoberfest Beer Festival
	Stellenbosch Food and Wine Festival
November	National Choir Festival
	Spier Arts Festival
December	Million Dollar Golf Challenge
	Cape Town Long Street Carnival

Government initiatives

South Africa was in political isolation until the late-1980s due to its policy of apartheid. The policy was removed and tourism development began to expand rapidly. The government has been proactive in strengthening the appeal of South Africa as a major international tourism destination.

Recent government initiatives include the creation of the Garden Route mega-reserve near Cape Town, bringing together three national parks, the Tsitsikamma National Park, Wilderness National Park and the Knysna National Lake Area, as well as forests and other conservation land. It is intended that the mega-reserve will provide a model for the future of ecotourism in South Africa.

The government wishes to ensure the quality of the tourism experience by encouraging more accommodation providers to join the voluntary grading scheme. They are considering making the registration of accommodation compulsory and grading all registered accommodation if more businesses do not join the scheme.

To recognise high quality and achievement amongst the South African tourism industry, the government launched an award programme in 2005. The 'Tourism Oscars' bring together examples of excellence and celebrate South African achievement.

In 2004 at the World Travel Market in London, the South African Minister of Environmental Affairs and Tourism described the challenge ahead in hosting the 2010 Soccer World Cup. Speaking about the preparations for hosting the event the Minister said:

> 'There is no doubt that the World Cup will offer massive prospects for international investment and partnership with South Africa. It will be the first time the event has been staged on African soil and will bring with it key exposure to more than 400,000 visitors and more than 40 billion viewers in 204 countries. Clearly this requires high levels of product investment to deal with the high visitor volumes. We are committed to coordinate industry, labour and communities to build the stadiums, to upgrade and expand our airports, public transport networks, and communications infrastructure. We will construct the hotels, guest lodges and B & Bs. We will train our staff and equip our tour guides. By 2010 we will stand ready to present our visitors with the most impressive Soccer World Cup ever staged.'

Source: South African Government Department of Environmental Affairs and Tourism

A comparison of costs and options for travel

Travel costs

Most travel to South Africa from the UK is by aircraft. Travel costs vary depending on the time of year and the airline. The cost of a return flight can vary between £500 and £700 plus taxes. A three-day short break in Cape Town staying in a 3-star hotel with return flight can cost from £580, with a three-day break staying in a 4-star hotel starting from £630.

Different options for travel

Most airlines fly direct to South Africa. Johannesburg International Airport is the major airport in South Africa and is the hub for 45 airlines from all five continents. Cape Town is also popular with visitors from the UK. Flights from the UK are generally overnight, with a flight time from London to Johannesburg of approximately 12 hours.

UK regional airports

Several regional airports in the UK offer flights to South Africa. These flights include both scheduled and charter services. Other flights are also available.

Table 3 Flights to South Africa from UK regional airports

CAPE TOWN	
Regional airport	**Airline**
Birmingham	Lufthansa, KLM
London City Airport	Lufthansa, KLM
Manchester	Lufthansa, Qatar, KLM

JOHANNESBURG	
Regional airport	**Airline**
Birmingham	Emirates, Swiss Air, Lufthansa
East Midlands	Emirates
Manchester	Qatar, Swiss Air, KLM

Different air routes and transport principals

South Africa is serviced with daily direct scheduled flights from London Heathrow flying with South African Airways, British Airways and Virgin Airlines to Cape Town and Johannesburg. There are also flights to Johannesburg from London Gatwick with Nationwide Airlines, Iberia and Qatar Airways. There are flights from Heathrow to Johannesburg with Iberia, Swiss Air and Kenya Airways.

Stopovers

The flights to South Africa are direct and do not require a stopover. Passengers choosing to fly to another destination such as Paris to create a stopover may add significantly to the cost. South Africa is two hours ahead of Greenwich Mean Time and as such passengers suffer little from jet lag.

> *Research and analysis of the appeal of the country for UK tourists, drawing on data showing visitor trends over recent years, including analysis of current coverage by UK tour operators*

South Africa has a relatively small share of the UK holiday market; it represents approximately 3 per cent of long-haul outbound holiday travel from the UK. The majority of inbound visitors to South Africa come from the UK and Germany, with visitors from the UK representing 18 per cent of all inbound visitors.

Most visitors from the UK are holidaymakers, although visiting friends or relatives and attending business meetings may be included as part of an itinerary.

The average visitor stays for 16.8 nights, although there is a global trend towards shorter visits.

Coverage by UK tour operators

Few of the major tour operators offer tours to South Africa, as the major tour operators specialise in large numbers of package holidays and prefer to offer alternative destinations where they are guaranteed higher numbers of sales. South Africa has a greater coverage by specialist travel agencies and tour operators. These have been successful in developing market expertise and offering a range of alternative destinations and experiences. South Africa is beginning to make an impression on the major tour operators such as Virgin Holidays.

South Africa is represented by 76 tour operators in the UK (2004). Some of the tour operators include:

- Arblaster and Clarke Wine Tours Ltd
- Bales Worldwide
- Exodus Travel
- Sunset Faraway Holidays
- Golf Africa

- Kuoni
- Saga Holidays
- Explore Worldwide
- Tradewinds
- Virgin Holidays.

Appeal of South Africa to tourists from the UK

What the Brits love about South Africa

South Africa receives the bulk of its arrivals from Africa. However, Europe accounts for the highest percentage of its international visitors, with the majority from the United Kingdom and Germany. Over 350,000 British visitors of all ages arrive in South Africa each year.

South Africa is known for its friendly people and warm welcome coupled with excellent value for money. The destination provides an unforgettable African experience with all the convenience that its world-class tourism infrastructure offers.

The over-50s enjoy world-class golf resorts and wine regions. Younger adventurers love safaris, sailing and surfing, and the nightlife of its cities.

Three-quarters of UK visitors to South Africa indicated that they had received advice from friends and relatives both in the UK and in South Africa. Just over a third of the UK visitors indicated that wildlife was a major attraction. Other attractions were scenic beauty, visiting friends and relatives, African culture, a desire to see the country after political change, business reasons, curiosity and value for money.

Some 76 per cent of international visitors to South Africa make use of South Africa's shopping facilities. In the case of British visitors, it is 83 per cent. This reflects the fact that the exchange rate is extremely advantageous for the British. The average British visitor spends £70 a day in South Africa.

UK visitors give South Africa the highest overall rating (9.3 out of 10) for enjoyment of their stay in South Africa. Just over two-thirds of UK visitors state that they would definitely visit South Africa again, while a further 21 per cent indicate that they would probably visit again.

Source: South African Tourism (2004)

Visitor trends

Table 4 Number of inbound visitors to South Africa

	2002	2003	PERCENTAGE DIFFERENCE
Europe	1,252,710	1,319,172	+5.3
North America	216,275	222,139	+2.7
Central and South America	38,311	40,357	+5.3
Australasia	85,775	89,062	+3.8
Asia	177,415	176,566	−0.5
Middle East	33,401	31,814	−4.8
Africa (including Indian Ocean islands)	4,455,971	4,453,250	−0.1
Unspecified	169,725	172,530	+1.7
Grand total	**6,429,583**	**6,504,890**	**+1.2**

Source: South African Government, Department for Environmental Affairs and Tourism

South Africa is becoming increasingly popular as a tourist destination. The number of visitors increased by 1.2 per cent between 2002 and 2003 to over 6.5 million visitors. In 2003 UK residents made 456,468 visits to South Africa, an increase of 3.1 per cent on the previous year. This compares with 350,000 visitors from the UK in 2000.

Future trends
It is likely that South Africa will continue to see an increase in visitor numbers from the UK. The country has a broad appeal, from the luxury holiday market to backpackers. The amount that a UK tourist spends in South Africa has grown on average 7 per cent each year since 1998, however as the currency devalued at a rapid rate South Africa was unable to capture a large share of this increase. A review of spending by the South African authorities led to a decrease in the marketing budget of South African Tourism. However as the 2010 World Cup is being hosted in South Africa, the government is committed to placing the country on a global stage.

It is likely that in time South Africa will widen the tourism products on offer and will develop new areas such as cultural and historical tourism in the townships and a greater variety of adventure tourism. It is also likely that UK visitors will be encouraged to regard South Africa as a gateway to the African continent, visiting other countries such as Botswana as part of an African experience.

Attitudes of stakeholders to the development of tourism
The benefits of hosting an international sporting event can bring many more visitors as well as promoting the country to the rest of the world. Companies will be willing to invest in new tourism infrastructure, hotels, attractions and facilities. Some groups, like Fair Trade in Tourism South Africa (FTTSA), aim to integrate fair trade and sustainable practices into the tourism industry by working closely with the tourism industry and providing examples of good practice. As tourists become increasingly more aware of the needs of local people, FTTSA hopes that more local people will be able to benefit from tourism. South Africa has seen high levels of unemployment in recent years, so an expected rise in the tourism industry is welcomed by most people as it will potentially provide jobs and services that not only benefit tourists but also local people.

For further information visit the following websites:

Department of Environmental Affairs and Tourism (South African Government)
http://www.environment.gov.za

Fair Trade in Tourism South Africa
http://www.fairtourismsa.org.za

South Africa National Parks
http://www.sanparks.org

South Africa.com
http://www.southafrica.com

South African High Commission (UK)
http://www.southafricahouse.com

South African Tourism
http://satourism.com

World Travel Guide
http://www.columbusguides.com

A destination profile for Australia

Information about location, features, facilities and amenities

Location

Australia is located in the southern hemisphere and is the world's oldest continent. It covers 7,772,535 square kilometres (3,842,675 square miles). Australia is surrounded by the Indian Ocean to the west, the Pacific Ocean to the east and the Southern Ocean to the south. The capital city is Canberra and the largest city is Sydney. Australia is a large country, see page 252, approximately the size of the USA, but has one of the lowest population densities in the world, an average of two people per square kilometre. There are 18 million people who live in Australia, with over 70 per cent living near the coast, the most developed area being the east coast. The island of Tasmania is part of Australia and is located 240 kilometres (150 miles) south of Australia, see page 266.

Figure 2 Location and key features of Australia

Features

Climate

Australia has a varied climate, see pages 252 and 253; approximately 40 per cent of the country experiences a tropical climate, the rest experiences a temperate climate. The country receives more than 3000 hours of sunshine a year, approximately 70 per cent of the total possible sunshine hours.

The northern coastal city of Darwin experiences high temperatures and high amounts of rainfall, which in turn produces levels of humidity that can become uncomfortable, especially in March.

Table 5 Darwin climate data

Month	Average sunlight (hours)	Temperature (°C) Average		Record		Discomfort from heat and humidity	Relative humidity		Average precipitation	Wet days (+0.25 mm)
		Min	Max	Min	Max		am	pm	(mm)	(mm)
Jan	6	25	32	20	38	High	78	71	386	20
Feb	6	25	32	21	38	High	79	72	312	18
March	7	25	33	20	39	Extreme	78	67	254	17
April	8	24	33	19	40	High	69	54	97	6
May	9	23	33	16	39	High	63	47	15	1
June	10	21	31	13	37	Medium	61	47	3	1
July	10	19	31	13	37	Medium	59	44	0	0
Aug	10	21	32	14	37	Medium	63	45	3	0
Sept	10	23	33	17	39	High	65	49	13	2
Oct	10	25	34	21	41	High	65	52	51	5
Nov	8	26	34	21	39	High	68	58	119	10
Dec	7	26	33	21	39	High	73	65	239	15

Source: BBC Weather Centre

Sydney is located on the south-eastern coast of Australia and receives hot summers and cool winters. Although Sydney has experienced a higher record temperature than Darwin, average temperatures and rainfall are less, reducing the level of humidity. As the climate is favourable around Sydney, more people have chosen to visit and live in this area than anywhere else in Australia.

Table 6 Sydney climate data

Month	Average sunlight (hours)	Temperature (°C) Average		Record		Discomfort from heat and humidity	Relative humidity		Average precipitation	Wet days (+0.25 mm)
		Min	Max	Min	Max		am	pm	(mm)	(mm)
Jan	7	18	26	11	46	Medium	68	64	89	14
Feb	7	18	26	9	42	Medium	71	65	102	13
March	6	17	24	9	39	Moderate	73	65	127	14
April	6	14	22	7	33	–	76	64	135	14
May	6	11	19	4	30	–	77	63	127	13
June	5	9	16	2	27	–	77	62	117	12
July	6	8	16	2	26	–	76	60	117	12
Aug	7	9	17	3	28	–	72	56	76	11
Sept	7	11	19	5	33	–	67	55	74	12
Oct	8	13	22	6	37	–	65	57	71	12
Nov	7	16	23	8	39	Moderate	65	60	74	12
Dec	8	17	25	9	42	Moderate	66	62	74	13

Source: BBC Weather Centre

Australia is one of the driest continents in the world, with the interior of the country being mainly desert. It covers approximately 70 per cent of the country and is known as the Outback. Australia has 10 deserts, the largest being the Great Victoria Desert that extends 176,000 square kilometres (109, 120 square miles), covering 5 per cent of the country.

Topography

Australia is a large continent and has a total landmass of 7.7 million square kilometres (4.8 million square miles) and extends from 2623 kilometres (1626 miles) north to south and 3278 kilometres (2032 miles) east to west. Australia is an ancient continent, with its present landscapes dating back over 90 million years. There are four main regions: the Coastal Plain, the Great Dividing Range, the Central Lowlands and the Western Plateau.

The Coastal Plain runs along the eastern side of Australia and contains the major cities of Brisbane, Sydney, Canberra and Melbourne, as well as providing some spectacular beaches that are popular with surfers. To the north-east of the coastline is the Great Barrier Reef, the largest area of coral in the world.

The Great Dividing Range extends from Cape York in the north to Tasmania in the south. It contains Australia's highest mountain, Mount Kosciusko (2228 metres/7300 feet), and a series of ancient volcanoes.

The Central Lowlands contains one of the lowest points in Australia, Lake Eyre, which is 12 metres (40 feet) below sea level.

The Great Western Plateau is mainly desert with several salt lakes. These are produced by water left over from heavy storms that evaporates in the intense heat to leave a hard salty crust. The most famous landmark is Uluru (Ayers Rock) that rises 867 metres (2840 feet) above the desert, see page 285.

Accessibility

The internal tourism infrastructure is well established. As the country is so vast many people rely on internal flights that cover the whole continent. All major cities and regional centres have airports or landing strips. Even Uluru (Ayers Rock) can be accessed by air. The major airlines that serve the popular tourist areas are Jetstar, Virgin Blue and QantasLink.

Sea transport is available and is mainly used to travel to the Great Barrier Reef and the island of Tasmania.

Rail transport is accessible but most people prefer to travel by air. Few services span the entire country; one that does is the Indian Pacific, which operates between Sydney and Perth, covering 4350 kilometres (2697 miles) and taking three days and three nights.

There are road networks within and between the major towns and cities although the vast distances between places can make driving impractical. Traffic drives on the left and maximum speeds outside urban areas are between 80–110 kilometres per hour (50–68 miles per hour). Car hire is available for those over 21 years old and a UK driving licence is valid for up to three months. Driving in the Outback during wet weather can be difficult as many roads are dirt tracks. Coach services operate between major towns and cities and are one of the cheapest ways to travel around Australia. Greyhound Pioneer operates the national coach network.

Travel times

The following chart gives approximate travel times in hours and minutes from Sydney to other major towns and cities in Australia.

Table 7 Approximate travel times from Sydney in hours and minutes

	AIR	ROAD	RAIL
Canberra	0.45	4.00	5.00
Adelaide	1.40	25.00	22.00
Brisbane	1.20	15.00	15.00
Darwin	5.00	–	92.50
Melbourne	1.10	10.00	14.00
Perth	4.00	65.00	56.00

Source: Columbus Guides

Language

The official language of Australia is English. Visitors from the UK are familiar with Australian culture through television, film, music, food and drink.

Disabled travellers

The needs of disabled visitors are well catered for in the major towns and cities. The 2000 Paralympics in Sydney highlighted sporting excellence amongst disabled athletes and promoted Australia's commitment to accessibility. Tourism businesses have a responsibility to ensure that they are doing as much as they can to increase access to all disabled groups under the Australian Disability Discrimination Act (1992).

Attractions

The top ten most visited regions in Australia are:

1 Sydney, New South Wales
2 Melbourne, Victoria
3 Brisbane, Queensland
4 Tropical North, Queensland
5 Gold Coast, Queensland

6 Perth, Western Australia
7 Adelaide, South Australia
8 Petermann Ranges, Northern Territory
9 Sunshine Coast, Queensland
10 Whitsundays, Queensland.

WORLD HERITAGE SITES

1 Kakadu National Park
2 Purnululu (Bungle Bungle) National Park
3 Riversleigh (Fossil Mammals)
4 Wet Tropics
5 Great Barrier Reef
6 Fraser Island
7 Uluru-Kata Tjuta
8 Shark Bay
9 Central Eastern Rainforest Reserves
10 Lord Howe Island
11 Blue Mountains
12 Willandra Lakes
13 Naracoorte (Fossil Mammals)
14 Tasmanian Wilderness
15 Macquarie Island
16 Heard & McDonald Islands

Figure 3 Australia's World Heritage Sites

Source: UNESCO

Visitors to Australia are attracted by its diversity: from rainforest, desert, and beaches to dynamic cities. Australia has 16 UNESCO World Heritage Sites (see Figure 3) and over 500 national parks. Popular animals include koala bears, kangaroos, emu, parrots and saltwater crocodiles. Care must be taken, as there are several species of poisonous spiders, snakes and jellyfish.

As Australia is such a large country visitors find it extremely difficult (or impossible) to see all the major sites within a two-week stay. Most visitors either opt to stay longer or to concentrate their holiday to one or two regions. A current tourist visa, the official permission to visit the country, is valid for three months. Working and study visas may be granted for those wishing to stay longer.

Sydney is the most popular destination for inbound visitors. Its harbour is dominated by the Sydney Harbour Bridge, known locally as the 'coathanger'. It is a single span arch that took eight years to build. The bridge is continually being painted. It takes ten years to completely paint it using approximately 30,000 litres of paint. As soon as one coat of paint is complete it is time to start painting the bridge all over again.

Sydney Opera House is a short distance from Sydney Harbour Bridge. Its unique shape attracts many visitors and has become the world's busiest performing arts centre. The building is not just a large theatre for opera, there are also several halls and stages which host all kinds of music and dance, as well as displays and exhibitions.

Sydney Harbour and Opera House

When visiting Sydney nearly 40 per cent of all visitors from the UK take a trip to the Blue Mountains, part of the Great Dividing Range. The Blue Mountains National Park is 65 kilometres (40 miles) from the outskirts of Sydney. It offers scenic tours, walking, spectacular waterfalls and Aboriginal heritage.

Two hours drive north of Sydney is the oldest wine-producing region in Australia – the Hunter Valley. Visitors can tour more than 100 wineries as well as play golf and take part in other activities such as cycling, hot-air ballooning or horse riding.

Beach culture is an important part of Australian life as there are over 7000 beaches to choose from, more than any other country. Sydney has over 30 beaches, the most famous being Bondi Beach.

The Gold Coast is one hour drive from Brisbane and has been developed with tourism in mind. It features high-rise hotels, casinos, nightclubs, shopping malls, bars and restaurants. Over 2 million tourists visit the Gold Coast each year, attracted by its tourist facilities, its surf and 42 kilometres (26 miles) of golden sand. There are four theme parks along the Gold Coast: Dream World, Sea World, Warner Brothers Movie World and the Wet 'n' Wild Water Park.

The Gold Coast of Queensland

The Great Barrier Reef is as large as the British Isles and contains more than 2000 islands supporting 1500 species of fish and 400 types of coral. It is the world's largest marine park. Tourists can visit the Reef by water taxi or view it from the air on special flights; they can also investigate the reef underwater by snorkelling or scuba diving. However, most visitors view the reef from a special glass bottomed boat or an underwater observatory.

The Great Barrier Reef

Uluru, or Ayers Rock, is one of Australia's most famous landmarks. It is situated in the Uluru-Kata Tjuta National Park in the centre of the country, 2340 kilometres (1451 miles) from Sydney. The rock is 3.6 kilometres (2.2 miles) long and is 348 metres (1140 feet) tall.

The entire area has special spiritual significance to the Aboriginal people. The Australian government handed the area back to the Aborigines and as a result its traditional name, Uluru, is now used.

Visitors can take walks around the rock, although climbing is discouraged. Pleasure flights can also be booked in advance to see the Uluru-Kata Tjuta National Park from the air. One special feature of Uluru is that the rock appears to change colour at sunrise and sunset, producing shades of dark orange and deep reds before the light fades turning it to black.

In the north of Australia the Kakadu National Park is famous for its rainforests, waterfalls, rivers and crocodiles. It is Australia's largest national park, covering 19,000 square kilometres (11,780 square miles). It has been designated a World Heritage Site for its natural beauty and for the ancient Aboriginal art that dates back 60,000 years.

Uluru (Ayers Rock)

Facilities and amenities available to tourists

Accommodation

There is a wide range of places to stay in Australia. Major towns and cities offer familiar accommodation provided by the main hotel chains. Motels and travel lodges are found along popular highways. The difference between a hotel and a motel in Australia is that a hotel must provide a public bar amongst its facilities. There are some motels that provide excellent standards of accommodation but cannot be called a hotel, as they prefer to provide a bar service exclusively to their guests rather than include the general public. Hotel and motel accommodation is graded by the use of a five-star grading system, similar to that used in the UK. These range from 5-star luxury hotels to 1-star basic accommodation.

The number of guesthouses and establishments offering bed-and-breakfast accommodation is increasing, particularly around popular tourist areas and national parks. Guesthouses are not allowed to serve alcohol as part of their facilities.

Pub accommodation offers bar facilities, food and basic accommodation. Traditional pubs in many of the towns and cites are large buildings that are sometimes mistaken for hotels. A room at a country pub can cost about the same price as staying at a hostel.

Backpacker hotels and student hostels is one of the fastest growing sectors of the accommodation industry. Some independent hostels offer incentives such as free breakfasts or courtesy buses to encourage business. Hostels do vary in quality from purpose-built hostels to converted low-standard motels. The Youth Hostel Association (YHA) owns over 140 hostels in Australia and is part of Hostelling International. These hostels are inspected regularly. YHA members in the UK can visit Australian hostels paying YHA rates.

Camping and caravan parks are found in most of the main tourist areas, around the coastlines and the national parks. Some areas require a permit before pitching a tent and in other areas it is forbidden outside the designated camping and caravan parks. Several companies offer camper vans and motorised trailers with which to tour Australia. This is an excellent facility for those who wish to explore beyond the limits of major towns and cities.

Food and drink

Australian cuisine extends beyond the stereotypical barbecue or 'barbie'. Sydney rock oysters, fresh *barramundi* fish, *yamba* prawns, home-raised beef, kangaroo and lamb are all widely served. One of the most famous and widely popular food items is Vegemite, which is similar to Marmite.

Australia is renowned for its cold beer and is increasingly recognised as a high-quality wine producer, with an extensive range of wines that are popular in the UK. Many vineyards offer wine tours and tastings. The largest wine-growing region is the Barossa Valley near Adelaide; other popular regions include the Hunter Valley in New South Wales and the Murray River region in Victoria.

Entertainment and events

There are many local events, festivals and celebrations as well as popular sporting events. Art and cultural events are increasing, especially those that celebrate Aboriginal culture. Australia is also known for hosting major international events, such as the Olympic Games and the Paralympics in 2000, and annually hosts a range of international sports from Formula One motor racing to tennis.

Melbourne is the location for the Commonwealth Games in 2006; between 4000 and 6000 athletes from 71 countries will be competing, including those from the UK. The city can cater for large numbers of visitors; there are 25,000 hotel beds within 5 kilometres (3 miles) of the city and nearly 3000 restaurants. Melbourne has an efficient transport system; it has the fourth largest network of modern trams in the world, with 450 trams moving people efficiently around the city every day. Over 40,000 international visitors are expected to attend the 2006 Games.

Australia hosts a variety of national and international events each year:

January	Australia Day (26 January)
	The Australian Open tennis tournament in Melbourne
February	Australia Cup yachting event in Perth
	Gay and Lesbian Mardi Gras Festival, Sydney
	Royal Canberra Show
March	Australian Surfing Open event
	Australian Formula One Grand Prix, FIA Formula 1 World Championship, Melbourne
April	Royal Easter Show, Sydney
	Melbourne International Comedy Festival
May	Adelaide Cup Carnival
	Riverland Country Music Festival

June	Sydney Film Festival
	Mildura International Balloon Fiesta
July	Sunshine Surfmaster, Geraldtown
	Melbourne International Film Festival
August	Sydney Marathon
	Toowoomba Australian Heritage Festival
September	Festival of the Winds (kite festival), Sydney
	Darwin Festival
October	Henley-on-Todd Regatta, Alice Springs
	Melbourne Writers Festival
November	Melbourne Cup
	Festival of Freemantle
December	Sydney to Hobart Yacht Race

Government initiatives

The Australian government has invested heavily in developing international awareness of Australia as a tourist destination. Through marketing in selected countries, including the UK, the aim has been to develop an image for Australia that focuses on the natural environment, the personality of Australian people, the lifestyle and culture.

The link between sport and tourism has been developed since the Olympic Games in 2000. The Australian government has included sport as part of its tourism strategy. In 2004 the government pledged a contribution of more than A$270 million towards the costs of the 2006 Commonwealth Games. The Games will attract the largest-ever Commonwealth athlete participation, and there will be a global television audience in excess of 1 billion people. It is also an opportunity for Australian tourism to be promoted to a global audience.

Seven countries have been identified as the main tourism generating areas. These are New Zealand, Canada, Singapore, Malaysia, South Africa, India and the UK. International sporting events attract large numbers of visitors who also spend money locally on food, accommodation and tickets. The Olympics in 2000 brought 1.6 million tourists to Australia and generated A$6.1 billion as a result, creating jobs and improving facilities and amenities. It is hoped that the 2006 Commonwealth Games will create similar benefits.

The government has also identified a growing interest in wine and food tourism. It has developed a national wine policy to encourage more people to visit places where local food and drink are produced and to widen the benefits of tourism to rural areas. The policy aims to bring businesses together, such as vineyards, hotels, restaurants, transport operators and wine merchants, and to encourage them to promote their products to other countries, including the UK. Nearly half a million international tourists visit Australia's vineyards each year.

The Australian government recognises the need for a coordinated approach in promoting tourism. In 2004 Tourism Australia was established. It brought together the Australian Tourism Commission, See Australia, the Bureau of Tourism Research and the Tourism Forecasting Council, to provide a single organisation for the promotion of tourism, see page 258.

A comparison of costs and options for travel

Travel costs

Most visitors travel to Australia by air. Travel costs depend on the time of year and the airline. The cost of a return flight can vary between £550 and £700 plus taxes.

A ten-night holiday in Sydney staying in a 4-star hotel, room only, with return flight, can cost from

£1099. A return flight, fourteen-night, three-centre holiday, staying in 3-star hotels, room only, in Sydney, Ayers Rock and Cairns, with a Great Barrier Reef cruise included, can cost from £1575.

Different options for travel

The most popular way to travel to Australia is by air. Flights from London to Sydney take approximately 23 hours and 30 minutes, while flights from London to Cairns take approximately 25 hours and 30 minutes. As it is a long time to spend travelling many visitors break the journey by taking a stopover.

Another option is to travel by cruise liner from the UK, which can take several weeks, or to fly to Australia and join a cruise (see page 260).

UK regional airports

Several regional airports offer flights to Australia. These include both scheduled and charter services. Other flights may also be available.

Table 8 Flights to Sydney

SYDNEY	
Regional Airport	**Airline**
Birmingham	Emirates, British Airways
Bristol	British Airways
East Midlands	Emirates
Leeds-Bradford	Virgin Atlantic
London City	British Airways
Manchester	Qantas, Malaysia Airlines, Singapore Airlines, Emirates, British Airways, Lufthansa
Newcastle	Qantas

Table 9 Flights to Melbourne

MELBOURNE	
Regional Airport	**Airline**
Birmingham	Emirates, British Airways
Leeds-Bradford	Singapore Airlines, Malaysia Airlines, United Airlines
Manchester	Singapore Airlines, British Airways, Qantas, Emirates, Malaysia Airlines
Newcastle	British Airways, Qantas

Different air routes and transport principals

There are two main routes by air to Australia from the UK. The most popular and cheaper option is the eastern route via the Middle East and Asia. An alternative route is via the USA and the Pacific.

There are seven main gateway cities to Australia. These include:

- Adelaide
- Brisbane
- Cairns
- Darwin
- Melbourne
- Perth
- Sydney.

The main travel principals that offer scheduled services to Australia from the UK are Qantas, British Airways, Singapore Airlines, Thai Airways, Malaysia Airlines, Air New Zealand, Cathay Pacific Airways, Emirates, Lauda Air and Virgin Atlantic.

Qantas is the Australian national airline and operates 27 flights from London to Australia each week. Qantas also operates 5000 domestic flights each week to 60 regional destinations across Australia.

Cruise liners that visit Australian ports are available from major companies such as P & O, Holland America, Hapag-Lyold, Saga Shipping, Star Cruises, Seabourn, Silversea and Cunard Lines. They offer a variety of routes, including round-the-world cruises and southern hemisphere cruises.

Stopovers

Stopovers are used to avoid jetlag. Given the long distances involved in travelling to Australia, the time spent travelling and the difference in time zones, many visitors break their journey by stopping over at destinations such as Hong Kong or Singapore. Flights from Singapore to Sydney take approximately 8 hours. If travelling the western route to Australia via Los Angeles, flights from Los Angeles to Sydney take approximately 13 hours and 30 minutes.

Stopovers are useful in allowing passengers to rest, have a proper sleep in a hotel bed and exercise by walking around and seeing places of interest. One of the concerns of long-haul travel is the risk of developing deep vein thrombosis (DVT), which is a blood clot in the veins. Regular exercise and movement whilst travelling may help to prevent this condition.

Time zones

There are three different time zones in Australia.

- Eastern Standard Time (EST): this covers New South Wales, Victoria, Queensland, Tasmania and the Australian Capital Territory. These are 10 hours ahead of Greenwich Mean Time (GMT) UK.
- Central Standard Time (CST): this covers South Australia and the Northern Territory. These territories are 9 hours and 30 minutes ahead of Greenwich Mean Time (GMT) UK.
- Western Standard Time (WST): this covers Western Australia. This is 8 hours ahead of Greenwich Mean Time (GMT) UK.

> *Research and analysis of the appeal of the country for UK tourists, drawing on data showing visitor trends over recent years, including analysis of current coverage by UK tour operators*

Australia has an established share of the UK holiday market. Inbound visitors from the UK represent 14 per cent of all international arrivals and account for 20 per cent of all visitor nights. The UK is the second largest market for visitors to Australia in terms of the number of visitors. Visitors from the UK spend more per visit (A$2998 in 2003) than any other country, making it a popular choice for Australian tourism. Visitors often travel to Australia for more than one purpose; the main purpose is for a holiday but many also go to visit friends or relatives and a smaller number travel on business.

The average visitor to Australia stays for 38 nights (2003), down from 44 nights in 2000. There is a global trend towards shorter visits.

Australia 'Favourite Country' in UK Survey

Australia has been voted 'favourite country' in a travel survey of over 15,000 holidaymakers from the United Kingdom.

Scott Morrison, Managing Director of Tourism Australia, today welcomed the results of the Trailfinders 100th Edition Readers' Survey, one of the largest consumer travel surveys ever compiled.

'This is more great news coming from one of Australia's most important tourism markets,' Mr Morrison said.

Trailfinders, the largest independent travel company in the United Kingdom, regularly conducts surveys in its *Trailfinders* magazine, asking readers to vote for their favourite locations and holiday experiences worldwide.

'Australia was not only voted favourite destination but Sydney was voted favourite city (long-haul), Bondi Beach was voted favourite beach in the Pacific and the Sydney Harbour Bridge was voted favourite icon worldwide,' Mr Morrison said.

'Visitors from the UK not only tend to stay longer in Australia and spend more money, they also tend to travel around the country spreading the economic benefits of tourism to rural and regional areas.

'In terms of total spend by any one market, the UK is by far Australia's number one market, so it is great news that over 15,000 UK travellers rate Australia as their favourite destination,' he said.

Australian resorts were also recognised with Hamilton Island in the Whitsundays voted best resort in the Pacific; and the award for best non-beach resort hotel worldwide went to Peppers Bloomfield Lodge in Queensland.

'These results not only show how popular Australia is amongst UK travellers but are also a testament to our word-class tourism industry, with a number of Australian resorts and a touring company also being recognised,' Mr Morrison said.

Australian Pacific Touring was voted favourite Escorted Touring Company worldwide.

'There is a strong affinity between Australia and the UK and Tourism Australia's activities in the market aim to ensure we continue to convert this interest into actual travel bookings and more people spending their holiday dollar here in Australia,' Mr Morrison concluded.

Source: Tourism Australia (2005)

Coverage by UK tour operators

There are approximately 100 tour operators in the UK (2004) that include Australia in their programmes. Some tour operators' brochures, such as Thompson Travel, Tradewinds, Hayes and Jarvis, Kuoni and Qantas Holidays can be found in high street travel agents.

There are several specialist tour operators targeting specific markets, including backpacking. The leading backpacker and student travel specialist for destinations to Australia is STA Travel. Some of the other tour operators that organise tours to Australia include:

- Adventure Tours Australia
- All Ways Pacific Travel
- Austravel
- Bath Travel
- Coach Tours of Australia
- Connections Adventures
- Freedom Australia
- Sydney Learning Adventures
- Trailfinders
- Travel2.

Visitor trends

Table 10 Number of inbound visitors to Australia

	2002	PERCENTAGE CHANGE 2002/2001	2003	PERCENTAGE CHANGE 2003/2002	2004	PERCENTAGE CHANGE 2004/2003
Oceania and Antarctica	905,000	-4%	956,500	+6%	1,155,000	+21%
Europe and the former USSR	1,180,500	0%	1,212,000	+3%	1,243,700	+3%
The Americas	556,200	-4%	537,500	-3%	561,500	+4%
Africa (excluding North Africa)	67,300	-6%	69,200	-3%	67,200	-3%
Middle East and North Africa	51,500	-8%	52,700	+2%	64,000	+22%
Southeast Asia	673,800	-1%	625,300	-7%	638,700	+2%
Northeast Asia	1,345,500	+6%	1,230,000	-9%	1,411,800	+15%
Southern Asia	58,900	-8%	61,500	+4%	73,100	+19%
Not stated	2600	-82%	1300	-50%	100	-96%
Total	**4,841,200**	**0%**	**4,745,900**	**-2%**	**5,215,000**	**+10%**

Source: Tourism Australia

The number of tourists visiting Australia is increasing. In total there were 5.2 million visitor arrivals during 2004, an increase of 10 per cent compared to 2003. This is a large increase and one that reflects confidence in Australia as a destination.

In 2002 there were 642,700 visitors from the UK, an increase of 4 per cent on the previous year. In 2003 there were 672,800 visitors from the UK, an increase of 5 per cent on the previous year. In 2004 there were 676,200 visitors from the UK, an increase of 1 per cent on the previous year. The increase in the number of UK residents visiting Australia in 2003 was partly due to supporters travelling to Australia to attend the Rugby World Cup.

Future trends

Several airlines offer routes to Australia. Recently there has been an increase in the number of flights offered by Qantas, Virgin Atlantic, Cathay Pacific and Emirates. The introduction of the new Airbus A380 on long-haul routes will add further capacity. It is expected that the number of visitors to Australia from the UK will grow at an average rate of 4.3 per cent each year to a total of 989,900 by 2013. This compares with the average expected annual growth rate of 5.7 per cent, with a predicted 8.6 million visitors to Australia by 2013.

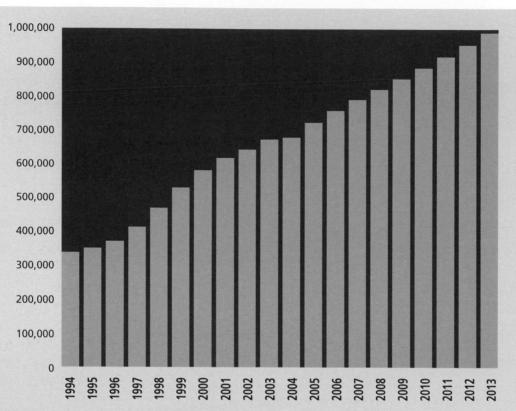

Figure 4 Visitor arrivals from the UK to Australia, actual and forecasted   Source: Tourism Australia

Attitudes of stakeholders to the development of tourism

As tourism develops, stakeholders are looking to new markets and emerging products. There is an increasing demand for sport tourism and ecotourism. More tourists are looking for nature-based tourism as well as learning more about local population and culture. Australia is in a unique position to promote ecotourism through its rich environment, as in places such as the Great Barrier Reef. It is important that both the environment and local cultures are recognised and appreciated by all who visit.

Correctly managed, ecotourism can have enormous benefits to rural indigenous communities such as Aboriginal groups. There is much concern over Aboriginal ways of life and culture, not only among the Aborigines themselves but also among visitors and government alike. Many inbound visitors are fascinated by Aboriginal culture and wish to learn more about it, and at the same time help to sustain and develop local economies and traditional ways of life.

Stakeholders are keen to expand the benefits of tourism, increasing visitor spend and extending the length of stay and educating visitors about Australian life and culture. Coordinated efforts are best to ensure that visitor flows are maintained and that opportunities are realised.

For further information visit the following websites:

Tourism Australia (public site)
http://www.australia.com

Tourism Australia (industry site)
http://www.tourism.australia.com

Tourism Research Australia
http://www.tra.australia.com

World Travel Guide
http://www.columbusguides.com

Australian Government, Department of Industry, Tourism and Resources
http://www.industry.gov.au

Australian Government, Australian Bureau of Statistics
http://www.abs.gov.au

292   OPTIONAL UNITS

> **An evaluation report for tour operators, recommending which of the two countries to include in their future programme**

South Africa and Australia benefit enormously from inbound tourism. Both countries wish to attract more visitors from the UK and are successful in offering a wide range of tourist facilities, attractions and amenities. Their success can be seen in a range of newspaper articles and publications for the travel trade.

Australia the most desired global destination

'Australia is the top destination for global independent travellers, according to an annual Lonely Planet Traveller online survey of 20,000 respondents' – *USA Today*

Australia voted No.1 holiday destination

'Australia has been named the top holiday destination for British travellers, according to a survey by Conde Nast Traveller magazines' – *London Evening Standard*

Rise in tourist arrivals to South Africa

'South Africa beat most of its competitors in the long-haul market including Australia and Thailand' – *Travel Weekly*

SAA EXTENDS ROUTE

'South African Airways is to add two more Heathrow–Cape Town services – on Saturdays and Sundays – from November' – *Mintel*

Standsted to gain Cape Town link

'South African airline Civair is planning to begin three flights a week from Cape Town to London' – *Travel Trade Gazette*

South Africa predicts 50% boost in UK visitors

'On the back of extra scheduled flights, South Africa is forecasting a 50% boost in UK visitor numbers within two years' – Travel Trade Gazette

Melbourne gears up for 2006 games

'The games will be Australia's biggest event since the Rugby World Cup and the country is expecting more than 11,000 Britons to visit' – *Travel Trade Gazette*

Sydney voted world's best city destination

'The Travel and Leisure World magazine's annual readers' survey has voted Sydney as the world's best city destination' – *International Herald Tribune*

As a consultant advising UK tour operators looking to expand their programmes in the southern hemisphere, it is first necessary to be aware of different types of tour operator: large-scale tour operators dealing with high volume sales or special interest tour operators dealing with smaller numbers of visitors. This may influence the decision being made.

Destination profile

Both Australia and South Africa have a varied topography. The landscapes offer a visitor variety, from coastal areas and forests to mountains and deserts. Australia has the additional advantage of having rainforests and a unique marine coral reef. These are considered natural advantages as they provide a broader range of experiences for the visitor.

Both South Africa and Australia have climates that are considered comfortable by tourists, although some might experience discomfort when visiting rainforest and desert regions. Rainforests rely on a regular supply of water and as such Australia receives more wet days than South Africa.

In terms of access, both countries have good road and rail networks. The Australian Outback is a remote location and as such many roads are dirt tracks that require extra care whilst driving during heavy storms. Both Australia and South Africa rely on internal flights to remote locations.

Access for the disabled is more widely promoted in Australia than South Africa. Although the South African government is making good progress in widening provision, there is still much work to be done in ensuring that tourism businesses comply with the government's own expectations.

The South African government is working hard to ensure that tourism businesses recognise the importance of high-quality service. Although excellent levels of customer service are rewarded, it is not perceived as being consistently high across the country.

Both countries offer a range of attractions, including national parks, wine tours, sports tourism, culture, beaches, towns and cities. South Africa has an advantage in terms of expanding its wildlife tourism based on safari holidays and the chance to see the big five: lion, leopard, elephant, buffalo and rhinoceros. Both countries offer marine wildlife but in different ways: South Africa offers whales and dolphins that swim close to its western shores whereas Australia offers the Great Barrier Reef.

In terms of hosting major international events, Australia has an advantage in terms of organising the Olympics, Paralympics, Rugby World Cup and Commonwealth Games. However, South Africa has great potential in offering a range of first-class football stadiums and tourist facilities in preparation for the 2010 World Cup.

Costs and options

The cost of flights to both countries is largely comparable. Special offers and other incentives by airline companies mean that prices fluctuate on a regular basis. South Africa is currently being marketed as a potential short-break destination with three-day or four-day holidays, compared to Australia where a minimum of two weeks is usually required. This makes South Africa more accessible in terms of overall cost compared to Australia.

More airlines in the UK operate flights to Australia than to South Africa. More regional airports are used for flights to Australia than to South Africa. However, as discussed on page 260, holidays departing from a regional airport may include a change at another airport to connect with another flight.

Many tour operators already include both these countries within their programme of activities. More tour operators include Australia in their programme of activities than South Africa: 76 tour operators include South Africa compared to approximately 100 that include Australia.

The flight time to South Africa is less than half the flight time to Australia. Therefore no stopovers are required and jetlag is greatly reduced. This is a definite advantage to South Africa in terms of distance and access from the UK.

Appeal of each country for UK tourists

Both South Africa and Australia appeal to UK tourists in different ways. Australia is an established favourite long-haul destination for visitors from the UK. Many people travel to Australia to visit friends or relatives as well as visit on holiday. The tourist attractions are well known and the British are familiar with Australian culture.

Part of the mystery surrounding the Australian continent is its links with its Aboriginal past. An understanding of Aboriginal culture is an insight into the spiritual landscape of Australia. South Africa is beginning to reveal the stories and experiences of traditional black Africans and so develops stronger links with its own historic past. Tours of the Soweto township are an example of this.

South Africa is less well known as a tourist destination compared to Australia. South African tourism authorities continue to present the image that their country is an 'undiscovered destination'. This provides great scope for future development of a wide range of tourism products.

UK visitors represent 14 per cent of inbound visitors to Australia and represent 18 per cent of inbound visitors to South Africa. However, UK visitors to Australia spend more and stay longer than visitors from any other country.

In 2003 Australia received 672,800 inbound visitors from the UK, South Africa received 456,468 inbound visitors from the UK. Australia experienced 10 per cent more visitors than the previous year but is expecting an average annual increase of 4 per cent. South Africa received a 3 per cent increase in visitors from the UK in 2003 compared to the previous year.

In conclusion, Australia appears to be the preferred destination for inclusion in tour operators' programmes. However with the approach of the 2010 World Cup, South Africa has the potential to impress a global audience and launch its international brand image for South Africa as a destination. There are special interest segments of the South African market that remain untapped. Specialist tour operators will see the immediate potential of this market and in the future South Africa may begin to significantly increase its share of the UK tourism market.

Resources

Jones, E. (ed) (2001) *Lonely Planet: Africa on a Shoestring*, 9th ed. London: Lonely Planet Publications Ltd.

Joyce, P. (2003) *Globetrotter: South Africa*. London: New Holland Publishers Ltd.

Pike, J. and Bell, B. (eds) (2002) *Insight Guide: Australia*. Singapore: APA Publications Pty.

Ross, Z. (ed) (2002) *Eyewitness Travel Guides: Australia*, 2nd ed. London: Dorling Kindersley Ltd.

Smitz, P. (ed) (2004) *Lonely Planet: Australia*, 12th ed. London: Lonely Planet Publications Ltd.

Index

loyalty 168
Lunn Poly 41, 42

Madame Tussaud's 12
main types of tourism 1, 2
management training 155
maps 166
market research 63, 175, 176, 178–85
market segmentation 174, 175, 186–9, 202
    age 186–7
    life cycle 186, 187
    lifestyle 186, 188–9
    social group 186, 187–8
market share changes 6
marketing and sales 147, 152, 153, 154, 155,
    174–204
marketing, definition of 175–6
marketing mix 175, 190–202
    place 190, 191
    price 190
    product 190, 191–4
    promotion 190
marketing objectives 175, 177–8
    SMART check 177
marketing policy 175, 177
marketing process
    application to travel industry 174
    importance for travel industry 174
    key stages 174, 175, 177–8
Marriott hotels 35
Maslow's pyramid of needs 62
mass tourism 19–20, 21
Mediterranean resorts 6, 23, 29, 38, 41, 87–8
mentoring 73
methods of market research 179–85
mission statements 165, 177, 178, 186, 232
motels/Travelodges 34
motor cars 32
    see also car ownership; car rental
motorway networks 29, 32, 115, 116–18
    European International Network 116
mountains 92, 94, 211, 212
multiple travel agents 41, 42
museums and art galleries 13, 57, 97, 101–2, 207,
    208, 209, 210, 241
music festivals 213, 236
mystery customers 170, 184

nannies 158
National Accessibility Scheme 216
National Express 33, 177
national occupational standards (NOS) 170
National Park Authority 224
national parks 4, 154, 211, 212, 213
National Parks and Access to Countryside Act
    1981 212
National Parks (Scotland) Act 2000 212
national tourist boards 4, 45, 114, 154, 229, 257
National Trust 13–14
natural attractions 86, 89, 92–6, 102, 255
natural beauty, areas of outstanding 4, 19, 44
natural disasters 15, 16, 91, 254
needs and requirements 7, 19, 26–8, 51, 52, 168,
    176–7
negative impacts
    cultural 18
    economic 17, 18
    environmental 18
negotiating skills 168
Network Rail 223
New Forest 212
New Zealand 253, 254, 261, 262, 263
niche markets 40
non-standardised nature of products and services
    10–11
Norfolk Broads 212
Northern Ireland Tourist Board website 229
Notting Hill Carnival 209

observation in market research 180, 184–5
observation of job role 145
oceans, location of 86
off-peak travel 3, 197
Office for National Statistics (ONS) 224, 225, 226,
    227, 244
    website 229, 263
Office of Gas and Electricity Markets (Ofgem) 223
Office of Water Services (Ofwat) 223
Olympic Games 45, 105, 113, 154
one-way communication 165
open communication 164
Orient Express 118–19
outbound tourism 3, 6–7, 37, 111, 115, 116, 154–5
outbreak of war 15
overseas travel 20, 24, 150

respect for customers 59, 61, 69
responsible tourism 18, 19
restricted communication 164
restricted mobility 70, 83, 102–3
retail complexes/shopping 209, 228
retail distribution chain 37
retail travel agents 37
rivers 92, 94
road transport *see* bus/coach companies; car; fly-
drive; motorway network; tunnels and bridges
Roman remains 100–1
Royal Automobile Club (RAC) 36
royal palaces and castles 5, 99
Royal Society for the Protection of Birds (RSPB) 14
Ryanair 29, 30–1, 121

safety and security 62, 63, 111, 113
Saga touring company 68, 186
sales promotions 198, 201–2
satisfaction of customers 58–9, 64, 191, 195
saving on costs 220
scenic railways 120
scheduled flights 108, 115
Scotland as destination 221, 227
ScotExchange website 229
Scottish Tourist Board (STB) 13
seaports 123
Seaside Award 221
seaside resorts 20, 29, 35, 211
seasonal pricing 196
seasonal work 17, 74, 148, 151, 158
secondary/desk research 145, 172, 179–80, 185
secondary sources of information 110, 111
Sector Skills Development Agency (SSDA) 170
sectors of the industry 30–46
different roles 1, 2
see also accommodation providers; transport
providers; and others by name
self-assessment 146, 171
SWOT analysis 171
self-catering 35, 36, 39, 102, 236
self-confidence 81, 168
self-drive 24, 27
self-packaging 27, 40
selling products and services 56, 80–1
increased sales 57
self-confidence 81
serviced accommodation 35, 39

services 2, 3, 10–12, 37, 40, 42, 46, 51, 52, 76, 242
Severe Acute Respiratory Syndrome (SARS) *see*
disease and tourism
Sheraton hotels 35
shift work 148
shopping expeditions 8
short breaks 8, 24, 27, 125, 217, 218, 233
short-haul flights 6, 7, 86, 87, 108, 120
sightseeing 8, 154
see also built attractions; natural attractions;
visitor attractions
size of organisations 2
socio-economic factors 20, 21, 24–5, 187–8
South Africa 254, 261, 262
destination profile 270–9
accessibility 270–1, 272
attractions 272–4
costs and options 276–7
coverage by UK operators 277–8
facilities and amenities 274–5
features 270, 271
government initiatives 276
location 270
tourism development 279
visitor trends 278–9
websites 279
South America 254, 255, 261, 262
South West tourism/Tourism 230–42
accommodation 236, 238
aims 232
cities 232
coastline 230–1
comparison with UK 237–8, 239
day visits 233
events and entertainment 236–7
history 230–1, 232
inland areas 231–2
key trends 233
local produce 231–2, 237
marketing brands 241
provision evaluation 239–42
sports 231
transport and accessibility 237
visitor attractions 234–5, 241
websites 231, 239, 240, 241
southern hemisphere as destination 249–96
Australia 280–95
costs and options 258–62

types of training 75, 146
transfers 108, 117
translators 152
transport providers 30–4, 237
transport types 85, 115–25
transportation 12, 25, 111, 215, 254–5, 257
    choice 31
    problems 46
travel agency consultants 147
travel agents 30, 37, 38, 39, 40–3, 46, 53, 155, 195, 258–9, 265
Travel Training Company (TTC) 164
travel cards 197
travel, definition of 3
travel destination 86
The Travel Foundation 266
travel in the area visited 3
    see also excursions
travel insurance 26, 40, 58, 81
travel principles 259, 260
travel routes and gateways 86, 108
    see also airlines; bus/coach companies; ferry operators; train companies
The Travel Show (on BBC) 200
travel times 86
Travel Trade Gazette 110
Travel Trends 224, 225, 226, 227, 244, 263
Travel Weekly 110
tunnels and bridges 32
    see also Channel Tunnel
two-way communication 165

uncontrollable events 15
underground railways 120
unforeseen events 15
uniforms and dress code 60–1
United Kingdom
    main flows 3
    range of destinations 4
    Tourism Survey (UKTS) 4, 233
    see also 19th century tourism; inbound tourism; National Trust; outbound tourism; visitor attractions; etc.
unsociable hours 148
US Office of Travel and Tourism Industries 113

vaccination see health regulations
value for money 12, 39, 46, 47, 57, 59, 97, 195, 197, 214

verbal communication 165
vertical communication 164
vertical integration 46–7
video conferencing 165
videos used in marketing 11, 201
Virgin Airlines 138, 177
visas see entry requirement
VisitBritain 153, 206, 218, 228, 230, 235, 243
    website 229
visitor attractions 8, 12, 30, 38, 44, 46, 110, 111, 112, 114, 194, 243–5
    working in 152
    see also historical interest; natural attractions; theme parks; etc.
visitor numbers 13, 150, 224, 243–5
visitors from USA 5, 113, 226, 238
    see also inbound tourism
visits to friends and relatives (VFR) 3, 7, 8–9, 31, 113, 121, 125, 218, 225, 228, 233, 237, 239
VisitScotland 229
VisitWales 229
visual impairment 70, 83
volcanoes 92, 95
voluntary sector organisations 2, 13–14, 147

Wales Tourist Board (WTB) 13
    website 229
war and tourism 15, 113
water pollution 221
waterfalls 92, 96
watersports instructors 159
wealth creation 17
weather 90–2, 111
websites for tourism statistics 229
weekend breaks 155
wholesale operators 37
wilderness areas 211, 213
wildlife disturbance 18
winter sports 27, 28, 90, 94, 221
work experience 145, 163
work-related learning 145
work-shadowing 145
Working Time Directive 163
World Travel Market 200
World Wildlife Fund 91
written communication 79–80, 165

youth hostels 34

Let the web do the work!

YOUR REF. NO.
S 666 SLT 08

Why not visit our website and see what it can do for you?

Free online support materials

You can download free support materials for many of our Leisure and Tourism products. You can sign up for free e-newsletters to get the most up-to-date news about our resources.

Lists of useful weblinks

Our site includes lists of other websites, which can save you hours of research time.

Online ordering – 24 hours a day

It's quick and simple to order your resources online, and you can do it anytime – day or night!

Find your consultant

The website helps you find your nearest Heinemann consultant, who will be able to discuss your needs and help you find the most cost-effective way to buy.

It's time to save time – visit our website now!

www.heinemann.co.uk/vocational

01865 888068 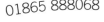 01865 314029  orders@heinemann.co.uk  www.heinemann.co.uk

Heinemann
Inspiring generations

939 R